The Memoirs of Lord Chandos

Oliver Lyttelton, Viscount Chandos

THE MEMOIRS OF

Lord Chandos

AN UNEXPECTED VIEW
FROM THE SUMMIT

by Oliver Lyttelton,
Viscount Chandos,

P.C., D.S.O., M.C., LL.D.

NEW AMERICAN LIBRARY

First publication in the United States, 1963
© The Trustees of the Chandos Literary Trust 1962
All rights reserved. No part of this book may be reproduced
without the permission of the publishers.

First Printing

Published by The New American Library of World Literature, Inc.
501 Madison Avenue, New York 22, New York

Library of Congress Catalog Card Number: 63–21512
Printed in the United States of America

To Moira, Antony, Rosemary, Julian and Adrian

FOREWORD

CHANCE HAS GIVEN ME a varied life and in the latter part of it even a role upon the large stage. If I could amend Virgil, I would choose as a foreword to this book the words "Quorum pars parva fui."

It has been my good fortune to have known many of the great men in the age in which I have lived. I have dared to portray some of them in the knowledge that descriptions by one man of another must at the best be subjective and are apt to give more insight into the painter than into his sitter.

I hope that those who look for jaundiced criticism or acid comments upon others will look in vain.

I wish to record my warm thanks to Miss Pamela Prior, who has made many valuable suggestions and who, with others, reduced my illegible manuscript to typescript; to Mrs. Thomas, who has been my secretary for the last twenty years and who was able to refresh or correct my memory of some of the events described; and to my sister, who has given me help over the family history.

I owe much to comments and corrections by Sir Denis Rickett, Sir Hilton Poynton, Mr. Angus MacKintosh, Mr. Jack Johnston and Mr. Hugh Fraser. All these gentlemen were at one time private secretaries in the offices of which I was the head.

I thank many others who have checked my memory of events in which they as well as I were concerned, particularly Sir Edward Spears, Mr. Christopher Sykes and Mr. Richard Talbot. I wish also to thank Miss Margery Weiner for such scholarly work, particularly in identifying and checking my quotations and for other valuable suggestions. She has also read the proofs with care and insight.

My sincere thanks are due to the following publishers for permission to quote from copyright material: Cambridge University Press for *M. Manilii Astronomicon* by A. E. Housman; Cassell & Company for *War Speeches* by Winston S. Churchill; Clarendon Press, Oxford, for *The Dictionary of National Biography;* Collins Publishers for *Lugard: The Years of Adventure* by Margery Perham; Wm. Heinemann Ltd. for *Lord Derby "King of Lancashire"* by Randolph S. Churchill; Odhams Press Ltd. and Charles Scribners' Sons, New York, for *World Crisis* by Winston S. Churchill; Sidgwick & Jackson Ltd. for *The Collected Poems of Rupert Brooke*. The permission of the Controller of H. M. Stationery Office has been obtained for quotations from Hansard, *The History of the Second World War*—Mediterranean and Middle East—Volumes I, II and III, and *The History of the Second World War*—British War Production.

—CHANDOS

CONTENTS

BACKGROUND

M R. RAYMOND CARR once said that he had read so many accounts of the early life of public men that he was considering writing a book on the subject to put a stop to them. I have no wish to spur him on to this distasteful task, and my first two chapters are consequently not episodic: they are intended to give some objective rather than subjective account of the family into which I was born, and of the environment in which I was brought up.

The Lyttelton family goes back a long way into English annals— into English history would perhaps be too high-flown a phrase.

The family crest of a Moor's head and the motto *Ung Dieu Ung Roy* show that an ancestor made a pilgrimage to the Holy Land or took part in one of the Crusades. His prowess is unsung.

The first Lyttelton whose name is recorded, in 1161, was John de Lyttleton or Luttleton. It appears that the family was established at Frankley in Worcestershire more than seven hundred years ago, about 1235. A certain Sir Thomas de Littleton (the spelling of the name remained variable and arbitrary until modern times) was Esquire of the Body to Richard II, Henry IV and Henry V. His grandson, Sir Thomas Littleton, 1402-81, was a judge and author of the celebrated *Treatise on Tenures*. This was written principally for the instruction of his son Richard, but was soon ranked as a work of authority. Though written in law-French, the style is easy and agreeable: "Probably no legal treatise ever combined so much of the substance with so little of the show of learning, or so happily avoided pedantic formalism without forfeiting precision of statement." [1]

[1] *Dictionary of National Biography.*

The *Treatise* became the foundation of the British law of property, and Coke's elaborate commentary upon it, *Coke upon Littleton*, had to be studied by any aspiring lawyer up till recent times.

John Lyttleton, Member of Parliament for Worcester, "respected for wit and valour" (Bacon) was involved in the conspiracy of 1600/1601, and was convicted of high treason. He escaped execution through the interest of Sir Walter Ralegh, but died in prison.

The law continues to run through much of the family history, and in the middle of the seventeenth century the Lord Keeper was Baron Littleton of Mounslow. According to Whitelocke he was "a man of courage and of excellent parts and learning." Clarendon says of him that he was "the best antiquary of the profession . . . a handsome and a proper man, of a very graceful presence and notorious for courage which in his youth he manifested by the sword."

Passing to the eighteenth century, George Lord Lyttelton, 1709–73, was a poet, author and patron of letters. He was a friend of Pope and Thomson. One of his poems was included, I think surprisingly, in the *Oxford Book of English Verse* until recent editions.

He became Chancellor of the Exchequer in 1755, but his qualities seem hardly to have been fitted to his office. Lord Chesterfield warned his son against the "distinguished inattention and awkwardness of Lord Lyttelton." Horace Walpole remarked, "they turned an absent poet to the management of the revenue and employed a man as visionary as Don Quixote to combat Demosthenes." He opened the budget of 1756 "well enough in general, but was strangely bewildered in the figures . . . never knew prices from duties nor drawbacks from premiums."

I have twice nearly been Chancellor of the Exchequer, and might well have opened the Budget of 1952. The account of my ancestor's speech of 1756 would have provided a disarming opening for a modern Budget Speech.

It was this Lord Lyttelton who built Hagley Hall, the ancient manor of Frankley having been destroyed in the Civil Wars. As a parenthesis I might add that my father had a golfing cottage near the links at Woking, and called it Little Frankley, upon which Gerald Balfour, a neighbour, said it should rightly have been named Frankly Little.

The next heir was the profligate Thomas, Lord Lyttelton. He was —or so it was said by the devout—visited by an apparition, warning him that he would be dead in three days' time. He was found dead in bed by his servant the morning after the third night.

My grandfather, the fourth Lord Lyttelton, was a classical scholar and an intimate friend of Gladstone. Gladstone and he married, on the same day, two sisters, daughters of Sir Stephen Glynne. Mr. Gladstone was thus my great-uncle.

My grandfather had eight sons. The eldest son, Charles, was a man of affairs, of superior intellect and disenchanted wit. He restored and greatly improved the fortunes of the family. He became Deputy Chairman of the Great Western Railway.

His wit, though it sounds mordant, left no wounds. One of my less popular aunts by marriage sat on one of the Charles II chairs in the gallery at Hagley. It broke under her portly form. She protested to my uncle: "I might have broken my back." He replied, with the ghost of a smile, "A great many backs like yours, very few chairs like mine."

My father regarded Charles as the best cricketer of this cricketing family, and he was one of the half dozen best game shots in England.

One of my uncles, Sir Neville, was a soldier of distinction and became Chief of the General Staff and First Military Member of the Army Council; another, Arthur, was Bishop of Southampton; another, Edward, Headmaster of Eton.

My father, Alfred, "was the finest player of his time at cricket, football, rackets, and fives," [1] and on his record could perhaps claim to be the greatest all-rounder in the annals of British sport: he represented his University in five different branches. At cricket he was the first choice for England after W. G. Grace, and one of the best wicket-keepers that ever put on the gloves. He played association football for England—a rare distinction for an Etonian. He was outstanding at rackets, and won the Gold Racquet for real tennis in 1882, 1884, 1885 and 1887–95 inclusive. He was a good shot and rode well to hounds.

He first married Laura, daughter of Sir Charles Tennant, and amongst his sisters-in-law were Margot Asquith, afterwards Lady Oxford, and Lady Ribblesdale, wife of the "Ancestor," so called from his Regency appearance, one of the best-looking and most picturesque figures in the hunting field or the drawing-room, as can be seen from Sargent's portrait of him. Although not entitled to by protocol, I addressed these ladies all my life as Aunt Margot and Aunt Charty. Laura died in 1886.

My father married my mother in April 1892, and I was born in March 1893. My mother came of the Midlothian family of Balfour,

[1] *Dictionary of National Biography.*

who claim David Balfour, the hero of *Kidnapped,* as an ancestor. The Balfours are closely allied to the Haringtons. The water closet was the invention of one of my ancestors, Sir John Harington, of Elizabethan times. He may well claim, by this humane contraption, to have conferred greater benefits upon mankind than the League of Nations or UNO.

My father, declining to captain England at cricket in Australia, devoted himself in early life to the law. He began to practise on the Oxford circuit and owed his chance—so the story goes—to his cricket. He had played a particularly sparkling innings in the Gentleman and Players match at Scarborough (W. G. once described his batting as "the champagne of cricket"), and the solicitor of the Great Western Railway Company had been a delighted witness. It so happened that, soon after, the counsel for the Great Western on the Oxford circuit was ill and, a case coming up, this solicitor decided to give it to young Lyttelton.

A man had broken his leg getting out of a train, and claimed damages from the company for negligence in lighting Paddington Station. My father cross-examined him. "Are you aware that there are two types of carriage in use on the railway?" "Yes." "Do you know that one type has two wooden steps, the other one wooden step, the single step being about six inches from the platform?" "Yes." "Which type was the carriage from which you alighted?" "The one with the single step." "How do you know, if the station was so ill lighted?" The witness, who was putting forward a flimsy, or even a fraudulent claim, lost his head, and instead of saying "I noticed it when I got in," could only mutter that he had guessed and might have been wrong. The railway company won the case, and, during the rest of his legal life, my father was frequently retained by them.

I suppose that he was one of the best-liked men in London society. He had great charm and gaiety: although very religious he was tolerant, and his judgements upon men and women were kindly and informed by his humour rather than by his own strict standards. His great friends were Lord Salisbury and Arthur Balfour.[1] At his dying request, Arthur Balfour acted as my mentor and guide.

My mother was catholic in her tastes and interests and was very widely read, especially in French. She herself was the author of several books and plays. In one, *Warp and Woof,* Mrs. Patrick Campbell played the leading part, but the play had no more than a *succès d'estime.*

After my father died, my mother's public activities were mani-

[1] Afterwards Earl Balfour of Whittinghame.

fold. She withdrew from the social life which she had followed with my father, and devoted herself mainly to three subjects: the foundation of a National Theatre, psychical research in conjunction with Gerald Balfour, and work for the League of Nations upon the opium trade and the white slave traffic. She was the British substitute delegate to the League on these subjects, and was given the Grand Cross of the Order of the British Empire as a recognition of her services.

I have carried on her work for the National Theatre partly as an act of filial piety, and partly because my deep conviction is that a National Theatre must be one of the foundations of British society.

Her work on psychical phenomena was of a scientific nature, and she published a book called *Our Superconscious Mind,* which was a serious and respected contribution to the subject.

I was devoted to both my father and mother. I had a hero worship of my father but stood in some awe of him. He was delighted by any success that I had, and diluted any reproof for my failures with benignant affection.

After my father's death, I discussed every aspect of life, every detail of my career with my mother. She treated me as a contemporary, and sometimes by mistake signed herself "Yours, Edith Lyttelton," then crossed it out and substituted "Your loving Mother," and added "I quite forgot that you are not a friend, but my son." Next to me in the family was my sister,[1] and, my younger brother having died in infancy, I was an only son.

Much against the tradition of those times, and indeed of today, I was not sent as a boarder to a private school, but attended Mr. Bull's in Baker Street as a day-boy. My cousin Gilbert Talbot and I drove to our studies in a hansom cab belonging to a Dickens-like character of the name of Gray. The horse was called Fire King, but showed no signs of deserving his name. One day, when likely to be late for school, we pounded his flanks with the butt ends of our pencils, and he broke into a sedate canter. The reins in front of us became as taut as bow strings. Fire King soon broke back into a trot and was quickly pulled up to a halt. The cabby dismounted and read us a lecture on the dangers of reckless speed in London, as well as on the cruelty to animals involved in the use of pencils as goads.

When I was sent to Eton I had never been away from home, had no friends of the same age in the school, and was shy and lonely.

My account of Eton which follows is written objectively, and

[1] Now Lady Craik.

may give the impression that I was studious and withdrawn from the ordinary life of the school. In some degree I believe this to be true.

My cricket was a disappointment. In his first summer at Eton my father was batting at the nets: the cricket professional ran across to Mike Mitchell, the cricket master, and excitedly exclaimed, "Come over 'ere, Mr. Mitchell, there's a little dark gentleman who 'its the ball like an 'orse kicking."

No such praise attended my début. I was soon written off as cricketing material, and though I became quite good as a junior, I never afterwards aspired to more than club form, and devoted myself, as a revulsion from the family tradition, to golf.

My sons refuse to believe that I was ever shy and scholarly, but bad judges though men are of themselves, I still hold it to be true. At the University I merely became social and an educated *flâneur*. It was the camp and the Army which turned me into a case-hardened man.

CHAPTER I

ETON

ETON IS A PLACE much misunderstood, and often deliberately misunderstood, by those who were not Etonians. Its society is humane and tolerant; the education it had to offer was unique in my time, and I believe still is: if you did not take advantage of it no one minded particularly unless you carried your indifference beyond the point of good manners, into an oafish ignorance.

In my third year I used to attend lectures on Plato by Mr. Broadbent, whose phenomenal memory made it possible for him, without glancing at the text, to recite a page of *The Republic* in Greek, then translate it into English, comment on it and then resume in Greek on the top of the next page.

Continuity is nearly always essential to a man's memory. I remember Maynard Keynes, at dinner one night at the Other Club, saying to me: "I have no memory: every morning when I wake up I have to regain my intellectual position." "Heavens alive!" I said. "Ah well," he went on, "it's not so bad as it sounds, because as I am working my way back I remember that I have been along the road before. But using the usual definition of memory, I have none. I am one of the best read men in England"—he never suffered from false modesty—"but I couldn't recite six lines of English poetry to you for all the money in Lombard Street, and," turning a baleful eye on me, "I don't suppose you could." "You would like to bet? A bottle of claret?" I retorted. When I had won the bottle without having had to look beyond Housman, whom I selected as a suitable medium between a King's and a Trinity man, he turned to me and said, "I should know at once if you misquoted—try." So I started off on something fairly hackneyed, but where it is easy to get a word or two wrong:

> *Thou wast not born for death, immortal bird* . . .

When I came to a certain line, I misquoted on purpose:

> *Perhaps the self-same song*
> *That crossed the sad heart of Ruth.*

"Stop! Stop!" said Maynard. "That's wrong: it doesn't scan." And then, so strange is memory and so necessary to mine are continuity and momentum, the thread was snapped and I could not remember the right words. Nor could Maynard, but, strangest of all, nor, after we had given him the false line, could Desmond McCarthy, who was sitting on the other side of him. We were at a loss, but catching sight of Eddie Marsh at the other end of the table we explained, and Eddie, in his reed-warbler voice, supplied the line in a flash. It is, of course:

> *Perhaps the self-same song that found a path*
> *Through the sad heart of Ruth, when sick for home,*
> *She stood in tears amid the alien corn;*
> > *The same that oft-times hath*
> *Charm'd magic casements, opening on the foam*
> *Of perilous seas, in faery lands forlorn.*

I am not usually much intrigued by manuscripts, first editions and the like, but I must say I was fascinated to find out from an article in *The Times* upon Keats that the last two lines were originally written:

> *Charmed the wide casements opening on the foam*
> *Of keelless seas in fairy lands forlorn.*

In that version the sense, though fantastic enough, is clear: no ships have furrowed those fairy seas. Yet Keats must have felt that the spondee in the second line dragged a trifle and that an anapaest sounded better. So he crossed out "keelless" and substituted "perilous," and wrote "faery" for "fairy." The sense disappears but an even more numinous music, an even more haunting poetry, is borne upon the air.

This is a digression springing from the phenomenal nature of Broadbent's memory, which could overcome interruption or lack of momentum. He was a beautiful scholar and displayed a caustic but not unkindly sense of humour.

Once, the Captain of the Boats, "Soccer" Williams, was found reading an evening newspaper at the back of the room during Broadbent's lecture on Platonic love, and was told to wait afterwards. I hung about.

"What was I saying, Williams, about Platonic love?" Broadbent growled at him, and Williams, whose knowledge of the subject had clearly been drawn from that very evening newspaper, launched out into a highly coloured and erotic version.

"Stop! Stop!" said Broadbent. "Your views on Platonic love, Williams, are more those which I should have expected from a divorced wife than from a dispassionate student of the text. Please go away."

My own education started from what I still think was the inspired teaching of two men, Cyril Alington and Hugh Macnaghten; the first, married to my half-aunt, was Master in College and afterwards Headmaster of Shrewsbury and then of Eton; the second, towards the end of his academic life, became Vice Provost of Eton. They both took what are called Select Divisions or, as they would now be described in a pamphlet by the Ministry of Education, "a class of twenty selected students from a certain age group, consisting partly of those who had gained scholarships and partly of those whose studies were not grant-aided, the latter in the Eton terminology being described as Oppidans."

I remember once, as a sort of relaxation from more twisted syntax, we read Caesar's Gallic War under Macnaghten. Everyone knows it begins: "*Gallia est omnis divisa in partes tres.* All Gaul is divided into three parts." "Has any one of you," said Macnaghten, "ever reflected on these words? Caesar, the inevitable co-respondent in every fashionable divorce suit in Rome, the author of many of the dirty jokes in Roman bath-houses, had been known as a politician, an orator and a wit, but not as a soldier. He is loaded with debts. He is forty-two—much older than it sounds now—when he is given command of the legions in Gaul. He writes his first despatch: these are his first words: 'All Gaul is divided into three parts.' Everyone in Rome knew that Gaul was divided into dozens of different parts, as many as the Balkans are today, in 1908. Caesar wanted to give society the impression that he had cast off the smart world, the luxurious triclinium, for the camp, and had left behind the fashionable epigram, to rap out the staccato, oversimplified military summary to which generals in the field are often addicted."

I am not very happy about the scholarship of all this, but I feel sure that it is good, even inspired, teaching. Not only was I amused enough to read a lot more about Caesar, but more than fifty years later I catch the very intonation of Macnaghten's voice: "co-wespondent, Wome," and so on. I have not forgotten.

Other memories are jogged. I can still smell the warm asphalty smell, with a faint tang of gas from the fives courts, which filtered into his classroom on a summer's day. We were reading Theocritus. A boy was construing: he boggled at ψιθύρισμα (psithurisma), and said he didn't know what it meant.

"Not know what it means?" said Macnaghten. "Listen," and he held up his hand, "there." And through the window came the unmistakable sound of the rustling of the trees. A boy next to the window looked out and exclaimed, "That's not the rustling of the trees, sir, that's the Windsor steam brush." "Get out of my woom, you gwubby little wationalist, and stay out in disgwace until I call you back. You are not fit to mix with scholars until you have puwified yourself by weflection on your cwime." [1]

I am quite proud to have been mentioned in Macnaghten's book; he says one of the pleasures which he recalls as a teacher was my construing and translating of Cicero. I may have been good at it, but it would have paid me well in after-life if I had studied oratory a little more deeply.

Eton is often spoken of by the ignorant as if it were one of the citadels of the Philistines, as if, for example, the only key to its hierarchy was athletics. The highest social distinction was to belong to Pop, the Eton Society, and though athletics was one of the things which helped, another, for that matter, was the secretaryship of the Musical Society. If you did not play games well, you had perhaps to be a little more amusing and a little more agreeable than if you did. Alec Cadogan[2] and my youngest son, Adrian, were both elected to Pop, although at the time they had no colours.

The whole atmosphere of Eton is much nearer that of a university than a school: no doubt one of the contributing factors is the system of single rooms, which gives to boys what they generally lack at the formative age, some privacy. This is a factor of primary, not secondary, importance.

Great attention should be given to these subjects. The privacy that comes from single rooms, the staircase layout in universities,

[1] Sir Osbert Sitwell describes this incident but wrongly attributes the remark about the steam brush to me.
[2] Now the Rt. Hon. Sir Alexander Cadogan.

the need to arrange the furniture in a drawing-room in the right pattern to discourage the *tête-à-tête* and promote general conversation, if that is what you want, are matters of importance. Light colours in factories to make work as cheerful as possible, the shape and size of legislative chambers, must be studied with attention, not only by engineers or architects but by humanists.

In later years, some new universities, in the name of efficiency, have wished to break away from the staircase layout, without which in my view the mixture of scientist and classicist, Right and Left, is less likely to be brought about.

Turning to democracy and government, the shape of the chamber will have a lasting effect upon the very nature and mode of government or Parliament. After the old House of Commons was destroyed, we were probably more cajoled than persuaded by Mr. Churchill into an oblong chamber. Mr. Churchill always—and as I think rightly—contended that two-party government becomes almost impossible in a circular chamber, at least if the intimate nature of debate is to be preserved.

The new House of Commons, like the old, cannot nearly seat all the Members. When showing American visitors over the House, I sometimes could not make them believe that every Member had not got his own seat and his own desk. They obviously thought this an incomprehensible example of inefficiency and an inexcusable departure from the tenets of "method study." I used to defend our ideas. "Madam," I would say, "if you owned a nightclub, would you have room for everyone to dance? If you did, the nightclub would go broke. A crowd is necessary for success. There is a lot of dull, humdrum business transacted in this chamber; the Members would look lost on most days in a chamber with 630 seats. On the other hand, on a great Parliamentary occasion the House is crammed: Members sit in the gangways and the galleries: excitement and tension are created."

Boys should be relieved of the strain of living constantly together in mass. Privacy develops the individual: the company of his fellows helps him to fit into the society in which he will have to move. As much attention should be devoted to privacy as to company.

It is to be hoped that economy will never lead to the abolition of the individual room at Eton; it is in my opinion one of the principal influences that make the place what it is.

It seems appropriate, when talking of my own education, to say something of what I think of it in general. Obvious though my thoughts may seem, I would in defence plead that only too often education in the nineteen-sixties is confused in the public mind with the acquisition of facts, or the ability to answer quizzes. I have tried to counter this whenever I am given the chance.

It falls to the lot of many public men to give away prizes at schools. I have done it many times, but have hardly ever been asked to do it twice at the same school. My argument and theme, though commonplace enough, are thought to be not quite seemly for the young, and of course most unseemly for their parents.

Say I, "What do you expect from education? To pass examinations? A knowledge of facts? Are there such things? Do you expect to know all the answers? If you do, you are far from the light: the hallmark of an educated man is that he doesn't know all the answers. He is uncertain, at a loss very often. The Chinese are said to have a proverb—though I can't trace it—'To be uncertain is to be uncomfortable, but to be certain is to be ridiculous.' Anyway, Montaigne says: 'The conviction of certainty is a sure proof of nonsense and extreme uncertainty.' No, education will, I hope, make you uncomfortable. One of the first things that education must teach you is to call into question everything which you are told, especially what is told you by the clergy, by schoolmasters and I need hardly add, by politicians, active or retired, alive or dead.

"The more educated a man is, the greater will be his humility in the face of the problem, and perhaps humility rather than knowledge is the parent of forgiveness.

"Provoked to an unusual orotundity, I once exclaimed in the House, 'The Hon. Member has used that most hateful of all dialectical weapons, the simplicity and certainty which can only arise from a profound and obdurate ignorance of the subject.'

"A certain humility in the face of the problem and a certain humility at all times is not a bad thing, though it is not a quality which would generally be ascribed to me by my friends. I cannot claim to be more than a seeker after it.

"What else can education give us? I would say that it helps us at times, and I would hope often, to recognise the authentic voice of the Muses. 'Fame runs before him as the Morning Star' [3] means very little, but if you cannot recognise in it the voice of the Muse you will never, or so I think, be admitted to the Grove of the Muse of Poetry.

" 'Corruption, the most infallible symptom of constitutional liberty,' a dictum which must have sustained many a colonial states-

[3] Dryden, *Absalom and Achitophel*, Part I, Line 734.

man faced by unsavoury incidents in adolescent governments, can only have been written by Gibbon with the Muse of History guiding his pen. She must have inspired Michelet's epitaph of Cardinal Richelieu: '*Il eut l'intention des grandes choses qu'il fit.*'

"When Hannibal ended his speech to his army in North Africa before they set sail to invade Italy, '*Le silence était si profond qu'au loin on pouvait entendre le bruit de la mer*'; in this we can surely hear the voice of the Muse.

"And to go back to poetry:

> *Wakeful beside her slumbering Antony,*
> *Pale Cleopatra gazes out to sea* . . .

sang Hilaire Belloc. The unprintable lines that follow do not disguise, nor, for that matter, would they disgust, the Muse.

"What pleasures are denied you if you have not got the education to recognise these voices, and into what errors you will fall if you start accepting what other people tell you."

I lived my life at Eton under two different housemasters. They both had good houses, but their methods of rule were strongly contrasted.

My house tutor when I was a new boy was Henry Bowlby, a cleric from the pages of Trollope. He was a great friend of Lady Desborough and of the Duchess of Sutherland, and when he introduced the Christian names of these two great ladies into the conversation, I fear that his boys were not above enquiring "Who is Etty, or Milly?"

All schoolmasters, at least in those days, were inclined to be slightly snobbish, and it may be that this vice could then be more readily understood and forgiven than in our own times. If they conceived their role in the state to be that of training and teaching those who were likely to shape its future, then they must have wanted to have pupils from the great families. The sons of those families would have a start in the race, a start given them, perhaps because the family could influence a safe seat, perhaps because to be backed by a substantial inheritance gives a man the time and independence to pursue a political career without worry or subservience to the Whips, perhaps because Cecils and Stanleys, Cavendishes and Fitzmaurices, Grenfells and Primroses and Vane-Tempests were none of them averse from recruiting candidates from one another's families if they could.

Henry Bowlby's pupil room was a pupil room of all the talents. It included Patrick Shaw-Stewart, Ronnie Knox, Charles Lister,

Julian and Billy Grenfell, Edward Horner, shining figures in a golden age of young men, and all killed except Ronnie Knox in the holocaust.

Under the Eton system, the lower boys used to attend "private business" with the stars, and I still remember the effortless scholarship and brilliance of this galaxy.

With all his Grantley-like worldliness, my tutor was devout and high-minded, and brought the Christian ethic to bear upon the daily life of his house.

During my third year Bowlby left, to become Headmaster of Lancing, and was succeeded by Gurney Lubbock. He was the rare combination of a schoolmaster and a man of the world, a competent scholar, a lover of music and a good player of games. He had means of his own and kept one of the best tables in a house at Eton. His methods were typically Etonian and smacked little of the pedagogue.

One of the boys, Sir Desmond Bagot, was suspected—and rightly —of going to Windsor races whenever a chance offered. I suppose he was seen one day in the paddock, and that this got to the ears of M'Tutor.[4] In every Eton house there is a sideboard at the entrance, known traditionally as "the slab," upon which letters and everything that boys have ordered from the shops are deposited, books, clothes, football boots, rackets, walnut cakes, strawberries or sausages.

On the morning of Windsor races, my tutor kept an eye on the slab, or planted a scout beside it. When Desmond's change suit was left there by his tailor, he removed it to his private house. Some time after the last race he said to Desmond, "Your change suit is in my house. You had better take it away." The lack of the change suit is, of course, check-mate to any Etonian who wants to go to the races.

Just as the old Parliamentary rule requires a Member to wear his top hat when raising a point of order during the progress of a Division, so that he is conspicuous and identifiable by the Speaker when Members are pouring in and out of the lobby, so a boy in a top hat, tail-coat and white tie can hardly fail to catch a master's eye in Tattersalls or the paddock.

In my last year I was captain of Lubbock's house, and he treated me as a partner and a friend. I used to smoke an occasional Balkan Sobranie up the chimney, but if his approach, which was never surreptitious, made me put it out, he only gave a warning sniff and

[4] The Etonian abbreviation pronounced *mč tutor.*

said no more. When he asked us to dinner, he gave his top boys the best of everything, a sound claret and a little good brandy to end up with.

His great interest outside his work was music, and he married, after I had left Eton, Miss Irene Scharrer, the pianist and well-known player of Chopin. Their lives were cast in different worlds and the marriage was not a happy one. He spent much of his private fortune on his wife, and after he had left Eton was obliged to continue teaching in a private school as an assistant master, a humble task for an ex-housemaster at Eton, but one which he fulfilled without complaint.

My uncle, Canon Lyttelton, was Headmaster during all my time. He had been one of the best of the Lyttelton brothers as a cricketer, and in a moment of revelation confessed that he never walked up the aisle of a church or a cathedral without bowling an imaginary ball down it and wondering whether it would take spin.

He was a saint and a man of transparent honesty, without any tinge of cant. On the other hand, he was a crank over matters of diet, was the strictest of vegetarians and was supposed by us, after a dinner of sour milk or curds, to sleep with his feet out of the window. He developed a cancer when he was over seventy, and had it cut out. This convinced him that his vegetarianism was a mistake, and soon afterwards he took to red meat and woodcocks. Whatever may be the clinical soundness of this diet, he was soon riding a bicycle again and lived robustly to the age of eighty-four.

He suffered from one rather serious disability: he was a poor scholar. He could often be shaken upon matters of syntax and even quantity. A. B. Ramsay, himself a fastidious scholar, attributed my uncle's lapses to lack of preparation and pointed out that the learned Rawlins never went into school without it.[5]

I was in sixth form during my last year under the Headmaster, and I fear we shamelessly exploited these weaknesses. "Surely, sir," we—heartless little brutes—used to say, "you can't scan the syllable short in elegiacs? We can't think of an instance, although the dictionary says that it can be scanned short or long. Or don't you think your second sentence in this Latin prose is a little monkish, or at least a little silver?"

One day the sixth form were reading extracts from Livy unseen. He is an author with a difficult syntax, and the extracts, which had been selected by Mr. Rawlins, the Lower Master, were cruelly tangled and obscure. The Headmaster could not manage them himself

[5] G. W. Lyttelton in a letter to the author.

and left us to do our best. Turning over a page, however, he came on the words "*Pheras rex cum omnibus copiis venit,*" and catching sight of this apparent half-volley, himself went on to construe and began: "King Pheras came with all his forces." This is a real schoolboy howler and was received in a shocked silence. Then someone, I think it was Benthall, K. S., objected that the word "*venit*" was left in the air so to speak, and anyway who was King Pheras? The Headmaster thought he was King of Thessaly. I have fortunately forgotten whether it was Geoffrey Madan or I who then asked, "Would not another and possibly more felicitous rendering be "The King came to Pherae with all his forces," particularly as Pherae was to be the base of his operations?"

Boys are cruel animals, and there was no escape for Uncle Edward, who could only mutter, "Well, go on, go on."

It so happened that "Dilly" Knox was to examine the trial papers of sixth form: he was doing it for the last time, after some disagreement with the Headmaster. An opportunity for reprisals thus presented itself, and the first paragraph of one of the Latin translation papers opened provocatively with the words: "*Pheras rex cum omnibus copiis venit,*" and of course nearly all of us did our part, and translated it "King Pheras came with all his forces." We had to write out a good chunk of one of the *Georgics* for our pains, because even the least vindictive of Headmasters could not let the joke pass.

His transparent goodness and lack of pretence, however, left him the master of the field on another occasion. We had been given a sonnet of Shakespeare or Milton to translate into Greek iambics, not an agreeable exercise in a golden summer week. However, a colleger said, "Verrall has done this into iambics," and gave us the reference. Most of us did not attempt to improve upon Verrall and copied his version.

Dick Durnford, the master who corrected our Greek verses, scored the first copy with red ink and comments such as "rather strained," "surely not permissible in classical Greek?," "please avoid ἅπαξ λεγόμενα (hapax legomena)," and so forth. He soon discovered that most of the versions were the same. The sixth form were duly summoned to the Headmaster, who looked like thunder, although tears were obviously not far away. We let him run on and he was, for once, in the usual vein of schoolmasters. "You who are the top of the school, upon whom I rely for so much in running it, have here descended to a mean and shabby practice—cribbing. Money and care have been lavished on your education, and you can find no better way of rewarding them than by putting up one of your number to do the work and then copying him. I am ashamed that you should have sunk so low, and I am deeply sorrowful as an Etonian that I should have lived to see it."

Then one of us, not I, interrupted. "As a life-long lover of iambic verse, Sir, I have always looked up to Professor Verrall as a master of the art of translation. We have been told, and by you, to follow him. We have. I did not think, nor did most of my fellows, that his version of this sonnet could be improved upon, although clearly Mr. Durnford would not agree with us. Anyway, I copied it out and would have thought it impudent to set up any version of my own as a rival."

The Headmaster's thunder disappeared, the sunshine burst through. He beamed, and with a benevolent chuckle he said, "You're all a lot of scamps. Now let's go to Upper Club and look at the cricket." His joy and relief were as transparent as his previous sorrow.

The other master under whom we sat in sixth form was the celebrated C. M. Wells. He had been a well-known cricketer and footballer, and acted as the cricket master.

He is a classical scholar of great learning in the Cambridge tradition so well exemplified by A. E. Housman. He is a fastidious judge of wine, knows a great deal about racing, and is devoted to fishing, at which in his ninety-first year he still excels.

His other principal hobby was confounding German scholars and pointing out, in the style of the famous introduction to Manilius, how often grammatical theories and explanations had been falsely established by them on the evidence of corrupt or amended texts. He might well have echoed Housman's sentences, which have consoled and lightened my path through later life:

> If nature, with flagitious partiality, has given judgement and industry to some men and left other men without them, it is our evident duty to amend her blind caprice; and those who are able and willing to think must be deprived of their unfair advantage by stringent prohibitions. In Association football you must not use your hands, and similarly in textual criticism you must not use your brains. Since we cannot make fools behave like wise men, we will insist that wise men should behave like fools: by these means only can we redress the injustice of nature and anticipate the equality of the grave.[6]

C. M. Wells also had an encyclopaedic memory, and was credited with the ability to recite *Paradise Lost* by heart. As a scholar

[6] From his introduction to Manilius.

he seldom lacked for a parallel quotation to illustrate his point. At other times he would quote, at length and from memory, one of the great poetical or dramatic passages from the classics in Greek or Latin in a rather dry and unemotional voice, and would end by saying, "Of course it's awfully gooood."

Mr. Rawlins, another well-known scholar, became so much interested in grammatical niceties as to regard the Greek testament and the Epistles of St. Paul mainly as a repository of fascinating grammar.

One of my contemporaries in sixth form was Geoffrey Madan, the most brilliant scholar of my day. He and I were great friends, and I am one of the few and lucky owners of a copy of his *Commonplace Book*, given to me by his wife, after he had died. In later life his scholarship led him into unlikely places for research, the suggestion book at Brooks's or Boodles, the bread-and-butter letter of Swinburne to a vicar who had given him luncheon. Every Christmas he used to give his friends fifty-two quotations or epigrams or some undiscovered treasures from private letters. He used to interlard them with pastiches of his own invention. Some of them seem to penetrate in an uncanny way into the very mode or mind of a nation. For example, his pastiche "Inscription on the Great Wall of China: 'The three Dreadful Things'—of which the first was 'Fear at Sea.'"

These Christmas gifts are mostly repeated in the *Commonplace Book*. He has included a sentence of Michelet which I gave him and, unfortunately, has chosen, much to my chagrin, a very poor epigram of my own. My collaboration helped in the quotation from the imaginary Abbé de Montfichet: *"Être d'accord c'est déjà vieillir."* Surely that has the very ring of La Rochefoucauld, but I am not sure that Geoffrey did not spoil it by adding, as an afterthought, *ou bien s'extasier.*

One day it was advertised that Madan would read a paper on Spenser to the Literary Society. Mr. Luxmoore and a master or two, well armed with questions and quotations culled by late night study to illumine the discussion and point their own learning, attended. Their annoyance was manifest when it turned out that Spenser was a Victorian poet, a creation of Geoffrey's wayward imagination, a man of dubious private life and some bawdy inclinations in his otherwise admirable and scholarly verses, all of course composed by Geoffrey. The evening was not a success.

We had to show up from time to time an original composition in

Latin or Greek in the style of one of the great authors. Geoffrey elected to write an account of a visit to Eton by Herodotus. I can only say it was Herodotus. It was so perfect that the authorities invoked an old Eton custom and sent Geoffrey "up for play," which meant a personal congratulation from the Headmaster and, if I remember right, a whole holiday for the rest of the school.

The only analogous event in my memory was when, in 1960, the only two All Souls fellowships awarded were both filled by Etonians, one of them my youngest son: the schools were then given a whole holiday. I was particularly gratified, because this distinction was gained a week or two after Bob Boothby had said in velvet tones, during a television programme, that parents did not send their sons to Eton for education, but merely from snobbery.

Various societies played a considerable part in our lives. In my tutor's house, as in others, there was a debating society which met on Saturday nights. Outside the house, the school Musical Society was the biggest, but the Political, the Literary and the Archaeological Societies also flourished.

An Eton audience, like that of most public schools, is polite, inquisitive and ruthless, and it is quite an ordeal for a Minister to address the Political Society. Courteous but disintegrating questions, posed with apparent innocence but backed up by a malicious knowledge of where the tender spots of an argument rest, come up from the body of the meeting. Not even experience of the House of Commons gives the speaker any lasting sense of security.

The clergy, in preaching sermons to schoolboys, do not always understand the need for picking their phrases with more than usually fastidious care. One preacher, and he was very small in stature, began a sermon in College Chapel in favour of the Melanesian Mission somewhat like this:

"Christianity has made such strides in these islands that you might mistake their inhabitants for our own countryfolk. For example, I myself last year married fourteen Melanesian women." At this point an ominous rustle nearly broke into undisguised laughter, and even though he went on, "and gave the sacrament of baptism to more than a hundred and fifty children," his sermon was irretrievable.

My father had been one of the legendary figures at Eton, the acknowledged leader of the school in almost all fields. He was Captain of the Eleven, Keeper of the Field (that is the captain of football), Keeper of Fives and Racquets, in sixth form, and President of the Eton Society (Pop). He lived to be a leading Counsel and a Cabinet Minister, but he often said no position in after life began to accord the *réclame* or prestige which he enjoyed at Eton.

During my first half at Eton, there was another such figure, though not so eminent, Denis Finch Hatton. It was he who introduced sponge-bag trousers to the Eton Society, and he followed his own rules of dress and discipline without interference by authority.

When I was a new boy I went up to Agar's Plough about noon to see the cricket match. There was a small tent set aside for house-masters' wives and the dames, that is the matrons of the houses. Although it was a day of blue sky, with the clouds riding high, a cold breeze was blowing across the ground and I was surprised to see all these privileged ladies sitting on chairs in the open.

Eton were batting, and I took up a position near the tent to watch the game. Suddenly a top hat, with the red seal of Pop on the crown, rolled slowly out of the tent. A sleepy but commanding voice drawled out, "Be a good fellow, will you, and retrieve my hat." Denis, who was supposed to have been at a London ball the night before, was taking a few minutes' sleep in the ladies' tent before changing and going in to bat.

In a less humane or more authoritarian society the ladies would have driven the intruder out, like Clodius from the festival of the Bona Dea, but no one dreamed of disturbing Finch Hatton. He was a sort of Sir Percy Blakeney of the place. The bridge which links Upper Club and Agar's Plough was built by his friends and is dedicated to this great Etonian.

I gained no successes at games and had only one colour, my house colours for football. I loved fives and was quite promising until I bruised the middle bone of my right hand.

After my first two years I had many friends and began to enjoy the daily life of the school.

It is difficult to catch the characteristic outlook on life of Etonians. Like port, it has matured in the bottle, and although new vintages are constantly added to the catalogue, they all retain the body, the colour and the bouquet of their ancient vineyard.

There is not a peppercorn of truth in the old parable of the charming young lady at the ball who had nowhere to sit. The Etonian saw her predicament at once and said, "Oh, let me get you a chair." The Wykehamist got it and the Harrovian sat on it. I would, however, claim that Etonians set a high store on good manners, develop as a rule an ease and urbanity in whatever society they find themselves; they are suspicious, like Talleyrand, of too much zeal, and carry a certain disenchanted tolerance into the hurly-burly. Eton, above all, seems to live in a civilised atmosphere, and although all boys are capable of excesses, μηδὲν ἄγαν (meden agan) is nearer the philosophy of the place than ἀιὲν ἀριστεύειν (aien aristeuein). Both these slogans—"No excess" and "Strive to be best"—were displayed in gold letters in my tutor's pupil room, which we thought was carrying things a little far.

The Greek for an early morning meal is ἄριστον (ariston) and the Greek for being the best ἀριστεύειν (aristeuein), and when as a small boy I was asked to translate ἀιὲν ἀριστεύειν (aien aristeuein), though I knew perfectly well what it meant, I answered, "Never go out without your breakfast." My tutor thought that would do just as well as the other.

I must resort to one other anecdote which sounds the same note. The harmonics may ring in Etonian ears.

I was a Cadet Officer in the Corps, and my company was commanded by an enthusiastic master, who I suspect had gained a running blue for the three miles. One grey, sultry and steamy day, we did an exercise against an imaginary enemy. After a couple of hours of short rushes we were bored, and tired, but at last the company came to rest in a small copse. We sank down and mopped our foreheads. The master, still charged with high-voltage energy, scanned the rear rank and said, "Fitzherbert, get up that tree and look if you can see the enemy." Fitzherbert gazed upwards, and then with a smile said, "Oh, I'm afraid I can't do that, Sir." No more was said on either side. Fitzherbert had reached the limit of cooperation and was unwilling to make himself ridiculous; the master understood that he had gone too far.

Few sincere people would subscribe to the cliché that their schooldays were the happiest days of their life. When he is told this, every wise man's son doth know that it is a parental subterfuge to make a boy go back to school with cheerfulness. I cannot say truthfully that Eton was the happiest time of my life. I preferred the holidays myself, and went back to school with no feelings of zest or exhilaration.

I have, however, a love of Eton, owe to her such education as I command, a great many friends, and a certain ease and confidence in the turmoil of life. I can never forget the magic of the place itself: the school yard, Brewhouse Yard, the great procession of the Thames, the smell of chestnuts in bloom, the crack of cricket ball and bat in the playing fields: the contrast between the bustling life of the present and the throng of today's Etonians and the benignant autumnal intrusion of the past.

My loyalty to her has remained unshaken and I always feel, unjustly and unpardonably, that my very numerous Harrovian friends are so particularly agreeable because they have survived an unpromising start to their lives. The only two days in the year when I would not run to catch up Lord Alexander of Tunis or Lord Monckton are the two days of the Eton and Harrow Match.

CHAPTER II

THE UNIVERSITY

Y FAMILY was a Cambridge family, my father inevitably had been Captain of the Cambridge Eleven and, as a matter of course, I went up to Trinity College as an undergraduate.

Freshmen at Cambridge in those days lived their first year or two in lodgings, and I settled in to an apartment, bedroom, sitting-room and bathroom, on the top floor of Hoop Chambers in Bridge Street, near the corner of Jesus Lane and almost opposite to one of the entrances to Hewell's Court of my College. My landlady was a billowing Jewess of maternal inclination to which she gave expression chiefly through the kitchen, for she was an excellent cook, almost a Cordon Bleu.

It was said that these rooms, which were at the top of some very steep stairs, had once been occupied by my first cousins, George and Caryl Lyttelton. Caryl was the Cambridge fast bowler and, like many fast bowlers, developed a painful corn. The two Lytteltons summoned the local doctor to cut and tend the corn, which he did with despatch and skill. Unfortunately, in leaving, he caught his foot in the carpet and ricocheted a flight or more down the stairs. George went out on to the landing and, looking over the well, exclaimed, "Physician, heal thyself," shut the door and returned to his room.

The advantages of being a member of a very big college are manifold: there is more to choose from; the hermit is undisturbed; the gregarious have the widest opportunity for society.

The disadvantage in my day was that the Harrovians, Wykehamists and Etonians tended to coalesce into a small clique. They were mostly members of the Pitt Club: the top-sawyer Corinthians affected the Athenaeum Club, the counterpart of the Bullingdon at Oxford, to which election was exclusive. It had twenty-four members, who professed themselves to be judges of wine, racehorses and cards. The Club had rooms in a Georgian house in Trinity Street, opposite the Great Gate of Trinity, and the Club held dinner parties at regular intervals, known as Athenaeum T's from the shape of the table. Owing to the proximity of Newmarket the members were generally to be seen in force in the paddock at the meetings, and enjoyed more credit from the bookmakers than their bank balances deserved. I was a member of both clubs, and spent a lot of my time playing bridge or racing.

One of the most famous bookmakers of my time was Mr. Pickersgill, a charming man who did nearly as big business as Ladbroke's, and accepted the most outrageous bets without blinking an eyelid. His son was at Cambridge with me, and one day took a very bad fall out hunting with the drag hounds.

At one of the Newmarket meetings there was a "match" between Hornet's Beauty, the outstanding handicap horse of that time, and Rillet for the Abingdon Plate, the latter clearly running for the place money. There was hardly any betting, and I was talking on the rails to Mr. Pickersgill and asking him how his son was getting on, when Lady de Bathe, formerly Lily Langtry, came up and asked how he was betting. "I'll take twenty-five to one Hornet's Beauty, my Lady," he answered. "All right," she said, "twenty-five thousand to a thousand." He booked it without a murmur, and I suppose regarded the certain loss of a thousand as an example of what we should now call public relations. Hornet's Beauty won on a right rein.

At one time the racing set at Cambridge had taken the knock at Ascot, and the cash flow of the Athenaeum was reduced to a mere trickle. It so happened that Gibby Johnstone, who was supposed to be part owner, had let slip in the Athenaeum Club that he fancied his filly Elaine in the first sprint race at Windsor. All the racing people except me were in the schools, and I was the only one who could conveniently go to Windsor. I was entrusted with the Cambridge commission and was to be allowed the best of the odds that I could obtain to £50. I had at that time, in June, £72 in the bank to last me for the rest of the year. I went to Windsor races and began my task by seeking out Harry Lewin in the silver ring. We used to have an odd pound at the end of the day at Newmarket with him, and though hardly at the head of his profession, he was a sportsman, a good better and friend of undergraduates, not, I think, to his financial disadvantage. "What'll you lay me Elaine?" I said. "Oh, six or seven to one, to you," he answered. "Well, seven to one, you mean." "Oh, all right." "I'll have £700 to £100." He nearly fainted, but booked it.

After executing the rest of the commission, I went to the bottom of the members' enclosure to watch the race. Elaine was left three lengths at the post, and I put back my glasses and thought, "That's that. I shall have to go to my father for help."

To my astonishment, however, she got up to win by a neck. I had a lot of cash bets to collect, and when I was done I was crackling with notes and clinking with gold sovereigns.

I left the course at once (unluckily as it turned out, for I should have backed another winner) and went to see the cricket at Upper Club at Eton before catching the train to Cambridge. In the train I worked out the average price obtained, which was around eleven to two, but I had £350 to £50 for myself, as well as a little more at the average.

When I got out at Cambridge Station, I was met by a brass band and a large escort of cars. The band struck up "See the Conquering Hero Comes." That evening we threw a tremendous party. One of my friends who had been in the worst mess and got out of it on Elaine lost £200 at roulette, which cancelled his winnings on the day.

As a relief from these academic activities I played golf for the University, and in my second year got my blue. The first time I was ever picked was to play against Mid Surrey, and my father came to watch. That day my ball appeared to be attached to the hole by a string. I played well enough through the green, and putted like a man possessed. I went out in thirty, which might have been twenty-nine if I had had to hole a putt of two or three yards, which my opponent conceded.

These matches round London were a severe strain on our endurance as well as on our golf. We left Cambridge in a saloon coach by a train shortly before eight, and by eight were down to bridge in a haze of cigarette smoke. We reached Sunningdale, Woking or Mid Surrey in time for a few holes amongst ourselves, had a good luncheon and took on the scratch players of the club on their own ground in the afternoon. It was great fun, and if on occasions I vanquished a local undergraduate-killer, I felt I had deserved the huge dinner and rivers of liquor with which we celebrated before catching the nine-something back to Cambridge.

In spite of these distractions I read spasmodically, though seldom the works recommended by my tutor, Walter Fletcher. He formed the opinion that I should not get through the preliminary examination for the Classical Tripos held by the College, but I confounded him by working fourteen hours a day for a fortnight and passing with ease, almost with distinction.

My great friends were George Llewellyn Davies, adopted son of Sir James Barrie, Rudolph de Trafford, C. D. Lawrence, Roger Chance, David Heaton, Gilbert Dunning, Alec Hardinge, Marshall Field, Valentine Castlerosse, Loraine Hill.

One night during my first year I was asleep in my bedroom when I was woken by a policeman standing by my bed. He urged me to get up because the rooms were on fire and the floor was about to collapse. I quote from the *Cambridge Review* of February 6th, 1913:

A fire broke out one night last week at No. 1 Hoop Chambers. The occupants, Mr. E. St. L. Bonvalot and Mr. O. Lyttelton, were aroused from their slumbers at 3 A.M. by a policeman. The house was already enveloped in smoke. At such crises as these the natural instinct of man bids him seize his dearest possession and betake himself hurriedly to a place of safety. Some such impulse appears to have actuated these two gentlemen. Mr. Bonvalot emerged with an astrakhan coat flung over his silk pyjamas, and a box of cigars under his arm; while Mr. Lyttelton, with characteristic sang-froid, lit a cigarette from the flaming wall-paper, and descended into the street clasping firmly in his hand—an Athenaeum tie.

My rooms were gutted, my clothes and books burnt, but the insurance money kept me going for a few months, even without the help of the bookmakers.

Alec Hardinge,[1] afterwards the most correct of courtiers, and the King's Private Secretary, was perhaps the wildest of our set. One day, returning from the Athenaeum T with our gowns over our arms, we were stopped by Stephen Gaselee, in later years the librarian of the Foreign Office, but at this time the senior proctor. "Put on your caps and gowns, gentlemen," he courteously ordered. Alec replied with a string of expletives. "Oh, Mr. Hardinge," said Gaselee, "that will cost you a pound." "Well spent, too, you old monkey." "Two pounds, Mr. Hardinge." "You're no more than . . . ," Alec went on, and the toll had reached £8 before we disengaged. I told this story many years later to the King, who was delighted and thought all the more of Alec after it.

I used to attend the University lectures on Shakespeare delivered by Sir Arthur Quiller-Couch. In these days women undergraduates

[1] Afterwards Lord Hardinge of Penshurst.

were not members of the University, but they used to arrive very early and seize most of the seats. There were many more petticoats than trousers in the audience. I often had to sit in one of the window embrasures.

Quiller-Couch affected loud checks, and often a bunch of violets in his buttonhole. But for his doctor's gown he might have been a successful bookmaker. He would look round for a moment and then, after a pause, begin "Gentlemen," at which an indignant rustle like the wind in the trees swept over the assembly.

His lecture on *Macbeth* was, or so it seemed to me, a masterpiece. He described the dark, malignant passions at work, shut off and sealed up in the castle. In the middle of the lecture, when he reached the climax, he stopped for a few pregnant seconds, and then loudly rapped the desk in front of him. It was startling. You heard the knocking at the gate. You understood the brusque intrusion of the outside world of reality into the sinister darkness of the keep. Surely this knocking at the gate must be one of the most dramatic moments in all the literature of the drama. Your blood runs cold, as it does for the opposite reasons when, in *The Turn of the Screw*, Quint is seen through the window, and when the malign, phantom world lays a cold hand on the two children and their companions.

Anyway the lectures set me studying Shakespeare in a desultory way from the works of scholars. How strange are the contrasts in literary scholarship and criticism. How ingenious and how convincing was Theobald's emendation in a corrupt text, where Mistress Quickly describes the death of Falstaff, an emendation from "a table of green fields" to "a babbled of green fields." If Shakespeare did not write it, at least he might have.

On the other hand, I remember a note from a Victorian scholar on the line "Or to take arms against a sea of troubles," which ran in this fashion: "This apparently mixed metaphor can be understood when it is remembered that the Vikings, before embarking on a dangerous expedition, were wont to rush fully armed into the sea." This is where scholarship without understanding can lead.

Sometimes, as in *The First Night of Twelfth Night*,[2] new fields of understanding and pleasure open before you, when you read what Orsino wrote to his wife, and how the Russian diplomatic mission to Queen Elizabeth's Court was dressed on Twelfth Night. In this book, as in *Shakespeare's Bawdy,* some of the suggestions

[2] *First Night of Twelfth Night* by Leslie Hotson, published by Hart-Davis, 1954.

seem to me to be over-elaborate and strained, but they can be forgiven for the new light shed on many an obscure passage.

I made the acquaintance of A. E. Housman. It was difficult to believe that an outward appearance almost crabbed in its aloofness concealed the poet of despair and the agony of *sunt lacrimae rerum* (is not "Nor feel the heartbreak in the heart of things"—a line from a minor poet—somewhere near the meaning?).

One golden June Saturday, my friend Geoffrey Madan was paying a visit to Trinity from Oxford. About half past three he said, "Let us go and carry Housman off to Fenner's to see the cricket." "If you feel you can intrude upon him, I'm all for it, but I don't personally know him well enough." Geoffrey reassured me.

We got to his rooms a few minutes before four, and found him deep in study. Geoffrey proposed Fenner's, to which A. E. replied, "What a good idea. I finish work on Saturdays at four, so sit down, you two, for a few minutes, and then we'll go." He resumed his studies, and when the College clock struck, collected his books and came with us.

Another well-known figure who was a friend of mine was Gaillard Lapsley, an American, and at that time one of the Senior Fellows of the College. He had become the very personification of a Cambridge don: his performance in this role was so perfect that it seemed as if it owed something to conscious art as well as to the influence of the environment. His curtains, his claret, his comment were all in harmony with his role, and often, but not perhaps so often as they might be today, his arrows were dipped in curare and aimed in accordance with the academic habit at his colleagues. Thus, after the war, of a history tutor of another college who had become a successful and popular chaplain in the Guards Division, he purred in his suave and gentle voice, "Yes, Oliver, I suppose that there he would not be handicapped by any intellectual disability."

The figure of Lapsley comes back to me again from a time when we were both staying with Mrs. Leo de Rothschild at Ascott, Wing. There were more than twenty people in the party. Just before luncheon we were walking together on the lawn when he said reflectively, "How dreadful it is when the French lose their sense of irony." "Gaillard, what a portentous thing to say just before the sherry!" "Oh well, it's in my mind. I have just been paying a visit to a French friend of mine, a professor who is the greatest authority on Byron now alive. I asked him if Byron had ever practised unnatural vice. His face dropped a foot, and he replied, '*Oui, mon ami, il faut avouer qu'il y avait des incidents homosexuels dans sa jeu-*

nesse, mais il a racheté tout ça par l'amour passionné qu'il a éprouvé pour sa soeur.' "

That evening at dinner there was a dispute about who was Prime Minister at the time of the Battle of Waterloo. Fred Cripps and I alone advanced the name of Lord Liverpool, but it did not find acceptance. Then someone said, "Why quarrel? We have the senior history don of Trinity College, Cambridge, at another table. Let's go and ask him." We put the question and he instantly replied, "Oh, I shouldn't know. You see, I only go down to 1485."

It is curious that very few people know who was Prime Minister in 1815, a date which marks one of the crossroads in European history. Yet Lord Liverpool held the office from 1812 to 1827, longer than anyone except Walpole and the younger Pitt (although Lord Malvern has beaten all three, if his entry is not disqualified). Every Prime Minister walking up the steps of No. 10 Downing Street for the first time should bear these chastening facts in mind.

At this time Monty James was the Provost of King's, a great classical scholar and, in his spare time, the author of the famous book of ghost stories. Himself, as all Provosts of King's used to be, an Etonian, he was particularly hospitable to Etonians. At this time there was a well-known don who was supposed to be largely synthetic, and to have a cork leg, an aluminium cranium and other artificial adjuncts.

Monty James said that one night he had been to call upon him rather late upon some university business. The professor had "sported his oak," or locked his door, and when Monty knocked there was no reply for some time, until "a still, small voice answered, 'Come in.'" Monty continued, "I went in, and there was all of the professor, hung up over the bed, except for one eye on the pillow which had answered me."

This extravaganza was well known to us, and one night we were dining at King's, and the professor was amongst the guests. After dinner the Provost pushed two decanters towards him and said, "Port or burgundy?" "No thank you, no thank you. I have no palate." This further omission from a normal equipment strained our manners almost beyond the breaking point.

I went down for the long vacation of 1913 with few cares on my mind, but during it I was to taste the first bitterness of sorrow.

My father had been induced by "Scatters" Wilson[3] to play in a cricket match for a charity. I had once seen him play in an exhibition match with W. G. Grace, but he could not have been on a

[3] Sir Mathew Wilson.

cricket field more than once or twice in fifteen years. He made between eighty and ninety runs in his best style against some first-class bowling including that of Hitch, the Surrey and England professional. He was hit in the stomach by a fast ball and there is little doubt that this precipitated although it probably did not cause his illness.

A day or two later, he was taken ill with violent pains at the Foreign Office party. When the doctor came, my father told him that he had had gall stones when he was up at Cambridge and recognised the pain at once. It is probable that both this and the earlier attack were appendicitis, and my belief is that with modern methods of diagnosis and surgery his life could easily have been saved. The critical days were, however, wasted. It was thought that the pain would soon pass off. He said to me next morning: "I was going to play golf for the House of Commons against the Wilderness on Friday and Saturday. I have arranged that you should be my substitute. Lady Hillingdon, your hostess, was delighted to ask you in my place. I think you will enjoy your first appearance for the House of Commons. I shall be up and about when you get back to hear how you got on."

So off I went and found a great party assembled. There were nearly fifty people, including ladies, staying in the house. After the golf and a rest we put on our tail coats and white ties. A gardenia was laid on every guest's dressing table, and after dinner there were two bands to which we danced, one of them Cassano's to play the waltzes, the other to play the new ragtime. I enjoyed it madly.

When I got home I found my father still in bed and still in pain.

After another day or two, they said they must operate and he was moved to a nursing home. The hour of the operation arrived. My mother, sister and I waited for more than two hours in one of those stark impersonal rooms amongst the old numbers of the *Tatler* whilst it was in progress. At the end of that time Sir Thomas Parkinson, the physician, came into the room with a drawn face and said: "Alfred had acute peritonitis: a burst appendix. I have never seen perforation so extensive. I am afraid his condition is very serious."

The world seemed to stop. Although I stood, as any son should, in some awe of my father, I looked upon him as my ideal and loved him with the admiration and intensity of the young.

I felt that everything was falling and my mother's stricken looks but brave face tore my heart-strings. At this moment I began to be grown up.

However, after two days my father appeared to be recovering and was said to be out of danger. I was sent off accordingly to see Chaliapin in *Boris Godunov*. I remember the great actor and singer clearly, but my most vivid memory is of the countless people who came up to me, many with tears of relief in their eyes, to welcome me because they knew that my presence should mean that my father was recovering.

The next day he had a relapse, and two days later he died. Only those who knew can imagine the desolation of his family. If I could have looked a year or two into the future I should have known that he had gone out on the full tide of happiness and achievement and had been spared the years when his world would come crashing to the ground.

It was in his memory that, for the first time, there was a two-minute silence. The Oxford and Cambridge cricket match was being played. *The Times* reports thus: "On the stroke of 12 o'clock, the hour of the memorial service at Westminster, the umpires took off their hats. The thirteen cricketers on the field did the same and stood reverently to attention for some minutes."

I prefer to say no more, but to quote the words used by Mr. Asquith in the House of Commons. They were delivered without notes and under the stress of great emotion, yet not a word is out of place.

It is a loss of which I hardly trust myself to speak, for, apart from ties of relationship, there had subsisted between us for thirty-three years a close friendship and affection which no political differences were ever allowed to loosen or even to affect. Nor can I better describe it than by saying that he, perhaps of all men of this generation, came nearest to the mould and ideal of manhood, which every English father would like to see his son aspire to, and if possible to attain. The bounty of nature, enriched and developed not only by early training, but by constant self-discipline through life, blended in him gifts and graces which taken alone are rare, and in such attractive union are rarer still. Body, mind, and character—the schoolroom, the cricket field, the Bar, the House of Commons—each made its separate contributions to the faculty and the experience of a many sided and harmonious whole. But what he was he gave—gave with such ease and exuberance that I think it may be said without exaggeration that wherever he moved, he seemed to radiate vitality and charm. He was, as we here know, a strenuous fighter. He has left behind him no resentments and no enmity: nothing but a gracious memory of a manly and winning personality—the memory of one who served with an unstinted measure of devotion his generation and his country. . . .[4]

[4] Extract from the Prime Minister, Mr. Asquith's, tribute to Mr. Alfred Lyttelton: House of Commons, July 7th, 1913.

I still feel acutely how far short I have fallen of the example which I was set.

If I had to excuse myself, which I do not, I should say that days were about to dawn which would confront humanity with its sternest and most cruel test.

If under the strains we fell short, as we did, we can only pray for mercy and forgiveness.

At the end of the long vacation I returned to my old life at Cambridge and began to read more attentively.

When we came down in June the next year—1914—I was twenty-one, and gained some experience of London at the height of the season. I dined out and went to a ball almost every night. It is difficult to recall the power and riches of the aristocracy in those days. Those born into this small society, which excluded divorcées and actresses from the Royal Enclosure at Ascot, never lacked for entertainment, and it must be confessed that I had little knowledge of how the rest of the country lived. I saw the yellow carriages of the Lords Lonsdale and Londonderry sweep up to Ascot with their postilions. I listened with attention to the ripple of elegant conversation of the society of those days. I sat through the vast dinners which accompanied it: Thick or Clear Soup, Fish or Lobster, Entrée, Sorbet, Game, Foie Gras, Ices, Fruit and Savoury.

There were few evenings when I did not put on a tail coat and a white tie, the uniform for the stalls of a theatre as well as for the ordinary dinner party. The Opera at Covent Garden was the most glittering scene. The Grand Tier coruscated with diamonds.

At the other end of the social scale the ladies of the town were to be seen in the Promenade at the Empire in Leicester Square. They were mostly built or padded out or pinched in to give the effect of spreading sails and ample proportions. In their way they seemed just as inhuman as some of the respectable models and mannequins of today, sometimes poured into sheath-like cylinders and more often than not with white, ash-blonde or daffodil hair with which Raymond and not nature has endowed them.

My aunt, Lady Frederick Cavendish, whose husband had been murdered in Phoenix Park, was a lady of the old school who said "Orficer" and "Yaller." Her saintly character and shining goodness were spiced by humour. As a nephew, I never felt the slightest constraint in her presence, although she seemed to me to be incalculably old. Her tea table, whenever I was a guest at Carlton House Terrace, was loaded with scones and jam and cake. She gave me a glimpse of what Victorian society had been like. She once wrote to *The Times* to protest against the advertisement for corsets, which could only have been described even by the most prudish as diagrammatic. She regarded them as indelicate.

I am sure she was unaware of the loose character of much of the great world around her at the time and of the certain young men or women who were known by everyone not to be the children of their legal fathers.

In truth, manners change very quickly and the strait-laced Victorian era gave way to one of laxer and lower standards. Outward appearances were maintained and reticence on even innocent subjects was preserved. Even in Edwardian days it would have been inconceivable that a newspaper should have announced that Lady So-and-So, who had been married for two or three months was "expecting a baby in the autumn."

Soon after the war the change in manners took a further step towards freedom if not to licence. Reticence gradually disappeared and subjects which were never mentioned in public in 1914 became general topics of conversation.

I prefer, myself, to live in an age when almost anything can be discussed, but it is perhaps a pity that privacy is largely extinct. It has been replaced by exposure both of the body and of the mind. It is amusing to reflect what my grandmother or my aunt would have thought of the young ladies wearing two handkerchiefs and a pair of sandals who can be seen any day in the summer on the Croisette at Cannes or, on rare occasions, even in Piccadilly.

In 1913 it was as easy to distinguish a duchess from a housemaid in the street as it is now to distinguish the effeminate from the normal. Today, the housemaids—if such persons still exist—would be as well-dressed as the duchess, perhaps even better. The streets and the parks are all the gayer and brighter for the high standard of chic and dress attained by many of the young ladies from the office or the factory.

On the other hand, all changes have not been for the better. The servants of my youth had a tradition of service. It was not thought servile to serve and many a butler and nurse or maid were the trusted and loved friends of the family. They taught the youth the standards that were expected of them, and who of my generation did not learn to fish or shoot from some keeper and absorb from him some of the lore and the lessons of the countryside?

It is difficult now to believe that when Lord Derby died in 1893 "he left £62,000 to be divided between his 727 servants, gardeners, and the staff of the various branches of his estate," [5] and still more difficult for me to believe that I lived in an era when such munificence was possible.

It would be the merest hypocrisy to say that life was not the greatest fun in those days and that the parties in the great houses like Devonshire House, Londonderry House and Derby House provoked any feeling of guilt, at least in me.

Politics were much more part of social life than they are today. The increase of public business and the decrease of hospitality and the shrinkage of the social round have brought about changes in political life not all for the best. Two examples may illustrate the point. In my father's time, a Prime Minister could, and usually did, know—to a clause—the precise position of each of his colleagues on any major political question, for example on Home Rule, Welsh Disestablishment or the Deceased Wife's Sister Bill, and so forth. He would know just how far he could go with the consent of his Cabinet and at what point collective responsibility would be strained. This was because Ministers constantly met outside the Cabinet room at dinner or supper parties, at Goodwood or Doncaster, at Bolton or Knowsley or Taplow, and discussed these matters at large.

One of the arts of government, as of the management of companies, is not to face your colleagues, unless unavoidably, with decisions upon subjects which have not been thoroughly ventilated in advance. Today, such is the pressure of public business, it sometimes happens that a small coterie of Ministers have to put forward to their colleagues the solution of some major question not previously discussed with them.

When the matter is not urgent, no harm is done because a decision can be modified or deferred, but when it is pressing, the "outside" Ministers may be much embarrassed and may have to choose between disloyalty or dissatisfaction.

I have a strong impression about a second change. I believe that a government at the beginning of the century had to carry with it educated opinion and the opinion of the drawing-room if it was to remain in power, to a greater degree than is now necessary, with universal suffrage and a more popular press. I do not think that the Labour Government, if it had been in office in those days, could

[5] Randolph S. Churchill, *Lord Derby "King of Lancashire,"* (London: Heinemann, 1959).

have survived the Gilbert and Sullivan tangle into which it got itself over capital punishment.

In the House of Commons, Mr. Chuter Ede[6] was known to be a life-long abolitionist. He was now Home Secretary and said that the Government view was that the time was inappropriate for any change. He consequently urged the House to retain capital punishment. The Whips were taken off—and the House decided, against the Government advice, on abolition by a majority of twenty-three.

In the House of Lords, the Lord Chancellor, Lord Jowitt,[7] declared that from his long experience at the Bar he believed that capital punishment should be retained. He none the less felt it necessary to advise their Lordships to follow the vote of the House of Commons, the elected body, and abolish it. The motion to abolish was defeated by a huge majority.

It may be a false impression, but I doubt if any Government of 1906 would have survived so ludicrous and humiliating a spectacle as its advice given by two senior Ministers against their own avowed convictions being rejected on opposite motions in each House of Parliament, even though the Whips were off. In the event it was a two-day wonder and few now remember that the debate took place.

It is true to say that probably no generation in this country has witnessed such a startling and permanent change in society as has been witnessed by mine. Yet the violent changes have taken place without violence. It has been shown that Arthur Balfour was right in his epigram or oxymoron, showing that the supreme, perhaps the only, virtue of democracy is the power to change without Revolution.[8]

Manners, society, power, politics, conversation are almost unrecognisable from the pattern of 1913.

[6] Rt. Hon. James Chuter Ede, M.P.

[7] Viscount (later Earl) Jowitt.

[8] To Sir Robert Horne, Chancellor of the Exchequer:

A.J.B.: "You know, my dear Bertie, democracy is a much better system of government than autocracy."

HORNE: "What a pretentious thing to say just before luncheon!"

A.J.B.: "Yes, you see, under a democratic system, if the people become displeased with their government, they only have to go to the ballot box and get another one; but under an autocracy, if the people become displeased with the autocrat, they have no alternative but to cut off the autocrat's head; and, my dear Bertie, the cutting off of autocrats' heads is an idea which is generally inimical to that of autocracy."

CHAPTER III

THE FIRST WORLD WAR: I

A T THE END of my second year at Cambridge I had changed
with some reluctance from the Classical to the Law Tripos; it must
be confessed that I had allotted not the first two but the last two
of my years at the University to work. I had wasted my time and
had nothing to show for my university career except a golf blue,
many friends and some debts.

Admiral Sir George Warrender, then Commander of the 2nd
Battle Squadron, lived at Leasam, a charming eighteenth-century
house near Rye and five miles from my home at Wittersham. He
and Lady Maud Warrender were more than kind and hospitable to
me. I often used to play golf at Rye with the admiral, and one day
he asked me to be his guest in his flagship whilst the Fleet were
on manoeuvres. I was to present myself at Queensferry on August
4th. I was engaged to play for the Zingari in one or two matches
at the end of July but was free in August and eagerly accepted.

Tuesday, August 4th had other things in store. The Fleet was
mobilised by Mr. Churchill on Sunday, August 2nd, my invitation
for the 4th was cancelled, and on the Monday I was taken by my
mother to the House of Commons. The tension of a deadly and
historic moment brooded over the building. Whilst we were in the
Central Lobby we were joined by Mr. Arthur Balfour, and a few
minutes later by Sir Edward Grey. We had a few words with them,
and they sadly confessed that war was now unavoidable. Our
ultimatum would not be accepted. I still retain a vivid impression
of their calmness and of their sorrow. War was declared on August
4th.

At that time Lord Salisbury commanded the Bedfordshire Mi-

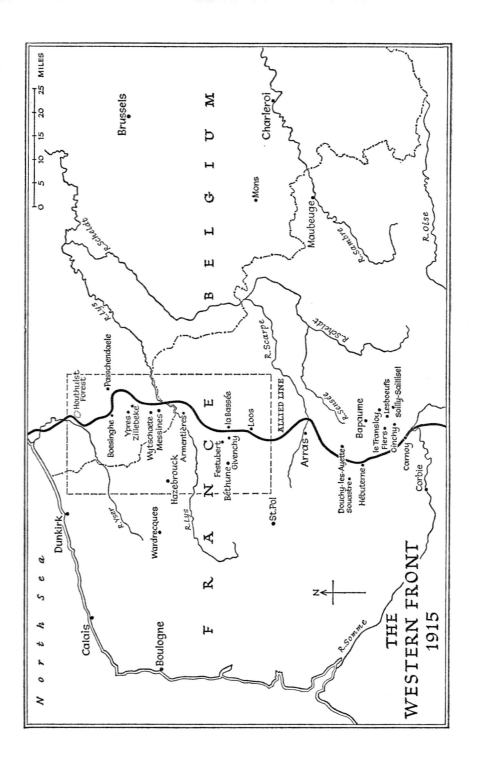

THE
WESTERN FRONT
1915

litia,[1] and Arthur Penn,[2] "Bobbety" Cranborne[3] and I were promised commissions within the month. Bobbety asked Arthur Penn and me to stay at Hatfield whilst we waited, and we spent a week shooting rabbits in the park and enjoying ourselves. The sights and sounds of that England,

> *And laughter, learnt of friends; and gentleness,*
> *In hearts at peace, under an English heaven,*

are still as fresh in my memory as if that August were yesterday.

It was hot and golden weather; the tang of the bracken, the hum of the insects, the benign and beautiful house all seemed to say, "Here is a moment of peace: remember it: it will be long before you will know it again." I think we realised clearly that these were the last days of the England which we knew and that the hundred years of peace, kept by the power of the Royal Navy, were to be succeeded by a struggle which would shake the world.

We all three had had some rudimentary military training in the Eton Corps (I had been a cadet officer myself), so that when we found ourselves commissioned in the 4th Battalion Bedfordshire Regiment and posted to Dovercourt, we did not find life in the regiment entirely new and unexpected. The officers were quartered in the hotel, and we patrolled the sea front in the search for spies. Mysterious signals were reported to be flashed from certain houses, but we never found anything to confirm these widely held suspicions.

Very soon orders were received by the battalion that over 1,000 recruits of Kitchener's Army were to join us and were to be trained and organised by us into a battalion. A day or two later they arrived: they were in civilian clothes and were mostly farmers, clerks, journalists and schoolmasters, although there was a smattering of workmen from industry. Picking the non-commissioned officers, which had to be done at once on intuition—and in my view intuition is at best a doubtful guide—organising the companies, pitching the camp, supervising the rationing and the interior economy and bringing some military order and discipline into this motley mass was fine training. They were a magnificent body of men, who learnt quickly and submitted kindly to being ordered about by a handful of young commissioned officers. I had

[1] Lord Salisbury commanded the 4th Battalion Bedfordshire Regiment.
[2] Afterwards Sir Arthur Penn.
[3] Viscount Cranborne, now the Marquess of Salisbury.

N

R. Yser

Houthulst Forest

Broembeek

BELGIUM
FRANCE

YSER-YPRES CANAL

Passchendaele

Boesinghe • Pilkem

Elverdinghe

Ypres • Potijze

Zillebeke •

Wytschaete •

Messines •

R. Lys

Hazebrouck

• Strazeele

Vieux Berquin

Bois
d'Aval
• Bleu
• Gars Brugge

le Cornet Perdu •
Vierhouck •
les Puresbécques •

Nieppe •

Armentières

• Neuf Berquin

R. Lys

Merville

la Gorgue

Picantin

Lille •

l'Epinette •

Neuve Chapelle •

• Aubers

Farm Cour de L'Avoué
×
Festubert •

Béthune • • Givenchy •

• la Bassée

o Hohenzollern Redoubt

ALLIED LINE

• Loos

• Lens

THE
YPRES SALIENT
AND
LYS BATTLEFIELD
enlarged from the previous map

0   2   4   6   8   10 MILES

special duties in musketry and saw many hundreds of these men through their arms training and firing.

I expect that the officers learnt as much or more than they taught, because everything had to be improvised and shaped from the very beginning, with few trained officers or N.C.O.s to help.

A month or two later we all three, Arthur Penn, "Bobbety" Cranborne and I, transferred to the Grenadier Guards and were posted to Wellington Barracks. We wore for the first time the gold-edged cap and grenade of the First Guards.

We were put "on the square," and were drilled or shouted commands all day. When Bobbety went sound asleep during an amusing evening at the Hippodrome, which Arthur and I were enjoying, I understood what a strain was already being put upon his physique.

I have seen many institutions in my life, universities, colleges, Government offices, joint stock companies, colonial administrations, Cabinets, but the best human organisation, the most efficient and the most closely knit of which I know is the Brigade of Guards.

The system is built upon a discipline as strict in its way as the Prussian; but the guardsman is taught that there is no one like him, and is instructed in the history of his regiment from the day he becomes a recruit. Pride and discipline, discipline and pride are the keys. The most rigorous standards of personal appearance and cleanliness, care of arms, drill and minor discipline are required. It is common today to talk of spit and polish in a derogatory sense, but those who wish to do away with them have, as a rule, little knowledge of war or battle for which soldiers are trained. Just as in a great industrial plant tidiness and good housekeeping make for efficiency, so a battalion well turned out, the men with their heads up, hair cut, shaved, in step and in some awe of their officers and N.C.O.s, will stand the strain of battle better than bodies which follow looser rules. It must be admitted that some flexibility, some initiative can easily be lost. The more highly educated soldier of today must be given much more information than we used to give to our men: he must be told why he is ordered to do something. We did not do that. On the other hand, it must be remembered that the men of 1914 were often those swept into the Army by unemployment or starvation, the two press gangs of those days.

It was often supposed that the Brigade of Guards was made up of picked men, but in fact their height was the only standard applied. When recruiting was brisk the height standard was raised, when it was slack it was lowered. I saw some of the recruits when they enlisted: they were often weedy and narrow-chested, but after only a few weeks of plentiful food, hard exercise and drill, they were almost unrecognisable. They were new men.

I have never forgotten this, have never criticised the "dole" for being too generous: for a long time it was barely enough to sustain life. I can remember the heartrending condition of many who presented themselves for employment in the zinc smelting industry at Avonmouth a year or two after the war. Only a small number were well enough nourished to stand the arduous manual work and high temperatures round the furnaces. Those who lasted for a few weeks began to pick up physically and became, after a few months, as fine a body of men as you could wish to see. Their wages had bought enough food to nourish them.

Time and again the Brigade of Guards have proved a bulwark in battle; time and again they have made the reputation of commanders; always they have set a standard at which to aim and which, though sometimes equalled, is never surpassed.

Again, contrary to widely held belief amongst the public and even in the rest of the Army, there is a high proportion of professional officers in the Brigade deeply versed in knowledge of war.

How lucky, and in our case, because we had been civilians, how immeasurably lucky, it was to have served through the war in a *corps d'élite*.

We duly passed off the square and in January 1915 the three of us were posted to the 2nd Battalion in France. At that time the odds against the survival at the front of a subaltern in the Brigade of Guards were very long: if he remained unwounded for six months he could count himself lucky; yet by the mercy of God all three of us were alive at the end of the war. Arthur Penn was wounded at Festubert in May 1915 and afterwards was adjutant of the 2nd Battalion. Bobbety Cranborne's health broke down in 1915: only his indomitable spirit had kept him in the front line for so long. I served with the 2nd Battalion in No. 4 Company until I became adjutant of the 3rd Battalion in 1915, and was not wounded till April 1918, by which time I was a brigade major.

We arrived at the base camp at Havre; it was cold, wind-swept and muddy. Our first night was not auspicious. We had all three been persuaded by a brother officer to buy sleeping bags lined with rubber. This was the first time we had slept in them, and when we woke in the morning, because of the condensation we were encased in ice, and looked like three *truites en gelée*.

As the war progressed, I gradually learnt never to buy in England things made for campaigning. An air mattress, or at the worst a hip-ring which you or your servant can blow up are worth all the specially designed sleeping bags that were ever made. The knife, fork and spoon in one tool were about as useful as the prong in the old pocket-knives for taking stones out of a horse's shoe. A folding India-rubber bath, designed for washing babies in a maternity hospital, is a good campaigning store to have in the mess-cart.

Our second day at Havre, the three of us went to early service, and it was very early, held in the Y.M.C.A. hut. Hardly had the parson mounted the wooden stage and begun the bidding prayer, when his batman appeared, carrying his false teeth on a plate. This gesture proved too much for the devout young officers, and even "Bobbety" Cranborne had to give way to some Cecilian giggles.

We were soon sent up to the front and joined the 2nd Battalion on February 23rd, 1915. By luck, it had had comparatively few casualties in the retreat from Mons, and in the first battle of Ypres. Its N.C.O.s were mostly men of long service: the discipline was of the strictest and the fire power of the battalion was unbelievable. The five rounds of rapid, aimed fire often made the Germans believe that they were opposed by a machine-gun battalion.

When we joined it, the 2nd Battalion was commanded by Wilfred Smith,[4] and the second-in-command was George Jeffreys,[5] known to all his brother officers as "Ma," but not from his maternal attitude towards young officers. When he joined the regiment in 1897, it so happened that a well-known *maison de rendezvous* had been kept by a Mrs. Jeffreys, known as "Ma," and the subalterns were quick to transfer the sobriquet to their brother officer.

The young officers were treated in the Grenadier manner: the slightest deviation from the highest standards was visited by reprimand or punishment, and I cannot recall that we were often praised. At the same time, we were aware that the commanding officer, second-in-command and the adjutant watched over us with deep regard to our interests and to our survival, provided we deserved it. One instance illustrates the point.

The month before I joined, the 2nd Battalion had relieved some Indian troops. My dear friend Jack Buchanan[6] had dug in his platoon in the middle of the night, according to his orders, in some flat and waterlogged country. The runner carrying his situation

[4] Lt. Col. W. R. A. Smith (18.5.15).
[5] Afterwards General Lord Jeffreys.
[6] J. N. Buchanan.

report at dawn had been killed or wounded and consequently Battalion H.Q. did not know where he was. The second-in-command "Ma" Jeffreys, accompanied by his orderly, in full view of the enemy and in broad daylight, strode out to find him, and did find him. By some chance, or probably because the enemy had started to cook their breakfasts, he was not shot at. Such actions are not readily forgotten by officers or men, and the very same second-in-command, who had without any question risked his life to locate a platoon, would of course have damned a young officer into heaps for halting his platoon on the wrong foot on the parade ground.

This phrase is worth explaining. In the Brigade we are drilled to give the word of command so that first the cautionary words—battalion, company, platoon, or whatever the unit is—are long drawn out, and secondly that the operative word of command reaches the men at exactly the right time during the pace. No absolute precision in drill such as that which we achieved is possible without the word of command being standardised in tone and exactly timed to the movement which it orders.

We stood in great awe of Wilfred Smith, who was one of the best battalion commanders in the Army. He had a steely eye and very soon made the young entry look something like the more senior officers: not the same, but something like them.

John Craigie, one of the patriots, as they were then called by the professional officers, and a good soldier, once elected to wear Newmarket boots, with leather soles and canvas uppers, on parade. He was made to feel as if he had turned his back on the enemy, and not only he but all the young officers were given a hearty damning and told that if they had not already disgraced the regiment they were obviously soon to do so.

When we joined the battalion, it was holding a position near La Bassée; the trenches linked up and ran between some brick stacks twenty or thirty feet high. Otherwise the position was a pattern of those with which we were to become familiar in the next three years. We soon learned the trench routine: stand to arms at dawn —the most likely moment for an enemy attack—stand down, except for the sentries, at full light, then cooking: the men particularly favoured cooking their bacon with the ration cheese at this hour. We all drank copiously of tinned coffee-and-milk, scalding hot. The smell—and smell is the most evocative of the senses—of coffee and milk and toasting cheese and bacon still takes me back to those raw, chilling dawns, and to my youth.

After breakfast, parapets, rifles, traverses, trenches, ammunition and equipment were inspected.

I had a lance-corporal in my platoon called Bryson, who seemed to me to typify the old soldier. He had at least twenty-five years' service, and wore the South African medals. He carried a hip-ring in his haversack, which was blown up for him by the young soldiers. In return, he instructed them in the lore of the Guardsman and of survival: how to avoid as far as possible punishment by the officers, and how to behave in the face of the enemy. He had only one tooth in his head, and I came upon him one morning after "stand down" while he was masticating a ration biscuit. He did this by inserting the tooth into one of the holes in the biscuit and working it backwards and forwards till a bit broke off. "Corporal Bryson." "Sir." "How do you manage that biscuit?" "Well, Sir, it's like a game of cribbage, Sir, a peg 'ere and an 'ole there, Sir."

My platoon sergeant, Sergeant Gambrell, was also, almost inevitably in those days, a long-service man, and was typical of the best of our N.C.O.s He knew the profession backwards: his manner and bearing remained precisely the same, whether he was in billets, in the trenches, being shelled or being drilled.

On the 12th March we moved to another sector round Givenchy, and our trenches were at the summit of a little knob or hill, and ran through an orchard which had been much fought over. In this context the word orchard means a pock-marked pattern of shell holes, one touching the other, some tangled undergrowth, and the stumps of the tortured trees standing out like Calvarys against the sky.

I used to do a good deal of patrolling. I personally feel braver in the dark, and in those days could see better at night than most. I rather enjoyed these patrols, and the thwack of an occasional bullet was not alarming if you were crawling on your stomach. It was exciting, but the horrible part of it was that we had to thread our way through decomposed corpses that still littered the ground. The cats of the village had gone wild: they looked fat and sleek and did some patrolling of their own.

I have some reason to remember my birthday, March 15th. The Germans apparently thought that we were going to launch an attack, so they started shelling our trenches at dawn, and kept it up nearly all day.

Trenches dug by the Brigade were narrow and deep, carefully sited for field of fire, and with very thick traverses. We could only sit still, endure the shelling and keep a look out. I spent my time counting the shells which fell within sight of me—they were a mixture of 77 mm. and 5.9 c.—but I lost count at 1,000. Only one shell hit the parapet full, and that beyond the traverse next to me. It killed one man, and we had to dig out three others; two men were nearly suffocated but untouched, the third was horribly wounded. I learnt that highly trained and disciplined troops cannot be shelled out of well-dug trenches, and that the casualties from shellfire are very small compared with those inflicted by machine-guns in the open.

We had some well-known characters in the battalion: the two outstanding company commanders were "Copper" Seymour[7] and "Crawley" de Crespigny.[8] Each had more than fifteen years' service. "Copper" Seymour, who had been recuperating from a bad Epsom or Newmarket with a dose of foreign service in Africa, had started his war earlier than most, and had been badly wounded at the head of his native levies. He was carried back some hundreds of miles, evaded the medical board and got out to France. His wounds were not fully healed at this time, and had to be dressed by his subalterns. He had red hair, brilliant blue eyes, and was a strict disciplinarian.

"Crawley" de Crespigny, his great friend, was soon my company commander, and I fell completely under his charm. He had been one of the best-known gentlemen jockeys of his day. Once, when he had taken a bad fall on a favoured animal, and was walking past the silver ring towards the enclosure, someone shouted out that he must have backed the other. Crawley jumped the railings and chastised the offender with his cutting whip.

He was, however, the kindest and most understanding of men, brave as a lion, most considerate and friendly to his subalterns. He was sometimes known to temper discipline with leniency, and when a young officer ran in one of his men for gambling in billets, he gave the man no more than a caution, and in private damned the eyes of the complainant.

He was wracked by the pain of a stomach disorder, probably brought on by wasting in earlier life, would not report sick, and sometimes used to lie groaning in the trench for the best part of the night. He usually recovered the next day, and took his glass of port or two as a sharp but unwise reminder to his stomach that he was having no nonsense with his digestion. He did not entertain a great respect for generals and the higher command, and was

[7] Major Lord Henry Seymour.
[8] Afterwards Brig.-Gen. Sir Claude Champion de Crespigny (5th Bt.).

reputed to begin most battles by cutting his own telephone wire. Both "Copper" Seymour and "Crawley" de Crespigny survived to command Guards brigades in the war.

The first battle in which I took part was the Battle of Festubert in May 1915. The 4th Guards Brigade, under the command of Brigadier-General Lord Cavan,[9] was not committed to the first assault: we were to exploit the initial success, and that often meant attacking some position which the first wave of troops had failed to take.

We had to move up in support at dawn, and my first day in a battle could not have opened in a more absurd manner. I was billeted in a small farmhouse: the farmer, his wife and two daughters of about seventeen or eighteen slept in a large attic, and I had to go through their room to get to mine. I was called by my servant, and dressed about 4:30 A.M., and when I passed through my host's room it was all too clear that the family had only just got out of bed. None of them had a stich on, but all politely bowed and greeted me with *"Bonjour, mon Capitaine."* I was a second lieutenant, but was too embarrassed to savour the compliment. After this unnerving encounter, I joined my half company: we fell in and made for the battlefield. Our company was deployed in line in a root field and told to await orders. Somewhere about 6:30 A.M., Crawley and I ate some hard-boiled eggs and drank some rum. I have never what is called "fancied" hard-boiled eggs since. We got mildly shelled, and were soon thoroughly bored. We never moved all day and marched back to billets as soon as it got dark.

The next day was different. The line had moved forward a few hundred yards. We had to march up in artillery formation across flat, featureless country, intersected by a few ditches. Artillery formation means moving in blobs: in this instance the blobs were platoons. The commanding officer was somewhere near the centre of the two leading companies, of which mine was one, and I heard him rebuking another platoon commander in biting tones because his rear rank was not properly closed up. We were met by salvos of low-bursting shrapnel, which cracked off in our faces, with a cloud of black smoke, at about twenty feet from the ground. The men had a disrespectful and unquotable name for these shells. They were more or less ineffective, but marching along through them, under the eyes of the commanding officer, is a frightening experience, and the complete nonchalance which it is necessary

[9] Afterwards Field-Marshal the Earl of Cavan.

for officers to exhibit is quite a strain. We were deployed into a support trench.

That day, Arthur Penn was wounded, and afterwards entered himself in his own game book under the heading "BEAT—Cour de l'Avoué: BAG—Self." We had a handful of casualties.

Just before the battle, Arthur Wiggins and another officer had gone down with chicken-pox, an event which I am certain had a marked bearing, as will be shown, on my military career.

We spent the night in burying the German dead, cleaning up our trench, thickening the parapets and awaiting orders. Very early the next morning we were told to take the Cour de l'Avoué farm, a heavily fortified strong-point in the enemy line, half a mile or so in front of us. It looked an ugly job, and we were warned that we should attack at about 9:30. At dawn, I took off my shirt and told my servant to throw a cup of water over me before I shaved. I felt very well, but to my surprise I saw that I was covered with spots. "Chicken-pox," I thought. I did not know what on earth to do. I happened to be only a hundred yards or so from Battalion H.Q., so I went along the trench and addressed the second-in-command, "Ma" Jeffreys, and told him of my discovery. He looked at me intently from about ten yards away, and rapped out, "Don't come near me. Get back to the advanced casualty clearing station."

I set out and had to pass through a very fair barrage. Major Billy Reid of the Irish Guards, who were in support close behind, asked me as I passed where I was off to, and when I told him, and why, he said, "You're a lucky dog." The casualty clearing station was full of wounded and smelt of blood, antiseptics and sweat. I had to wait for twenty minutes or so before I could show my spots to the medical officer. He did not hesitate over his diagnosis, merely said, "Parasitic," and turned away. I had some difficulty in getting him to mark my card.

So back I had to go. By then—about 9 A.M.—the barrage had got very thick, and I had a most unpleasant time, with shells bursting all round me.

However, the attack had been postponed, and I was soon able to rejoin and report to the second-in-command. I had the feeling that he had not expected to see me again, or at least not so soon, and he unbent enough to ask me what I had been doing the previous night. I said, "Burying some dead Germans and clearing up the trench." "That's where I expect you got the lice."

The attack was repeatedly postponed, and it was not till 4:30

in the afternoon that we advanced. The first part of it was frightening. My two platoons were not to be immediately deployed, and were in Indian file in an old communication trench, which ran into the enemy trenches at right-angles. We were heavily shelled in enfilade. We expected a direct hit at any moment, and could only sit and suffer. One of my section commanders, Lance-Sergeant Hunt, was buried, but we dug him out in time. We had two or three men wounded. Sergeant Gambrell was imperturbable, and the men remained completely stoical, though their curses rippled and snarled along the ranks. I have a prejudice myself against dying with a foul word in my mouth.

Eventually we deployed, and under a thin artillery barrage captured an enemy trench or two. It was at this moment that we heard that our commanding officer had been killed, and a little later that Barrington-Kennet[10] had also been killed.

The main attack on the farm was soon called off, because no progress had been made on the flanks by another brigade, and we were told to dig in as soon as it got dark. I was standing above ground supervising some of this digging; a few bullets were cracking through the darkness. The men had got down three or four feet when, for some reason, I jumped into the trench. "Are you hit, Sir?" said Sergeant Gambrell. "No, I don't think so, but something made me jump." I was up again in a moment, and we were soon well dug in. Nothing much more happened, except that we were well shelled and had a few more casualties.

The next night we marched back to billets. We were very tired, and when we regained the road were marching at less than two miles an hour when a staff car nearly scattered my two rear ranks. I pretended that I did not know that there was a senior officer inside, and let fly with a good stream of oaths and abuse. A voice said, "I am Major Gathorne-Hardy" [11] (a Grenadier) "and from the language, you must be from our 2nd Battalion." "Sir."

The officers were now dressed and equipped exactly like the men, except that we did not carry rifles, and I used to keep my Russian cigarette case in the entrenching tool carrier. When I took it out that night, I saw that a bullet had passed right through it: the entrance and exit holes were as if they had been drilled. Doubtless it was this that had made me jump: another quarter of an inch, and I should have had a shattered thigh bone.

My company was billeted in a farmhouse, and we slept for

10 Major B. H. Barrington-Kennet.
11 Afterwards General the Hon. Sir Francis Gathorne-Hardy.

twelve hours, only to be woken by the farmyard noises and by the smell and flies of the large midden. Rumours always sweep through armies like a bush fire. At this moment the story was that the Germans were about to give in. We were wakened one morning by loud cheering from all the men. This is the end of the war, we thought, and it was disappointing to find that the cheers were for an old boar who was making amorous advances to a sow.

After the battle our routine was monotonous, two days and nights in the trenches, two days in billets, two days in support.

We used to have big concerts in Béthune or La Gorgue when we were out of the line. One of the most popular turns was tap dancing by Captain Alexander[12] of the Irish Guards, who had attained a professional standard in this difficult art.

We got plenty of drill during our rest, but we were young and gay and a closely knit society. All officers in the Brigade are on Christian-name terms automatically, except the commanding officers, and sign themselves "Yours ever."

The Grenadiers had perhaps a closer affiliation with the Scots Guards than any other regiment, but we were all guardsmen first, had the same standards of discipline, the same professional training, the same pride, and the same kind of jokes. I learnt that in war all front-line officers are of the same age, whether they are forty or twenty, because they are all the same distance away from death. This abolition of age is another thing which knits the fraternity of fighting regimental soldiers together and which seems to widen the cleavage between staff and troops.

In those days each battalion had two Vickers machine-guns mounted on tripods and one specialist machine-gun officer. Much to my surprise, and it was my very first hint of promotion, I was selected as a potential machine-gun officer and sent to Boulogne for a three weeks' course. I studied machine-guns and their wayward temperament with great attention. In 1961, I am sure that I could still clear the No. 2 Stoppage, but I doubt if I could still take the Vickers machine-gun to pieces and reassemble it as we were taught.

My mother succeeded in getting over to France, like Gronow to Brussels in 1815, and I saw her several times and had dinner with her in the hotel at Boulogne.

Some time after I had finished this course, I heard to my amazement that Lord Cavan, who had just been given a line division, had asked for me as his A.D.C. I was to be released at once. Lord

[12] Now Field-Marshal Earl Alexander of Tunis.

Cavan, who was a retired officer in my regiment, had made a great reputation for himself as a brigadier-general in command of the famous 4th Guards Brigade during the first Battle of Ypres. In January or February 1915, Sir John French had arrived at Brigade H.Q. and offered Cavan a division but upon one condition, that he would promise to stay in the Army after the war. Cavan refused and said that he proposed to leave and hunt his hounds as soon as ever the last shot was fired. In consequence, he did not get his division until three or four months later. The incident throws light upon two things. First, the professionalism of the Army, which would not countenance an appointment unless it was held by "one of us," and secondly, and more disastrously, it was clear that if a retired professional had to promise to stay on to be promoted, no officer who was not a professional—or serving officer —whatever his battle experience, was likely to rise far in this hierarchy, almost as closely limited as the College of Cardinals.

In the Second World War, one of the reasons why the subordinate commanders were so much better was because youth and a determination to leave the profession of arms as soon as there was no one to fight were not an impediment to promotion.

I joined the major-general in the back area and found that Cuthbert Headlam,[13] his brother-in-law, was the other A.D.C.

The division held a line round Armentières, and the corps was commanded by Lieutenant-General Sir Charles Fergusson, another Grenadier and the very image of a guardsman: tall, good-looking, beautifully turned out, white moustache, and a quilt of medals. One day, Sir Charles came into our H.Q., which was in a villa in the much-shelled town, and I saw him take the major-general on one side. I could not help hearing that he was taking the general's name for wearing the gold spurs of a guardsman. "You are no longer a regimental officer, please remember that, 'Fatty.'"

Cavan was very kind to me. Cuthbert and I used to exercise his horses, which was not an unalloyed pleasure as one or two had been picked up cheap on Mr. Soapey Sponge's example. A.D.C.s in those days were glorified butlers, looked after the mess, kept the troops at H.Q. up to the mark and rode about with the general. Otherwise they had no professional duties whatever. They were not employed to keep touch with the troops during a battle, they ran into none of the dangers that faced the A.D.C. of Wellington's days, who "galloped" for their generals on the battlefield with orders,

[13] Now Lieutenant-Colonel the Rt. Hon. Sir Cuthbert Headlam.

generally to the hottest part of the fight. In short, A.D.C.s of my day were despised.

For about three weeks I enjoyed the comparative absence of danger and the comfort of divisional H.Q., but I soon became restive and began to seek ways of being returned to duty. My moves, which only just stopped short of insubordination, were not successful at first, because Cavan was told that a Guards division was to be formed, that he was to command it and that one or two battalions, including the 3rd and 4th Battalion Grenadiers, were to be sent out from home to complete it. The Guards brigades and battalions were to be withdrawn from the line divisions in which they were serving at this time, and from immediate fighting, in order to organize themselves as a division in a back area. There was therefore no object in returning an officer to regimental duty while the division was being formed.

By the beginning of August 1915, though still an A.D.C., I was back amongst my brother officers of the Guards division. I found that the Prince of Wales was an extra A.D.C. He was the most charming and delightful human being that I had ever known. He, too, chafed at being at H.Q., and all the more because he recognised that he was unlikely ever to be allowed to serve in a battalion. He never stopped trying.

It was a hot and sunny month and our duties at H.Q. were light. One morning, H.R.H. came into the divisional staff office and asked whether I was also dining with Desmond FitzGerald,[14] his great friend, then commanding the 1st Battalion Irish Guards. "If so, we will go together." I said, "Yes, Sir, I am the other guest," and was delighted because Desmond lived three or four miles away, and the road was nearly all up hill. The Prince's car would get us there in under ten minutes.

About 6:30 he arrived again in the staff office and said, "By the way, you have got a bicycle, I suppose? If you haven't you had better get one, because we ought to start. Dinner is at 7:30." The ration bicycle was a much worse ride than was the worst of Lord Cavan's hunters: it was heavy, and built for wear rather than comfort.

It was still very hot when we set out. "I never get off," said H.R.H. as we faced a mile or two of hilly road. "It is one of the ways that I keep fit." I was in good training, but after a mile I had sweated through my Sam Browne belt and had begun to entertain

[14] Lieutenant-Colonel Lord Desmond FitzGerald.

some republican inclinations. However, we had a gay and delightful evening: the Prince was happy, and in the highest spirits; we replaced our lost tissue with some old brandy, and free-wheeled home to our cage like schoolboys.

It is rarely that I am given a chance to pay my respects to him in these days, but for me his spell has never been broken.

He used to lend his large grey Daimler to any brother officer who could find the courage to ask for it. After I had returned to duty, I later got some leave and asked to borrow the car to get to Boulogne, because by this means you could get an extra day in England. He sent me a slip of paper agreeing at once, but asking me whether I would take a letter to "my people" at home. This was how he described the King and Queen.

I had some trouble with the French territorial guards at the road barrier at the entrance to Boulogne, and it took a few minutes of my fluent French and some bluff to get through. As I reached the quay the leave boat had just cast off, but I was not the Prince's messenger for nothing and, waving his letter to the King, I persuaded the embarkation officer to order the ship to put back. I swept up the gangway in triumph, and delivered the letter at Buckingham Palace in a few hours.

The first battle in which the Guards division was engaged as a division was the Battle of Loos, October 1915, but I saw little of it, because I was still on the staff.

Early in October, the newly formed Guards division was ordered to attack a complex of enemy trenches known as the Hohenzollern Redoubt.

At this time the higher command of the Guards division was dissatisfied with the handling of the 3rd Battalion Grenadiers by the commanding officer; unfortunately for him, some senior Grenadiers had also taken exception to the march discipline of the battalion whilst moving back from the trenches: a man had been seen short of a haversack, and the rear section of No. 14 platoon was not in step. There was hell to pay.

It so happened that the adjutancy of the battalion was vacant, and to my astonishment I was chosen to fill it. The G.O.C. was asked to release me from Divisional H.Q. and was, I think, quite glad to do so. My appointment caused much criticism: I had not been a regular officer before the war.

The commanding officer had been in conflict with Sir Douglas Haig[15] during the retreat from Mons, when he had unpardonably

[15] Afterwards Field-Marshal Earl Haig.

criticised to his face the dispositions which he had been ordered to take up: he had been sent home. The battalion had one or two company commanders who were thought to be too old; new brooms were wanted, but one new broom—myself—was obviously far too new. I joined the battalion on October 15th.

I left divisional H.Q. almost with elation—an elation which was somewhat deflated when I discovered that on the very afternoon of my posting the battalion had to relieve another in a boiling part of the line, and carry out a difficult though limited attack. I joined it on the line of march.

I was junior to most of the subalterns, although I was comparatively veteran in war experience. It was only too true that our commanding officer, who belonged to the old school, had lost confidence and thought he was a marked man. He was not slow to complain to me at having a young adjutant thrust upon him, but at least absolved me from blame: indeed, he leant upon my so-called experience.

We attacked our objective at night. The situation was confused, the shelling very heavy, and his orders, I thought, were contradictory. I made them at least clear and consistent, but the C.O.'s lack of confidence and hesitation had imperceptibly communicated itself to the junior commanders, and the attack, if not bungled, was not the crisp, decisive action that the Grenadiers expect.

Soon after these operations were concluded, after severe casualties, the 11th Corps, which included the Guards division, were allotted the task of holding a line from a point about 1,000 yards south of the Cour de l'Avoué northward to Picantin. This was not new country to us. The defensive system ran through low-lying country, which often became water-logged. The Germans held the Aubers ridge above us, and as usual had all the advantages of observation and drainage.

I remember, when out of the line, pointing out to the commanding officer some deficiencies in the interior economy. He agreed there were such, and on my suggestion called the company commanders together.

"The adjutant tells me," he began, "that there are some weaknesses in the interior economy about the issue of rum rations, the corporals' mess fund and—er—other things. Send for your company quartermaster sergeants and give them hell—give them hell!" I wondered if this lecture on the interior economy was adequate.

About the 14th November we were back on the old routine. As usual, and I regret having to say as usual, the trenches which the

Guards division inherited were a disgrace. The parapets were falling to pieces and the revetments were dilapidated: in a flat country
communication trenches are of great importance, and they were
already full of water. The strong points and defended localities in
depth had been shamefully neglected, and most of them were crumbling to pieces.

We quickly realised that as soon as the weather got worse, we
should have no defences. We accordingly set to work night and day
with the aid of the Royal Engineers to get trenches and communications into a guardsmanlike condition. We were only just in time,
and had to work feverishly against the clock. When we were relieved, the trenches were habitable, the defences were repaired, and
the whole system was "solid and secure."

We held the front line lightly. The routine for each battalion was
three days in the trenches, three days in close reserve, and twelve
days in billets in Merville, where there were divisional baths, a de-
lousing station and a concert hall, where we saw an occasional
film.

One night we were due to relieve our 2nd Battalion. It was wet
and cold as we moved off, but the gunners on both sides were evidently huddling in their dug-outs of the rain, for less than the usual
ration of shells rumbled or whined overhead. Battalion H.Q. was
in a farmhouse called Red Farm: it was in ruins, but one room had
been made more or less habitable, and heavily sandbagged.

I was soon busy taking over from my opposite number, Bill
Bailey,[16] adjutant of the 2nd Battalion, checking and signing for the
ammunition and rations, being shown the signal dugout, and so
forth. The two paraffin lamps of the outgoing battalion had been
taken away, and until ours were mounted the main room was lit
only by two candles stuck into bottles. They made no more than
a pool of light round the table, and the rest of the room was in
darkness. "Ma" Jeffreys, by then commanding officer of the 2nd
Battalion, said to me, "Oliver, I don't think you know Churchill,
do you?" I knew that their medical officer had been wounded or
gone sick, and I thought I was to be introduced to his successor.
Out of the darkness, however, emerged that well-known domed
head and stocky figure. It was Winston. It was a great surprise because we had thought that he was still a member of the Government.

That very evening, whilst we had a meal during the relief, he
started to enlarge upon his ideas of a land battleship. We listened

[16] Afterwards Col. Lord Glanusk.

—we had to—but we were sceptical about the views of a new-comer who had never even seen No Man's Land. We could not believe that anything could be designed to get across the country to which we were accustomed.

He brushed all this aside, and continued enthusiastically to pro-claim that these steel animals—tanks they might be called—were the way to break out of trench and positional warfare.

The three pillars of "Ma" Jeffreys' beliefs and loyalty were Eton, the Brigade of Guards and the Conservative Party, and it says much for Winston's charm that he overcame the handicap of being an Harrovian, a Yeomanry officer (at that time) and a Lib-eral. It did not take long before they were firm friends. "Ma" wanted the Brigade of Guards to be composed only of the three oldest regi-ments, and when after the war Winston used to thunder, "Star, Thistle, and Grenade! they should be the only guardsmen," I recog-nised whence the inspiration had been derived.

Winston went round the trenches the very night he had joined: he wanted to see everything and was obviously enjoying himself. He was not over-pleased, it is true, with the teetotal régime of "Ma's" H.Q., but otherwise betrayed the greatest enthusiasm for all features of his old profession. In a month he was the most popular officer in the Guards division.

In January 1916 our second-in-command was killed, and we had severe casualties: my C.O. was superseded. "Ma" Jeffreys appeared as the temporary commanding officer; he was shortly to get a brigade, and the intermission was occupied in an overhaul of the 3rd Battalion. The adjutant was subjected to a close questioning: the battalion stores were checked, the regimental sergeant-major was cross-examined, the drill sergeants were put through their paces. The quartermaster had to produce the mess accounts and to show that the battalion's handcuffs were present and correct. The company commanders had to report on a host of matters. I soon learnt that there was nothing, literally nothing, about a bat-talion that "Ma" did not know, and in a few days I had gained an insight into "how it should be done" that few senior officers could have imparted in weeks.

We had a man on the strength who had in peace time served two sentences for robbery with violence. I will call him Private Lee, although that was not his name. He was brutish and hardly sane. He took ill to the discipline of the Brigade, and was never out of trouble. His particular hobby was clubbing corporals with his rifle in billets when checked for some offence. He committed one of these atrocities the very day that "Ma" took over command. He was marched before the commanding officer, who directed that he should be tried by court martial; the summary of evidence was to be taken; when sentenced he was to be put on bread and water and kept in irons. I had studied the Army Act closely and suggested in private that this was beyond a commanding officer's powers, even in the field. "Ma" said sternly, "You may take it that I know the Act," and of course he did, but I was forgiven for my intervention because these restrictions could only be imposed after the man had been sentenced, and the commanding officer was anticipating an unfavourable verdict by the Court. The sequel to this incident will be recounted later.

After a detailed and exhaustive scrutiny of men, equipment, interior economy, N.C.O.s and company commanders, "Ma" pronounced that there was little wrong. What was wrong he quickly put right. He said I had done well in my short term, but obviously suffered from inexperience, particularly over my orders concerning the issue of the rum ration. If a man did not take his ration, it was to be poured out on the ground in the presence of an officer: otherwise a residue would remain that might be a temptation.

It was a peerless performance by a highly trained expert, and it taught me things which greatly advanced my education as an officer.

Lieutenant-Colonel B. N. Sergison-Brooke,[17] who had been brigade major, 4th Guards Brigade, in 1914, succeeded as commanding officer on February 9th. He was one of the best soldiers who ever put on a Sam Browne belt, and he soon made the 3rd Battalion one of the two or three best in the division. In addition to his extensive knowledge of regimental soldiering, he had passed the Staff College, and was versed in all the higher problems of staff work and command.

He and Billy Lambton[18] of the Coldstream shared one characteristic: neither, unless obliged to, ever spoke before luncheon. Before luncheon they were unapproachable. Their intimidating silences, when the most that could be expected was a curt order delivered between clenched teeth, derived from a slow-acting digestion, which clothed the world in a bilious haze until the first glass of port brought a ray of sunshine. After luncheon, both were charming, helpful and humorous.

I was "Boy" Brooke's adjutant until September 1916, when he

[17] Now Lieutenant-General Sir Bertram Sergison-Brooke.
[18] Afterwards Major-General the Hon. Sir William Lambton.

was hit. I was by his side. After I was wounded in 1918, I returned to become his brigade major in October 1918, and we finished the war together.

He was a man who inspired affection as well as respect: he was not accustomed to water down his opinions when they were asked for by senior commanders: he would never permit any criticism of his subordinates by others, but would reply, "He was quite right: blame me." Then he would say in private, "You bloody young fool, you ought to have posted the piquet line five hundred yards further out, not on that feature, but on the next one, as I told you. I thought you knew enough about war for that. Anyway you know more about it than the major-general, and I told him so, but don't do it again."

In a few weeks the reputation of the battalion was on a pinnacle.

After our rest and refit we were destined for the Ypres salient, and we spent most of the winter in the Potijze area, towards its left or northernmost sector. The reliefs were the most trying part of our duties; they involved marching by platoons, spaced out at 100 yards, down the main *pavé* road that led almost due north from Ypres to Potijze. The road was under direct observation by the Germans from the Pilkem ridge, and was therefore impassable for troops by day. Occasionally an officer and an orderly would use it in daylight, and they were not always shot at. Sometimes, however, it amused the German gunners to snipe even so small a party as two with a few salvos of 77 mm., and since they knew the range to a hair's breadth, it was necessary from time to time to cower in the ditch.

Of course old soldiers—that is those with more than one year's experience of war—acquire a sort of second sense of where and when shells are going to fall. I remember a senior officer, who had been wounded in August 1914, and who had only just got back, asking me why in God's name I was leading a party of details through some very bad, waterlogged country and not making use of the road and the cover afforded by some garden walls. I had hardly said, "Because that is a likely place to get shelled," when several salvos of 5.9s came roaring and rumbling over and knocked the walls to pieces. My party would have had a dozen casualties or more if they had taken the route suggested; as it was, we had a splinter or two and a nose-cap amongst us, but no one got hit. I cannot say how many times this sort of sixth sense of the hunted animal saved my life.

At one time I was due for a week's leave in England and, with the commanding officer's permission, was trying to scrounge an extra day by starting soon after dawn. I set out down the Ypres road, with my orderly, in broad daylight. You could almost have seen that our ears were cocked. Sure enough, here they come, we thought, and we were in the ditch in a flash; an excellent bracket, followed by another salvo pretty close to us, then a pause, which we used to make a hundred yards, by using the ditch; then another salvo fifty yards behind us. We made a small diversion round a few ruined houses, and woomph, woomph, woomph, another salvo in the middle of them. We were undamaged. It is particularly annoying and frightening to be pursued in this way when you are going on leave.

Our usual routine was two days and nights in the trenches, then back down that accursed road to billets in the ramparts in Ypres. The ramparts were several feet thick and excellent cover. Our billets were in the prison, which was protected by them, and though not a very cheerful place, was safe from anything but a very large shell. A road ran along the west side of the ramparts, and we used to do platoon and arms drill when we were resting. Ypres rang with our words of command, and a company or two of Canadians from the neighbouring division looked on in amazement and, occasionally, cheered. They thought it a ridiculous example of spit and polish.

Everything in Ypres was, of course, in ruins, but the old buildings gave some cover from shell fire, and enabled some movement to take place. The Germans shelled us spasmodically every day, and occasionally put down a heavy concentration, but did no more than make life uneasy.

After two days in this rather gloomy resort, we had to plug back up the road, soon after dusk, to the trenches. Parties from the first-line transport with limbered wagons, or leading horses with ammunition and stores, probably had the worst task of all. When the road was shelled, some of the poor animals went nearly mad with fright, broke loose and were difficult to get back on the road again. The marches, even to those without pack animals, were quite bad enough: you had the sensation that you were marching straight down the jaws of some Wagnerian dragon which was only waiting till you had got well inside to snap his teeth on you with a click. Moreover, when there was shelling, you could see a semicircle of flashes all round you, and to the north and south on the flanks of the salient some of the flashes were well behind you.

The days and nights in the trenches were mostly spent in improving the line, revetting the parapets and communication trenches, laying duck-boards and thickening the cover with sand-bags. The great difficulty in this work arose because the country had been pounded by the shell fire of two years into a soupy marsh, and all the drainage had been destroyed. Our line was well below the level of the Pilkem ridge, and some of the surface water from the German lines drained into the valley. This digging and strengthening and sandbagging was something of a labour of Sisyphus, because if it appeared to the Germans that we were making too good a job of it, they would drench our position with shells for a whole afternoon, blow in the trenches and oblige us to start afresh on our work.

This tortured piece of country had a kind of awful and sombre majesty: the majesty of death. The stumps of trees, the ruins and slime, seemed to make a picture fitting to man's folly; the stench of corruption which came from the many hundreds of unburied corpses added a Dantesque horror. But we were young, and thought more of our professional duties than of the decay and doom-laden landscape which stretched before us.

We were not attacked during the whole time we were in the line. All we had to do was to dig and repair, dig and repair and endure the shell fire. Sitting still and being shelled is a sort of gnawing experience. When two or three officers were talking and they heard the rumble of a 5.9, or the higher whine of a 77 mm., there would be a momentary, almost imperceptible pause whilst trained ears and senses judged how far away the shells would fall. If very near, we crouched against the parapet, if more than 25 yards away, the conversation went on. It sounded like this. "I see Blank won that race at five to four, a very fair price, because at eight stun . . .' (the shell bursts) '. . . seven, she was well in the handicap. Cecil said he fancied the filly."

Our headquarters were in a cellar in the garden of the Potijze Château, and looked out over a slimy pond. We made ourselves as comfortable as possible, had a red cloth with blue edges (the Brigade colours) to eat off, and there was a row if the cook overcooked a woodcock which had been sent out to us from home. We drank, of course, very sparingly, but always had a glass of port after dinner, before going round the line.

It was during these and many similar days that deep attention to comfort finally took root in me. As life has progressed, I have become less afraid of danger and more afraid of discomfort, but even in those days we paid more attention to the second, because the first could not be avoided.

Professionally, we thought little of the policy of the higher command. The front-line trenches were in full observation by the enemy, and enfiladed by artillery from one flank or another, in our case chiefly from the left flank. No one who spent some weeks in the salient could have been persuaded that it was sensible to hold this battered sea of shell holes and those stark ruins of a town: but hold it we did.

The weekly drain of casualties underlined the folly of the dispositions. By this time the Germans were far too wise to attempt to pinch out the salient: they knew that they would inflict more casualties by just pounding us, day and night, from the flanks. In the month of March 1916 alone, the Guards division, which was only engaged in routine duties, lost ten officers and 323 other ranks, and in April 400 of all ranks.

CHAPTER IV

THE FIRST WORLD WAR: II

T HE Battle of the Somme began on July 1st, 1916, and lasted till November 18th. It was a battle of attrition and both sides nearly bled to death. After it we could not maintain the same numbers of men in the field. On the enemy side, the German Army was never the same again: their problem of man-power was even more acute. The last flower of British and German youth was sacrificed in those four and a half months. Amongst these young men, there were the leaders who might have fashioned a different Europe and might have averted a second war. By Christmas they were nearly all dead.

The Guards division was not committed in the opening phases: with our high standard of training, and with our high proportion of professional officers, we were allotted the role of either exploiting success in open warfare, or of tearing apart the last resistance before the break-through. The military art and military tactics are at a discount in set-piece battles: they come to life in open or near-open warfare.

We did much marching about in the hot and dusty weather of August: we were to attack here, when the first attack had failed, or there, where the possibility of exploiting a success or a break-through was opening up. At the last minute the orders were always countermanded.

One day, just before we expected to make an attack, the commanding officers, seconds-in-command and adjutants of all battalions were ordered to a small copse some way behind the line. The barrage had already begun, and its ominous but muted thunder and thud charged the air with doom. Outside the little wood stood a dismounted corporal major of "The Blues," carrying the Royal Standard.

The King, for he was the reason for our summons, stood in a clearing and shook hands with each of us. *Morituri te salutamus,* I thought.

We expected and feared a battle speech, but the King talked to us in the most down-to-earth way—an example of timely tact. He asked Sherard Godman of the Scots Guards, the senior commanding officer present, what sort of food we carried into the attack. "Cold chicken?" he suggested, and when Sherard Godman replied, "Mostly bully beef, Sir," he rightly looked a little incredulous, and repeated, "Cold chicken, I expect." Once again, the attack was called off.

For three weeks or more we never heard a shell or the rattle of machine-gun fire. At the end of this unexpected pause it would have been difficult to match the Guards division in any army, in peace or war. Once when I was watching a battalion of the Grenadiers on the line of march, we passed and saluted a French general. He beckoned me and said, *"Alors, ce régiment vient d'arriver en France?" "Non, mon Général, c'est un bataillon de la Garde qui se bat depuis dix-neuf cent quinze."* A proud moment. The troops were sunburnt and looked as fresh and professional as you could have wished. Their equipment and turn-out were perfect.

Eventually we got orders that we were at last to be committed. We were first to capture part of the Flers ridge, a tactical feature which commanded the approaches to Bapaume to the east, and then press on towards Lesboeufs. The assault was to be made by several divisions, and was to be supported by tanks for the first time in history. Our furthest objectives, as marked on our operational maps, were distant, and we cynically supposed that few of us would be alive to reach them.

The cavalry were to be brought forward ready for the breakthrough: we thought that they would do little galloping and that the weather would have broken long before their chance presented itself.

We in the 3rd Battalion reconnoitred our position and the assault trenches from which we should issue. Zero hour was to be at dawn on September 15th. In the meanwhile, the weather was clear but windy, and the sky fleeced with cotton-wool clouds.

On the 14th, about 5 P.M., when the barrage had grown to a roar and we were sitting about with cramp in our stomachs, I wrote a letter—I thought it would perhaps be my last—to my mother, and told her that she would hear more from me in a day or two. I fear she guessed, like many in England, that a great battle was impending.

About 11 P.M. we moved off across the pockmarked battlefield. An occasional Verey light lit up the scene for a moment or two. Nothing but the riven stumps of a few trees or the rubble of a ruined house relieved the utter devastation. We made our way up a gentle slope, pitted with shell holes. It was pitch dark, and we marched slowly in our heavy equipment. There was a sensation that this slowness was prolonging our last night on earth and drawing out our last living hours. A few salvos of gas shells, unmistakable because of the different noise they made on bursting, fell near us. The battalion was ordered to halt and to put on gas masks; we moved off again down the far slope. Pitch dark; a Verey light or two; a little shelling; silence; curses.

We took up our position with our usual smoothness and began to improve our temporary assault trenches. Battalion H.Q., that is the commanding officer, Colonel Sergison-Brooke, and myself, and the signal officer, sergeant-major, drill sergeant and H.Q. Signallers, were established in a few shell holes between the first and second "waves" of our attack.

The regimental sergeant-major appeared out of the darkness, stamped to attention, saluted. "Battalion present, Sir; two men seeing the surgeon" (meaning that two men were in hospital), "one man, Private Lee,[1] missing." He saluted, turned about and joined the rest of H.Q.

"Well," said "Boy," "we had better pay a visit to these chaps on our right and find out what they are like." We stumbled along in the darkness and eventually came on a company commander, the left-hand one of the division on our right, and asked him about his immediate objective, his orders and so forth. "Oh, God, Sir," he said, "I am sure tomorrow will be the death of all of us." We reassured him, and we then walked back. "Boy," said, "I don't like the sound of that very much; those fellows are supposed to capture the Quadrilateral, and if they don't we shall know it. The bloody place will enfilade us, but that poor chap will probably be all right when once he has started."

Half an hour before zero we checked our watches again. It was cold, and I drank a good tot of rum and blew on my fingernails. Funk, I expect. 5:25 A.M. Five minutes to go, then two, one, thirty seconds, whistle. Advance. It was light enough to see the troops for

[1] See pp. 49-50.

three or four hundred yards on either side of us. They were all bent forward, like men walking into a strong wind and rain, their bayonets fixed and their rifles horizontal. Troops always, in my experience, unconsciously assume this crouching position when advancing into heavy fire.

A few yards after leaving our trenches we were met by a withering fire. Our friends on the right were soon brought to a stop, and the rattle of machine-gun fire from that flank showed that our fears of being enfiladed had been well founded. At this moment, the commanding officer was hit through the thigh, a very severe wound, and the drill sergeant killed. Although they could not have been more than a yard or two from me, I was unaware that either of them had fallen.

The Germans, who had been severely hammered by shell-fire in their trenches on the top of the ridge, had pushed forward a company or two to the foot of the slope in front of us, and were firing at us from a group of shell holes.

Suddenly the men saw them and, with a hoarse blood cry which I can still hear in my dreams, rushed this line and before we could stop them had bayoneted or shot most of the defenders. I say before we could stop them, because my confused impression is that the enemy shot at us till we were less than ten yards away, and then put their hands up.

After that, nothing would have stopped the Grenadiers—nothing. We stumbled forward, under increased fire, up the glacis. I was myself in a great state of excitement and for a few minutes fighting mad. We took the trench at the summit, and some prisoners, got our breath, and looked around. I found the units much mixed up: some Coldstreamers, Grenadiers and Irish Guardsmen were on either side of me. I could not find an officer at the moment, so I organised about a hundred men and put myself in command.

"Get this parapet straight," I ordered, "and dig like hell, or I'll put the lot of you in the report. Sergeant, take a party down these dugouts and clear anyone out you find; take some Mills bombs with you."

While we were mopping up, a galling enfilade fire was turned on us from the Quadrilateral, and although this had much less effect than when we had passed through it in the open, two or three of my men were hit. At this moment a German doctor, wearing a Red Cross brassard, appeared under escort from one of the deep dug-outs, blinking in the sunlight. I could not see where the enemy fire was coming from, and rather angrily said to the doctor,

"Do you speak English?" "Oh yes," he said. "Well, where is that fire coming from?" He pointed to his Red Cross and said, "I am non-combatant, and I do not know." "Well, if you don't tell me, I shall shoot you," I said, bringing out my revolver.

At this he burst into a half chuckle, half laugh, and said, "I am quite sure you will do nothing of the kind." He could not conceal his amusement. I also could not help smiling, and said, "Get out of here, and quick," pointing backwards, and as he scrambled up the rear of the trench, I kicked him not very hard in the behind to restore my self-respect. He merely grinned and made off. I afterwards heard that he spent the rest of the day in a shell-hole in the Ginchy valley below us, which was seething with shells, tending the wounded and doing what he could with a small stock of field dressings which he carried. A brave man: he was not even afraid of me.

I next saw a battalion of Coldstream executing a flank attack almost across our front. They were held up by some machine-guns which I could see. I found two sergeants and a few men, and with four Lewis guns I crawled out of the front line to give them some covering fire. One of the sergeants had the badges of Hythe on his sleeve—a Lewis gun expert, in short. We were in some dead ground and crawled forward quickly and safely. I could see two enemy machine-guns silhouetted against the skyline, and I clearly observed one man righting the No. 2 stoppage. I gave the range to my party as 150 yards, and we let them have four drums. First I lengthened to 200 yards, then dropped back to 100, still without the slightest effect. I have never believed in Lewis guns since that day.

I went back to our front line to collect a proper machine-gun, when I stumbled into Lieutenant-Colonel Guy Baring of the Coldstream Guards. He said, "Where's my battalion?" "I've just been trying to give them some covering fire, Sir: there is one company trying to get forward now." "I must join them at once," he said, and started to climb the trench. "Not that way, Sir, go round a little, you will get hit here. No, please, Sir," I said. "Please." He paid no attention and clambered up the trench. I hard a bullet strike him, and he fell back dead into my arms.

A minute or two later, I saw John Campbell [2] with his head-quarters in a shell-hole a few yards behind our line. He had a hunting horn, which he was blowing from time to time, though for what reason I could not guess. He was full of fight and enthusiasm. He saw me, and shouted, "Come here, Oliver." I joined him in the

[2] Afterwards Brig.-Gen. J. V. Campbell, V.C.

shell-hole. We argued about exactly where we were, and I convinced him that it was not where he thought. "Those bastards in that redoubt are holding us up; go and get a few men and bomb them out."

This was not far from a sentence of death, but needs must when you get an order. Back I went, collected a dozen men and a few boxes of bombs, and started bombing down the trench. The method I employed was the conventional one of rushing to the place where the last bomb had exploded, with a couple of men overground on either side of the trench.

We had made about forty yards or so in this way, when I heard the drum of feet making towards us down the trench. I pulled the sides of the trench down and rapped out an order to one of the men to mount our Lewis gun. The first German to appear was shot dead at about five yards' range; he had his hands up, but it was impossible to see this in time to stop. "Cease fire!" I shouted, and then appeared eighty or ninety others, all with their hands up. I passed them quickly down the trench, rather in fear that they might knock us on the head when they saw that we were only twelve. Of course forty yards away there were quite enough men to deal with them.

In less than an hour I reported back to John Campbell in his shell hole. "The redoubt is cleared, Sir, and I've captured about a hundred prisoners." "By God, that's the best thing I've seen done in the war!" he shouted. "Damn me if I don't get you a V.C. for that! Damned if I don't!" "Oh," says I, "I'm afraid they all had their hands up." My V.C. vanished.

I afterwards used to say, as a joke, that if I could only have kept my mouth shut, I should have been wearing the V.C. Even if I had been dishonest enough to keep silent, I would surely have been found out. We were careful in the Brigade that decorations were not given to those who were only lucky.

The redoubt being cleared, I decided I must try and attack the next objective with my hundred men, although our barrage had long passed far beyond us. The enemy was obviously in great confusion, and I thought we might pick up something cheap. I found a communication trench leading away from the line to the east, down the hill, which gave us a covered approach to the next objective. We filed down it; the shells were now falling well behind us, and we were suddenly carrying out an exercise in peace in the sunshine. We took a trench with only a few Germans in it, and most of them wounded. The outskirts of Lesboeufs were just in front of us,

and I could see a well-head in the garden plot of one of the houses.
I dared not commit my hundred men to the village with both my
flanks in the air, so I ordered the men to put our newly won trench
into a state of defence, and sent back a message that I was in the
outskirts of Lesboeufs, and that I thought reinforcements of a battalion or so could rush it with small loss. Shortly afterwards, I
came on Major Rocke, a senior officer who had also led a detachment down the hill. He was clearly enjoying himself and was full
of fight. He was thenceforth in command. I talked to "Piggy" Hirst[3]
of my battalion, who had posted himself with a Lewis gun or two
to protect our right flank. He appeared to regard the proceedings
like a Newmarket habitué regards a country meeting: anything
might happen in a mess like this, but really, one can hardly call it
a proper battle. "I've got two Irish Guardsmen, a few Coldstreamers and a dozen of my own company," he said ruefully. He was
quite unmoved.

An hour passed. The sun was warm; we were not shot at; we
thought we had been enterprising, and that at any minute we
should see some fresh troops coming down the hill to join us and
rush the village. I spent the time looking through my glasses and
saw to my chagrin a couple of German batteries collecting their
baggage, limbering up and moving off. They were about a thousand
yards away on my left flank and were quite unhurried and unmolested. I thought, "If our reinforcements appear quickly, we might
put them in the bag."

I could also see some infantry units moving back in some disorder, and I was sure that if we had even a brigade handy, we
could go for a mile or more without a casualty.

Two hours passed. Still nothing. I crawled forward and attracted
a deterrent volume of fire. Three hours passed. Four hours passed.
Then about 3 P.M. a large body of Germans—I judged at least three
strong companies—appeared in line a hundred yards or so away
from us in extended order and attacked my party.

I fired all six rounds of my automatic straight into their faces.
Nobody even flinched. It was a confused jumble; they got into the
trench with us. We were all mixed up. One German soldier got
down on his knee and drew a bead on me with his rifle from about
five yards' distance. I threw my empty revolver at his head. He
thought it was a bomb, dropped his rifle and covered his head with
his arms. We were hopelessly outnumbered, and I scrambled up
the back of the trench and blew my whistle to retreat. We went

[3] G. F. R. Hirst.

back in what the books call good order, but which does not look so tidy in fact. "Piggy" Hirst gave us some covering fire. The Germans, instead of sitting still in their trench and shooting us in the back, came after us up the hill with the bayonet; we gave them a few rounds as a reminder that this was bad tactics, and soon regained our front trench.

It was the experience of this morning and afternoon which finally convinced me that it was no good having reserves in the hands of a corps commander, or even a divisional commander. The chances were so fleeting that never would the rearward commanders be able to exploit the unforgiving minute. They would never know in time what was happening in the front line, and the holes made in the enemy line would nearly always be jagged.

Once in our line I heard some terrible news about our casualties, and some terrible rumours, most of which proved true. In our battalion, "Piggy" Hirst and I were said to be the only officers intact, although John Hopley was no more than nicked in the leg.

Little progress had been made on either of the flanks of the Guards division, and we were ordered to stand fast and put our lines into a workmanlike state of defence.

I soon heard an explanation of my haul of prisoners. By sheer chance our 2nd Battalion had started a bombing party on the other flank of the redoubt, a few hundred yards to my right. It had been organised and led by Bill Bailey. The Germans in the redoubt, whose officers were all casualties, heard the bombing beginning on each flank, thought there was a concerted movement to pinch them out, and threw in their hands.

Things are never what they seem in a battle, and the one inviolable, unshakable rule is never to give in—never. The fog of battle often wraps the brave in its mantle and hides their weaknesses and their mistakes. Never give in: never acknowledge that you are surrounded, outflanked or outnumbered, keep up some sort of line, some sort of defence, however feeble: these are the rules of battle. If you keep them, you will get some surprising successes: you will earn glory or the grave—generally the first.

I heard of several other officers in other regiments who had been killed, among them my great friend and brother golfer, Mark Tennant, killed by a shell in the front line. The casualties in the 3rd Battalion amongst the men were thought to be very heavy.

The enemy counter-attacked. Five minutes of the brigade's type of rapid fire soon put an end to that. The slope was littered with bodies, and the attack melted like butter in front of the fire.

Two divisions of determined men could not have turned out the remnants of our brigade.

I was ordered to report to brigade H.Q., a few hundred yards behind us, to give an account of what I had seen of Lesboeufs. The brigadier was the famous John Ponsonby.[4] His H.Q. was in an old trench covered with a few galvanised sheets and camouflage. After I had made my report, he gave me a glass of port, made some joke about the bullet hole through the seat of my trousers, which I hadn't noticed, and asked me which way I was facing when I got it. He then suggested I should have two hours' sleep under the office table in his dug-out. "Becky" Smith,[5] his brigade major, said I was sound asleep in twenty seconds, and snoring like the lower notes of a cathedral organ. We were heavily shelled next day, but at night we were relieved. I had no company to command, and made my way back with a few details.

I ran into Cecil Boyd Rochfort of the Scots Guards, who was also marching out with some details. We tramped across the duckboards through the Ginchy valley, which was being heavily shelled, without getting more than frightened, plugged along in the darkness and reached a sunk road where, to our delight, we found our grooms and some ponies. They also handed us a mail from home. Cecil had a telegram. "God in his Heaven!" he said. "Look at this! Portia is going to marry the Prince of Wales." He handed me the telegram. "Office of Origin: Buckingham Palace. 'Am engaged to Portia. Edward.'" It so happened that Edward Stanley,[6] Lord Derby's eldest son, and a Grenadier, had been on the King's Guard at Buckingham Palace at the time of his engagement, and had handed in his telegram through the equerry's office. Portia Cadogan, a friend of ours, was also a friend of H.R.H., and it was not surprising that we got it wrong. As we rode home we wondered how the Princess of Wales would treat us when we made our bow.

I left Cecil Rochfort and arrived at our backward camp. It was a grim moment when I sat down to dinner alone. Piggy Hirst had not got back, and arrived later with his company. The next morning, Lord Cavan, the corps commander, rode into the lines and told me I was to receive the D.S.O. as an immediate award. I do not think I should have been given it if nearly all my brother officers had not been killed or wounded.

[4] Afterwards General Sir John Ponsonby (d. 1952).
[5] Afterwards Major-General Merton Beckwith Smith (d. on active service 1942).
[6] Lord Stanley (d. 1938).

In the action the commanding officer was severely wounded. Of the twenty-two officers who took part in the battle, nine were killed or died of wounds, and nine were wounded. Four only, including myself, survived. We lost, in the two days' fighting, no fewer than 395 other ranks killed or wounded, more than half the effectives.

Amongst the officers killed were two of my dearest friends, "Sloper" Mackenzie[7] and Raymond Asquith. The former was a brave and simple soldier, a charming and generous friend, who died at the head of his company. Raymond, the son of the Prime Minister, was no professional soldier. He should have been spared, but he had shaken off with a shrug a staff appointment which would have made a proper use of his outstanding qualities. He returned to duty and to his brother officers with undisguised satisfaction.

In him England lost one of its rarest men. Even a stranger could have seen that his good looks and noble profile disclosed a man of the finest character and powers. His astringent but kindly humour many times illuminated our darkness, but with all this brilliance he was simple and unselfish enough to take his chance and make the sacrifice with men who were not his equals.

Let me add that the death of the Prime Minister's son in action at last convinced the French that we were with them to the very end. But oh, Raymond, the waste, the senseless waste that you should have died this day.

The next day we received a telegram that Major A. F. A. N. Thorne[8] had been appointed to command the battalion, and would arrive the following day, about noon, from the 1st Battalion Grenadiers, where he had been serving as second-in-command. Although, of course, he was a Grenadier, I only just knew him. His reputation was high. He arrived in a car with Major Lord Gort,[9] who was serving at that time on the staff at G.H.Q.

Hardly had we finished luncheon when "Fat Boy" Gort said that he and "Bulgy" Thorne would like to go over the ground over which the 3rd Battalion had fought two days before. I should act as their guide. I cannot say that the proposal attracted me. I thought we could ride under cover to a point below the western slopes of the Ginchy valley, but then I thought we should have to pass through the valley itself, which had been boiling with shells when I had last seen it. A number of new batteries had taken up positions in it, and the enemy counter battery bombardment was likely to be in-

[7] A. K. Mackenzie.
[8] Now General Sir Andrew Thorne.
[9] Afterwards Field-Marshal Viscount Gort, V.C.

tense. There was nothing to stay these two enthusiasts, and obviously it was desirable for the commanding officer to reconnoitre the ground in case we were again ordered forward.

It was not an afternoon upon which I look back with any nostalgic pangs. We got well shelled, reconnoitred the Flers line, and crawled about in the open. I was able to give some account of the fighting. We had some tea with "Copper" Seymour, whose headquarters were in a hole dug under a disabled tank. At last we started back, and had reached the duck-boards in the Ginchy valley, when one of our fighter aircraft came wobbling across the line at a hundred feet or so, and crashed on its nose two or three hundred yards from us. I saw the pilot get out of the cockpit and start to collect his map and other equipment. "Come on," my two seniors shouted. "We must see if he is all right." "He looks to me quite unhurt," I mumbled, but off we went, to be greeted of course with salvos from a battery of 77 mm., searching for the crashed plane. Fortunately without direction, their shooting was bad, and the ground was soft.

The pilot was in good order, and soon we were on our way, and out of the shelled zone.

While we were resting, Private Lee, the ex-criminal to whom I have already referred, and who had been reported missing on the night of the 14th, was marched into our camp under escort of the French police. He had been arrested ten or twelve miles away in the back area. He had cut off the grenade from his cap and the buttons from his jacket, and he was ordered to be tried by court-martial. I took the summary of evidence.

The penalty for desertion was death. I sent for his platoon sergeant and told him to read the summary of evidence. Lee was to be put on every wiring party and every patrol whilst awaiting trial.

The second night we were in the trenches he was reported missing. I found out a month afterwards that his comrades had told him to walk out in front of his section at night, and that they had then shot him. Long after this macabre incident, I was reading the names of guardsmen admitted to hospital in London, and amongst them was Lee. I reported to the 3rd Echelon that he was awaiting trial by court martial, but they had mislaid the records, and he could not be charged. He had been wounded in three or four places, and had crawled into the C.C.S. of another division. He duly recovered from his wounds, and after he left the Army, as a war hero, probably resumed his profession of robbery with violence.

On September 25th, the other Guards brigades stormed Lesboeufs and secured the slopes beyond it. The casualties were pitiful, especially amongst the officers. During this attack, the 2nd Guards Brigade and the 3rd Battalion Grenadiers were in support, but were not committed, since the objectives were gained.

After the successful attacks of September 25th, and after the line had been consolidated east of Lesboeufs, the division was relieved. Congratulations couched in the most laudatory terms on our conduct in the two battles were received from Sir Henry Rawlinson, G.O.C. Fourth Army, and from Lord Cavan, commanding the XIVth Corps.

The campaigning season was drawing near its end, and in the early days of October the Guards Division was withdrawn into the back areas, to absorb its reinforcements. We were allotted the duty, for a month, of building a railway in the valley of the Somme. At this point in its course, the river spreads out into several channels, which form some small islands, one or two of which are joined by causeways to the mainland. In the autumn light, the valley was a place of great beauty and peace; the reeds and bog myrtle, and a few trees, gave it a subdued charm, and a heron or two, an occasional mallard and some reed warblers shared it with us. We established ourselves on one of the islands and quickly made ourselves a comfortable camp. The pioneers built us a brick fireplace at the end of the mess; at night we had a roaring fire, at dawn the various parties moved off to their fatigues.

It was a wholly enjoyable interlude, and we were soon in good spirits. I liked my new commanding officer, who was a highly trained soldier, and the battalion appeared to be in fine shape. The river swept majestically past us; the lagoons and the little streams glowed rufous or silver at sunrise or sunset, and we heard "the wheeling kite's wild, solitary cry." [10]

Winter was approaching and we were soon back in the line on the monotonous routine of two days in the line, two in support, two in billets. Our sector was reasonably quiet, and we had few casualties. I got some leave at home and now, wearing my D.S.O., felt a true veteran.

Soon after I arrived in London, Arthur Balfour, then First Lord of the Admiralty, asked my mother and me to luncheon in his house in Carlton House Terrace; we were alone with him. He was supposed, for the first time in his life, to have begun reading the newspapers and wanted, so he said, to understand the recent bat-

[10] J. Keble, *The Christian Year:* 20th Sunday after Trinity.

tles, of which he had read in *The Times*. He asked me a series of questions. How did you deploy for the attack? I told him that we were crammed into a fairly dense mass, and opened out after zero hour like a concertina. "How very odd," he said. "Why would that be?" "It's because the enemy always puts down a very heavy protective barrage behind the front line of attacking troops, to prevent or hinder the movements of the next wave or of reinforcements. By massing the attacking troops well forward, it was expected that we should escape a lot of the shell-fire." "Do you approve of this tactic yourself?" he said. "It seems to me to be quite contrary to the sort of precepts of the Duke of Wellington." "Well, to be frank, I think it's a mistake, and the remedy can easily be worse than the evil." "I suppose that if the very first line is shelled, the casualties are heavy?" "Yes." "And wouldn't the regiments get mixed up?" "Except with very highly trained troops, that does happen."

"Now tell me about wire." "It has to be cut by artillery fire: there is no other way; it must be done by a concentration of batteries, and even then it takes several days." "So the enemy must always know exactly where, and I suppose when, to expect an attack?" "Yes, that is roughly true, but there are feint attacks and short bombardments, and the use of tanks that is beginning to develop."

He had clearly not thought about these matters very much but at the end of my cross-examination he had grasped the main tactical problem, and my answers had been filed away in his memory. I was deeply impressed by the way he gently reduced the subject to its essentials.

His detachment—and it was his most marked characteristic— was for some reason never chilling or unsympathetic, and he had the peculiar gift of making all those to whom he talked feel as if they were as clever as he. Sometimes his detachment caused a momentary embarrassment. He was said to have been dining one night with a constituent, and was no doubt thinking of his forthcoming speech, when a dish was put on the table. Forgetting that he was not at Whittinghame, where his sister, Miss Alice Balfour, kept house for him, he exclaimed abstractedly, "Tapioca pudding! How disgusting!" and a little later, "What, no cream? How preposterous!"

These few days of leave were wonderful, but going back, and the farewells, were like beginning the war all over again.

In the middle of November we did a short spell in the trenches on the old Somme battlefield and, behind the new line, sadly inspected the graves of many of our brother officers and our men who had fallen in September.

We next side-stepped to the south, to relieve the 9th French Corps, and the 3rd Battalion Grenadiers were to take over from a French reserve regiment, holding a sector near Sailly-Saillisel. The siting of the line was good, although we were overlooked in the immediate back area. We had a good field of fire. Otherwise the conditions were foul: the front line consisted of a string of posts which could not be visited by day and the mud was the worst which we had ever experienced. We used to move within a short distance of the front line overground; a man in the Scots Guards, who slipped off the duck-boards, drowned in the mud before he could be rescued.

The relief by the 3rd Battalion Grenadiers was to be accomplished on two successive nights, which meant that battalion headquarters shared a dug-out with the French regiment for one night, one day, and the next night up till 1 A.M. We could not move about in the daylight, and had to sit together, knee to knee, in the cramped quarters until dusk.

The French adjutant was a small, rather stunted Parisian, full of argot, and no great respecter of his commanding officer, Colonel Dolce. He and I slept from 1 A.M. till dawn, under the table in the small chamber, about 10 ft. by 10 ft., that served as a mess; the two commanding officers were in a sort of alcove which had two wire bunks, one above the other.

About dawn, one of the wire bunks creaked; the French adjutant jumped to his feet. "*C'est vous, mon Colonel?*" "*Tch, tch, tch,*" came the reply, "*je fais ma toilette.*" The colonel, who had slept in his breeches, got up ponderously, put on his jacket, which had a *faux col* round the neck, stretched himself, did up his collar, and then drew the index fingers of both hands along it, yawned, slapped his hands together and, in a cheerful voice, exclaimed, "*Eh bien, le petit déjeuner, s'il vous plait.*" As far as we could find out, he had not left the dug-out or its immediate environs for over a fortnight, and we were not sure that the toilette was quite adequate.

Breakfast over, the day had to be passed somehow. My commanding officer's French was rather of the public school variety, but he was nothing if not brave. "*Excusez-moi, mon Colonel, mais est-ce que vous avez des bombes dans le ligne?*" Colonel Dolce's face was blank. "*Je regrette infiniment, mais je ne comprends pas; des bombes, qu'est-ce que ça veut dire? Comment? . . . Ah, les grenades à feu. Donnez-moi cette carte là, s'il vous plaît. Où sont mes pince-nez? Tch, tch, tch, où sont mes pince-nez? Ah, les voilà. Bien,"* spreading out the map. *"Aujourd'hui nous nous trouvons ici. Voilà mon p.c. au point dix-neuf cent soixante-deux, ici."* "Non, mon Colonel, pas là, mais ici," said the adjutant, swivelling the map round. *"Oh, pardon, mais je ne vois pas très bien. Oui, oui, ici. D'ici à chaque compagnie dans la ligne nous avons une liaison téléphonique, et chaque compagnie a un dépôt qui contient trois mille deux cent cinquante grenades à feu."* There was not a grenade in the line that we could find. A pause.

"Mon Colonel, est-ce que vous avez des filles dans la ligne?" "Ah, ah, Colonel, vous rigolez, des filles, ah ça, c'est bien, c'est très bien," laughing, *"des filles. Moi, je suis père de famille, mais une fois, quand j'étais lieutenant à Limoges, mais c'est une autre histoire, et je me rappelle . . ."* Seeing that the situation was likely to get a little out of hand I interjected that my commanding officer was enquiring about the *fil-de-fer barbelé.* *"Ah, nous avons le fil-de-fer barbelé sur toute la ligne du front—très fort, très fort."* Not a strand of wire other than a few coils in the shell holes could we find.

On the last night of the relief, when one of our companies was approaching the front line, the Germans put over a sharp raid, which caused some confusion in the darkness, and a French detachment was driven back in some disorder down the short trench up which Fryer's company was advancing. He quickly drove the Germans out of the front trench, but a French machine-gun and one or two of their men were missing. We captured two or three Germans.

Our French friends at regimental H.Q. were pretty quick with a report to their division that the Grenadiers had lost this gun and been responsible for the confusion. At first light, however, we found the gun in the arms of a dead German whom we had shot about five yards out in No Man's Land. We returned it with compliments and some indignation: it was a more effective reply than any amount of written reports.

When the relief was reported complete, Colonel Dolce stood up and made a charming little speech in French, wishing us luck and victory, saluted—the hand held perpendicular—pulled aside the gas blanket and was gone. The adjutant picked up the map and a pair of gloves which the colonel had dropped, stopped at the gas blanket, made a typical Parisian gesture, drawing his index finger upwards across his nostrils, and then said to me, *"Au'voir, mon pot, tu sais que c'est un gaga,"* and slipped into the night.

This regiment was, of course, a second-line or reserve unit and was used to hold quiet sectors of the line at times when no attack could be expected. They were not typical of the French Army, for which I had great admiration; they were adequate for a passive role. Moreover, one of the French military adages at that time was *"Nous ne faisons pas la petite guerre."* I always thought that this was a wise saying, and a wise policy, and it meant "we only stir the pot when there is a battle on: we don't believe much in raids, or disturbing sleeping dogs." I never met an infantry officer who believed much in raids as a means of keeping up the offensive spirit of the troops, although they had their uses when an identification was wanted by military intelligence.

The winter of 1916–17 was the coldest and bleakest that I ever remember. Even the back areas, where we rested in support, were a sea of mud, and even when resting we were under canvas. The horse lines at Carnoy were so deep in mud that "horse-drawn sledges had to be used to get the forage from the road to the horses." It nearly always blew, and the razor-like wind brought scuds of snow through the camps and set the canvas billowing and flapping with a noise like cannon-fire.

I do not remember having a meal all the winter, in or out of the line, without wearing an overcoat, although we tried to huddle over our braziers. We never got dry, except in a sleeping bag, and week after week the discomfort was indescribable. I remember one day riding six or seven miles to inspect our first-line transport; the rain beat into my face as we slithered along, ran down my neck, got under my mackintosh apron, and in a quarter of an hour I was wet to the skin.

Most of us caught colds in the head; bringing out a handkerchief from under our sodden mackintoshes, with blue hands, seemed to be the final straw.

The distances from the front line to these camps were very great, and until we had improved the duck-boards, the men used to arrive completely exhausted after their tour of duty.

On New Year's Day, 1917, we were relieved, and never more thankfully marched into billets round Corbie.

We were back again at the front in a neighbouring sector ten days later. The trenches were again in very bad shape, and our work was soon stopped by a heavy fall of snow and a severe frost, so severe that the men could not get shovels into the ground.

In the first week of March I was told that I was to be promoted to be the next staff captain of the 2nd Guards Brigade; in the meanwhile, I was to act temporarily as the staff captain of a brigade group. It was thought that the Germans were about to shorten their line by retiring, and the brigade group had been given the role of pursuing them.

In the middle of March, sure enough, their retreat began. It was very well carried out, like most German military manoeuvres, and covered by some of the heaviest shell-fire I remember. Arranging supplies and seeing them forward through the barrage was a dangerous task, and made all the worse because there was no element of the heroic to be found in it. I wished heartily that I was back with the battalion, a few hundred yards further forward, with at least the chance of seeing what was going on.

All the same, advancing into new country was exhilarating. We felt real soldiers again, and although we had to be careful of the countless booby traps laid by the enemy, and were heavily shelled, we did not suffer many casualties.

When the advance was halted, we had to work hard as navvies at making roads, filling in shell-holes with débris from ruined houses, laying duck-boards, repairing bridges and getting the area into a workable and defensible shape, but it was a change from that foul winter. These large working parties were occasionally attacked by aircraft, the first time that I ever saw this.

In mid-June I was duly appointed staff captain, 2nd Guards Brigade, and put on the red tabs. The staff of a brigade at that time was a brigadier-general commanding, a brigade major, that is his senior general staff officer (G), a staff captain, or administrative staff officer on the Q side, a signal and an intelligence officer, sometimes a chaplain. A certain amount of general staff work is done by the staff captain, particularly in battle, and at that time an appointment to this post was considered a step towards being a brigade major, which is a very responsible position, only ranking below the command of a battalion.

The brigade was commanded by a famous character, John Ponsonby. He was the central figure of innumerable stories and incidents, and had a highly developed sense of humour and of the ridiculous. It is very rarely true to say that the men loved a particular officer, but it was true if said of John Ponsonby.

The general had two Arab ponies. On parade he rode one of them, a stallion, which often gave unmistakable signs that he was thinking of other things. The general suffered from a severe impediment in his speech, and it had taken us a long time to find out the names of the two Arabs. In fact, it was only by a subterfuge of "Becky" Smith, formerly his brigade major, that their names were ever discovered. The brigade had a new dug-out in the line, and "Becky" said that the general must christen it after his two Arabs. "A good idea; write out the notice board." "Oh, no, Sir, you must do that yourself; it's half the point." Down went Saint Cloud and Bimbashi.

The orders at this time about wearing steel helmets were very strict, and John Ponsonby loathed them. He bought a pith polo helmet, had it covered in khaki canvas, mounted the Coldstream badge in front and, since we all used to have coverings to our helmets, it passed as steel.

One day I was going round the trenches with him in a high wind when the pith helmet blew off and went bowling off at high speed into No Man's Land, in full view of two or three hundred men.

As a soldier he was rather old-fashioned, and relied much upon his staff in planning and drafting orders. His brigade major, upon whom most of the responsibility fell, was one of the best of the younger officers in the brigade, "Budget" Loyd [11] of the Coldstream, who had only just missed a V.C. during the Battle of the Marne. He was a veteran, had a clear brain and was deeply versed in his profession. To these qualities he added an imperturbable calm, a strong character and a pervading and rather disenchanted humour. We were indeed a very happy H.Q., and "Budget" and I have remained firm friends ever since.

We usually had a chaplain attached to us. One of these had just joined us, and I hardly knew him. One Sunday, when we were resting out of the line, I went into the brigade mess after church parade, and found the chaplain standing in the corner, to which he had just been ordered by the brigadier. The reason for this punishment was that he had preached a sermon on the text "they cast lots for his raiment," and used it as a platform for launching a severe diatribe against gambling. This appeared to the brigadier to be quite an unnecessary refinement of the Christian ethic in the middle of the war, and should in his view have been left to more peaceful times. The sermon had also exceeded the usual length permitted.

The chaplain did not seem to mind this treatment. Although he was unmercifully chaffed and kept in his place by the brigadier,

[11] Now General Sir Charles Loyd.

and although he had to listen to language not often heard in the vestry, I believe that he was happy and contented. He learnt more about humanity than most of the clergy, and succeeded to high preferment in the Church after the war.

A great offensive to capture the Messines-Wytschaete ridge was now planned by the 2nd Army, of which the Guards division formed a part.

Our role was to pass through the leading waves and capture the final objectives, if they should fail. We trained intensively in the Wardrecques-Renescure area for the battle; large-scale models of the ground were constructed and the most careful study of the terrain was carried out daily. We were confident that we should succeed, but thought that we should incur heavy casualties.

The barrage the day before the battle seemed to us the heaviest that we had heard. On the day itself, June 7th, we were ready at dawn to move off, and expected that the approach march would be the worst part of our task.

A situation report: 2nd Army has captured first objective. A little later: 2nd Army has captured second objective. About noon: 2nd Army has secured whole line of last objective. A most welcome anticlimax to our preparations: not a casualty; not a shell nor a bullet anywhere near us. We marched back to billets and started a big party of rejoicing, followed by some bridge and gambling for high points: a not infrequent reaction. I won handsomely, and we went happily to bed at 3 A.M., at a time when most of us thought we should be patrolling somewhere beyond the final objective. We were loud in our praises of our comrades in front, who had got on without us.

The next battle projected was in the north, and on June 10th we heard that we should make the critical assault on the extreme left of the British line, and next to the French corps, the Corps de Fer.

The Boesinghe Canal divided our front line from the German; the ground was flat for a thousand yards behind the enemy position; it then rose gently to Houthulst Forest. There were numbers of farm houses turned into strong points in the enemy defensive system in depth. Moreover, we were under direct observation from the Pilkem ridge, and the whole of our forward communications round the village of Boesinghe and back to Elverdinghe were overlooked.

It seemed a tough task, and our chief concern was how to cross the canal. The bed of the canal was about seventy feet wide, and except for a small stream of water which ran down the middle, was filled with soft mud, in which a man sank quickly. The German trench ran along the eastern bank.

Whilst we were in the line preparing the position for assault by improving the communications and the trenches, Brigade H.Q. was established in Elverdinghe Château, a well-built stone house which had been badly knocked about by shell-fire, but which from a distance looked solid and intact. It was in range of the German field guns, but apart from a few salvos which fell in the garden, we were left alone for the first three or four days.

The brigade intelligence officer was Henry Dundas of the Scots Guards, a splendid type of Scotsman, twenty years old and full of brains and enthusiasm. Just before dusk we used to play an imaginary four holes round the garden with imaginary clubs. At dusk there was always some shelling of the Château, and the first shells stopped our round, and we returned to the brigade office, which was at least safe from splinters, though from nothing else. Henry and I shared a large bedroom on the first floor. I never fancied being above the ground level: when shelling begins, you feel as if you are taking unnecessary risks and sleep is fitful. On the other hand, if you are in the safest place available, however poor that may be, you are fatalistic, and it takes something to burst very near to wake you. We soon had to move down and sleep in the brigade office, and when an unpopular battery of our 60-pounders started registering from our garden the Château became very unhealthy indeed and suffered several direct hits, which shook the teeth in our heads.

Our left battalion complained that they were being shelled by some high-velocity French naval guns. The French denied this hotly, and pointed out that a salient was a salient, and that it was the Germans who would seem to be shooting from behind us. We had several casualties from these shells, and after further protests by the Guards division a test was arranged.

I was to meet a colonel of the French artillery at the left junction between the British and French positions, and a trial salvo was to be fired to reassure us. I duly took up my position and soon the colonel, accompanied by some signallers, arrived. The wire had been unrolled behind him, and after some courtesies, communication with the suspected battery was obtained.

Holding up his hand, the colonel said into the telephone, *"Arrosage général,"* an expressive term for harassing fire. We could hear the six guns go off, then the rumble like six trains at full speed, and then woomph, woomph, woomph all round us: a perfect bracket. Never have I seen a telephone wire wound in so quickly. The colonel made a grimace, shrugged his shoulders and departed. We were never troubled again by this battery.

It had been determined by divisional H.Q. that we should cross the Boesinghe Canal by unrolling some narrow mats with wooden cross-pieces: a hand-rail was to be rigged so that when the mats were below the water level a man could guide himself across. The R.E. also constructed a number of light pontoon bridges, supported by petrol tins, which were to be run across as soon as a few men had gained the other bank.

The enemy shelling of our communications and back areas was sustained and intense. At night we patrolled across the canal vigorously and soon found out that the front trenches opposite were always lightly held and sometimes evacuated altogether. In broad daylight a battalion of the Coldstream crossed the canal and gained a foothold, which was rapidly extended. The French came into line on the left of the 3rd Guards Brigade, and because the 38th Division on our right could not advance, we threw out a defensive flank.

The attack now seemed to be of a more conventional character, but still looked tough. We could expect a heavy barrage upon the canal crossings, and the movement of reinforcements was going to be an ugly business. My own role as staff captain was to lead a string of mules, loaded with ammunition, wire and other stores, across the canal and up to the battalion H.Q. of my old battalion, the 3rd Battalion Grenadier Guards, as soon as they had reached their objective. I cannot say that I relished the prospect.

By the time I had to set out I expected that the shelling would be heavy. Mules are allergic to shell-fire, and if anything bursts close to them, they are apt to behave in a most tantalising and un-Guardsmanlike manner.

The heaviest barrage of the war was fired by our artillery. We had never heard or seen anything to match it. On that morning it was said that £18,000,000 worth of 18-pounder ammunition was fired; the whole sky flickered with the flame of the discharges, and the enemy lines appeared to be drenched with the explosions of salvo after salvo. We had to wait for the 38th Division to get into line and then advance. This we achieved in perfect order, but the left flank of the 38th were held up by some pill-boxes and heavy machine-gun fire. We were able to help by attacking these in flank and reducing the most troublesome. We captured an officer or two and about fifty men. The rear companies passed through the forward troops and captured the final objective.

The time had now arrived for my expedition, and I set off with my ears well pricked. To my astonishment we were able to pick our way in driblets across the numerous bridges which by then had been flung across the canal. I can only remember one casualty. The man was hit in the left bicep by a splinter: it was a superficial wound, but bled profusely and we could not staunch it. I sent him back and I can still see his delighted face, with a grin from ear to ear, as he made off, holding his field dressing in place with his right hand. He had got the ideal "blighty," just bad enough, he thought, for a month in England.

Once across the canal, we had some salvos round us but nothing nearer than fifty yards away, and in the soft, churned-up ground, the fragmentation was low. The mules hated it even more than I did, and the poor beasts shied and played about and became nearly unmanageable. This is the kind of operation of war which is the most trying to temper and calmness, and has no element of *élan* to offset it.

We advanced across the shell craters, spurred on by our own barrage of oaths and imprecations, which apparently had a soothing effect on the mules, and we duly gained the H.Q. of the 3rd Battalion Grenadiers. There was "Bulgy" Thorne, the commanding officer, with his adjutant and signallers round him, in two large craters. I was, of course, greeted with a stream of chaff. "Hullo, Oliver. How's our muleteer? How's the gilded staff? I bet they put the wind up you round the canal. How many mules are in the report?" and so on. "How did you get on, Sir?" I asked. "Well, we've had a few casualties, but not too bad."

We unloaded quickly and started back. The mules knew that they were making for home, and almost dragged the men along who were supposed to be leading them. We only had one salvo anywhere near us, and no one was hit.

It started to rain that very night, and it rained steadily for the next few days. The battlefield, which could not have been much above sea level, became an almost impassable quagmire. A day or two later, when I was up the line, I saw that the difficulties of supplying the troops were appalling. I talked to one or two battery commanders at dusk, when their ammunition was arriving by pack animals. The intensity of our own barrage was one of the principal causes of the sea of mud; the banks of the Zillebeke had been breached; every shell hole was filled with water, and we were literally bogged down.

The battle pursued its dreary and exhausting course. We were relieved on August 7th, were back again on August 27th and squelched our way forward under heavy shellfire, with orders to assault the line of the Broembeek. The Germans, however, mounted two or three counter strokes, one of which led to fierce fighting, and our attack was postponed.

CHAPTER V

THE FIRST WORLD WAR: III

I N SEPTEMBER I was sent home to do a staff course at Cambridge. I therefore took no part in the successes achieved by the brigade in crossing the Broembeek and capturing the final objectives. Losses were heavy: twenty-six officers and 537 other ranks in the brigade.

The course at Cambridge was an intensive one. We were comfortably lodged at Caius College and given the run of the college. Although we had to ride ration bicycles on the numerous staff rides, it was an enjoyable interlude.

I was back at the front early in 1918. At this time Great Britain had insufficient reserves to fill the ranks, and rather than reduce the number of divisions the High Command decided to reorganise brigades into three instead of four infantry battalions, and thus reduce the number of effectives in the infantry by 25 per cent. The Guards division had three battalions to spare. They were formed into a 4th Guards Brigade. The brigadier was to be Lord Ardee,[1] formerly a Grenadier but now of the Irish Guards; I was appointed brigade major, and Eric Mackenzie of the Scots Guards staff captain. The brigade was composed of the 4th Battalion Grenadiers, the 3rd Battalion Coldstream and the 2nd Battalion Irish Guards. The then commanding officers were Lieutenant Colonels Pilcher, Longueville and Alexander. The brigade was complete on February 2nd, and was assigned to the 31st Division. We were played out by the massed drums and fifes of the Guards Division, and departed very sorrowfully to a line division on the 11th February.

I shall never forget the turn-out and appearance of the troops as

[1] Afterwards the Earl of Meath.

we marched into our new quarters. We were watched by many men of the other two line brigades. They looked with astonishment at our gleaming equipment and pipe-clayed rifle slings.

The 31st Division had been fulfilling a passive role for some weeks, and we soon relieved one of the brigades in the line. Our presence was suspected by the Germans, who put over a strong raid a night or two after our arrival, doubtless to obtain an identification. They got more than they reckoned for, and we captured a handful of prisoners; although there was some hand-to-hand fighting, in which the imperturbable Fryer's company of my regiment distinguished itself, the Germans did not get the identification for which they sought.

I was not impressed by the command or general staff of our new division. That night, when an intensive barrage came down on our front line, they kept ringing me up to know what was happening, and whether we were still there. I asked the G.S.O.[2] I what it was all about; no attack had yet developed; no, we did not want any reinforcements; there really was no need to get windy; "What are your plans?" "We haven't got any beyond maintaining our line intact," and so on.

The general air of relief and the congratulations which we received from H.Q. over this small action struck me as quite out of place, and left an unpleasant feeling that the professional standards were different from our own.

We were relieved, and the division was placed in G.H.Q. reserve. On March 21st we were engaged in a training exercise in open warfare near St. Pol. This day was the beginning of the great German offensive.

The very next day, we received orders that the brigade was to come under the orders of General Sir Aylmer Haldane, commanding the VIth Corps, and was to be rushed to the front in lorries. The brigade embussed late that night and the following afternoon the brigadier and I were ordered to precede them in a staff car and to report to the corps commander. When we arrived at his H.Q., I asked the B.G.G.S. for maps. The German penetration had been so deep that all the big-scale maps were no longer of any use. All I could be given was one map of the scale 1/100,000. The line we had to occupy was marked on this map. It was about an inch and a half long, and, in a devastated country, the map was on far too small a scale to be of any use in identifying natural features.

My brigadier, Lord Ardee, who had been wounded in 1914 and

[2] General Staff Officer.

who had only just got back, looked at the map with amazement. We were neither of us particularly reassured by the atmosphere at Corps H.Q., which was busy packing up, and we had the uncomfortable feeling that something near a rout had taken place, and that the general no longer had any control over the battle. We heard afterwards that the whole Corps H.Q.—administrative staff officers, provost marshal, police, A.D.C.s, cooks, scullions, typewriters, signallers and sundry details, which ran to the number of much more than a hundred—had poured back with their transport and had blocked the road up which the brigade was advancing. The spectacle of a general clearing out in some disorder is never very encouraging to troops, but the guardsmen only laughed and made some caustic and blasphemous comments.

We got some kind of orders to relieve a brigade "in the line" and stop the rot. Our position was to be in the neighbourhood of the Sensée switch.

At this time the 4th Guards Brigade in their lorries were still two or more hours away. I asked the B.G.G.S. how we were expected to find the trenches in this devastated country at night from a small-scale map. He said the brigade which we were to relieve (and which I guessed was much shaken) would send guides to a certain rendezvous on the road which he pointed out. I thought inwardly that this was a very remote chance. I suggested to my brigadier that he should send back an order for the troops to debus near this point, and that I should immediately go forward and reconnoitre the line which we were to occupy. He agreed, and I left at once with an orderly. I found my way, largely by questioning a number of men who appeared to be wandering about behind the line, and eventually reached the front line, held by the three or four battalions which we were to relieve. It was under desultory shell fire.

I did not like the look of the situation in any way, but if we could get our men into the line—the Army reserve line which was only spit-locked but which had a little wire—I knew we could at least put it into a state of defence. I felt very unsure about our flanks, but had no time to reconnoitre them.

It was still light when the leading battalion arrived in their buses. I gave the brigadier's orders to debus by word of mouth, and we soon had the three battalions dispersed in artillery formation, and in touch with one another. Darkness fell: no guides. I sent some bicycle orderlies to look for them, with no result. An hour or two passed: no guides. It was dark. "What do we do now?" asked the brigadier. It certainly was a puzzle. "Well, Sir, this has got me beat as an operation of war, and all I can suggest is that, if you will take the risk, we should get the brigade into Indian file and I will lead them to the extreme right flank of the troops which we are to relieve, and then wheel left until I have reached the left flank. When we stand fast, at least four companies will then have to be dropped back to form a support line. I am the only officer who might find the way, and if I am killed or wounded we shall be in a pretty pickle. Sir," I added, "every man must be told to keep his right hand on the pack of the man in front of him, and that if he lets go he is for a court-martial."

The brigadier thought over this astounding proposition, but then agreed. Verbal orders were issued accordingly, and nearly two thousand men got into Indian file with the brigade major in front and the brigadier at the rear, every man with his hand on the pack of the man in front of him. Shades of the Staff College and Hamley's *Operations of War!* But that was how it was done. I dare say it would be safe to claim that this was the first time in history that a Guards brigade had been led into battle within a few hundred yards of the enemy in Indian file.

It was pitch dark but by the light of some Verey lights that were fired from time to time I found my way, reached the right flank, wheeled to my left and went down the front trench until I found the left-hand company. The relief was completed. About 3 A.M. the four companies were dropped back and dug themselves in in support.

At dawn troops were seen falling back on our right and soon a rabble of British soldiers appeared and retreated through our lines, headed by an officer. When questioned, he said that his troops "had broken" the previous evening. I had him placed under arrest and sent to the rear. Soon after this humiliating incident the G.S.O. I of the division sent up a message which plaintively asked why two or three platoons of the front-line troops had not been relieved. He said that the division had been asked the reason by the outgoing division and it really was a serious matter. I told the G.S.O. I exactly what I thought of the complaint, of the staff arrangements, of the outgoing troops, of the absence of guides, and suggested a destination for their complaint. We were afterwards treated with the greatest respect.

The next day no orders arrived; we were attacked and beat off the enemy; our right flank had to be refused; then some details on our left decamped and we had to refuse our left flank.

The following day our dispositions looked more like a large hairpin on the map, so far thrown back were our two flanks. Type-written orders which had no bearing whatever on the situation reached us from the division but eventually telephone connection was established and we were ordered to fight some kind of rear-guard action, though we were not told whom we were to cover, nor where the line of resistance was to be.

By then we were almost surrounded and first had to disengage. So far had the Germans lapped round our exposed flanks that we extricated ourselves by night in columns of fours on a frontage of one or two hundred yards. To go into battle in Indian file and dis-engage from the enemy in columns of fours must have been a unique experience, but that is just what happened.

By this time we had had three and a half days of marching and fighting and had not seen much of either of the other two brigades in our division. We were told, however, that there were now other troops in front of us and that we were in reserve. Up till this moment, I had had no sleep at all, because I had had to spend the nights in locating our troops and seeing that they were in touch. I had covered a great many miles on foot. I was, moreover, naturally anxious about the situation and felt no confidence in any of the troops on our flanks. We had had some casualties, but they were not severe, and here at last we were in reserve.

The staff captain, Eric Mackenzie, had established brigade H.Q. in a Nissen hut, which had originally formed part of a divisional school far behind the front. As I returned from the line, my third consecutive night without sleep, I realised that my brain was work-ing in a different compartment from my body. I looked down from outside at myself, and above me I saw the heavenly host and the angels of Mons. My physical reactions were no longer spontaneous, they had to be thought out first and the link between my brain and my hands and arms and legs was broken. When I stumbled on to the Nissen hut, I could not remember how a door opened, and had to sit down and think it out. Then I remembered that doors had handles, and worked out how they could be turned. I almost fell into the hut. Inside there was light and a meal, which I needed as much as sleep. I ate voraciously and drank one small glass of port which put me to sleep as if I had been poleaxed. I lay down on the floor and was out for a couple of hours, but only for a couple of hours, because at 2 A.M. the staff captain woke me up and said, "Divisional Orders." I shook myself awake and drew out from the pouch a long typewritten document. The orders read to me like a scheme on Laffan's Plain. The two line brigades were to conduct a series of complicated manoeuvres, were to retreat and were to put out patrols and get into touch with this and that. I could not make head or tail of it, but I did in my half-awake condition seize on the fact that we had to do nothing before dawn.

"I can't make head or tail of this," I said to Eric. "Don't wake the brigadier; give me another two hours under the table, get ready six orderlies with bicycles and throw a bucket of cold water over my head at about 4 A.M.."

I was duly called, read the orders and by the time I had extracted from them our intended role we had little time to spare. I wrote the orders on a field message pad in pencil: "At 5:30 A.M. the 4th Battalion Grenadiers will retreat down the road A–B, the 2nd Battalion Irish Guard down the road C–D. Staff officers will meet them on these roads and direct them to their new positions. The 3rd Battalion Coldstream Guards will be in reserve in the area E–F. Acknowledge." I sent off the bicyclists and went to sleep.

Eric and I disposed ourselves on the two roads at dawn and led the very tired troops into their new positions.

The next order we got was that we were to fight a rearguard action on the line of the high ground near Douchy-les-Ayette. Fighting rearguard actions means something quite different from holding a line, and like a fool I thought that the orders meant what they said. We accordingly thinned out our front line and kept the bulk of the troops in reserve, ready to deploy and counter-attack when the front screen was penetrated.

The brigadier was slightly gassed that night, and in the morning could hardly speak. He would shortly have to go sick. I tried to get in touch with the 31st Division, but there were no signs of them. At that moment, to my amazement, I got a message from "Crawley" de Crespigny, commanding the 1st Guards Brigade of the Guards division, that one of our two line brigades was marching about in the back area of his brigade, with orders to hold the Brown Line. There was no Brown Line marked on his map nor on mine. "They are buggering up my communications and anyway there is no Brown Line. They don't appear to have a clue."

This message gave me the only cheerful bit of news I had heard since the battle began. By a strange chance the Guards division were on our left; I found out where Divisional H.Q. was located. I could not get in touch with our own division and I therefore determined that we must place ourselves under the orders of the Guards division. It was clear that the brigadier must go sick at once: he had been much worse gassed than he would admit.

I rode over to the H.Q. of the Guards division and asked for the major-general. He was unfortunately up the line. "Well, I must see the G.S.O.I." "I'm sorry, but he is playing badminton." This simple statement was a real tonic: it showed that everything was under control, everything was normal. He appeared at that very moment, sweating gently from his exercise. He was Ned Grigg.[3] I explained our predicament, and he said that the major-general would be glad to have us on his right flank, and would doubtless try to sort out the command difficulties. At least we were now able to anchor our left flank on the right of the Guards division.

I sent a message to Colonel Alexander, commanding the 2nd Battalion Irish Guards, that the brigadier had reported sick and that as the senior commanding officer he was now in command of the brigade. He answered that he could not leave his troops at the moment, they were being heavily attacked; he would come back as soon as he had driven off the enemy.

That afternoon a divisional order from 31st Division arrived: it was clear that they had intended no rearguard action, but had meant that we should hold the high ground in front of us in strength, and stay there. We were to stretch a hand to the 42nd Division, said to be on our right. Our dispositions had been designed to fight a rear guard action in accordance with the previous orders. Instead, a yawning gap had to be filled and held. No time was to be lost, so I rode off, accompanied by my groom, to re-dispose our troops. The enemy was already attacking, and I had to ride through a thick barrage. The horses were terrified, and my Irish groom was calling on the protection of every saint in the calendar. Shells burst all round us and I thought that we should not get through. The air was full of splinters, the scream of the shells drove the horses mad; my flask of port beside my saddle was broken by a splinter, the port ran down the poor brute's quarters. He whipped round, thinking it was his own blood, and nearly un-shipped me.

It was about the hottest ten minutes I can remember, but we arrived safely. I explained our new role, and Colonel Longueville and I personally led the Coldstream to our right flank, spread them out and got in touch with some elements of the 42nd Division. This move of ours looked more like a counter-attack than a re-grouping, because a few Germans appeared on the slopes and we were subjected to a very hot barrage of low-bursting shrapnel. By

[3] Afterwards Lord Altrincham.

nightfall we were properly re-disposed on our new line. As soon as it was done, according to Longueville I fell asleep whilst giving him and his reserve company commander a situation report.

The next day an attack developed on our left: we beat it off and we still had some kind of touch with elements on our right. Later, the enemy launched a heavy attack on the Guards division on our left, but suffered a bloody reverse. Two German regiments were cut to pieces.

We were not seriously attacked in the afternoon, but were covering a lot of ground, with a defensive flank thrown out on our right and no more reserves at our disposal. We were now in telephonic communication with our division, and at 3 P.M. received a message. "Following from 3rd Army. Enemy has broken through near Hébuterne and is advancing on Souastre." This was not a very happy message for us, because it meant that the enemy were a mile or two behind our right flank. "Well, this is it," I said to Eric Mackenzie. "There's nothing else we can do, we have no troops in reserve. We should get all the signallers and officers' servants lined up, facing backwards. We sell our lives dearly, and all that."

I tried to telephone to the 31st Division, but the signallers reported, "Line dis." No shells had passed overhead, so I said to Eric, "Divisional H.Q. has been overrun, of course." At this moment we saw men streaming back on our right, like the crowd off Epsom Downs after the last race, and an infuriated gunner major leading out his battery on foot, with the men carrying the breech blocks of their guns.

Nothing happened for an hour or more; then a staff car carrying a D.A.Q.M.G.[4] came down the road from our rear. "Where have you come from?" we asked. "Hébuterne," he said. "You don't mean it: we were told the Germans were already there." "Oh no, I have only just left, and everything is quiet." "What about the Division?" "Well, the G.S.O. I has put Divisional H.Q. into a state of defence, and when I saw him he had felled two trees across the road. Unfortunately they came down on to the Divisional telephone lines and broke them: a proper mess."

We afterwards found out what had caused the panic on our right. When the line had been miles away, the French had established a farm in the back areas to supply fresh vegetables to the troops. It was manned by old territorials. When the battle swept forward, they were told to leave their farm. They accordingly

[4] Deputy Assistant Quartermaster General.

drove down the road in some sort of tractors, and such was the morale of the rearward troops that they had been mistaken for Germans in armoured cars.

Soon after these incidents we were relieved and were once again back in billets in G.H.Q. reserve, that is to say, we were part of a division which could only be committed by the orders of Sir Douglas Haig himself.

We received a divisional order that a conference was to be held on the lessons of the recent battle. It was to be attended by brigadiers and their brigade majors and by commanding officers and their adjutants.

When we were assembled, the G.S.O. I began by saying that he wished to refer in particular to the night of March 26th, which was the night that I had had the glass of port. My heart sank.

He began with a short summary of the situation, which ended, "At about 10 P.M. it was necessary to issue orders to the three brigades to withdraw. The divisional orders reached them at about midnight. What orders were given by the brigades?"

At this point he plunged his hand into the Divisional pouch and extracted two or three typewritten foolscap papers. "These," he said, "are the orders of the 91st Infantry Brigade and they reflect great credit on the brigade major. I will read them to you." He did. "I have only one comment to make. The left battalion of the brigade should have been withdrawn first, because it was not in touch with other troops on that flank." My heart sank still further.

He again fished some more typescript from out of the pouch. "These," he said, "are the orders of the 92nd Infantry Brigade. They seem to me admirable, but the reserve battalion was not ideally placed and should have been astride the road.

"Now we turn to the orders of the 4th Guards Brigade. I would remind you that these are veteran troops, commanded and staffed almost entirely by professional officers. It is midnight, and a dark night; the troops have been marching and fighting for three days; the commanding officers are tired; what orders are given?"

At this point, he pulled out a rather crumpled sheet of a field message pad, about the size of an income tax demand note, and read out:

At 5:30 A.M. the 4th Battalion Grenadiers will retreat down the road A–B, the 2nd Battalion Irish Guards down the road C–D. Staff officers will meet them on these roads and direct them to their new positions.

The 3rd Battalion Coldstream Guards will be in reserve in the area E–F. Acknowledge.

"There you are, gentlemen, the professional touch. Everything is there: no trouble to understand those orders in the middle of the night. That's how to do it, and that's the first lesson I want to drive into you."

I felt quite built up, and I knew, of course, that even without that glass of port, the orders would have been just the same.

We had emerged from the recent battle with little confidence in the command, and still less in the staff of our new division. We had not seen much of either of the other two infantry brigades composing the division during the fighting, and we did not know the quality of the troops. We suspected that they had received some incomprehensible and conflicting orders, and that was why they had never been where we expected them.

The battle had been exhausting alike to patience and physical endurance. Nothing is more tiring than confusion: order, counter-order, disorder. At least we were thankful that the casualties of the 4th Guards Brigade had not been crippling by the standards of those days: they amounted in all to fourteen officers and 372 other ranks.

The acting brigadier was Colonel Alexander, then twenty-eight years old to my twenty-five. We immediately started on our usual routine of training.

The Divisional Commander, Major-General Robert Wanless-O'Gowan, called upon us at our H.Q., which had been established in a well-built stone house, the second day after we had come out of the line. Just before he was leaving he said in his broad Irish accent, "Colonel Alexander, we have all the best harriers—cross-country runners—in the Army in the other two brigades, and we've organised a cross-country race for Saturday. Ye should enter, yourself." "I have entered," said Alex, "and I think I shall win. Of course," he said with a grin, "you may have a champion, and then I shall only be second." The major-general was much taken aback by this, and did not know whether it was a joke or a boast.

On the day of the race a few of us, including the major-general, assembled round the finishing line of the seven-mile cross-country race and, a minute or two before we expected, a figure, five hundred yards in the lead, was seen topping a rise and making across a ploughed field. It was Alex: he ran in an easy winner. "Oh, dear, I'm puffed," he said. "I wouldn't like to do that again." The team race was won by a team of professional harriers, but somehow I do not think that the popularity of the 4th Guards Brigade was much enhanced in high quarters by Alex's victory.

We were soon in good trim, and the situation reports seemed to show that the front between the junction of the 3rd and 5th Army, where we had been lately engaged, had been stabilised. The brigade that had relieved us had made a spirited attack and had mopped up the Germans in Douchy-les-Ayette, taking more than 500 prisoners. The enemy thus paid the penalty for disregard of military principles and a piece of sheer tactical effrontery. "That's that," was our feeling.

Meanwhile, on April 5th, Alex was relieved by Brigadier General the Hon. L.J.P. Butler, and resumed command of the 2nd Battalion Irish Guards. Butler, too, was a highly professional officer, who had passed the Staff College and was as delightful to serve as Lord Ardee or Alex.

We were not to be left at peace for long. On the 9th the Germans directed an attack on the Lys front with nine divisions. They overran the Portuguese Corps. At noon on the 10th we got news that their offensive was meeting with dangerous successes; their penetration was deep, and getting deeper. A glance at the map (see pages 31, 33) will show that this thrust might have had deadly results.

In the March battles it was possible to give some ground without endangering points of primary strategical importance. Apart from the disorganisation of some of the troops—rout might not be too strong a word—I never had the feeling in those battles that the very issue of the war depended on our immediate success in holding the enemy.

In the Lys salient, however, first the great rail centre of Hazebrouck was at stake, and then, not far away, the Channel ports. Vital strategical objectives lay within a few miles of the enemy's spearheads. I had, all through the operations in which we were about to be engaged, the gripping anxiety that unless this thrust could be contained we might well lose the war, or at least might have to fight it out for another year or more, with the odds against us.

Once contain the attack, and it was clear that the Germans would be in a vulnerable posture, and would be subject to the daily drain of casualties which we had experienced in the Ypres salient. In short, we were playing for the highest stakes.

We soon got our orders. We were to embus at midnight and were to be engaged somewhere in the Merville area. We accordingly marched to the rendezvous on the main road, and before midnight were ready to get on board. No buses. We spent a miserably cold and uncomfortable night beside the St. Pol-Arras road. 4 A.M.: still no buses. The brigadier and I managed an hour and a half's sleep on a heap of granite stones by the side of the road. The troops got some rest in the ditch, but it was too cold to sleep for long.

Dawn: and no buses. Full light: no buses. They eventually arrived just before midday; we were packed in like sardines and jolted off, already far from fresh.

Our orders were to debus somewhere east of Merville. As we rumbled along, we received one or two very alarming situation reports which seemed to show that the front was crumbling, and that the Germans were rapidly advancing into an increasingly confused and fluid front.

A staff car arrived at the head of our column, with orders that the brigadier and I were to report at once to the corps commander of the XV Corps at his H.Q. in a small château north of the Bois d'Aval. We accordingly left the brigade and motored ahead. When we arrived, the château was being shelled by 5.9s, a grim indication that the front was not far away.

We were shown into the staff office, and into the presence of Lieutenant-General Sir Beauvoir de Lisle and his B.G.G.S.[5] De Lisle was a spare, lithe figure, and an ex-cavalry officer. His demeanour was very different from that of the other corps commander under whose orders we had been placed in the previous battle. He might have been described as unpleasantly rude and confident in a drawing room but this was the staff office. He radiated courage, energy and decision, all conveyed in a rather overbearing manner.

He asked the B.G.G.S. for the big map. He indicated two points on it, and rapped out, "Between these two points there are no British troops. The best German corps on this front is pressing through this gap and, gentlemen, unless you do something before morning there'll be no more fox-hunting. Good evening, gentlemen."

These picturesque and incisive orders were all we wanted: they left us a free hand, but also told us that Hazebrouck and even the Channel ports were threatened.

The first thing to do was clearly to find out by reconnaissance how far away resistance was being maintained on the flanks, and

[5] Brigadier-General, General Staff.

to deploy the brigade somewhere in the gap, stretching a hand to right or left to get into touch with other troops. I was ordered to make a preliminary reconnaissance eastwards along the Haze-brouck road with a couple of orderlies, and judge how far forward we could debus. "Do your best, Oliver," said the brigadier, "but it will be dark very soon, and if you can't find any troops, find a place anyway where we can debus. I shall bring the troops along the road to meet you. They should be here in an hour or two."

So off I set, and before I had gone a mile I could see little or nothing in the gathering dusk, in this flat, featureless country, except the road. We ran into a small German bicycle patrol who, seeing us, at once rode off. Not a very auspicious sign. I decided at once that this was quite far enough to bring the lorries, and I sent back a report to this effect. The brigade arrived and debussed; the commanding officers were called and were told to deploy with the 4th Battalion Grenadier Guards resting about the road junction east of Gars Brugghe; the 3rd Battalion Coldstream on the right were to deploy in the general direction of L'Epinette. Both battalions were to send out patrols to try and gain touch with other troops on their flanks. The 2nd Battalion Irish Guards were to be in brigade reserve and were to place two companies in echelon behind the Coldstream right.

The official accounts of our dispositions give, as such accounts always must, a much clearer impression of a tidy, carefully worked out plan than was the fact. We had no time or light in which to reconnoitre or pick a line of defence; the words of the corps commander rang in our ears, and we just had "to do something before morning."

A company of the Irish Guards was sent to reconnoitre forward, and was soon fired on from some houses near Vieux Berquin. We could also see the flicker of machine-gun fire in the darkness over a wide arc in front of us.

We established Brigade H.Q. in a school in Neuf Berquin, and could issue no more orders till light. Just before dawn the brigadier said he would go out to the left flank and find out the situation of the Grenadiers. I was to go to the right flank and discover how the Coldstream were disposed, and if their right was in touch with any British troops. The brigadier and I would meet at Brigade H.Q. within an hour.

I set off and soon found the Coldstream. They were already being shelled, and the back areas were being sprayed by machine-gun

fire, which made movement dangerous. I went towards their right
flank, which rested on a little stream. I could see no British troops
on their right, and was scouring the country with my field glasses
for any movement, when I was horrified to see a German engineer
company running a cable across country about 500 yards to my
right. They were already nearly opposite our right flank, and unless this was a more than usual piece of effrontery, it meant that
some troops were ahead of them, and that we were already outflanked.

I hurried back to Brigade H.Q.; the brigadier was already there.
I reported, and he said, "The Grenadiers are deployed, but I'm
damned if I could see anyone on their left."

By this time heavy artillery fire and the rattle of machine-guns,
and all the sounds of a sharp engagement broke out. "What do we
do now?" said the brigadier. "Well," I answered, "I suppose we
had better disengage as soon as we can, and come back a mile or
so behind the Bois d'Aval, and send out some patrols to find where
our friends are." "Yes," said Butler, "but I doubt whether we can
disengage: it sounds pretty hot in front. I think I shall ring up the
Division and tell them I'm going to attack; it's bluff, but it might
come off."

Personally, I did not like the plan, and said so, but the brigadier
soon decided on it. Meanwhile, we received reports that the enemy
attack had developed all along our front, but had been beaten off.

Orders were given to advance, with patrols well thrown out in
front, and to seize every opportunity of exploiting any success. We
heard that troops of the 50th Division were definitely in the neighbourhood of Les Puresbécques. We decided to seize this hamlet if
possible, and join up with them.

At about 11 A.M., the two battalions advanced in perfect order.
The Coldstream pushed forward a few hundred yards, but were
heavily fired upon from the houses of Les Puresbécques, and there
were no signs whatever of the 50th Division. The Grenadiers advanced towards Vierhouck-Le Cornet Perdu, but the road was swept
by artillery and machine-gun fire. The left company, however,
most gallantly led by Pryce, seized a few houses in Pont Rondin
after hand-to-hand fighting. Thirty Germans were killed in this
spirited attack, and we captured two or three prisoners and two
machine-guns.

The Germans, seeing fresh troops advancing in perfect order on
a 3,000-yard front, evidently thought a big-scale counter-attack was

developing, and did not press home their own attack. In fact they withdrew on both our flanks; they renewed their heavy shelling, and again sprayed the back areas with machine-gun barrages.

Our situation was critical. Both flanks were in the air; a gap had developed between the left of the Coldstream and the Grenadiers, and our front of about 3,000 yards could only be lightly held. At this moment a pioneer battalion, the 12th Battalion K.O.Y.L.I.,[6] was placed under our orders by the Division. They were found to be holding a line on our left, and a company of the Irish Guards was sent up to effect a junction between them and the Grenadiers, who were brought back to the road junction just north of Gars Brugghe.

The country where we were fighting was as flat as a table: the only features were some scattered hamlets, a farmhouse or two and some hedges and ditches.

We could not help admiring the tactical handling of the battle by the enemy: they pushed forward their machine-guns with great boldness into every empty farmhouse and, sometimes from the cover round the farmyard, sometimes from the upper windows, sprayed the roads and the country with bullets, which made movement very dangerous behind our line, whether for single officers, or for parties of men. The enemy infantry boldly followed the machine-gun teams and pushed forward in small parties under their covering fire.

No actual attack developed in the next few hours but one was clearly being prepared. Our only satisfaction was that the day was passing. Soon it was 4 o'clock and the best part of a day had been gained.

At 4:30 P.M., however, the Germans attacked all along our line and shelled us over open sights. At Brigade H.Q. we could see little, but it was clear that our volume of fire was very heavy in reply. Pioneer battalions are not intended or trained for the kind of role which the 12th K.O.Y.L.I. had to play, but the battalion fought gallantly and only had to give a little ground. Elsewhere we held fast.

At dark our line was intact, and we breathed again. Our casualties had been heavy: my own regiment alone lost eight officers and 250 other ranks, and the Coldstream losses were only slightly less. The two battalions fired more than 200,000 rounds of S.A.A.[7]

During the night, the troops, who were very tired, improved their

6 Kin's Own Yorkshire Light Infantry.
7 Small Arms Ammunition.

line, but could do no more than construct a series of detached posts. The line was stretched like a bowstring.

April 13th dawned. Soon after 6 A.M., the Coldstream were attacked, and an armoured car tried to push down the road. I happened to be visiting the Coldstream at this moment, and saw the armoured car withdraw under fire. It was a foggy morning, and some parties of the enemy had infiltrated between the posts on our extended front. A company of the Irish Guards were detailed to mop them up and had some success.

At about a quarter past nine, another very determined attack was pressed home, but it was bloodily repulsed. Further to our north, the enemy succeeded in driving back some elements of another division, and penetrated into Vieux Berquin, uncovering our left flank.

This was perhaps the most critical moment of the battle. The enemy were round both our flanks; a fresh column of infantry of about two battalions was seen by an artillery observer from the top window of a farm house, debouching from Bleu; the enemy artillery started to fire at us over open sights; the immediate rear areas were under continuous machine-gun fire. We moved Brigade H.Q. into the firing line; we had no more reserves to speak of. I said to the brigadier, "This is what is known as a soldier's battle. 'La garde meurt et ne se rend pas,' and all that." "I make the same answer as Cambronne," he retorted.

Soon after noon the brave K.O.Y.L.I. were blown out of their position and pressed back, finally uncovering our flank. The left company of the Grenadiers, under the gallant Pryce, was thus isolated and surrounded. Our last reserve of one company was thrown in with orders to try to help Pryce and to form a defensive flank on his left. Pryce's company fought to the very end, and when last seen he was charging the enemy at the head of seven men. He received a posthumous V.C. The company of Irish Guards fought with great courage and were almost wiped out.

Brigade H.Q. was in a sunk road, with our signallers and details in the firing line, and things were getting very hot indeed. At this moment an Irish guardsman, sweating profusely and calling upon all the saints, was seen picking his way down our road, over which shells were continuously bursting. He handed me a message: it was a characteristic one from Alex and read, "Dear Oliver, I am running very short of soldiers. Alex."

The Coldstream companies on our right flank fought on with the utmost gallantry, but they too were nearly wiped out. At this point in the battle, the 4th Guards Brigade were reduced to a number of isolated posts or pockets, still refusing to give in, and clinging to their positions whether surrounded or not.

In the afternoon, I saw a number of stragglers from other divisions streaming back down the main road to Hazebrouck. I hastily improvised a post across it, and ordered them sharply to spread out, dig themselves some cover and be prepared to shoot. This they readily did: they only wanted orders to become soldiers again.

Meanwhile the H.Q. details of the Grenadiers and Coldstream, including the orderlies and signallers, beat off yet another attack.

At this moment—it would be about four in the afternoon—the fire of the enemy slackened; there was a sensation of pause. It was true. The day was nearly spent; the vital time had been gained, the enemy was still far from Hazebrouck, and along the road came marching the leading companies of the 1st Australian Division, which had just detrained at Hazebrouck. Each company was over 200 strong. These magnificent troops advanced down the road, sometimes in a rather unconventional form of artillery formation, and most of them carrying some unconventional equipment. They were superb, and their language, learnt on the sheep stations of their country and matured in a hundred engagements and patrols, was like the battle cries of other days. By itself it would have driven back any but the most determined enemy.

Yes, the day was saved; we had fulfilled the task; the Germans had been fought to a standstill; there would be more fox-hunting.

The price for us was awful. In this soldier's battle, the Grenadiers lost fifteen officers and 504 other ranks, the Coldstream fifteen officers and 490 other ranks, the Irish Guards nine officers and 250 other ranks. Less than 400 fighting men remained when we were withdrawn.

Late in the afternoon of the 13th, the Australians had taken up a strong position behind our so-called front. Nearly all fighting had ceased, and some of our posts could be withdrawn. I went out to some of them to tell the men where to rejoin the remnants of their battalions. At one moment I was talking to the second in command of an Australian battalion, who said to me, "My men report some Guards stragglers in a farmhouse in No Man's Land." "That is not true," I answered. "What you call No Man's Land has been the battlefield for the last three days, and anyway you will bloody well come with me and find them." Three or four hundred yards away, find them we did, in a farmhouse. The "stragglers" consisted of about eleven badly wounded men and two stretcher bearers, one of them wounded, who had not abandoned their comrades. "Now," said I to the Australian, "you will eat your words." He did, with a good grace.

This afternoon was my first experience of Australians, and they have always, ever since, had a place in my affections which has never been shaken. They are perhaps not the best of troops to handle when there is no one to fight, but let them get a sight or scent of a battle, and they are superb.

When we were withdrawn on April 14th, the whole 4th Guards Brigade on the line of march looked no more than one battalion, and a weak one in numbers at that. We got back into some billets, and the brigadier and I and the rest of his staff were having some dinner when an A.D.C. in a steel helmet came in, saluted, and declaimed in a loud voice a personal but rather flamboyant message of thanks and congratulations from the corps commander himself.

It was a typically British incident, because we were all somewhat embarrassed and could only reduce the histrionic tension by offering him a seat and a glass of port. Later the corps commander, and it was good of him, forwarded an account of the battle of the 11th–14th April to the G.O.C. 2nd Army. In it he said that nothing finer was recorded in the annals of the British Army than "the glorious stand against overwhelming odds made by the 4th Guards Brigade."

I must repeat that this was a soldier's battle, the Command could do little but improvise; there were no tactical features except a small wood and a hamlet or two; we were soon deployed on too wide a front and had soon committed most of our slender reserves. We could thus exercise little influence on the course of the battle.

The iron discipline and long fighting tradition of the Guards regiments stood the strain and won the day. The individual soldier fought to the last, and once more showed that the greatest of all military rules is "Never give in." We had beaten off and chewed up two divisions of well-led German troops. When the battle was over, for the first time in the long history of the Brigade of Guards, we had to form a composite battalion of Grenadiers and Coldstream. The 2nd Battalion Irish Guards had just enough men to make up a pitifully weak but separate battalion.

CHAPTER VI

THE FIRST WORLD WAR: IV

ON APRIL 19th, 1918, the reinforced but still depleted brigade relieved the 2nd Australian Brigade on the eastern edge of Nieppe Forest. On the 22nd I was writing some orders at Brigade H.Q. in a woodman's or gamekeeper's cottage in the forest for a raid to be carried out the next day by the Irish Guards. We were being shelled by gas shells, and one of them hit the cottage. I had on my gas mask, but I was spattered with liquid mustard and had a few small superficial wounds; no more than scratches. The warmth of your body vaporises the gas, and in an hour I was blind, and huge blisters began to appear in my groin and in my armpits. I was evacuated to the casualty clearing station, but I never saw it because I was completely blind then and for the next three or four days. My blindness did not frighten me particularly, because I thought I could feel that the eyes themselves were undamaged. I believed that I could not see because my eyelids were so swollen that they had closed over my eyes.

All I remember of the C.C.S. is that the nurse had pince-nez which rattled. I was sure from the touch of her hand that she was not young, and when I asked her if she was in her twenties, she replied, "Get along with you, I'm over forty."

My burns nearly reached the limit beyond which you die, and the journey in a bumpy train to the base hospital at Boulogne was agony. My kit was sent down separately, and an orderly who went through the pockets of my service dress jacket and appropriated my cigarette case and a pound or two got so badly gassed from the jacket that his pilfering was found out. He was severely punished as well as having to suffer some painful burns.

The most trying part of extensive gas burns is that you cannot sleep, and your resistance to pain becomes impaired. However, the pain soon got less, and I was evacuated to England. After a very rough and painful crossing, I found my mother waiting for me at Victoria Station with the news that I had got the last bed in London in Lady Evelyn Mason's hospital in Bruton Street.

Dressing my wounds was an interminable business and I have never forgotten the skill, patience and gentleness with which the Sister gradually applied the liquid wax which was then the treatment. It was an orthopaedic hospital, and I was in a bed next to a splendid Northumbrian, who had been a dentist before he joined the Army. He had lost a foot, but was recovering and wanted someone to talk to about his profession.

I learnt quite a bit about "boof and poomice," which he thought was a sovereign beginning for the treatment of teeth.

The Colonel of the Regiment, the Duke of Connaught, personally saw every wounded Grenadier officer, but when he came to see me I was in such pain that he did no more than shake my hand and congratulate me.

One of my early visitors was Eric Mackenzie, the Staff Captain of the 4th Guards Brigade, who told me that the brigadier would recommend me either for a bar to my D.S.O. or a Military Cross, whichever I preferred. At that time I thought another bit of ribbon would fill out my chest better than a rosette on the ribbon of my D.S.O., and I have mildly regretted my choice ever since. However, I have the satisfaction that both my decorations were Immediate Awards: that means they were given, so to speak, on the battlefield.

The system adopted for giving decorations in those days was faulty. There was no decoration which could only be gained by fighting regimental soldiers, other than the V.C. General Staff officers and administrative officers could, after a period of admirable service at, for example, G.H.Q., expect the D.S.O. The M.C., which at the beginning of the war was only awarded for bravery on the battlefield, was given to many who had never heard a bullet or a shell. The chief baker at Boulogne was said to mount one.

Beside the V.C. I have always believed that there should be a routine decoration exclusively reserved for fighting troops, which could only be won under fire.

Honours and awards in war and peace loom large in men's minds. Only those who have been Ministers will know to what lengths some people will go, or to what depths of importunity they will descend, to get even the smallest decoration.

The other two visitors whom I particularly remember were Lady Moira Osborne, whom I thought an exquisite and attractive girl, and Winston, then Minister of Munitions and a very busy man. He was sure mustard gas was a humane weapon, and as by then I was out of pain and rapidly recovering, I agreed with him. If the shell which hit my little cottage had been a high explosive, I should not have survived.

I was up and about in a month, and appeared before the Medical Board. The doctors, although I did not know it, were inclined to disbelieve officers who said they were perfectly fit, and give them a month's leave. Those who said they had not properly recovered were apt to be given duty at once.

Although I wanted to rejoin the regiment, I fell into the trap, said I was fit, and got a month's leave. At the end of it I reported to Lieutenant-Colonel Lord Francis Scott, commanding our reserve battalion. He had received a crippling wound in 1914. I saluted. "Oliver, how are you?" "Very fit, Sir." He turned to the adjutant. "What do you say?" "He looks bloody awful, Sir." "Three weeks' leave, and then you can command a training company. Enjoy yourself, and don't overdo the staying up late, or the parties. We will now go to the ante-room for a glass of port and congratulate you on your medals."

My gas wounds left no ill effect, and only where the scratches had become infected can I discern any scars today.

In three weeks I was commanding a training company about 250 strong, and mostly composed of the last call-up from the mining districts of Wales. We had a week or two at Chelsea Barracks, and I had some trouble in getting my Welshmen up to the brigade standards of cleanliness in clothing and equipment. I had as many as a hundred men "showing articles" the first morning, but they soon learnt. Otherwise they were the best lot of recruits I had ever seen. It was impossible to overwork them; they were always cheerful; they sang songs in eight parts on the line of march, and they could dig like moles. I felt, if they were typical, that labour relations in the coal-mining industry in Wales must have been badly handled in peace-time, both by unions and employers. I became much attached to my Welshmen and thought very sadly that many of them would be killed or wounded, but although I did not guess it, they were not trained soldiers until too late for the fighting. I had the great satisfaction of seeing the first draft of my company, a hundred or more men, arrive in Maubeuge on November 11th or 12th.

We were soon moved for field training to Tadworth, and my company took shape very quickly. I enjoyed training them. They also made an almost clean sweep of the football, boxing and athletic finals, and by backing them for modest sums at long odds, I found myself richer by £200.

Every evening I had a round of golf at Walton Heath. Life was healthy and idyllic. It is, however, a strange thing that when you are wounded, you breathe a sigh of relief that you are out of it and, you hope, for a long time, but after a week or two you begin to chafe and wish to get back to fighting.

The famous Edinburgh dentist Dr. Girdwood, who used to treat me when I was a boy, overworked himself and took a month's fishing holiday. He came back in a fortnight, and I asked why. He said, "I just couldna keep away from the teeth." The pull of the craft applies also to soldiers.

Early in October, I was appointed Brigade Major, 2nd Guards Brigade, commanded by my old commanding officer, now Brigadier General Sergison-Brooke. When I got off the boat at Boulogne, I had some difficulty in making my way to the front because the Army had just made a rapid advance, but by some judicious lorry-jumping I caught them up in about twenty-four hours.

When I reached the front and got out of the divisional car, I saw in front of me a green, undulating landscape, unscarred by war. An orderly led the way. The brigadier was standing on a small mound with his brigade major, Billy Wynne Finch,[1] who had just been promoted, and whom I was to relieve. It was a clear evening, and the brigadier was watching a skirmish through his field glasses.

I was soon given a situation report, and Billy was told he could go off to his battalion. The brigadier turned to me and said, "Orders now: troops are to stand fast. Put out the piquet line, Oliver. Line of resistance along that feature," pointing to it. It was all that was necessary to someone who had learnt his mind and methods long before. He turned away. I was truly back, and soon writing the orders.

Open warfare was a wonderful sensation, but it was a dangerous business for brigadiers and their brigade majors, because we had continually to move about in the open, under fire, in order to keep in touch with the troops and with the rapidly developing battle. Orders often had to be given by word of mouth.

After a few days, we did a tricky piece of deployment by night;

[1] Afterwards Colonel Sir William Wynne Finch.

it would have been well-nigh impossible if a sunk road had not provided an assembly point; even then the road was not square to the position which we had to assault, but ran diagonally at a gentle angle across our front from left to right. This meant that at dawn our right flank had to advance first, and pick up the left. The movement was perfectly executed, and although it was a brisk fight, with some quite heavy casualties, we drove the enemy out in no time.

That afternoon we were to exploit our successes still further, and the brigadier and I made for forward Battalion H.Q. It was one of those unlucky days: my orderly was killed; the Germans had got a new weapon, or new to us, a quick-firing one-pounder pom-pom, with which they sniped the general and me. It was a nasty weapon, because the little shells arrived in coveys, almost simultaneously with the sound of the discharge, and there was no time to take cover.

We got to the Battalion H.Q. of the 3rd Battalion Grenadiers, then commanded by Lord Lascelles.[2] They were in the open, under a sloping green bank, and as we arrived they were being heavily shelled. Several signallers were killed or wounded. Harry Lascelles was quite imperturbable, and was smoking an Egyptian cigarette, which he held in the very tips of his fingers: he might have been playing bridge at the St. James' Club. "Really," he said, exhaling smoke with obvious pleasure, "a most unpleasant and unfortunate afternoon. We have captured the village, but I have had quite a few casualties, and I'm afraid Carol Carstairs has been very badly wounded. And now they won't leave my H.Q. alone. There you are," he said, as another salvo crumped round us. "What did I tell you? And there's another poor fellow wounded." He apparently thought it quite unlikely that the enemy would have the effrontery to kill or wound the son of a real English earl.

We transacted our business, and then had to go back a few hundred yards to Brigade H.Q. We got sniped again by the pom-poms, and a few salvos of 77 mm. In addition to the usual sensation of being an exposed target, we had also the feeling that we were now on top of the enemy and that it would be a pity to be put in the bag in the last few days of the war.

Some bitter news awaited us at H.Q. The brigadier's wife was critically ill; her life was despaired of, and he was to go home that very night. He arrived in London just before she died, and

2 Afterwards the Earl of Harewood.

was back again in three days. The blow was all the more poignant because we were all beginning to think of home and peace.

On November 4th, in what proved to be our last battle, we had to mount a most complicated and difficult attack. Our whole corps was to be engaged, and there was only one road on the corps front from which to deploy, or along which to pass artillery or reinforcements.

At zero hour, or shortly after, we had to cross a river; bridges would have to be improvised very quickly or a bottle-neck would be formed and congestion caused to the artillery and troops marching forward. The staff work had to be timed to a minute, and all the troop movements calculated to a fine point of accuracy.

The action in the early morning was spirited; the staff work proved adequate. We had some trouble at the only stone bridge, across which we had to pass a battery or two of field artillery. At one moment, when there were two guns on or near the bridge, a shell fell near the parapet; the horses shied, and one gun was thrown into the river ten feet below. The coupling of the limber parted, the limber blocked the road, and the horses' kicking and plunging added to the confusion. The block was soon cleared, and we advanced rapidly.

The next two days we made further advances, although the enemy machine-gun detachments clung to the ground with determination, and caused us delay and casualties. These detachments, as usual, were skilfully and bravely handled. The Germans seldom fought badly.

Then there was a pause of nearly a day, whilst we brought up supplies. We again advanced, against strong enemy rearguards, and reached a position astride the main *route nationale* leading eastwards and about four or five miles from Maubeuge. Night was falling as we established Brigade H.Q. in the stationmaster's house alongside the railway. It was November 8th, and we were to be relieved by the 3rd Guards Brigade soon after midnight. At about 5 P.M., Kenny Digby[3] of the Coldstream sent in a German prisoner, an N.C.O., who, they said, had been carrying orders in the turned-up sleeve of his jacket; they could not translate them, and sent them on to us. Colonel Vickery, who was at our headquarters commanding an artillery brigade, soon produced an English version. We found that the orders set out the whole of the German dispositions on several miles of front, and the present positions of

[3] Now Lord Digby.

the units were marked in. We learnt that the orders for the next day were to fall back, fighting tenaciously, to the high ground east of Maubeuge; the town itself was to be abandoned.

This was too good to miss, and we obtained permission from the division to push on and delay the relief till the next morning.

The brigadier took the boldest action: the 3rd Battalion Grenadiers, with an advanced guard and a "point," marched straight down the road to Maubeuge in fours, and reached the town at dawn. At Brigade H.Q. we had received no news by 6 A.M. and were anxious, although we heard no fire, that something had gone wrong. The brigadier and I accordingly rode down the *route nationale* to get in touch, leaving orders for the other two battalions to be ready to move at a moment's notice.

After a mile or two we felt very lonely: there was not a soul in sight. We could hear a battle going on a mile behind us, on our left flank, and one or two spent bullets, probably our own, fell harmlessly on the road. At last we came on a reserve company of the Grenadiers, and shortly afterwards rode into Maubeuge. The inhabitants surged out of every cellar and house: the enthusiasm was indescribable. We were smothered with flowers and soon had to hand the bouquets to our grooms. In a short time all that could be seen of them were their horses' legs and their grinning faces sticking out of a riot of flowers which would not have disgraced Moyses Stevens.

We established Brigade H.Q. in a comfortable house, and when the 3rd Guards Brigade relieved us, we got down to some sleep. We expected to be left alone for a day or two before we should in our turn have to leap-frog through the 3rd Guards Brigade, who had seized the high ground east of the town.

At about 3 A.M. on November 11th, I was woken by divisional orders. The message was laconic: "Following from Army begins: Hostilities will cease on all fronts at 11 A.M. November 11th. Acknowledge." I did not wake the brigadier. I went off to sleep again and was first in to breakfast and, forgetting that he did not know the news, a minute or two passed before he said, "Anything from the Division?" "Yes, Sir, this: the war is over."

About 10 A.M. one high-velocity shell roared into the town about 500 yards from our house, and frightened the life out of us. Then silence: silence that is, except for the clucking of chickens, the creaking of cart wheels, mooing of cows and other sounds of a country town on market day.

We rode round the troops; everywhere the reaction was the

same, flat dullness and depression. Winning in war is a most exhilarating sensation, and we had not had many days in which to
savour it; we had some scores to pay off, and now they would
never be paid.

We began to wonder what England would be like, whether we
should have enough to live on, what promotion would be like,
what our account at Cox's might be.

This readjustment to peace-time anxieties is depressing, and we
all felt flat and dispirited. We decided that a party and some gambling might cheer us up.

The attractions of Maubeuge were not great and we were
thrown back on our own resources. We rode about the country;
we tried a little shooting, but there was no more than a smattering
of partridges; we played bridge and gambled. Just as boredom was
setting in we received orders.

The B.E.F. was to march into Germany with all military precautions as if engaged upon an operation of war. We received the
general order of march for the Guards Division. The distance from
Maubeuge to the Rhine is about 140 miles as the crow flies, but
our route, which would take us through the Ardennes, seemed to
involve nearer 200.

We set off. For the first few days the weather held and it was
exhilarating to be on the line of march with these magnificent and
victorious troops.

The first large city which we entered was Charleroi; it had only
been evacuated by the Germans a few hours before. They must
have been much disorganised for they left everything behind them
in filth and disorder. The military hospital at Charleroi presented
one of the most revolting spectacles which I can remember. The
yard was filled with all the debris of the operating theatre: blood-
stained bandages, here and there a dismembered limb or two,
excrement, two unburied German soldiers, broken windows, mud:
an example of how quickly soldiers may become a rabble when
discipline is removed.

We were glad to leave Charleroi and the coal-mining district and
debouch into some clean country.

We were rapturously received by the inhabitants and soon became accustomed to being bombarded with flowers without losing
our composure. In some villages the school-children in their first
communion clothes greeted us with cheers and sang the Belgian
national anthem, which may have merits though brevity is certainly not one of them. In others, the mayor or the local land-

owner laid on a feast for us and delivered eloquent speeches of welcome. Apart from these feasts, we subsisted on our Army rations for the first time since the war began, and found them monotonous.

We marched into the Ardennes, a beautiful country of mountains and forests, but sparsely inhabited. The billeting of a brigade group was a long and exhausting task. Once I rode nearly a hundred miles in two days trying to find barns, outhouses, farms, villages, which would hold a company or a couple of platoons, and the staff captain must have covered even larger distances. As we approached the valley of the Meuse, it started to rain and then the enjoyment of seeing a new country and the pleasures of peacetime soldiering ceased. Mud was our old enemy, and here it was again. The maps were inaccurate. One day near the German frontier we marched for hour after hour and long after we should have reached our billets we saw a signpost marking still another twelve kilometres to our destination. The rain beat steadily down and the men were very tired as darkness fell. I calculated that we had marched more than twenty-six miles, although on the map our route measured no more than eighteen. Twenty-six miles in a day falls into the category of a forced march for fully equipped troops. Stonewall Jackson's famous march in the Shenandoah Valley was only twenty-eight miles.

A day or two later at about nine in the morning, we were sloshing along a muddy road; it was a grey sullen day, there was a wind in our faces which blew the rain through our clothing and we were already wet through. The area to which we were marching had only a few scattered farms. It looked as if some of us would sleep in the open. The brigadier and I were riding at the head of the column and occasionally cursing, when we heard the chug-chug of a motor bicycle threading its way past the troops. The despatch-rider dismounted and handed me an order from Divisional H.Q. Summarised, it stated that rioting had broken out in Cologne and that the brigade was to entrain in a certain area four or five miles to our flank that very night. There followed the details of the number of trains, times and the usual routine details of troop movements.

The news was welcome; we should soon be in a city and we did not think that the rioting would be very serious once our troops were on the spot.

We marched to a wayside station; there were several railway officials in smart uniforms to greet us. The German organisation was quick and efficient. The trains, made up of cattle trucks, arrived according to the march-table and the next morning we rumbled off.

Brigade H.Q. and our three battalions arrived in the early afternoon at the Hauptbahnhof, Cologne. The Oberbürgermeister and the Town Council were there to greet us. They explained how the rioting had begun: the demobilised soldiers of the German army had been allowed to keep their uniform jackets and trousers but not their forage caps, and a few of them had started breaking the shop windows to help themselves to caps. This had led to further disorder and quite serious rioting. In short, we were welcome. The brigadier enquired where the troops were to be billeted, and we were told that officers and men were to be accommodated in barracks which had only just been evacuated. It was feared that there was little furniture or bedding. We said that this would not do at all and that we should distribute ourselves as we thought fit the next day. Six limousines and guides would report at 8 A.M. the next morning at the barracks to carry the billeting parties. "There are no cars," said an official. "There will be tomorrow morning," said the brigadier grimly. We fell in on the platform, battalion by battalion, and marched off through the streets, played out by the drums and fifes. The battalions looked superb. The whole city had turned out to look at us; there was an air of relief. Many civilians marched alongside the men. It took a long time fitting in the troops and making them reasonably comfortable. By 6 P.M. we had found no suitable place for Brigade H.Q. and were directed by the Oberbürgermeister to a small house near the barrack gate. The door was opened by a young German lady, who welcomed us politely and placed two bedrooms at our disposal. The rooms were well furnished, comfortable and spotless. Our hostess said she regretted she had no food to offer us. Should she ring up for a table at the Excelsior Hotel? This one sentence did more to make me feel that the war was really over than all the speeches of the mayors and all the cheers of the school-children in Belgium.

We went off to the Excelsior and clanked into the restaurant. The band almost stopped; everyone stared; the headwaiter and several others bustled up to take our orders. Some civilians were moved out of the way without ceremony; we were officers and civilians clearly did not count for much in German eyes. We were embarrassed. The black bread and thin soup testified to the shortage of food in Germany.

The next day we billeted ourselves more comfortably. Frau von Obelmann had offered us her large, comfortable and hideous house as Brigade H.Q. on condition that she was undisturbed on one floor. She expressed some anti-imperial sentiments, but I fancy that our welcome owed more to her fear of having her belongings pillaged than to any warm feelings for the invaders.

The city was still supposed to be in some turmoil and we received orders to prepare a defence plan for keeping order if riots broke out.

While I was drafting it, the brigadier noticed that the orders began with the word "Secret." He said, "Strike that out. I shall publish the orders in the post office."

I remember that the defence plan read after this fashion:

In the event of serious rioting breaking out in the area of the Domplatz and Hohenzollern Bridge, two batteries of field artillery and a machine-gun battalion will be ready to sweep the approaches. Three battalions will patrol such and such an area, and so forth.

Of course, a lot of troops which did not exist at that time were detailed in these orders, but the publicity was worth a division. Unbroken tranquillity reigned over the city.

For a few days before the arrival of Lieutenant-General Sir Charles Fergusson, the Military Governor, the Brigade Group found themselves in control of a great city of nearly three-quarters of a million inhabitants. It was a heady sensation. I do not think that we abused our power.

Conditions in Germany outside the zones of occupation were unstable and disordered.

A number of well-known singers from other opera-houses found their way into Cologne, and the Municipal Opera, at other times not one of the best known, was thus reinforced and re-established almost within a day of our arrival. The director, for obvious reasons, thought that *Mignon* should be one of the first presentations. We secured the Imperial box for H.Q. and attended. The soprano, whether from nervousness or lack of practice, was out of tune. I could not resist sending for the director of the Opera next day, and expostulating. "The British," I said, "are a very musical people and cannot endure a performance like that of last night, when the soprano was always unsteady and often out of tune. *Mignon* is hardly in itself an opera of the class that commends itself. Herr Direktor, you must submit your programme in advance to this H.Q., and please see that this excruciating performance is not repeated."

He was speechless and never realised that he was having his leg pulled, partly no doubt because he knew that the strictures on *Mignon* were well founded and partly because German officials in those days took themselves very seriously.

The next day, the civil authorities asked for the Hohestrasse, a smart shopping street, to be reopened to wheeled traffic. It had been closed by the German military authorities. I shrugged my shoulders, and said, "Well, by British standards it is far too narrow, but here where the administration appears more lax I suppose we can consent, but if it leads to traffic jams it will be closed again."

These were the only reprisals in which we indulged and, considering that Germany had invaded Belgium in 1914 and caused us a lot of trouble during the next five years, I hope we may be excused.

After a few days the Military Governor arrived. The whole brigade was drawn up in mass in the square facing the main station. At 12 noon precisely, the doors were thrown open and framed in the doorway was Lieutenant-General Sir Charles Fergusson, whom I had first seen at Armentières in 1915.

"General Salute;" "Present Arms;" the massed drums struck up the "Point of War;" the Military Governor, faultlessly turned out, mounted, and escorted by a squadron of the Ninth Lancers, with their pennants flying from their lances, rode off to the Town Hall to receive, so to speak, the keys of the city. An officer who was present described the scene. The Oberbürgermeister obliged with a long speech. He traced the history of Cologne from early times through the Archbishopric to the present, and claimed that it had always been an anti-imperial city. He went on to describe the dreadful scenes of disorder and bloodshed which he thought might soon be witnessed. It was a long speech, made all the longer by having to be repeated by the interpreter, sentence by sentence.

The Military Governor stood up, the very personification of a senior general. With the ghost of a smile he said, "I am a soldier, and therefore the political history of Cologne does not concern me. As for the rest, my troops will keep your city in order. You may go now."

The Oberbürgermeister and the Town Council filed out in some dejection and seemed aware that they had taken no tricks.

We soon began to be bored by garrison life. Exercise was difficult; we had to ride through the streets and the tram-lines for a long way before we got into the country, and even then it was flat and uninteresting. We were entertained to a kettle drive or two in some vast root fields. A wide circle was made of guns and beaters. At the beginning each man is perhaps ten yards from the next, and then the circle is gradually contracted. The partridges flew in all directions and offered some good sport. When the circle got really small, I thought I had not been in such danger since the battle of the Somme.

We ignorantly drank Rhine wine at every meal and this régime and the lack of exercise led to some quarrels between brother officers who had never spoken a hard word to one another throughout the campaign.

In February 1919, I got some leave. A senior admiral came to dinner at Brigade H.Q. and offered Aubrey-Fletcher[4] and me a lift in a destroyer from Boulogne to Dover. They were going to take a look round the Ypres salient on their way and we had to be at Boulogne by a certain hour.

"Flick" Fletcher and I hired a Minerva car and set out. Somewhere near Ypres—and it was raining—it gave out, and we looked like being stranded for the night. Mercifully, the admiral and staff swept up a few minutes later and packed us into their cars. We reached Boulogne and witnessed the way in which destroyers are handled when they are carrying an Admiral of the Fleet. In one second after the last officer had gone on board, we were under way and soon making high speed through the shipping in the harbour.

A vast tea was laid on and almost before we had time to enjoy it, there we were at Dover. We were given another lift in a special train to London.

[4] Sir Henry Aubrey-Fletcher.

CHAPTER VII

IN THE CITY: I

I FOUND London in a state of great gaiety. There were parties every night. I had just begun to enjoy myself and feel at home in blue serge, gold spurs and some medals, when I was struck down by the influenza. It hit me at a dinner party at Lady Essex's in Brook Street, and one other guest, Lady Moira Osborne, looked as ill as I felt. She also succumbed.

I got sick leave, and since the Brigade was soon to return from Cologne, I was not to rejoin them. Demobilisation was beginning quite rapidly. I found myself in the happy position of being a brigade major in the Brigade of Guards without a brigadier or a brigade. I gave myself plenty of leave and joined my friends at every lighted candle in the town.

I also went racing a good deal and, surprisingly, had a run of success which made me think that I could defer a decision about my future for a few weeks.

However, I soon fell in love with Moira Osborne and love turned my thoughts with the urgency that nothing else can to the grim problem of money and subsistence.

I had a few hundred a year and my pay and nothing else. I looked likely to return to being second-in-command of a company with promotion much clogged by the expected contraction of the Brigade of Guards. Moreover, you could hardly get into the Guards' Club for officers.

Should I be called to the bar or launch out into some other career? I clearly could not propose to a duke's daughter without some prospect of being able to support her. In the meantime, I danced almost every dance with her and she was the best dancer I ever remember. My condition was getting more and more serious.

I remembered my father's injunction to me on his death-bed: "When you want advice on anything, go and ask Lawrie [Mr. Justice Lawrence[1]]. He is the wisest man I ever knew."

So I rang up and asked him if I might come and have tea with him in his house in South Street. The dear old judge received me like a son, and over the cucumber sandwiches I told him all, or nearly all, and asked him the great question, Should I be called to the bar?

He pursed up his lips and with a pensive look, which I had observed in court, said, "Oliver, this is a very serious matter. I must reflect upon it deeply. I will reserve judgment and deliver it tomorrow at tea, if you can come at the same time." When I returned he summed up: "The law has got into very few hands. Your father's connection is too long past to be of much help. You are twenty-six, and that is a bit late to begin. You can't count on earning more than a pittance three or four years from now. But, Oliver," he said with a smile, "there is something even more important. I suspect that you can work hard enough when the work is there and has to be done, but I doubt, with your temperament and the social pull from London which you will feel all the time, whether you are the sort who will continue to work hard reading your law and waiting for briefs whilst your friends are racing, shooting and enjoying themselves. In short, my judgment is: Don't touch it."

I knew from what he had said that he had collected some evidence which I had not given him myself. I unquestioningly accepted his decision.

I thought that with several dances and parties in the offing at least I should not have to interrupt my fun at that moment, and the urgency seemed even less when that week I found a winner at 100 to 6.

A little later, I thought of my first cousin, Melville Balfour, a rich and successful stockbroker, fond of hunting and racing, a man of mature judgement and a friend who had often given me a good time. I said I fancied becoming a banker in the international field, and he smiled at this naïveté. He did more, however; through Sir James Leigh Wood he got me a place as a learner in Brown Shipley & Co. This rich and old-established partnership originally op-

[1] Afterwards Lord Trevethin.

erated as an offshoot of an American banking house and still worked closely with Brown Bros. of New York, Boston and Phila- delphia. I was to join as a clerk in the postal department at the beginning of August and would be moved round from one depart- ment to another to learn the banking function.

The firm was of the highest standing, and not over large in numbers. It specialised in foreign exchange, particularly in the dollar exchange, and in commercial credits. My salary was to be £180 a year and a bonus at Christmas.

So my future was settled and there were still a few weeks more of the London season, which had become even gayer.

Towards the middle of July, I learned that Moira was soon to leave for Scotland. I knew I ought not to, but I decided to put all to the test. I wrote on a certain Friday and told her that I wanted to talk to her on a serious matter: would she come to tea on Sunday?

Once I had posted the letter I began to suffer the agonies of suspense. I went to the Guards' Club and got in touch with my great friend, Eric Mackenzie of the Scots Guards, who had been staff captain of the 4th Guards Brigade when I was brigade major. He was known to the young ladies of London as "Mother."

I told him everything. His response was immediate: "You are to place yourself in my hands. We must fill in the time till Sunday evening. It is now twelve. Your glasses are in the hall, I expect; we leave for Hurst Park at once."

He never left my side. We were put on a good-priced winner by a friend, and I had a larger bet than usual. Anyway, the afternoon passed and we returned a hundred or two the richer. He stood over me while I dressed for dinner. We dined well on champagne and quails and swept to the music hall. By this time, I had begun to think that my succession to Ernest Cassel would be quick and that my impending fortune might increase my matrimonial chances. We went to bed late and happily. I was roused from sleep by Eric on the telephone the next morning: "Sherry at the Guards' Club when you are ready, say eleven-thirty. I have ordered a car and we're going racing again."

We came away small losers, at which I was much relieved be- cause I thought, "You cannot be lucky on the race course and in the drawing-room." Eric had collected some friends for dinner and bridge at the Club, and that passed the evening.

Meanwhile, my mother had heard from me of the state of affairs and proposed to make a kind of financial hara-kiri for my sake.

The morning of the day arrived, and there was Eric. He never left me and although we could not go racing he kept me distracted with a slap-up luncheon and some bridge.

That evening I was accepted. I could not believe it and was in the seventh heaven of happiness, and I was right to be.

Moira had to go to Scotland in a few days and I had an engagement to stay at Brighton with Lady Meux for Goodwood, which I dared not chuck at such short notice. Fortunately, Lady Meux was Moira's aunt and knew from her daughters what was toward. She released me readily after the first two days' racing. I came away a winner over the two days of nearly £400.

Soon after, Moira and I parted, she to a party of Lord Northampton's at Lochluichart, and I to Brown Shipley & Co., Founders Court, Lothbury, E.C.

Founders Court had a sort of Galsworthy aroma about it. The staff referred to the partners as Mr. Ted or Mr. Laurie; the partners' room gave on to a small courtyard in which a fig tree protested against its environment.

The change from being a guardsman and a brigade major, under whose eye every knee stiffened, to being a clerk in the postal department was marked.

The department had a staff of three or four and, other than having to know the postal rates to every part of the world, its duties were mainly in producing reports on the credit standing of the bank's customers and answering enquiries on more general matters in the economic field.

My very first morning, all the staff were out on enquiries, when a request was received from New York by the partners, asking for an assessment of the liquidity of the German banks. I was told to go round to Samuel Montagu & Co., who were the acknowledged authority. Brown Shipley were in close relations with them, especially on foreign exchange.

I presented myself in the hall, and the porter asked for my name and whom I wanted to see. I replied "Brown Shipley & Co." to the first, and "one of the partners" to the second question. The name of Brown Shipley opened the door in a trice, and I was ushered to my surprise straight into Lord Swaythling's presence. I had occasionally played bridge with him when a guest of "Cardie" Montagu,[2] and he realised that my face was familiar.

"Ah, how do you do," he said. "We have often met in the part-

2 The Hon. Lionel Montagu.

ners' room of Brown Shipley & Co., I believe?" I said, "Oh, no," in a tone of voice which might have conveyed that I was expecting to be invited to be a partner at any minute. I put my enquiry, and he gave me a detailed survey of the subject. I was a little surprised when almost every sentence began: "You know as well as I do, my dear Lyttelton, that . . ."

I reported back as much as I understood, which was not much.

I soon settled down, and after a fortnight or so reached the conclusion that the department was trying to do something impossible. There were 4,000 names on the cards and a simple calculation showed that without a vastly increased staff the information could not be kept up to date year by year, or even triennially. Moreover, much more than three-quarters of these cards related to customers who no longer had active accounts.

I pointed out these absurdities in a memorandum and suggested that the customers should be divided into two categories, the active accounts and the non-active, and that we should only be required to keep up to date the information relating to the active accounts: a few hundred at the most.

This piece of administrative percipience was greeted first by astonishment, then by obstruction and soon after by acceptance. Even then we had to work hard to keep the information on the active accounts up to date within a year.

One day an enquiry was received from Philadelphia about the standing of a well-known British firm in India which was attempting to open a credit with Brown Bros., Philadelphia. The matter was urgent and important, and I went out on the road and made extensive enquiries lasting three or four hours, during which I found out that the company in question was already much extended and had been refused further lines of credit in London.

I went into a post office without returning to the office and cabled one word to Philadelphia: "Avoid." I got into hot water for this, even when I explained the evidence upon which it was based. I was told that this laconic message would never have been authorised by the partners. One of the directors was a close personal friend of one of the partners. "Anyway," they asked, "how did you manage to send a cable without coming through the postal department?" "Oh, I paid for it myself," I said. This appeared quite astounding, but I was allowed to claim the cost.

I was told not to do this sort of thing again, and some more guarded telegram was subsequently despatched which evidently did not remove the impression of the first. I was not forgiven until the Indian house failed for a large sum and when it was found that our American associates had given it no credit.

I was soon moved into the commercial credit department and began to learn the intricacies of consular certificates, manifests, bills of lading, insurance policies: in short, of documented acceptance credits. The acceptance commission was 2% per annum or ½% for a three months' bill, and I was amazed that my colleagues could read off the ½% without apparently resorting to arithmetic. It took me a week to learn the trick.

One day, during the luncheon interval, I was alone in the department when a porter said that there was a customer outside. I went out but at first could see no one. Then I noticed some fingernails stretched out on the counter at some distance from me. They belonged to a smiling but diminutive Japanese gentleman who could not see over the counter.

He said that he wanted to open a credit for about £180,000 in favour of some exporter in London. How could it be arranged?

I said, "Oh, that is quite simple: we are here for that purpose. You write us a cheque for £180,000 and we handle the documents for you for a half of one per cent."

To my astonishment, he wrote the cheque which I had "fated" and the transaction was completed in the afternoon. I could not resist the joke of telling the manager that I had opened this credit.

He said, "What! How could you? This is awful, I must see the partners." When I was sent for, I explained that the credit was covered by cash in the Westminster Bank. Then all was smiles, but they were a little shocked by the charge of ½%, which seemed high; it should have been ¼ or ⅜, but even this was forgiven.

I studied the theory and law of banking every night into the early hours of the morning, and absorbed *Hales Law of Banking* and *Chalmers on Bills of Exchange* and other standard books. I never worked so hard again until I became a Minister.

Perhaps the most baffling intricacies of banking concern foreign exchange. There was at that time one small part of the theory which was not covered by any text-book, but which was afterwards explained by Keynes in a famous passage. The question is: What, in theory, puts one exchange at a premium over another three months hence? Thus if spot sterling is, say, $4.60, why in theory is three months sterling, say, $4.60½? The answer lies in the disparity between the different rates for money ruling in London and New York, but it is too intricate a subject to be worth discussing. In any case, the theory is overlaid by the practical laws of supply and demand.

I eventually got to the bottom of it, and much else on the way, and found some of my theoretical knowledge of great advantage when I was transferred to the Foreign Exchange Department. At that time Brown Shipley & Co. was the only bank in London which operated a common book in the four centres, London, Boston, Philadelphia and New York, and which therefore paid no commission on dollar/sterling transactions. This gave us an advantage of a sixty-fourth or a thirty-second in the rate and in consequence of this and some other ancillary advantages, almost all the dollar transactions in London were eventually cleared through our books.

The dealings in "telegraph transfer" were done by Mr. Pirie, the head of the department, who sat surrounded by banks of telephones. Telegraph transfer means that the pounds or dollars are bought or sold for settlement on the same day. For example, the contracts used to read "H & T the 10th," meaning here and there. It is a business for which you have to have nimble wits, and it is a great strain. Mr. Pirie chain-smoked all day and when uncovered in a rapidly changing market and unable to get through to some bank to cover, he occasionally threw the instrument on the ground and danced on it from exasperation.

The underlings in the department had to make the calculations and send out the contracts, which kept us hard at it from 10:30 in the morning till late in the evening, often until 9 P.M.

The juniors were occasionally allowed to deal in cheque, which was a much more sedate business and which anyone at all competent could safely do.

To give an idea of the hold which we had on the dollar exchange: one day the English branch of a very large American concern wanted to remit its annual dividend to the United States. The manager came in person and asked the rate at which he could buy a cheque for something over $3,000,000. We quoted 3.66. "Well," said the American representative, "I must test the market." "We don't recommend you to do so," we told him, "because this is a very large cheque; it will be identified—unlike T/T [3]—and you will move the rate against you." "Well, that's the way it is," he answered. In an hour's time he came back and was a buyer of a cheque for less than $2,000,000. We quoted 3.65, which he accepted. We said, "We gave you good advice this morning. You

[3] Telegraphic Transfer.

made a mistake in going round the market. You bought $500,000 at 3.65¾ from A. B. & Co., $250,000 from C. D. & Co. at 3.65½ and $500,000 from one of the big five at 3.65⅛." "Gosh, how did you know," he exclaimed. "Oh," we replied, "we have just sold them the dollars."

We employed, amongst others, a well-known firm of "running brokers," whose only duty was to put us in touch with the enquiries for exchange. They charged, for this menial function, six shillings and eightpence for every $100,000 of business transacted. At the end of one year their account amounted to £12,500. This gives an idea of the size of the annual transactions and why the clerks were kept busy.

I spent a short time in the Paying Cashier's Department and learnt that this business is no mere routine. The Paying Cashier was Mr. Chapman, an urbane philosopher, with a wing collar and a bow tie, interested in Spinoza. He paid out on demand as if celebrating a sacrament.

One day, an open (uncrossed) cheque had been presented for payment by a rather seedy-looking young man. It was drawn for forty-odd pounds in favour of Lockwood Brown & Co. in Jermyn Street. Mr. Chapman said, "How would you like it, Sir, seven five-pound notes and the rest in ones?" "Yes, please." "One moment." He then rang the bell hidden under the counter, which brought the messengers to the door of the bank. The young man, guessing that things had gone wrong, made a bolt for it. He was caught.

"What on earth made you do that?" I asked, when I heard the story. "Well," said Mr. Chapman, "there were three main reasons. First, the easiest forgery is from four to forty. Secondly, an open cheque is unusual: when it is examined it will probably be found that the crossing has been taken out with chemicals. Thirdly, Lockwood Brown is a well-known firm of athletic outfitters and the drawer of the cheque, an elderly American customer of ours, is hardly likely to have spent such a large sum in buying tennis racquets, golf clubs or the like."

It turned out that Lockwood Brown's post box had been robbed the night before.

I learnt from this that there was more in being a paying cashier than meets the eye and that Mr. Chapman knew a lot about the world that you would not find in the pages of Spinoza.

I spent some time in the Securities Department and consulted Mr. Oldfield about my meagre investments.

I had inherited about two thousand shares in the Mysore Gold

Mine, a Tennant concern. These shares had originally come to my father in the marriage settlement of his first wife, the daughter of Sir Charles Tennant, who had made a large fortune in Victorian times. The mine had been a wonderul payer, but was now thought to be dying out on the lower levels. I decided to sell at somewhere just above two pounds, and said to Mr. Oldfield, "I have a sentiment about these shares, and if they go below a pound I want to buy them back."

Some months later, Mysores had a considerable fall. One day, I was in Throgmorton Street on my way out to luncheon when I met a half-commission man of my acquaintance. "What are Mysores?" I asked. "Oh, about either side of the figure," he said (meaning 19s. 9d. to 20s. 3d.). "Well, you can buy me two thousand, if you can get on below a pound."

I got back to the department after luncheon to be greeted by Mr. Oldfield, who said, "Captain Lyttelton, I've got you your Mysores back at 19s. 9d." Hardly had he spoken, when the telephone rang and my friend said he had bought two thousand at 19s. 10½d. So I had twice what I wanted. The market, however, could not deliver them: there were very few free shares, the great bulk being held by the Tennant family and their connections.

As the Settlement Day approached, Mysores crept up to 22s. 6d., 23s., 24s. 6d., 27s. 6d. and eventually a jobber turned up in the Securities Department, explained the situation and asked me at what price I would let the market out. I said, "Oh, 32s. 6d., I suppose." He thanked me profusely and accepted the price at once.

This is probably one of the rare instances where a clerk at £180 a year has cornered a market at 19s. 9d. and been thanked by a leading firm of jobbers for letting them out at 32s. 6d.

All this time Moira was immured at Hornby Castle in Yorkshire, the home of the Leeds family. I was most unpopular with my prospective father-in-law, mainly I hope on the grounds that I had no money and only an uncertain future. He would not hear of our being married. I was, however, allowed to spend an occasional weekend with the family.

It was a long and, for that matter, expensive journey after work on a Friday evening, and the Duke would only meet me at Bedale. This meant a tiresome delay and change at Northallerton, which itself was ten or twelve miles from the Castle. On my return journey I had to leave on Sunday evening from Bedale, kick my heels at York for three hours or more, before catching the London express at 1 A.M.

The Duchess and Moira's sisters were much on my side and put the Duke into Coventry, or near Coventry, when he persisted in his obstinacy. I had some rather acid interviews with him. I would point out that I had about £1,400 a year and should soon make my way in the City. The Duke said, "Why, getting in and out of the City every day alone will cost you 10s. in taxi fares." When I retorted that I went by Underground for 6d. a day, he was not mollified. He was aghast at the thought of his daughter having to face life with an adventurer on my pittance, and when I said that Duff Cooper and Lady Diana Manners had married on much the same, I made matters considerably worse. "Look what's happened," he exclaimed. "She has fallen through a skylight and broken her leg. How's that to be paid for?"

When you are very young, delays of the kind which confronted me appear interminable. In fact before very long he relented, under family pressure, and somewhere about November he reluctantly agreed to our being married in January 1920. He added a very small annual settlement.

After I was officially engaged, and when Moira's family returned to their house in London, in Grosvenor Crescent, I went to call on them at tea-time. As the footman preceded me up the stairs I was aware of wisps of sacrificial smoke and some smell of burning eddying down the well of the house. The drawing-room appeared to be in a thick fog. The reason for this unusual phenomenon was that the Duchess was burning away a large slice of Christmas cake in the fire. The cook was under the illusion that the family liked Christmas cake and had made a large example covered with sugar icing. Rather than offend her, a slice of this was cut off every evening and sacrificed as a burnt offering to her susceptibilities.

The drawing-room itself had some of the finest pieces of French furniture in the world: pieces which the Louvre would have been glad to acquire. The fireplace, on the other hand, was graced by a green japanned tin coal-scuttle, on which lilies of the valley had been painted. This monstrous and incongruous object had been bought by the butler from some store, and caused my mother-in-law endless amusement. It was not removed; better to suffer it than hurt anyone's feelings.

We were married at St. Margaret's, and drove away in the ducal brougham, clip, clop, up Constitution Hill to Grosvenor Crescent.

My mother had decided to turn the two top floors of her large house at 16 Great College Street into a flat where we could live, and we went on our honeymoon with an assured residence to which to return. In those days it was thought a most unusual arrangement. The flat was charming. Our establishment consisted at first of an outrageous Irish butler, not allergic to whisky, a lady's maid, a housemaid and a cook, and on a little over £1,400 a year we judged ourselves to be very poor.

I worked harder than ever, but we really enjoyed ourselves. We were widely entertained in London, and often spent Saturday to Monday at Grimsthorpe, Taplow, Hatfield, Trent, The Wharf and so forth. I made an odd hundred or two by underwriting and mild speculation, but there was no doubt that we put a big strain on our income, even though we were housed nearly free.

I still retain enough of the reticence of my era or period not to write of my private and family life other than to say that I have been blessed far beyond my deserts and that Moira and I and our children have always been a closely knit family. Our four children have been endowed with brains superior to those of their parents. Moira and I have long ceased to make incautious remarks on literature, philosophy, music, history or, for that matter, business in front of them. "Parents should think before they speak" has been our enforced rule.

My long hours of work and study began to give me, after a year at Brown Shipley, a solid grounding in the theory of banking, in its law and in its practical working. At first, even the simplest terminology is baffling; such terms as "placing the proceeds against the accruing liability" and so forth are now so much part of my vocabulary that I can hardly conceive that I found them puzzling.

I have forever been grateful to Brown Shipley, with their splendid tradition, for giving me the chance to study as a learner. Amongst other things I found out was how skilled is the profession of bank clerk and what charming people bank clerks are and with what patience and forbearance they are willing to answer the most elementary questions.

In my days they were certainly underpaid, and it is a satisfaction to know that in 1962 their conditions are far better and that they can look forward to pensions which, though hardly adequate recompense for their services, at least are enough to keep them in reasonable comfort when they retire.

I still claim to know the banking function intimately, and it has stood me in good stead.

Since those days I have always felt that training, either of a general character or in a form of business in which a young man does not intend eventually to make his career, is a wise course.

If a man begins at the bottom of a company in which he hopes to spend his working life, all that he knows will have been learnt either from his seniors or from his competitors. It is what the other man does not know that puts the knowledge of one who does at a premium.

Again, if I had my way, a large proportion of men with honours degrees in, say, engineering would normally spend another year at the university in studying the general theory of business. It is the theory that counts in most walks of life. "Study the campaigns of the great captains," said Napoleon.[4] A knowledge of the theory of war will simplify the problems even of a company commander in a way which experience alone never can.

One thing is clear: the man who invented the slogan "An ounce of practice is worth a pound of precept" should have been put in the stocks. It was a cruel thing to say, especially to Britons, who err too often on the side of empiricism. We all know, of course, that, in the world of affairs, action and execution are the touch-stones of success, but both stand the test more often when founded upon theoretical knowledge.

In the late summer of 1920, the British Metal Corporation were looking for a young man. The Managing Director, Sir Cecil Budd, had been grossly over-worked in the Ministry of Munitions during the war and wanted help and an eventual successor. He enlisted John Hugh Smith, afterwards a managing director of Hambros Bank and a member of the famous business family, to find him one. John had also been educated at Brown Shipley and made enquiries of the partners. "Yes, we've got a chap who will probably suit you," they said.

I was asked to luncheon by Sir Cecil Budd. He was a large, ponderous man in form, but he had not only nimble and flexible wits but a chuckling sense of humour and a kindliness which shone in his face.

He offered me the job of being a learner in the Metal Corporation. At the end of twelve months, if they liked me and I liked them I was to become General Manager. He told me that the Corporation had been formed at the request of Lord Ashfield, President of the Board of Trade, to replace the German dominance in the Empire in non-ferrous metals.

4 *Napoléon: Pensées pour l'Action,* ed. Driault (Paris, 1943).

"What do 'non-ferrous metals' mean?" I asked. "Well, mainly copper, lead, zinc [then known as spelter] and tin. The principal shareholders of the company are Lloyds Bank, Morgan Grenfell, Central Mining, the Rio Tinto Company, Cookson's and British Aluminium. The company carries on a merchanting business in the finance, shipping and sales of these metals and are large dealers on the Metal Exchange."

"But I know nothing about metals," I demurred, "and I have no technical knowledge on these subjects. All I know about is a bit of banking."

"Yes," said Sir Cecil, "but you won't have to know much technically; you will soon learn enough."

I had not wanted to leave the financial or banking world, but the prospects of this new job, that is to say the pay, pulled me the other way.

"What am I to be paid?" I asked.

"Well, £600 a year as a retainer for the first year."

I accepted, and was to begin work in August, just a year after my first entry into the City.

Three weeks after I had accepted, I was offered a managing partnership in a well-known bank—evidence of how short the country was of young men. I thought I had unluckily missed the chance and distinction of a lifetime. In fact I was blessed by fortune. I should have disliked the critical nature of banking, and it would have been many years before I earned in the bank half of what I was to make at the Metal Corporation.

CHAPTER VIII

IN THE CITY: II

I JOINED the British Metal Corporation in Abchurch Yard as a learner in August, and found myself in the dealing department. It was under the management of a small, perky, balding little cockney called Henry Arthur Buck. He had started life as a solicitor's clerk, had been secretary of the Metal Exchange and had been secured after the war by Sir Cecil as the principal dealer of the new Corporation.

Apart from being a delightful character, he was the sharpest-witted dealer in the business. He could smell a buyer or a seller a hundred yards away. If the other dealer was suspected of being a buyer, he assumed an expression of bounding cheerfulness: you could feel how strong the market was. On the other hand, if the dealer was judged to be a seller, Henry Arthur's steps dragged, his eyes became dull and glazed and obviously no one could ask a man in such a state of depression to take anything more on to his book except at a considerable concession in the price.

We became firm friends, and remained so till the day of his death.

At this time, he was just beginning to earn good money and it was exhilarating to see him tasting pleasures which he had denied himself in youth. He often told me how he had saved up to buy his first bicycle and was just ready to put down the cash (there was, of course, no hire purchase in those days), when the uppers came away from the soles of his boots. It was summer weather, but there would be another month's saving before he could ride out into the country. "The sadness of it, Pendragon [his nickname for me, for some reason], the sadness of it."

I learnt from him the mysteries of dealing, of contangos (the premium by which forward metal exceeds the price of spot), backwardations (the discount by which forward falls below the price of spot in certain conditions of the market), landing charges, assay values and the whole paraphernalia. I also learnt his shrewd summing up of all his customers and competitors. "As straight as a corkscrew, Pendragon." "Bone, just bone." "Straight but touchy." "Thinks he knows everything. I always tell him so, it's worth a good 2s. 6d. a ton," and so on.

A year or two later, I reckoned that he spun between £50,000 and £100,000 a year for the company out of his agile brain by buying and selling, and by his lightning quickness in closing up contangos when they exceeded the running rate of interest, and so forth. His success never went to his head, and he remained a simple and lovable character.

I had been in the dealing department for a few months when I was sent for by the managing directors. They explained that they were worried about the exchange risks involved in their purchase of copper in the United States. Would I work out a plan to eliminate the risk? This, of course, was child's play to someone trained in foreign exchange: I made a report in an hour. The dollars must be sold forward against the spot purchases of metal and the forward sales of dollars covered in as the copper was sold out in sterling.

It would be tedious for the general reader if I were to trace in any detail my business activities or my business career between 1921 and 1938. There are some features of it which, however, I must record; they have certainly formed or affected my whole outlook on affairs; their circumstances destroyed any insular inclinations which I may have entertained in my youth.

The British Metal Corporation was more than a mere money-making machine. It had an "over-all strategic concept." This was to make the British Empire self-supporting in the non-ferrous metals, not only for economic but also for defence reasons. It had been formed under Government inspiration for this purpose.

It was clearly not enough that these important minerals and metals should be of Empire origin; we should aim at directing the raw materials into Empire smelters and refineries, and as far as possible secure that the control of the resultant metal was in British hands for sale, and if possible in those of the British Metal Corporation.

I count it as a piece of fortune that I should have been concerned with a company which had to be conducted with a dominant theme. It added point and spice to the more pedestrian task of making money for the shareholders and a livelihood for myself.

The sums invested in mining, smelting and refining in the British Empire were huge, and it was quite obvious that the necessary control could not be gained by a single company, or even by two or three of the biggest acting in concert. The practical policy had to aim at a loosely knit federation.

Our part was to provide the finance, shipping and sales organisation. Our position could not be secured unless the British Metal Corporation was itself prepared to take some financial interest, particularly in new ventures. We must, I thought, provide other services in the field of mining and metallurgical processes. Beyond this, a system of interlocking directorships and personal ties with some of the great companies engaged in the business pointed the way to our federal objectives.

At the end of my year of probation I became General Manager. All through these seventeen years from 1922 to 1939, first under the leadership of Sir Cecil Budd, and then under mine, aided and wisely advised and kept in check by my two friends, William Mure[1] and Jack Budd,[2] this is the policy which we consistently pursued. When the war broke out in 1939, the British Empire was self-sustaining in these vital metals and I claim that we had played a major role in bringing this about.

At this time the Corporation was (and still is) the agent of the Broken Hill group of mining companies in Australia. The Australian interests in this large group were managed in London by a remarkable man, W. S. Robinson, with whom I thus became closely associated, and for whom I entertained the greatest admiration and affection. He, no less than ourselves, was pursuing the theme of a self-contained British Empire in metals, and he and I were soon working in the closest harmony, which none of the stresses of war or peace has ever disturbed. At first I was merely a lieutenant.

W. S., as he is known the world over, was not only the most completely equipped business man that I have known, but on the broader aspects of economics and monetary policy he had an originality of thought far in advance of his times. He has lived to see many of his ideas, which the more orthodox considered in those days to be outrageous, accepted as conventional, or even as axiomatic.

[1] Now Managing Director of the British Metal Corporation.
[2] John Cecil Budd.

I was and am deeply devoted to him, and all that I know about business which is out of the ordinary I have learnt from him. He was the most widely travelled man in those days, and was as closely in touch with the American as with the Imperial or the continental scene.

The first advance that we made towards our "over-all strategic concept" came about through him. A financier and industrialist called Tilden Smith had been largely financed by Lloyds Bank during the war. He was a man of great imagination and vision, but with grandiose ideas, who was apt to regard figures as a matter of opinion. He owed the banks some millions and was eventually persuaded to sell us his zinc-smelting companies at Swansea and Avonmouth and four million shares, carrying virtual control, in the Burma Corporation, the great zinc–lead mine east of Mandalay.

There was one moment in these negotiations which will be stamped for ever on my memory. We had rivals; their offer was on the point of being accepted; we put in a counter bid. We went to see Sir Robert Horne, who was acting for Lloyds Bank. We waited tensely. After some pregnant minutes Sir Robert said our terms were reasonable, but further negotiations with Tilden Smith would be necessary. This was the first hurdle surmounted. I had been sitting with both hands on the table and, when I got up, I could see their damp imprint on the shiny mahogany. It is quite wrong to suppose that business is not sometimes very exciting.

The National Smelting Corporation[3] was born, and I was one of the seven signatories. For the British Metal Corporation, there is no doubt that this deal was the "break-through." Two great companies entrusted us with their sales. We had already gained a predominant position in the metal trade. I was appointed a Managing Director of the British Metal Corporation, and also joined the Board of the Burma Corporation. I, too, was beginning to emerge into a larger field.

It is here necessary to describe the international metal trade. It is supported by one of the largest blocks of capital, probably the largest after oil and steel, in the world. In spite of this, not more than perhaps twenty-five men really counted in the industry.

It is not, in the usual sense of the word, a competitive business, since most of its products are broadly identical in quality, such as electrolytic copper and zinc, and soft lead. Moreover, providence or chance has put these minerals, from which the metals are derived, into the ground in widely different proportions, and asso-

[3] It has since become part of the Consolidated Zinc Rio Tinto Group.

ciated with other minerals in many diverse ways. The great por-
phyry deposits of copper in South America, owned by U.S. companies for the most part, run from one per cent of copper, and
even under, up to two per cent to the ton. The Rhodesian mines
would be on the average about three times as rich. Some mines,
notably these same low-grade porphyries, are mined by quarrying
or open-casting; others, like the Rhodesian, by shaft and deep-
level mining. It can thus be seen how different is the industry
from those which draw their raw materials from the same sources,
and which depend upon design or quality of their product to survive.

The metal trade is truly international, for no country is self-
supporting in all the non-ferrous metals. Thus the United States
have no tin, the United Kingdom—if classified apart from the
Commonwealth—has no significant resources of any of them. All
the great industrial countries have to import some of their needs
from their colonies or from overseas. Metals must be exchanged
across all the international frontiers.

No one amongst the twenty-five men whom I have mentioned
could play a part unless he was well known to the other twenty-
four, unless he had travelled widely over the world, and unless he
had been a regular figure at the numerous international conferences, and a signatory of the international agreements which
covered and sought to control the production and disposal of the
principal metals.

I hope that I am not elevating myself to an unjustifiable emi-
nence when I say that, after the retirement of Sir Cecil Budd, I,
later, was one of the twenty-five who could claim to have a say in
this world-wide industry.

The British Metal Corporation in the early nineteen-twenties had
already gone some way towards its objectives. We controlled very
large amounts of Empire lead and zinc, but not any large tonnage
of copper. Opportunities to improve our position soon presented
themselves. A short time after the discovery of the Rhodesian
copper field, Mr. Chester Beatty, who was a colleague of mine on
the board of the Burma Corporation, offered us a participation
of about £1 million in the Roan Antelope mine, then in course of
early development. From diamond drilling it had all the marks of
being one of the great copper mines of the world although the ore-
body was not proved by cubication. The participation naturally
carried with it the sale of the metal.

I tried to persuade my board to accept his offer—and was

backed up by my executive colleagues—but we were judged to be young and sanguine. Moreover, Chester Beatty reeled off such startling figures of the grade and ore reserves which were likely to be opened up that they thought he was romancing. He certainly gave the impression of high-pressure salesmanship. I failed to persuade the Board, and by far the greatest opportunity in a century was missed.

Every figure and estimate given by Chester Beatty was either fulfilled or exceeded as time went on. My feelings in this small field of contest, when I had to pass on their decision, were like those of the Duke of Marlborough on the great field when he was thwarted by the Stadtholders and Dutch generals. I cannot even now bear to calculate what our holdings would have eventually been worth: it would have been more than £20 million, and our position would have been unrivalled.

We also had the opportunity of financing the Noranda Corporation in Canada and were offered about $5 million in bonds, convertible into ordinary shares at $7 a share. Again the board burked at the size of the investment and we took only $500,000. This time we secured the agency. The shares soon stood at $53 and since then have been split more than once.

In those days, agencies and merchanting business were often carried out through the link of personal connections and friendships. As the size of companies tended to grow, and their needs became more varied, more and more attention had to be paid to the nature and scope of the services rendered by merchants, and the British Metal Corporation were in essence merchants. It was, of course, clear that mining companies did not wish to speculate in the price of metals, and that the merchant could cover the risk by taking on to his books the daily output of the mine at the pithead, so to speak, at that day's price. The merchant would get rid of the metal in two ways, either by selling it direct to the consumer, or by selling it on the Metal Exchange. Conversely, if demand from consumers exceeded the intake on any day, the merchant would buy on the Metal Exchange to cover his short position. These, in simple terms, are the essence of merchanting business, whether in metals, rubber, wheat or cotton, or in any commodity in which there is a terminal market. Allied to this is straight-out agency business, where the broker takes no risk other than the solvency of his customers or the integrity of his client.

Both merchanting and agency business were going to be difficult to secure if finance was the sole service to be given. We were

accordingly determined to build up two technical departments concerned with mining and metallurgy.

On the broader theme we set out towards two objectives of our
"grand design." The first was to consolidate the British hold upon
the British market by a merger with our rivals and competitors,
Henry Gardner & Co. The second was to seek Continental affiliations. I was the negotiator in both cases.

Henry Gardner & Co. held, and still hold, two important agencies
of Empire companies, that is of the International Nickel Company,
American-controlled but mining nickel and subsequently copper in
Canada, and the Consolidated Mining and Smelting Co. of Canada,
half-owned by the Canadian Pacific, mining chiefly lead and zinc
in British Columbia. Our relations with Gardners, if not hostile,
were at arm's length.

I put myself in touch with Mr. Gardner, and gained his confidence. We got on well together and he was receptive to the general
idea of the merger. In the end the Amalgamated Metal Corporation
was formed. It held all the shares in both companies, and still
does. This merger made the two concerns dominant in the British
Empire in these metals, but of course this dominance could be
weakened or destroyed by penetration of the Empire markets by
Continental concerns, and by German or Belgian concerns in particular.

With the reluctant consent of the new board, upon which Mr.
Gardner sat, I was permitted to negotiate first an exchange of
shares with Metallgesellschaft, and secondly, to acquire a block
of shares in Norddeutsche Raffinerie, managed by Metallgesellschaft, operating the largest copper refinery in Europe. The principal negotiator on the German side was Richard Merton. He had
strongly European and international inclinations, and was a member of the well-known Jewish family which had founded the
Metallgesellschaft. We became friends. He was a man of great
flexibility of mind, and of wide vision. His command of English
and French only just fell short of being perfect, and his knowledge
of the European metal trade was unrivalled. As time was to show,
he was endowed with the greatest human quality—courage. The
exchange of shares meant implicitly but not explicitly that we
should use the Metallgesellschaft for our purchases and sales in
Europe, and that they would similarly use the Amalgamated Metal
Corporation in the British Empire. These negotiations were protracted, and at Mr. Gardner's insistence there was a clause under
which the shares were to be re-exchanged if there was ever war

between Great Britain and Germany. Our respective holdings were held by a Swiss company in Basle. I became a director of Metallgesellschaft and of Norddeutsche Raffinerie.

Similar negotiations took place with the Société de Minérais in Brussels, the protagonists on the Belgian side being M. Pisart and Mr. Micholajack. I joined the board.

Such knowledge as I had of European affairs was derived from these connections. I visited Brussels several times a year, and Frankfurt hardly less often.

When the arrangements with Gardner and the Continental affiliation had been concluded, the "over-all strategic concept" had been largely achieved. It can be well imagined that I was then known to every *contrôleur* on the European expresses, and knew myself every restaurant in the Rue Grétry and elsewhere in Brussels. My taste in burgundy to this day is not slipshod.

Besides these frequent visits to the Continent, my duties took me to Burma and Australia. The undertaking of the Burma Corporation was one of the most fascinating. Originally it had been a Chinese penal settlement, and the convicts had mined it for silver. The large mounds of tailings pointed to primitive smelting operations, and probably to a rich ore body. The mad English rediscovered and developed the mine in this remote country, infested with dacoits, and carried in the first equipment on elephants. When we bought control, the management required much strengthening. The mine is six hundred miles from Rangoon, north-east of Mandalay, and was linked to the Burma Railway by a spur railway belonging to the Company. The smelting plant and headquarters were at Namtu.

It was an exciting experience to take your place in the observation car on our railway at Namyao. The line wound its way through majestic scenery, steep mountains rising from the valley, covered by jungle in its primaeval state. You would catch sight of monkeys and tropical birds, peacocks and jungle fowl. A few miles from Namyao complete solitude descended on the traveller. On my first visit we approached Namtu as the sun was sinking; no human being, not a farm nor a settlement could be seen. Then, suddenly, as we reached the base of a mountain rising steeply to five thousand feet above the valley, the town burst into view, a blaze of electric light, houses and bungalows everywhere, the great smelting plant and the hum and hustle of a community of fifty thousand people. It looked like Paris from Montmartre, in the scene from *Louise*. Every one of its inhabitants depended upon the Company for their existence. All the food and clothes and stores were brought in by the Company; we set up the shops and were the land-lords; the fan-tan saloons were no doubt carried on in the Company's premises.

It is not enough, of course, in these isolated communities to provide the pay; it is also necessary to give people the opportunity of spending it, and of not only buying what they need, but also what they want.

At that time the labour was Chinese. They came across the Yunnan frontier to make their fortunes. Some of them returned to carry on banking, shopkeeping or money-lending on their savings of a few silver rupees. A small number prospered greatly. Our buying agent in Rangoon, who was also the representative of the British American Tobacco Company, had started life as a coolie in the mines, and had already amassed a fortune of some £40,000.

During the cold season the climate is exhilarating. At noon the temperature is between 90° and 100° Fahrenheit, but in the evening the mist forms a cap over the valleys and the nights are very cold. We would have breakfast, muffled up in two or three pullovers. By the end of the meal we had shed two, and by nine or ten o'clock were in tropical shirt and shorts.

W. S. Robinson had found the man to run this great undertaking. It had not been easy. The manager had to be more than a mining and metallurgical expert: he had to be an administrator and leader of a high order. If he was faced by any technical problem, he could consult no one: he and his staff had to find the answer. There are very few who can combine all these qualities, but in selecting Percy Marmion, Robinson had made no mistake. He was an Australian, short of stature, of somewhat Napoleonic cast of countenance and gait, well-equipped technically, confident and decisive, if not autocratic. He gradually made the Burma Corporation one of the great mining companies of the world. His heart was broken when Burma was overrun and his life's work was submerged by war and invasion and finally by the virtual nationalisation of the mine under independence.

I spent some time in Australia. I have made many trips there, and the country today is unrecognisable from what it was in those days. Perhaps the aeroplane has been the greatest instrument of change. When I first visited the Broken Hill mines, it took us about thirty-six hours to reach Broken Hill from Melbourne; the present directors fly up in two hours, leaving at dawn and breakfasting in Broken Hill. The last part of the journey in those days was over the Silvertown tramway; the heat was intense and the dust choking; the rolling stock as far from the Blue Train as a buggy is from a Rolls-Royce. We arrived impregnated with dust, stiff and unshaved. We stayed at the Freemason's Arms in Broken Hill, which in those days was only surpassed for discomfort by the Grand Hotel at Zeehan in Tasmania.

The township was inhabited by about thirty thousand people. The breadwinners were entirely employed in the mines by the four great companies, the North Broken Hill, the Sulphide Corporation, the South Broken Hill and the Zinc Corporation. Much of this labour force was foreign, at least in origin. A number of Poles, for example, had been brought in to break a strike. What are now known as labour relations were bitter, but the foreign element was not the only cause.

When we arrived, it had not rained in Broken Hill for seven years. Not a blade of grass, not a tree relieved the brown scorched desert of the town and its surroundings. A fine dust from the tailings was blown by the prevailing wind through the township and settled upon—hit, I think, is the better word—the houses, the clothes, the food and the throats of the inhabitants and produced a thirst which I have never experienced in any other part of the world.

The water for working the mills and for the use of the town was brought from a reservoir about fifteen miles away. The mines at lower levels—the ores are sulphide—are hot, and each stoping team had one man carrying the beer in quantities which even the Germans would have envied. The teams consumed it, but it came out through their pores almost as quickly as it went down their throats.

By this time I was a director of the Zinc Corporation, though in no executive position. I was privileged to see the transformation brought about largely by the inspiration of W. S. Robinson. He had several ideas which he persuaded the Zinc Corporation to put into force. The water from the concentration plants was filtered. Amidst the derision of Australia a belt of trees five hundred yards wide was planted as a wind-break. It had a row or two of citrus trees nearest the township, and more than five hundred varieties of gum trees in the main plantation. It was watered from the filtered effluent of the plants. W. S. appointed the principal "red" in Broken Hill as the warden. The plantation sprang up quickly. Some of these trees today are 100 feet high.

Swimming is as near to the heart of every Australian as cricket or horse-racing. A huge swimming bath was constructed; it was filled from the same source. New houses were built; later, air-conditioning was installed, and a new shaft sunk which brings the miners up, not into the open but into a building equipped with the latest shower baths. Tens of millions of tons of tailings were co-agulated with bitumen, to stop the dust from blowing. A liberal lead-mining bonus was negotiated, depending on the price of lead. For over thirty years no labour troubles have rent Broken Hill.

In the great cities of Australia in the nineteen-twenties the visitor became aware of the bitter and stubborn struggle between capital and labour. For example, the manners of the men and women assistants in the shops were harsh and hostile.

Since those days all is changed. Australia has found her feet, and though the average Australian has an unrivalled command of bad language, he does not use it on the innocent stranger.

Nothing short of invasion can prevent, in my opinion, the continued and accelerated growth of this wonderful country, which is endowed with abundant natural riches, and inhabited by a magnificent people.

The measures which we had undertaken had been directed chiefly to securing the British control of copper, lead and zinc mined in the British Empire. It is now necessary to turn to tin. The British Metal Corporation, through Vivian, Younger & Bond, were the selling agents of two tin-smelting companies: the first, the Cornish Tin Smelting Co. at Redruth in Cornwall, smelted the Cornish ores which had been mined there since the days of the Phoenicians, and some imported ores from Bolivia: secondly, the Eastern Smelting Co. in Penang smelted the Malayan and Siamese concentrates from the alluvial deposits of the peninsula. The Patiño family controlled the Williams Harvey Company in Liverpool, a rival smelting concern, though in friendly relations with us.

The number of men in the world skilled in the smelting of tin was small—a mere handful—and one of them, Ernest Pearce, was a friend of Sir Cecil Budd. We had long sought to amalgamate our interests in Redruth and Penang with those of the Williams Harvey Company in Liverpool; by these means, a very large supply of tin concentrates would be tied in, and we could smelt them more economically in one plant in the U.K. rather than in two. It was planned to shut down the Cornish plant and to concentrate the operation in Liverpool.

The Patiño family was immensely rich; the head of the family, Simon Patiño, had founded the family fortunes at Llallagua in Bolivia. He was now the Bolivian Minister in Paris, and was installed in a large house in the Avenue Foch, sumptuously furnished and hung with Gobelin tapestry. I soon became acquainted with him. He hardly ever trusted anyone, and even then not for long. He came to repose some fitful trust in me, partly I believe because I dealt with him with a candour that hardly fell short of bad manners.

His Excellency, though he had lived in Paris for many years, did not speak French, and I observed one day at luncheon that he did not know the word Gruyère. Conversation and business had to be carried on through an interpreter, generally through Señor Vargas, a sardonic and swarthy Bolivian of great ability, with a tough and disenchanted view of men and affairs, and of his employer in particular.

One day, I was talking to His Excellency in his office. I was perched on an elaborate gold chair "after" the Italian renaissance, and was looking intently towards him. The reason for my interest was his personal jewellery and décor: a blue suit, with white cloth top-boots, a black-pearl pin the size of a pigeon's egg, a superb blue diamond ring on one finger, and an equally striking emerald on another. His watch chain had diamond and emerald incidents. He observed my scrutiny with some distaste, and asked with asperity why I was staring. I replied, "Your Excellency would not care to know." "But I wish to know," he replied. "You tell me, at once." Thus absolved, I answered, "I was wondering, if I bid £100,000 for you as you stood up, whether I should make a profit or a loss." He was a formidable figure, and no one had ever spoken to him like this before. At first he seemed much offended, but then the nature of the compliment percolated through, and he ended by being amused. I still think I should have made a substantial profit, especially since I suspected that his waistcoat concealed a Fabergé watch.

Jokes in business are dangerous currency. A year or two later my company and the Patiños were engaged in a large operation to support the tin market. They were to put up a million pounds or two in London, we were to match it with a similar amount, we were to manage the business, and stability was to be restored to the market, which was in a sad state of collapse.

The negotiations were protracted, and I had to fly to Paris three or four times. Eventually His Excellency affixed his signature— Don Simon Patiño R— to the contract, and handed it to me. I said to the interpreter, "You will kindly express to His Excellency my gratification that this business has at last been successfully consummated, a result largely due to his wisdom and comprehension. Tell him that we are very happy to be associated with him and add"—here my innate frivolity got the better of me—"that we shall treat his money as if it was our own."

He saw the *double entendre* and nearly snatched the contract out of my hand. In a minute or two it was explained that this was a proverbial expression of trust in English, and he was placated.

I am very careful about using jokes as cement to a negotiation, although they have served me in good stead in Africa, because Africans like them, and there they are one of the catalysts of intractable subjects.

To return to tin. It so happened that the manager of the Williams Harvey Company, a skilful smelter but a self-made man, had been affronted by being treated as a mere employee by the Patiños. He resigned, and a successor was difficult to find. Ernest Pearce had the qualifications; he was in the good books of the Patiños, and through him the amalgamation was effected, and a company called Consolidated Tin Smelters was founded.

About this time I was sitting next to a lady at dinner. She was rich in her own right, and had been persuaded by her husband, who was a stockholder, to buy twenty-five tons of tin for her own account. She said, "Oliver, do you know anything about tin?" "Know anything about tin, indeed!" I replied and, ascending to hyperbole, "Why, *l'étain, c'est moi!*"

I have only made two other jokes in French as far as I can remember. I have repeated them so often with unjustifiable pride that their provenance has even been attributed to others. Both were original, and all my own work. Curiously enough, the wild duck comes into both.

As an international conference was just ending, the secretary rushed up and asked us in French what we were going to give to the press. I answered, *"Un canard à la presse, comme toujours."*

The other joke defiled my own dinner table at home. Moira and I were dining alone with the children. On the menu the cook had written *"Canard sauvage au porto,"* but a fat, white duck, obviously of Aylesbury origin, was put before us. "I don't believe," said Moira with some distaste, "that this is a wild duck at all." To which I replied, "No, I am afraid it is a *mallard imaginaire.*"

For those readers who have not at this moment thrown this book into the fire, I must continue on the theme of tin politics.

A company promoter, John Howeson, had started by floating tin companies in Siam and had formed the London Tin Corporation and the Anglo-Oriental. Some of his early flotations were at inflated figures and he was ill regarded, both in the City and the metal trade. He soon extended his interests into Malaya.

When his group began to get into trouble because of a fall in the price of tin and some rather rickety finance, instead of shrugging his shoulders and leaving the companies to extricate themselves as best they could, he started to organise the world production of tin so as to secure a livelihood for the producers and some stability of price for the consumers.

He was introduced to me by my great friend, Murray Graham, and though I thought the edifice which he had erected was shaky and bore the marks of company promotion rather than industrial policy, I formed the opinion that he himself was changing into a serious figure in the metal world. We started to finance him and his two companies on a large scale, always upon ample security. I also became interested in the International Tin Agreement, and was the author or origin of much of its fundamental policy and rules. It aimed to reduce production when the price fell below £180 per ton, to collect a buffer stock of any temporary surpluses, and sell the stock to prevent the price rising above £210, at which price production became unlimited. Although it attracted criticism, sometimes bitter criticism, I have not the slightest doubt that the policy was to the advantage of both producers and consumers.

The Netherlands Government, and the great Banka Company, deriving their supplies from the Dutch East Indies, were induced, largely by Howeson's negotiations, to join the scheme. The Patiños adhered to it and, through the London Tin Corporation, which controlled most of the Nigerian tin, the Nigerian Government also joined. I became the representative of the Nigerian Government on the International Tin Committee.

Many of the critics of the scheme of the International Tin Council in those days would be astonished to learn that the price of tin in 1961 had reached £990 per ton, and might be inclined to acquit us of exploiting our power at £180, even though the currency in which the price was expressed has depreciated perhaps threefold.

The London Tin and its allied company, the Anglo-Oriental, carried on the largest dredging operation in the world. They controlled, by shareholdings in many companies in Malaya, more than forty dredges producing large tonnages of tin concentrates. Our finance and help to this undertaking was not only to assist an important Commonwealth undertaking, but also to tie in supplies of tin concentrates for our smelters.

An opportunity also occurred to buy a large block of Malayan tin-mining shares which were held in Australia. A new company was formed, called British Tin Investment Corporation, which bought these shares, together with a large holding of Patiño's. I became chairman.

It can now be discerned how large a hold we had gained over the mining and smelting and sale of tin, all of course in harmony with the objects for which the company had been formed.

Soon after these combinations had been completed, Howeson and some of his associates attempted to corner pepper. This was slipping back to his old life with a vengeance. Millions were invested in this gamble, but the more they bought, the more pepper came out of hidden stocks. Financially the Howeson Group, though aided by one of the banks, was rocked back on its heels. More money had to be found from somewhere, and Howeson bought a company of metal brokers, James & Shakespeare, and proceeded to try to float it on the public, and raise some hundreds of thousands in this way. I had come to like Howeson, and highly regarded his services to the cause of tin. I had gone down to my house in the country for a holiday in August, when an express letter arrived, asking if the British Metal Corporation would underwrite a substantial part of the James & Shakespeare issue.

Although at this time I did not guess that pepper was at the back of it, I knew the company, which was a member of the London Metal Exchange, as a small and respectable firm of metal brokers. When I read what they were made to look like in the prospectus I was amazed: they had been blown up to a great size, and their profits appeared to me to be inflated beyond anything that I could think was correct.

There and then I wrote to Howeson a letter of such candour that it did not stop short of brutality. I told him that his début in the City had earned him a bad reputation as a company promoter, that gradually this reputation had been improved by the serious part which he had come to play in the industry and that he had collected some powerful support, including our own. This rotten flotation would at one blow destroy all that he had built up, and irretrievably ruin him. I begged him as a friend to drop the whole matter, and ended by saying that on no account or in any way, direct or indirect, would the British Metal Corporation or the Imperial metal group have anything to do with it.

He wrote back a charming letter, in which he appeared both to accept my strictures and to follow my advice. Would that he had. The flotation was made and some months later he and some of his colleagues were prosecuted for the issue of a false prospectus; he was convicted and sentenced to a year's imprisonment.

Before these sad events we had become aware that the finances of the London Tin Corporation and its subsidiary, the Anglo-Oriental, were in disorder, and, although our loans to them were well secured, that drastic action was necessary.

I enlisted the aid of Mr. Montagu Norman,[4] the Governor of the Bank of England, and suggested that I should be given the task with my friends, Mr. de Trafford,[5] Major Baring,[6] appointed by the Association of Investment Trusts, and Mr. Ivan Spens, my golfing partner and one of the leading accountants of the day, senior partner in London of Brown Fleming & Murray, to assume control of the board and put the finances on a sound foundation.

The task brought us into close touch with Mr. Norman. Whatever he may have been as a central banker, as a man of business he was incomparable. He combined charm, wisdom and adroitness, even cunning, with the most disarming courtesy and good manners. He had also a vein of eccentricity, which he consistently exploited. He would stick his ticket into his black Homburg hat when travelling on the Underground, and would pass into a brown study until roused at the Bank station. He lived in the barest room and slept on an iron bedstead, with some good modern pictures, propped up with their faces against the wall.

He made no disguise that although the Bank would help us, he would take no responsibility whatever, and that if we either slipped up or shielded anyone of the old management, he would disown us completely and in public. When saying this, he used to cover his face with one hand, with outstretched fingers, and twinkle at us through the gaps. He was careful to repeat his warnings, that no one was to be shielded, in front of the Bank's solicitor, Sir William Leese, of Freshfields, Leese & Munns. We all knew, however, that he did not want another City scandal after the pepper, and that as far as possible no dirty linen should be washed in public.

I remember that after one of these conferences he helped one of our young lawyers on with his coat and then, taking him by the

[4] Afterwards Lord Norman.
[5] Mr. Rudolph de Trafford.
[6] Major T. E. Baring.

arm, walked with us through the long corridors of the Bank to the front entrance. The solicitor remained a captive to the Governor's charm for life. I came to know Montagu Norman more intimately later when I was a Minister, and though I disagreed with him on many matters of policy, never escaped from the circle of his charm.

When Howeson was convicted, the Bank nominated a neutral chairman of the London Tin Corporation, Mr. Bunbury.[7] He was faced not only with the complexities of tin politics, but also with conducting some stormy meetings.

I had told my friends that six to eight weeks of intensive work would be necessary, that the company had assets of great significance to the British Empire, and that it was a national duty to save it. I was far out concerning the time. It took us fourteen months before we could disentangle the interlocking interests of the various companies, confirm the value of the assets at a proper figure, and organise the management.

The reconstruction of companies is often a thankless task. Shareholders whose interests have to be written down become highly critical and suspicious, particularly when the nominal value of equity shares is altered downwards. After about a year Bunbury retired, and I became chairman.

Thus the British Metal Corporation, first through its finance of London Tin and Anglo-Oriental and of the British Tin Investment Corporation, had large interests in the mining companies in Malaya and Nigeria, and through my chairmanship of both companies had an important voice in the mining and smelting policy of the Commonwealth.

The above account shows that I gained a wide experience in business, at least in metals, had become the director of many companies and was inured to negotiation, both local and international.

I claim no more as a business man than to be a trained professional. Judgement is another subject, and I have always been too expansionist. There are business men who deal very seldom, and who discard twenty propositions before they pick one. They are often the authors of great enterprises built up from small beginnings; they are enterprising *à l'écart*, so to speak.

There are others, and I am one, who deal fifteen times out of the twenty, and are wrong many times. We hope that our successes are in a bigger sector than our failures. Both types are needed. There must be pessimists and careful pickers, as well as opti-

[7] Mr. E. J. Bunbury.

mists whose creed is expansion. One of the great weaknesses of nationalised industries is that often the decisions are in the hands of one man. If he makes a mistake, by pressing forward too soon, or by hanging back too long, there is no compensating "hedge" either by the over-cautious or the over-certain. In the dispersed power and amid the competition of private enterprise, a balance is more likely.

It is curious that nationalisation should be a belief held so earnestly by elements of the Left. Democracy is the dilution of power, and they are ever ready to proclaim it. Nationalisation, however, is in effect its centralisation. This statement would be both bald and untrue if the nationalised industries were in reality under Parliamentary control. In theory they are, in fact they are not. No one has yet been able to evolve a system of control by Parliament of the countless day-to-day operations of a great industry like coal or transport, without making its practical control impossible.

All we know is that "Why was the 12:05 from Colchester late yesterday?" is an inadmissible Parliamentary question, but we are not sure whether the question "Why has the 12:05 from Colchester been more than fifteen minutes late on twenty-three days out of the last thirty-one?" can be disregarded by the Minister of Transport.

After I had left politics I was often asked, "What is the main difference to you in the change?" I used to answer, "The shareholders do not meet almost every day; they only meet once a year. Negotiations by a Minister are much more difficult than negotiations by a business leader. Not only does the House of Commons become restive unless they know something of what is going on, but often flanks are exposed, tender spots made raw, impossible targets insisted upon and the atmosphere clouded by the need to tell the legislators something of what is passing."

All those who, like myself, have spent their lives in negotiation know how much they depend upon establishing an atmosphere in which essentials can be insisted on without a breakdown, or concessions can be made without eroding principles. Often the negotiator is conscious of a moment when the parties are getting nearer; sometimes this moment has taken weeks or long hours of discussion to reach. The iron is hot. It is particularly maddening when at this moment the private secretary comes in to say, "The Chief Whip asks you to come at once to the House; there is to be a division on the suspension of the ten-o'clock rule." For twenty minutes, while you are away, the parties have time to think up some new objections, and to shrink back from the precipice of agreement.

The effect of the last joke—and jokes can be powerful solvents for all that I have said—has worn off. The authoritative aura which surrounds a Minister or a Secretary of State is dispersed; there is a pause; the negotiations begin to lack focus. The Minister himself returns in some irritation to find that the atmosphere for agreement has been dissipated, objections have hardened. Again and again this has happened to me.

The other part of the Ministerial life which is irksome is its disorder. To those who have been accustomed, as I have, to get their legs under the desk early in the morning, to have a more or less orderly arrangement of the day's business, and to take their legs home at six or seven of an evening, it is infinitely distracting to have to pack up and move over to a cell in the House of Commons and to be cut off from the base of your Department, or to have your work interrupted by sudden calls to answer a Question which you did not think would be reached, or to have to reply to a motion for the Adjournment on some trivial matter when the Parliamentary Secretary is not available.

These distractions are all the more frustrating when there are frequent Cabinet meetings. The Cabinet is the most important part of a Minister's life. A departmental Minister must read all the Cabinet papers carefully; often the subject will be unfamiliar to him, and often has no bearing on his responsibilities for his Department.

The increase in the public business has imposed, and is imposing, an ever greater strain on Ministers, and some action must be taken to relieve it, such as the delegation of some matters, perhaps concerning local government, to another body. The present Prime Minister once said to me that government was becoming increasingly a physical rather than an intellectual test. Moreover, the Ministerial function in many departments has been changed into an administrative function, and the old conception that Ministers are policy-makers and that the role of the Civil Service is to put these policies into effect has almost disappeared. The Ministry of Aviation, the Ministry of Supply, the Ministry of Pensions and National Insurance, the Ministry of Transport, the Ministry of Power, most of the Board of Trade and the Ministry of Health have become largely administrative. These offices are likely to be held by those without wide administrative experience. I remember, when I was a boy, that the President of the Board of Trade hardly ever went to London for six months in the year and, if there were red boxes[8] on two successive days, he was apt to complain of the burdens of office.

Even at the Treasury, the Foreign Office and the Colonial Office, much administration is involved. The control over the Civil Service exercised by the Treasury is largely administrative. The Foreign Office is concerned with wide matters of administration affecting the embassies and the national intelligence; the Colonial Office with capital development, credits, the Colonial Department Corporation, colonial education and agriculture.

In short, the functions of Government have immeasurably increased; the complexity of the modern world and the speediness of modern communications have added incessantly to the subjects and to the task with which Ministers are concerned.

[8] The name given to the red-leather boxes that are issued to ministers for carrying confidential documents under lock and key.

CHAPTER IX

CONTROLLER OF METALS

I N 1935 Italy invaded Ethiopia. Our relations with her steadily deteriorated and when oil sanctions were mooted the possibility of war began to loom.

One day, rather to my surprise, I was asked if I could make it convenient to call upon the Director of Army Contracts. In peacetime it was the custom of the War Office to advertise their requirements of copper about once a fortnight, and to invite tenders. The quantity was usually 500 tons, on rare occasions 1,000 tons. The price at which the cheapest seller got the order had some effect upon the general sentiment of the market: it was regarded as a sort of barometric reading.

I duly went to the office of the Director of Army Contracts[1] in Victoria Street, and was shown into his presence—a charming, courteous man with a strong though inhibited expression.

He lowered his voice. "We face a crisis with Italy." I am afraid I said that I was well aware of this from the newspapers. "Well," he went on, "the Government is very short of copper." I am afraid I said that I was fully aware of that also, especially as I had several times advised them to buy for stock at the low prices which then prevailed. He said that he sought my advice upon an important matter. The Government wanted forthwith to buy 50,000 tons of copper, without alarming the public, and without moving the price. How should they go about it?"

I have little natural cunning, but on this occasion I had the sense to ask, "Well, Sir, what is your own idea?" He replied, "We had a meeting of some of the heads of this department yesterday

[1] F. C. Bovenschen, afterwards Sir Frederick Bovenschen.

and we thought perhaps that we had better pursue our ordinary course of putting it up for tender. What do you think?" [2]

When, metaphorically, I came round with the aid of sal volatile, I replied that I could not think of a worse way of attaining his objects. The amount of copper was about about a hundred times that for which the War Office usually invited tenders, the public of course would take fright, and this advertisement of the Government shortage of copper would send the price rocketing.

"How is it to be done then?" he asked.

"There is only one chance, and that is to give the order to one of the biggest dealers. I suppose my own company is the biggest. The market would not be surprised if we were big buyers; they would take quite a time to appraise whether we were covering in against sales abroad, or running up our own stocks or that of the many consumers of copper who buy their requirements through us." I said I thought the price was bound to move somewhat owing to the large size of the order, but I did not suppose that the public would be particularly alarmed.

After some further discussion, he gave me the order to buy 50,000 tons of copper as best we could, but bearing in mind his two hopes. So bad a business man am I that it did not occur to me to tell the Director of Army Contracts that our minimum commission (for which we guaranteed delivery and quality) was ⅜ of 1%, i.e. just over 3s. per ton, for very large orders of this nature, and ½ of 1% for smaller business.

Our dealers during the next few days successfully bought about 7,500 tons without it being noticed and without any appreciable movement in the price.

Then the Mussolini crisis collapsed, and with it came the cancellation of the balance of the order. We put in our account, including the commission of ⅜ of 1%, and although the copper was paid for, the department would not agree to the commission. I asked them what they thought it should be, and they replied, "3/16ths." That annoyed me, because it looked as if they had just divided by two. Anyway ⅜ of 1% is the very lowest rate at which any reputable metal merchant would do business; it is a cut rate and it had to stand.

After some acrimonious correspondence I said irritably that I would sue the Government for the commission by a Petition of Rights—a most cumbersome procedure—and was prepared to fight

[2] It is only fair to say that the Director of Army Contracts was clearly not satisfied with the usual procedure or he would not have sent for me.

the matter as far as the House of Lords if they appealed. The department then paid with a good grace, no doubt secure in the knowledge that the Public Accounts Committee would applaud their efforts to get away with half the minimum charge.

The lesson which I learnt over this transaction left a deep impression on my mind. As I shall show later on, part of that lesson had to be ignored when war really did break out, but the rest of it has helped me.

I should sum it up by saying that the ignorance of Government Departments of the "market," or of the impact of quite simple transactions upon it, is only matched by their brazen commercial methods. In the end, however, they are grateful for any help given.

In March 1939, Hitler invaded Czechoslovakia and this time war seemed almost certain. I was told that if it came, it might be the intention of the Minister of Supply to ask me to become Controller of Non-Ferrous Metals.

I therefore began to formulate a plan for the purchase and eventual licensing and allocation of the four principal non-ferrous metals: copper, tin, lead and zinc. In war perhaps copper and zinc are the most important of the four, because cartridge and shell cases are made of brass and brass is an alloy of copper and zinc. Copper, too, is used for the driving bands of shells.

My plan started from something said to me by W. S. Robinson. This was an occasion when an important and new line of commercial policy derived from some of his passing remarks.

He had said: "Many great mining companies are wholly responsible for large communities in remote parts of the world. Noranda in Canada, the Broken Hill Companies in Australia, and the Burma Corporation are examples. They don't know, if war breaks out, whether they can sell their metal at all, if so in what quantity, they don't know whether they can ship it and they don't know whether buyers can be found who can pay for it. You should think of this, and if there is a war and you can help them there would doubtless be a reward for the Government in the prices at which they could buy."

I did think of it deeply, and conceived a scheme which was intended to resolve all these doubts.

It was the best piece of commerce I have ever done or planned, but the credit for it goes to the profound, ingenious and original mind of my friend.

The scheme was that the British Government would buy from each and every producer in the Empire the equivalent of their previous year's exportable surplus, free on board, at the usual port of shipment and would pay for it whether a ship was alongside or not. In return the metal was to be supplied at the current market price ruling just before the war with a variable price clause to cover increases in the cost of fuel, labour and transport to the coast. For the lay reader, an explanation is perhaps called for.

The three doubts of the mining companies are resolved.

First, they can rely on selling the equivalent of their whole last year's output, less the amount required for local consumption.

Secondly, they are to be paid if they can get the metal to the port: they have no responsibility for finding the ships.

Thirdly, they know that the buyer can pay, because the buyer is the British Government.

There are some arresting facts in the history of copper in war. The German preparations for the First World War were supposed to be extensive, but before the end of 1914, less than six months after its outbreak, the directors of the Metallgesellschaft (a company of which I became a director between the wars) were sent for by the General Staff and told that the Army was running out of copper and that emergency measures of the most drastic kind must be put in hand. Every brass fitting, door handles, fire irons, taps, church bells, everything containing copper was requisitioned and turned back into copper.

During the year which followed the Munich crisis, I pestered the Ministry of Supply to buy copper. They did nothing. I bombarded them with figures. They did nothing. I told the Foreign Office of the abnormal purchases of copper by Germany. They did not deduce anything.

I became so alarmed that I took private measures. I persuaded Mr. Robert Stanley, an American citizen and President of the International Nickel Company, which was a large producer of copper in Canada, to hold his working stocks (which the French call expressively *le stock de roulement*) in the United Kingdom. I warned him that I thought war was imminent and that on its outbreak the Government would certainly requisition his stocks. He was not deterred, and quickly built up a stock of 15,000 tons in this country.

This was something, but still not very much in face of what we were likely to consume. However, whilst the factories using copper were getting into their stride and producing at a low rate, it would keep them supplied for three weeks or possibly a month.

A few days before the outbreak of war, I had to go to Holland on business; it was hot weather and the Hague was stifling, so I went out to Scheveningen to spend two nights and get a breath of sea air. I cannot say why, but this journey and the empty watering place produced a sense of impending doom upon my mind, so deep-seated that I can still remember it.

I returned home to my house in Kent, and it was there that I heard the news that war had broken out. It was also confirmed that I was to be Controller of Non-Ferrous Metals, that the British Metal Corporation was taken over by the Government and that it had been ordered to move to Rugby.

My colleague, Mr. William Mure, had completed the arrangements for the move which had been partially planned. He implored me not to come to Rugby for two or three days because until the staff had moved in we could transact very little business.

I had been asked by the L.C.C.[3] whether I would voluntarily take into my house at Wittersham some children who were to be evacuated from the East End, and if so, how many. I had replied yes, and had put the number at ten, which Moira and I thought was the maximum we could accommodate. In the event, the L.C.C. gave notice that they were sending down thirty-one infants, their average age being between four and five, with some junior nurses. I thought this not only scurvy reward for my voluntary gesture, but also that there would be dangerous overcrowding. They duly arrived, some suffering from childish illnesses and one or two from impetigo. I was afraid of infection spreading amongst them, but we did our best and packed them in. I got a shock: I had little dreamt that English children could be so completely ignorant of the simplest rules of hygiene, and that they would regard the floors and carpets as suitable places upon which to relieve themselves. I was still more surprised when some of their parents arrived in motor-cars to see them at the week-end.

The day came when Rugby was ready, and I set off early in the morning for London to see the Minister of Supply on my way to Rugby. Action was a relief, but I did not like leaving the family to dangers which I could not assess. However, when I saw the balloon barrage clustering round London, I was glad that at least they were in the country.

Arrived at the Ministry, I found my fears about our shortage of metals fully confirmed. The Government had started the war with 7,000 tons of electrolytic copper in stock: towards the end of 1940 consumption was at the rate of 50,000 tons per month. They had

[3] London County Council.

already requisitioned the 15,000 tons belonging to the International Nickel Company. I pointed out that this was a mere stop-gap and that I must get busy on the cables to put into force my scheme —of which the officials were sceptical—and negotiate some contracts urgently.

So to Rugby, where I found the hundred or so of the staff of the company clustered round the Grand Hotel. The reception rooms had been turned into offices; my office was in a small bedroom, and we had a conference room in another.

We worked at white heat and were perhaps more surprised than we should have been that my plan worked. The great Empire companies producing copper, zinc or lead had no wish to profit by the war. Just before the war they had been trying to perfect schemes by rationing production which would keep prices at a point where they could live. From my intimate knowledge of the industry, I knew what these prices were, and they formed the foundation of my proposals.

Copper is perhaps the best and easiest example. I bid by word of mouth or cable £42 10s. free on board port of shipment to every Empire producer I could reach. H.M.G. was to be the buyer and the quantities each year were to be not less than they had exported in the previous twelve months; the contract was to continue until the end of the war with Germany.

They all accepted in principle, but there were many details to be worked out and negotiated. Meanwhile, the price of copper soared; the international market thought the British and French Governments were uncovered; the price reached £92 10s. delivered into works in Birmingham, a price, after deducting the freight and charges, more than double the equivalent price which the mining companies had agreed to accept in principle.

I was also successful, through our international connections, in laying my hands on about 40,000 tons which were in course of shipment to various parts of the world.

We began to breathe again; we had no right to. The Ministry had to satisfy the Treasury on the terms of each contract; the Treasury solicitors did not like the contingency clauses, hardly thought that the contract was in the best legal shape and complained that the definition of labour, fuel and transport was imprecise, and so forth.

My feelings of rage and frustration can be imagined. No contracts had been signed; no one, other than the directors of the various companies, even knew that any agreement was mooted. On the rise in the price of copper, the prices of the International

Nickel Company shares were rising a dollar a day on Wall Street, and Stanley, the President, could say nothing. He could have repudiated his telegram of acceptance in principle without the slightest breach of the best commercial practice or morality. However, he never budged from this flimsy bargain. He did become impatient and cabled the whole terms of the contract *en clair* at the "urgent" rate. The cable cost £1,650, but I could give no quick answer.

Just before these events, I was in the Ministry talking about licensing, sales of copper and the thousand and one things that had to be done. The two officials principally concerned were Sir William Palmer and R. D. Fennelly, afterwards Sir Daniel Fennelly. They were first-class, and were fighting to get the contracts through the Whitehall labyrinth. One night, I was just leaving for Rugby and had got to the door when I stopped in my tracks and exclaimed, "Good heavens, I have forgotten to tell you that I bought 40,000 tons of copper yesterday." (This was the copper referred to earlier.) "But," they exclaimed in dismay, "you have no sanction from the Treasury, or from us for that matter, to do anything of the kind." "All right; put it down to me," I said, and shut the door and left.

I wish they had. I should have made a profit of £1,600,000.

I addressed the staff at Rugby. When I said that in my opinion they would be stuck there for at least three years, they gasped.

At the beginning of the war we were told that we could pay our staff an extra 30s. a week as a lodging allowance, because they could no longer live at home. Six weeks later, to our astonishment, the Treasury cancelled the allowances. Sir Andrew Duncan called together the Controllers' Committee. We were indignant. He asked the Establishment officer at the Ministry to attend. He was not available; a deputy would be sent.

He came in. He was a tall, fresh-complexioned Scot. The case against his department was overwhelming. He did his best to present some façade of reason but he could make little of it. At the end, Sir Andrew said in very Scottish accents: "Well, it is just not going to happen. My personal worrd is engaged and it's just not going to happen. Will you please tell the Minister; and, forgive me, may I ask your name?" "Oliver Franks," [4] was the reply.

It did not happen; we won the day and the allowances continued.

After about six weeks we were covered for our probable require-

[4] Now Lord Franks.

ments of these important metals; the British Government did not appear in the open market as a buyer, and the international market fell.

The savings to the Government during the war from these contracts for the four metals can hardly have been less than £250,-000,000. It is interesting to reflect that in the first war our purchases from the U.S. averaged a little over £180 per ton and the corresponding sum formed part of the debt which we owed to them.

The purchases described above were at £42 10s. per ton, free on board, or under £50 at the port of discharge. In 1956 copper reached £436 10s., and the average price in 1961 was £230.

So much for the supplies. I had left the matter of allocations and rationing mainly to my very able colleagues, who had gradually been perfecting a licensing system. Every pound of these essential metals that was to be used required a permit. Of course, where the metal was to be used for the manufacture of munitions, the Government contract had only to be produced for the permit to be forthcoming, although some intricate calculations were necessary in almost every instance.

At the same time the ordinary life of the community on some scale or other had to continue and we had to decide how much metal was involved.

Accordingly, we started a long series of negotiations with all the trade associations using these metals that we could identify. I was astonished to find how many there were. Since the largest number were in Birmingham, we went there twice a week and saw several each day. The so-called negotiations had to be conducted in a rather staccato manner. We had the metal and we had the last word. To give an idea of the scope of these associations, they included the Coffin Manufacturing Association, the Flushing Cisterns and Copper Balls Association, the Household Brass Furniture Association, and so on.

"Now, sirs," I would say to the coffin makers, "no more coffins with six handles. I fear we must cut you down to two, so on that score you get a third of what you were consuming last year. Then, no lead linings to coffins."

"Oh, but Captain Lyttelton, there are corpses and corpses," said they.

"Well, all right, lead linings only on 'medical certificate.' "

To the next association I said, 'No more copper balls, I'm

afraid, for the cisterns of water closets and bath tanks; they will have to be made of plastic, so your allocation on this account is nil." And so on and so on.

We also advised the Ministry on the capacity of the manufacturing industry so as to avoid one plant being overloaded and another starved of orders. The necessary measures took a long time to become fully effective.

We were also responsible for keeping the smelting plants in the Empire supplied with their smelting materials; these are generally known as concentrates—copper concentrates, lead concentrates and so forth.

One of the sources of zinc concentrate for smelting into zinc in this country was Newfoundland, and the port from which the concentrates had been shipped for some years was called Botwood. I was engaged in sending shipping instructions by cable to the producers when one day the messenger informed me that a Colonel So-and-So, with an official pass, wished to see me cn an important matter.

He came into my little room. He was in his forties, lean and rather stern. "Are you Captain Lyttelton?" "Yes, I am the Controller of Non-Ferrous Metals." "How long have you held the position?" I replied rather testily, "Since the beginning of the war, but I am a busy man and I must ask you to come to the point."

Taken a little aback, he said, "Do you know of a place called Botwood?" "Yes, of course, it is a port in Newfoundland from which we ship zinc concentrates for the smelters in this country." "Are you aware that there is an important air base at Botwood?" "No, I am not, but what on earth are you getting at?" "Did you send this telegram?" I looked at it. "Yes, I did."

By then, of course, I had realised that I was suspected of being an enemy agent, and clearly a well-placed one.

I thought perhaps that being a member of a family that had been settled in England for seven hundred years, an ex-officer in His Majesty's First Guards, decorated for having fought on the right side in 1914, and now a senior civil servant, I might have been absolved of these sinister suspicions. If these easily obtainable facts had been verified the colonel might have been spared his journey and the taxpayer might have been saved his fare.

I rapped out, "Now, please don't be silly, or there will be trouble. I'm very busy. It's now half an hour before the time for luncheon. Please leave me alone now and later have luncheon with me. I will do my best to make it a good one." He accepted.

The long-term contracts which had been negotiated, the licensing and allocation system which became essential if we were to conserve our supplies for war uses, inevitably involved closing the Metal Exchange by Government Order. At first the members were resentful, especially as the British Metal Corporation, and for that matter I myself, were members and appeared to have been unduly favoured. We were permitted, however, by the Government to pay commissions to the merchants and brokers for handling the licences and internal transport under the direction of the control. The metal dealers were able to survive, but on very short commons. In the end, they patriotically accepted the undoubted hardships.

Of course, our own business as agents for many of the principal mining companies depended entirely upon whether the Government would permit us to charge the usual commission. Notwithstanding the large savings which we had effected for them, they were extremely reluctant to give us any compensation, and months of negotiation had to pass before we received anything. Eventually, an annual sum, quite inadequate to the size of the task which we were undertaking, was agreed.

Before the lull in the war was over, I had to go on a mission to Paris. A meeting was to be held concerning supplies of metals for the Allies. I was to be accompanied by a senior official of the Ministry of Supply, who, no doubt in the kindest manner, was to act the part of the political commissar under other constitutional systems, and make sure that I did not enter into embarrassing commitments.

The meeting was convened one morning. The Minister of Supply, Mr. Leslie Burgin, opened for the British in almost faultless French, which made a great impression on the delegates, and we got down to work.

There were some delicate niceties to be negotiated. Aided by my own French, which is fluent at least on technical matters, although rusty in conversation with a *femme du monde*, I got most of our way with, as I thought, some adroitness. To my horror my companion elected to cross the *t*'s and dot the *i*'s in a French of the most excrutiating grammar and accent. Apart from the outrages inflicted on the language, he violated one of the first principles of negotiation, which is never to recapitulate an agreement when it has been reached: there will always be enough difficulties when the agreement is drafted. He nearly wrecked the ship, but no doubt had the satisfaction of not having remained mute.

After two days in Paris we flew back to England, but when we sighted the coast somewhere near Brighton, we saw that a heavy snow-storm was sweeping the south coast. We turned back and were tipped out of our plane on the downs above Dieppe. A razor-like wind cut into us, and to add to our discomfort we were quickly surrounded by a menacing body of French territorials who pointed their rifles at us and showed some inclination to shoot us out of hand. It was a strain to us to keep our tempers in the icy wind.

We got a taxi and went down into Dieppe, booked a passage on the boat and reinforced ourselves first with Pernod and later with an excellent dinner, in which *fruits de mer* were prominent. About midnight we got on board and had the roughest and coldest passage imaginable. We disembarked at Newhaven about 4 A.M., and again the wind moaned through the snow-covered station and set our teeth chattering. A train was promised in an hour or two, and there was nothing to do but wait.

At this moment, my servant, Horne, who had brought my car from London, appeared with a thick coat and a thermos flask of hot coffee and some sandwiches. In ten minutes I was snugly on my way to London. Such service at such a time is unforgettable.

Early in 1940, I was asked to become Controller of Diamond Dies. Diamonds are used for the drawing of very fine wires, which are an essential component of certain electronic and radar devices vital in war; the thinnest wire has to be drawn down to 0.0005 of an inch: the dimension is technically called triple o five. Now, the diamonds were pierced by a few skilled craftsmen who had to know by experience the crystalline structure of the stone. It was an entirely empirical art: there were in the world only about five men who could make a hole in a diamond as small as triple o five, and all of them were in occupied territory.

I was lucky to obtain the services of Ronny Prain[5] as Deputy Controller, and I was delighted to see that he had every intention of supplanting me and himself becoming the Controller.

Extraordinary measures had to be taken. We could have done with the services of James Bond or the leading agent of Smersh. However, with the aid of Van Cutsem & Co., one of the leading diamond brokers in the world, we were able to trace the craftsmen. We had at one time to fly an R.A.F. machine to Lyons, then occupied by the Germans, to pick one of them out, and soon two or three others reached this country by devious and secret routes.

It may be added that the lesson was learnt and that a new in-

[5] Now Sir Ronald Prain.

dustry was founded in the United States and in this country, which was not dependent on these empirical methods.

Ronny Prain took over the full control just before I left Rugby, and showed his great skill and ability in handling these delicate problems.

The work of the Non-Ferrous Metal Control during the first year of the war, when we had to improvise and perfect a very large-scale piece of organisation, had indeed been massive.

I was back and forth to London by road about twice a week, and drove my two-seater Jaguar almost to destruction. Then suddenly the phoney war ended. Germany invaded Holland and Belgium, the news on the French front worsened daily. On my way to London, I used to stop at St. Albans to buy the evening paper. Every day the news got worse and I felt the gnawing grip of fear for our country and France and the future.

It is useless to say that it is no good tearing yourself with anxiety over events which you have no power to control or in which you play an insignificant part. In my experience, these are the worst anxieties; once you feel that you can do something by your own efforts, the substance of the danger, hard and finite, takes the place of the phantoms which imagination can conjure up: action is the anodyne of fear.

I could read between the lines of the darkening news, could conjure up in my mind the disorganisation which looked more and more like a rout. I would not have stopped short of despair if I had not fervently believed that an Anglo-French counterstroke was imminent. Surely, once again a Mons or Le Cateau would be followed by a Marne.

At this time, M. René Mayer arrived in London; he had been vice-president of Chemins de Fer du Nord and was my opposite number in France. We concerted plans for moving some of the stocks out of France, especially the stocks of copper and cobalt, a necessary metal for certain hard steels. We had little time, as it turned out, and were only partially successful.

I still recall with a sharp pang the stricken look in Mayer's eyes when it was reported that General Georges, upon whom he, and for that matter many of us, had pinned our hope of victory, had been captured.

Shortly afterwards, the French asked for an armistice. We were alone. The feeling of relief could hardly be believed. In some almost supernatural way the Prime Minister had felt the pulse of the country and heard its heartbeat; this cannot have come from knowledge, for he was necessarily much out of touch in these deadly times with public opinion; it was inspiration that dictated the famous broadcast. His words were what he felt and he somehow knew we all felt the same.

Everyone seemed to have had a burden lifted from his shoulders; the sense of unity was unmistakable: Britain was one country again. Her finest hour had struck when the miracle of Dunkirk was accomplished. How sure was the Prime Minister's instinct. It would have been natural and, as many thought, an overdue encouragement to describe it as the first faint gleam of victory, the birth of hope. He knew otherwise and the truth that we had suffered perhaps the greatest reverse to our arms in our long and tempestuous history again seemed to bring to every man and woman in the country the courage, if not the words, of St. Crispin's Day.

In my own small sector of the war, the defeat of France brought no new or startling problems. Our supplies of metals were brought across the sea from Canada, Australia, Burma and America. The Germans, it is true, found some useful supplies, particularly of copper, in France; some were saved from them by Elizabethan adventurers like Lord Suffolk, who shipped them out under the very noses of the enemy. Our lifelines were not cut, although anyone could see that the German occupation of the Channel ports brought them into the greatest danger.

I wondered what our military plan was to be. I thought I knew that it would be to hold the front in England, that is to say the beaches, with a screen; to organise a striking force ready to hurl itself at the invaders at the moment of their greatest weakness when they were so to speak half ashore, and before they had time to build up their supplies. Phrases like "throw them back into the sea" ran through my mind.

I spent a week-end at Chequers and there learnt that, though this was the general plan, we had no modern tanks and that there were not even enough rifles to arm more than a part of the infantry. The Prime Minister told me that he had secured 750,000 rifles from the United States and that he could not breathe until they arrived. He found out that they were all to be shipped in one vessel, but at the last moment and at the cost of some searing delay they were distributed over several cargoes.

My eldest son, who was slightly lame in one leg from the effects of polio but who had otherwise made a complete recovery, failed to get into the Air Force as a rear-gunner. He then thought he might work his way in by the back door, so to speak, by becoming an aircraftman.

The day that he presented himself at the recruiting centre, it so happened that the candidates were to be interviewed by a warrant officer. He was asked: "Can you do shorthand?" "No." "Can you typewrite?" "No." "Illiterate," rasped out the W.O., and it was entered on his particulars. Notwithstanding this, he soon became a signaller in the Army, a private soldier of course, and was posted to G.H.Q. at St. Paul's School. We saw him occasionally. He was in high spirits and was amused to learn from the G.H.Q. notice-board some of the dangers which beset him, and the instructions as to how to counter them. Thus: "Troops are warned that they must not drink any water that has not been previously passed by the Medical Officer," and "Leave to the Channel Islands is suspended until further notice"—the latter a somewhat unnecessary warning, since the Channel Islands were occupied by the Germans.

He was most anxious for a more active role and, pulling some strings through Brendan Bracken,[6] I got him transferred from the Army into the Navy—into the Marines. He lasted longer than could have been expected, but the standards of physical fitness which turned back so many others proved also insuperable for him and after six months of the war he was passed as unfit for military service.

Again, through the kind offices of "Pug" Ismay[7] I got him a commission in the Intelligence Service, and he soon left for Cairo. I was proud of his performance. No one could have tried more than he to get into the firing line.

[6] Afterwards Viscount Bracken.
[7] Now General Lord Ismay.

CHAPTER X

CHURCHILL

S HARED ACTION, common tastes, ties of blood are powerful influences in giving one man an understanding of another, but obviously conversation is the most important.

Conversation is generally spontaneous, and amongst friends, unguarded. Once spoken, it cannot be revised. Conversation is affected by little things as well as by big: the sex and nature of the company; the time of day; a glass of wine; and above all of course by the mood of the person who is talking.

So I approach some account of Winston Churchill first through the gateway of my memories of conversations with him. The key to his friendship is that he has to be amused: he is averse to the exegetical, or the ponderous.

President Roosevelt shared this characteristic. It is no doubt a weakness not to attach quite the same weight to an opinion from someone who bores you as from a boon companion. If it is a weakness, both these men had it.

By a bit of luck, Winston liked my sort of jokes and, I believe, enjoyed my conversation. I give an example at random. When I was first President of the Board of Trade, and just after I had introduced clothes rationing, I gave a mixed luncheon party for him at Claridges. He was chaffing me. "You must have a policy as a Minister, Oliver. You're no longer in that bucket shop of yours in the City. Administration is the handmaiden of policy in Government. Clothes rationing! It may be all right, but what is the political inspiration behind that, I ask you? All these ladies"—pointing to Clemmie[1] and Freda Casa Maury[2] and Moira—"would like an answer." "Strength through misery," I retorted. This is the sort of joke that tickles his fancy, and he repeated it under his breath once or twice with apparent relish.

In common with most of my family, I have certain powers of mimicry, and he seemed to enjoy my impressions of a sort of eighteenth-century conversation between Fred Woolton[3] and Fred Leathers.[4] Both these noblemen knew that I imitated them, but I do not think they minded. The imitations, though a trifle malicious, were not intended to wound.

Winston had a deep, almost an emotional friendship for Max Beaverbrook.[5] The causes were manifold. Max was the only leading member of his government near him in age who had shared experiences in the First World War and in politics outside the span of the rest of us. His support had been powerful; his achievements at the Ministry of Aircraft Production during the deadly days of the Battle of Britain need no telling. He added the gift of being able to amuse and entertain the Prime Minister; his talk has a zest, a mixture of enthusiasm and cynicism, of kindness and harshness, but above all an original twist which makes it astringent and exhilarating.

Describing himself as a conversationalist, Winston once said, "I am either sunk in a sullen silence or else I am shouting the table down." There is a grain of truth in this. I have often seen him sitting silent beside some embarrassed woman at dinner, the fingers of both hands but not the palms on the table, a frown on his face, his head pushed a little forward and downward, his expression clouded and sombre. These silences seldom lasted beyond the fish, or the first glass of champagne, and by the meat course he had usually begun to talk and had often swept his neighbour into the stream of argument.

His conversation was like that of Macaulay or Lord Curzon: it erred no doubt on the side of copious monologue; it was not like that of Arthur Balfour, who made the most stupid and Boeotian neighbour feel clever. When the sails started to draw, the great ship, with every stitch of canvas set, heeled over to the wind and ploughed through the waves; the rigging sang and the spray broke

[1] Now Lady Churchill.
[2] Marquesa de Casa Maury.
[3] Now the Earl of Woolton.
[4] Now Viscount Leathers.
[5] Lord Beaverbrook.

unheeded over the prow. The listener had the vivid impression that he was living at a time of great human struggle or, to change the image, stood upon some battlefield at a turning point in history.

His oratory was sometimes called to do duty in private as well as in public. An example was when he first met Harry Hopkins at Ditchley. They had met officially the day before, but this was the first full-scale meeting at leisure. America was not yet in the war. Harry Hopkins was a slight, emaciated figure; his health was bad and he was liable to constant pain, but he was a man of pervasive charm, with the rare gift of seeing the essential. The President at this time was devoted to him and watched over his health with almost maternal care. Brendan Bracken had told us all, and the Prime Minister in particular, of the great influence that Hopkins exercised upon the President. Although constant telegrams had been exchanged between the Prime Minister and the President, it was of high importance that something more personal, a state of greater intimacy between the two countries should be established. We should try to bring the President into full understanding and sympathy with us; he should be able to hear the harmonics as well as the notes.

The meeting took place at dinner on January 11th, 1941. When the ladies had left the table, Winston sprang into a majestic monologue, tracing the origins and course of the war up to that date. If it had been taken down, it would have been recognised as the substance of his first two volumes of the Second World War. His sonorous eloquence, his sense of history, of man's destiny and Great Britain's part in it were enthralling. He turned at the last to our war aims. "We seek no treasure, we seek no territorial gains, we seek only the right of man to be free; we seek his right to worship his God, to lead his life in his own way, secure from persecution. As the humble labourer returns from his work when the day is done, and sees the smoke curling upwards from his cottage home in the serene evening sky, we wish him to know that no rat-a-tat-tat"—here he rapped on the table—"of the secret police upon his door will disturb his leisure or interrupt his rest. We seek government with the consent of the people, man's freedom to say what he will, and when he thinks himself injured, to find himself equal in the eyes of the law. But war aims other than these we have none."

He paused. "What will the President say to all this?" Harry Hopkins did not reply for the best part of a minute—and how long that seems—and then, exaggerating his American drawl, he said, "Well, Mr. Prime Minister, I don't think the President will give a damn for all that." Heavens alive, it's gone wrong, thought I. There was another pause, and then Harry said, "You see, we're only interested in seeing that that goddam sonofabitch, Hitler, gets licked." [6]

There was loud laughter, and at that moment a friendship was cemented which no convulsion ever undermined. Some credit for the unity of purpose between the United States and Great Britain is due to Harry Hopkins.

This example of Winston's conversation gives perhaps too rotund an impression. Amongst a few friends his fun and humour were delicious.

At one time the Labour Government, whose achievements in building houses were not striking, wished to improve the figures by bringing into account the number of reconditioned houses and flats that they had added to the total. These were lumped in with the newly built houses and the whole were termed "accommodation units." It can easily be seen with what derision this hideous phrase was greeted by the man who had changed the name of the Local Defence Volunteers into just simply the Home Guard. Winston began to sing, in his somewhat toneless voice:

> *Accommodation unit, sweet accommodation unit,*
> *There's no place like accommodation unit.*

Whilst the war was still going on, a long and complicated discussion was in progress on the general subject of "Ever normal granaries" and "Buffer stocks." The theory behind these devices is, shortly, that in times of prolific harvests the surplus over the current demand is put into granaries and kept to supplement supplies when the harvest fails. Or again, when the demand for metals is slack a stock is built up to be released against a surge in demand.

Max Beaverbrook and I opposed the principle of buffer stocks which was then advocated, and we described it as the "bears'" paradise, providing unlimited opportunities for speculators to sell short against the accumulating supplies. The argument swayed this way and that. The Prime Minister, never avid of economic discussions, was obviously bored and even inattentive. His mind was on the war. "The buffer stock, Prime Minister," said someone, "will have to be—" "What did he say?" interrupted the Prime Min-

[6] The accuracy of this story is denied by my great friend, the late Robert Sherwood, but I was present when the remark was made.

ister. "Buffer stock," answered someone. "Oh, I thought he said butterscotch." This effectively stopped any further discussion, and we went back to strategy and the war.

Some of Winston's daily habits struck his friends with envy or admiration.

He believes, as I do, that champagne is an excellent item of staple diet. I would say that it becomes better with advancing years, and I genuinely believe that some of Winston's astonishing vitality is due to a régime which has always included a prescription of Pol Roger. I find old brandy a good end to the day, and if I am put to it I have a capacity for absorbing it without much effect other than the general feeling of *"Courage, mon ami, le diable est mort."* This formed another link between us.

Often when food rationing or supplies of food were under discussion, he would say with a smile, after urging the Minister of Food to greater efforts, "And after all, I do like my meals."

Once I was due to address a learned body at luncheon, and from experience I knew that they were both a highly informed and disconcertingly unresponsive audience. On the morning of this event I was rung up by the Prime Minister and asked to luncheon at Downing Street. I told him of my engagement. "Nonsense," he said, and ordered me to send my parliamentary private secretary, Somerset de Chair, to perform in my stead. Somerset was of the rabble-rouser type of speaker, and his methods did not appear ideally suited to the occasion. But there it was.

So at 1:30, with some buoyancy and sense of relief I went round to No. 10. I found the Prime Minister in splendid spirits, and saw that the reasons for my invitation were already on the table: they were a large tin of fresh caviar and a bottle of vodka, sent by the Russians. Neither the dish nor the liquor stood much chance. It was well after four o'clock before the Prime Minister left for his afternoon nap. The conversation, it must be confessed, was concerned more with the First World War than the Second.

After the war the Prime Minister answered parliamentary question three or four times a week. The questions were not usually intended to be helpful. Sometimes I had luncheon with him on a day when they would have been a strain upon the nerves or the digestion of any ordinary man. Yet he was completely relaxed. The Prime Minister's number on the Order Paper was usually in the early 40's, and he knew with uncanny precision when he would be reached. Sometimes a bottle of champagne stood on the table, and he and I drank a glass or two of it. Once or twice during luncheon he would ring the bell for a private secretary, add to an answer or polish a phrase with a relish only equal to that with which he attacked the luncheon. At about ten minutes to three the private secretary would come in and say, "They have reached 23." "Good, there's plenty of time," and he would pour out a small noggin of old brandy. At this moment I would become rather restive and anxious lest he should be late. A quarter of an hour later, "Number 36" would be announced. "We must go at once," he said and, with that, shot out of the room into his car and was in his place about two or three questions before his own were reached.

One of his greatest parliamentary gifts was his skill in answering questions. He revelled in them, and his relish communicated itself to the House. I give an example. It was after the war, in 1952. Mr. Callaghan, who was seldom conciliatory and who had a manner which the House thought was a little more assured than was warranted, was pressing the Prime Minister one day upon the subject of the Allied Naval Commander in the Mediterranean. The Prime Minister appeared to have inclined slightly in one direction when Leader of the Opposition and in another direction in office. Things were getting somewhat uncomfortable as the crake-like voice pressed the point: didn't the right honourable gentleman say this in June and now this in October? At last with a beaming smile the Prime Minister replied: "My views are a harmonious process which keeps them in relation to the current movement of events." [7] Callaghan shrugged his shoulders and sat down, as if to say it's no use bowling googlies to W. G. Grace.

One of his most signal virtues is his magnanimity. He seldom carries forward from the ledger of today into tomorrow's account. It has befallen me more than once to have a sharp and almost bitter argument with him of an evening, when hard blows were exchanged, and to find him the next morning benign and smiling and affectionate. He regards these bouts with friends as dialectics and not personal contests. He often scorns the Queensberry rules himself, and if you too discard them when you have been hit a little low, he cares not a hang the next morning. It is difficult to describe how endearing this can be.

I remember two incidents at Ditchley which illustrate his magnanimity. This beautiful house was owned at the time by Ronnie and Nancy Tree. Her exquisite taste had set it off to perfection. The furniture, the carpets and the pictures had been chosen with

[7] Hansard: House of Commons May 5th, 1952.

fastidious knowledge and discrimination, and all the embellishments were placed with an unfailing eye and contributed to a gracious, aristocratic but lived-in harmony. From the moment you went into the high stone-floored hall, typical of the architecture of the early eighteenth century, you felt a certain pride and satisfaction at having been asked.

In the war it was considered dangerous for the Prime Minister to spend the week-end of a full moon at Chequers. Although the main drive had been turfed over to make the house less easy to pick out from the air, it was still thought to be vulnerable. It was typical of Nancy and Ronnie's civilised form of hospitality that they entertained the Prime Minister at Ditchley on the week-end of every full moon and insisted that he should propose any guests that he wanted. I often went there.

When Minister of Production I had found, as others have, some difficulty in getting the leading scientists and academic figures who had given their services to my Ministry to sing in harmony. I hoped to make them sing in unison. I proposed to appoint three scientific advisers to the Ministry who were men of calm temperament, of high scientific attainments and who were widely respected. They were Sir Thomas Merton, then Treasurer of the Royal Society, Mr. William Stanier,[8] President of the Institution of Mechanical Engineers, and Professor Sir Ian Heilbron,[9] the distinguished chemist.

The proposal irritated the Prime Minister, who wrongly thought that I was trying to expand my "empire" and invade some of his. I got nowhere at first, and the question was unsettled at the time of one of these week-end parties. Some pretty and charming ladies were talking to Winston and me after dinner when unluckily he remembered my request that I should appoint this triumvirate. "Here's Oliver, always avid of power, now wanting to run the scientific side of the war; he's going to take it over from me. He first has a spearhead of three graces, and so we may expect to see everything in the scientific field better run."

Without much difficulty he made me look rather foolish and I could hardly answer back because I was quite sure that the Prime Minister did not want any detailed Cabinet business ventilated in public. So my hands were tied behind my back, and in front of these ladies I got something of a drubbing.

8 Now Sir William Stanier.
9 Professor of Organic Chemistry at the Imperial College of Science and Technology.

The next morning at about ten, I was asked to go and see him. The scene was a familiar one. He was in bed; a discarded breakfast tray of coffee and rolls still lay on the counterpane; five or six morning papers were lying about. Soda water in a glass; a long cigar, a woollen vest under a quilted bed-jacket; smooth, rather pink face; delicate, well-cared-for hands; spectacles slightly advanced on his nose complete the conversation piece.

"Good morning, my dear. I hope you are not vexed with me?" "Well, I was vexed, but I've got over it," say I. "I know I shouldn't have chaffed you so much, but why do you want to run everything?" "I don't, really I don't, but it does require people of the *métier* to compose some of the quarrels amongst the scientists. A won't talk to B, because B has invented something A thinks he ought to have invented, and so on. That's all there is to it." "Oh well, go ahead. I don't like it, but if you want it I suppose you had better do it." Then to other subjects.

Another example of his magnanimity comes to my mind. "Cardie" Montagu had said that a rubber of bridge at the Dorchester with two ladies would be a good relaxation. Would I choose a night? So after careful research I selected a date when the Prime Minister was to be in Rosyth, and when therefore the chances of being called to a committee or to No. 10 seemed remote.

We had an excellent dinner, without an air-raid warning; we had finished and I was exchanging some pleasantries with Clare Tennyson; the cards were spread out when the telephone bell rang. "Mr. Lyttelton?" "Yes." "The Prime Minister has called a meeting of the Defence Committee at ten P.M." "Please send round a pool car at once," I ordered. "Well, that's that, as far as bridge is concerned," I said rather sadly.

When I arrived in the underground War Room below the Cabinet Office, I found the Chiefs of Staff and Service leaders, Anthony Eden, Clem Attlee and some others already there. The Prime Minister soon came in, in a boiler suit, smoking a cigar. His chin was out. This was a sure sign of impending conflict and of a late hour for bed.

A proposition was put before us by the Prime Minister involving military action of an unusual kind, and for some reason he turned upon me and said, "What do you think?" I answered that it would obviously take six to eight weeks to prepare the military action and that I thought during that period we should try to obtain our requirements by diplomatic means. This infuriated the Prime Minister. "I have never heard in all my life," he said, rounding on me, "a more idiotic suggestion advanced by a senior Minister of the Crown. Always an excuse for doing nothing," he growled, like a wounded lion. I thought sadly of my bridge, which I had left only to be exposed as a sort of Fabius Cunctator to a large company, and could only reply, "I'm sorry, but that is my opinion and you asked me for it." Anthony Eden, who took the same view as I, was extremely annoyed, and a sharp argument ensued. It went on far beyond midnight and then suddenly the Prime Minister grinned and said, "In short, we unanimously adopt the idiotic suggestion of the Minister of Production." Who can be angry with such a man?

There were, it must be confessed, certain fields into which he would not allow his natural magnanimity to stray. Once a man in public life had taken up a position concerning a major issue which Winston, the sole judge, thought was against the interests or dignity of Great Britain, or was wrong or niggardly or cowardly or a hedge, that man was excluded from his esteem for ever. Sometimes this inflexible attitude extended even beyond these points. For example, he never forgave Malcolm MacDonald for his White Paper on Palestine, which ran counter to his strongly held Zionist tendencies. He even cast his intolerance back a hundred years: the name of Thomas Babington, Lord Macaulay, was greeted by an angry snort; he could hardly be mentioned, because Winston thought that he had treated his ancestor, the Duke of Marlborough, in a scurvy manner.

Talking of the Duke of Marlborough, I recall a fragment of conversation. He pointed out to me, with some mischief in his eye, either an infelicitous or ungrammatical phrase in a memorandum which I had written for him. I had to admit that he was right. I am usually rather fastidious on these matters, so a little nettled at being found out, I said, "Well, we can't always write with absolute propriety or felicity; even the last page of the first volume of your life of the Duke of Marlborough has a slight blemish." The Prime Minister turned his head like a bull in the bull-ring when a banderilla has been stuck into its neck. "Oh, what is that, pray?" So I quoted, " 'In his last years he had woven Marlborough into the whole texture of his combinations.' " This did not go well.

The next characteristic of the Prime Minister which begins to fill in the portrait is his eye to history and to his part in it. This and his patriotism; his defence of the fame, honour and mission of the British race are the thematic part of all his works; the variations may be countless, some cadenzas may seem irrelevant, though they are seldom trivial, but at the last he returns always to the dominant theme.

He will, I expect, prove to be the best documented Prime Minister that ever held the post. It will be surprising if these documents, when examined in a few years by historians, do not give a highly subjective view of the scene. The replies of his Ministers and his correspondents hardly find a place in his own history of the Second World War.

Time and the scholars will gradually adjust the balance. If it is thought, however, that here was a man so filled with his own ideas, so set upon a course which he alone had plotted, that every other view was set aside unheeded, the conclusion would be false; in fact, in a long experience of him, I have never known an opinion firmly expressed by a colleague go unweighed and unconsidered. Within the limits of the general policy they were more often adopted than discarded.

Sometimes you thought that he had brushed aside what you had said. His method to extract and test a man's opinion was to react violently and provocatively. Heat, he believes, refines the metal. More than once I had gone away with the feeling that my opinion had been trampled down, only to find that he had modified a speech or a telegram to meet the point.

One night at Chequers he was dictating a telegram to the Middle East, from which I had just returned. It was late and he was tired, and the telegram was not coming off the press at all readily. Most of it was finished when he turned to me and asked what I thought of it. I demurred and said that I was sure he did not really want my opinion. He jokingly ordered me to give it and I again asked to be excused. When pressed again I was forced to say that I thought the telegram was nonsense. The reaction was violent. "You speak to the Prime Minister like that! Nonsense? Preposterous!" He was angry for about a minute before he recovered his temper. We then had some whisky and soda and soon after went to bed. No sign of the telegram appears on the official files; I suppose that he looked at it again in the morning and did not like it.

This habit of listening to objections is, of course, one of the sure signs of strength. In public affairs strong men discard readily from weakness. All this is not to say that his relations with his fellow Ministers and the Chiefs of Staff were always sunny; at times they were sultry. He was exceedingly tenacious of important points of his policy, and when things were going badly in a logical or dialectical contest, he fell back upon obstinacy, oratory, invective and late hours. Against this, however, he had a deep-rooted respect both for Cabinet responsibility, and for what was due to the House of Commons. He did not get angry because others opposed him, but because he could not persuade them.

I have described the subjective nature of the Prime Minister's documentation. I had an amusing example of it in my own experience.

When I was Minister of State in Cairo, the Prime Minister asked my personal help in arranging that two ships carrying tanks should be unloaded with the utmost despatch, one at Alexandria and the other at Port Suez.

One day after the ships had arrived, I got a telegram from him which, so to speak, burnt my blotting paper. He said that an intolerable delay had occurred, for which he held me personally responsible. I had let him down and the country down, and so forth.

I was extremely angry and replied after this fashion: that both ships were unloaded at rates never before reached in either port— and I gave the rates—and, I went on, that the tanks could have been unloaded in a couple of hours in Alexandria and in a little more in the quarantine port of Suez, but that not even the Minister of State could withdraw the tanks from underneath 15,000 tons of supercargo. I ended my telegram by saying that his telegram was most unfair and should be immediately withdrawn.

Silence.

Two years after the war was over, General Pownall,[10] who was helping Winston with his archives and documents while he was writing his great work on the Second World War, rang me up to say that he wanted my permission to publish the first telegram described above. I answered, "Of course, but on one condition—that he also publishes my answer." In fact the telegram was never published.

He had wished to show the unceasing pressure to which he subjected his colleagues. He had not the slightest intention of being unfair, and I am sure he had entirely forgotten my answer. Only when he saw it did he judge that it would not favour the particular context.

I have mentioned this documentation at some length because it is evidence of his great respect for history. He looks back on the story of Great Britain and the English-speaking races with the eye

[10] Lieutenant-General Sir Henry Pownall.

of an historian, he looks forward to its future with the eye of a prophet and a statesman. He has seen that his part in it is recorded. No one will deny him his glory.

At this point it is necessary to say something of the Prime Minister and Minister of Defence as a strategist. Strategy has become an elastic word. Sometimes it is used to describe plans which belong properly to the grand tactical field.

Taking the true definition of the word, the Prime Minister's grasp of the strategical problem, and of the political objectives which are bound up with it, was at once profound, experienced, bold and successful.

In the grand tactical field, an area over which the head of a Government should, or so it seems to me, have a more remote control, he did not appear to be so effective. Both these statements require to be examined.

Three or four major strategical decisions were due to the Prime Minister and Minister of Defence. A digression is here necessary. He always held, and it appears correctly, that in war these two offices must be discharged by one man. Strategical and political objectives cannot as a rule be distinguished or separated, and consequently in war the head of a government must also be Minister of Defence. Moreover, the ultimate decisions upon the use of manpower to sustain civilian life on the one hand, and military defence or striking power on the other, must be interlocked.

Thus one of my terms of reference as Minister of Production was the allocation of national resources (other than labour) between munitions and the daily requirements of the people. Whilst this involved the closest collaboration and harmony between the two Ministers concerned, the Minister of Labour (Ernest Bevin) and the Minister of Production (myself), matters of policy quickly arose which far transcended the powers of anyone except the Prime Minister, acting as himself and as the leader of the whole Cabinet.

In the strictly strategical field, two or three of the Prime Minister's decisions altered the course of the war; our ultimate victory can in part be ascribed to them.

The first of them was the decision in 1940 to send the two armoured divisions to Egypt and to build up an effective Expeditionary Force based on the Nile Delta. It was a bold decision, even for someone who had grasped that the invasion of England was a fading possibility; it appeared foolhardly to some who had not.

General Sir Alan Brooke,[11] the C.-in-C. Home Forces, opposed the despatch of these armoured divisions. It is not far from the duty of the C.-in-C. Home Forces to demur upon such a matter. The extraordinary prescience and soundness of Alanbrooke's strategy is rightly brought out by Sir Arthur Bryant. On this occasion, however, he advised the Prime Minister and the C.I.G.S.[12] that these two divisions could not be spared. Events seem to have proved that their despatch was a justifiable and constructive risk.

I was always a profound believer myself in the African strategy. The German Army, swollen by the manpower released by its conquests, towered over the war scene. Served by a General Staff of unequalled professional attainments, and fresh from victories swifter and more comprehensive than any ever witnessed in Europe, not excluding Napoleon's campaign in Italy, it was at that time clearly invulnerable on the mainland of Europe.

From our point of view the decision to reinforce the African theatre seemed to me to have been completely sound. If a man trained to the hour and weighing 16.7 stone challenges you, who are not in very good health and who weigh 8 stone, to some contest or other for money, it is unwise to challenge him at weight-lifting or try to see whether you can push the door open when he is pushing on the other side. The best chance of taking his money is to challenge him at bridge, billiards or spillikins, games at which his physical superiority may even be a disadvantage.

War in the Middle East, based on the Nile Delta, can only be a small war in terms of numbers. At no time in the Western Desert was battle engaged between more than about ten divisions on each side. The Germans had 145 divisions available for Barbarossa, the code name for the attack on Russia. Looking at the northern flank of the Middle Eastern theatre, and supposing Turkey to have been overrun, the maximum deployment by the enemy south of the Taurus mountains would not, according to the advice of the General Staff given to me in Cairo at the time when I was Minister of State, initially exceed five to seven divisions. I have lately had the advantage of reading an analysis of the German plans, given me by Brian Melland of the Historical Section of the Cabinet Office, which confirms the justice of this appreciation. On the assumption that Russia was to be speedily defeated, Directive 32 of the O.K.H. called for a total of nine to ten divisions, one corps going into Syria, another into Anatolia, down the Euphrates and

[11] Now Field-Marshal Viscount Alanbrooke.
[12] Chief of the Imperial General Staff.

the Tigris, and through Azerbaijan to Bagdad. These plans of 1941 were of course formed on the assumption that the Russians would collapse and that Malta, Gibraltar and Tobruk would be eliminated.

Any deployment by the enemy on the Northern Mediterranean littoral involved the use of sea communications highly vulnerable against a predominant sea power, and if made in the Levant, even longer and equally vulnerable communications either by sea or through the territory of a resolute and sullen Turkey.

These appreciations are easy to make at the Staff College, and their justice can be readily appraised by the historian from his rooms in the university. They are not so easy at the time. Many mistakes which seem obvious in the light of after events are still made in war. There are few battles that have been won solely by the genius of the victor; it can often be seen subsequently that elementary mistakes by the vanquished have contributed.

This decision to despatch two armoured divisions to Egypt and to build up a front in Cyrenaica was one of the greatest and boldest contributions to ultimate victory made by the Prime Minister. He was no doubt fortunate that Hitler fell so easily into the trap, but the conclusion that the African operations weakened and bled the victorious German Army to a point where an invasion of the Continent by Anglo-American armies became a practical operation of war is inescapable.

This strategy was later to involve the invasion of North Africa from the west. The Americans were never convinced of the soundness of this plan, and regarded it to the end as rash. They had the suspicion that the Straits of Gibraltar would become the Gates of Gibraltar, and that the gates might be shut behind them with a clang and their forces cut off. That this continued to be the American view is proved if it is remembered that no American warship passed into the Mediterranean itself at the outset of these operations, and that the landings inside the Mediterranean, although carried out exclusively in ships of the Royal Navy, were made far to the west of the points which the Prime Minister and the British Cabinet considered desirable. Finally, the landing on the west coast of Africa, made only by American troops, though perhaps a useful diversionary blow, can now be regarded largely as a blow in the air.

Having conquered North Africa,[13] an event signalised by General Alexander's famous telegram:

[13] February 1943.

Sir, the orders you gave me on August 15th, 1942, have been fulfilled. His Majesty's enemies together with their impedimenta have been completely eliminated from Egypt, Cyrenaica, Libya and Tripolitania. I now await your further instructions.

the Prime Minister's next moves, first to disregard Sardinia and invade Sicily, and then to attack the under-belly of Europe through Italy, appeared then and appear now to have been equally sound and imaginative. Whether the tip of Italy was in fact too near and Salerno too distant a point of impact will remain doubtful, or whether a blow at the extreme range of fighter support from the air, based on Sicily, would have led to quicker decisions will always remain a point of argument. The Prime Minister was an advocate of the second course.

Only two more strategical conceptions of the Prime Minister need to be discussed. The first is that he was entirely opposed to the American invasion of France by the Rhone valley. It now seems in the light of history that, although many prisoners were taken, this attack reduced the effectives at the decisive point in the north, and was no more than a supporting operation. Secondly, the Prime Minister favoured strengthening rather than weakening the Allied Armies in Italy, thereby making the liberation of Central Europe through the Ljubljana Gap a feasible operation of war.

Time and again he drew attention to the advantages to be gained if the Western Allies rather than the Russians were the liberators and the occupying armies of some of the capitals, Budapest, Prague, Vienna, Warsaw, which are part of the very foundation of Europe. On this occasion he did not get his way, and his views were not accepted. The political balance was overset, and we are still feeling the effects today.

No further proof of the general nicety and justice of his grand strategical designs seems to be called for.

It is a common and on the whole justifiable criticism that he was over-fond of diversionary attacks. Norway, even late in the war, always lured him. Rhodes and the Greek islands were attempted, and led to unnecessary dispersion and failure. In 1944 he urged invading the tip of Sumatra, which seemed to most to be an ill-conceived and untimely plan.

I think that his fondness for isolated diversions will be counted as serious blemishes upon his record. It had its origin from his deep conviction, which I humbly share, that the strategic concept of the attack on the Dardanelles in the first war was sound, and that we only failed because we were half-hearted and ill-served by our commanders.

Here and there he may be blamed, but his grand strategy will stand the test of time and history.

His influence on grand tactics was less felicitous. The Prime Minister sought to intervene almost on the battlefield itself. I saw at first hand many an interchange between him and Auchinleck, C.-in-C. in the Middle East. The Prime Minister was impatient of delay and kept pressing an actual date for attack upon the reluctant Auchinleck. If these exhortations had come to the unfortunate C.-in-C. through his military chiefs they would have been hard enough. But they sometimes came direct. I had advised Auchinleck to consult me upon any telegrams he sent direct to the Prime Minister, not of course upon the substance, but upon the presentation. The tone of one or two of his drafts was such that if they had not been otherwise expressed, he would have risked dismissal. It is no doubt difficult for a man of the aggressive and courageous temperament of Mr. Churchill to restrain himself from trying to influence every event. The Prime Minister's signals to keep close to the enemy, his exhortations to seize the enemy by the throat, his impatience at delay, his belief that vigorous action can often redress the balance of inferior numbers or equipment, acted as a spur. He bore down the Safety First mentality, regularly stressed the dangers of inflexible plans worked out in advance, but I cannot think it wise to address them direct to the C.-in-C. in the theatre of war. It is also dangerous to form tactical conclusions, as distinct from strategical, from so great a distance.

On the other hand, victory had withheld her hand from us for so long, the test of battle was urgent, the will to win had to be built up, the fighting spirit fostered. War cannot always be judged by arithmetic. Sometimes the fight must be taken to the enemy in spite of everything. The real issue facing a Prime Minister and Minister of Defence is whether a Commander-in-Chief is irresolute and unwilling to put battle to the test from lack of courage. This was not true of Auchinleck. It is a matter of confidence; when confidence has been forfeited the Commander must be superseded, when it exists he must be supported.

It is notable that after Rommel's attack against the 8th Army had been squarely defeated in the battle of the El Halfa ridge, and when Alexander was Commander-in-Chief, the Prime Minister was amazed that the successful defensive battle was not at once followed by a decisive counter-stroke. He went through agonies of impatience; yet his impatience was overcome, though narrowly, by the confidence which he had in Alexander and Montgomery.

My summary would thus be that the Prime Minister in the field of strategy can claim to have made two or three war-winning decisions; if he interfered too much in the field of grand tactics, and tried to make his influence felt on the very battlefield itself, which led sometimes to failure, as it did in Wavell's attack to relieve Tobruk, he had as a credit, to set off against errors in time and space, the birth of a much more aggressive spirit throughout the forces. "I will make them fight," he thundered at me more than once.

There are two more attributes of Mr. Churchill which must not be passed in silence, because they played an important part in the war. The first was his eager readiness to listen to new, sometimes to fantastic, ideas thrown up by scientists, engineers and academic figures. This receptivity in a man over sixty, with small claim to be regarded as a good listener, had, or so it would seem, long and deep-seated origins.

That his interest was fanned and cherished by Lord Cherwell seems undoubted. The Prof could explain with lucidity and explore with imagination the ever-widening horizons of discovery and knowledge in these fields. From his explanations the Prime Minister gained a rough and ready grounding in physics and electrical phenomena which he turned to good use. His interest, for example, in R.D.F.,[14] in radar generally, the bending of the beam, the countermeasures of WINDOW,[15] ensured that the inventor or discoverer gained an immediate, informed and sympathetic hearing. Once convinced, the P.M. could clearly secure Treasury approval and action more speedily than could any other Cabinet Minister.

I would put the Prime Minister's help in these matters very high amongst his contributions to victory. Indeed, I think it would rank only just below one or two of his grand strategical designs.

The Prof's contribution was thus a great though indirect one. My own relations with the Prof were always unclouded. I had a deep and genuine affection for him and I think he was one of the two cleverest men whom I have been lucky to know well. The other was Maynard Keynes. I must add that I put some bounds to my definition of the epithet. Cleverness can espouse unworthy as well as worthy causes; it can build but it can also pull down. In

[14] Radio Direction Finding.
[15] Tinfoil strips used to confuse German radar.

my definition it does not necessarily embrace imagination or power of negotiation and management of other people.

An example may serve to illustrate how well grounded Winston was in radar. By virtue of being Minister of Production, I was a member of the Anti-Submarine Committee. Towards the end of the war the Germans had developed the Schnorkel submarine, which could be submerged without its engines running and breathe through its snout. It could not be detected by Asdic when lying on the bottom, and the Prime Minister asked why we could not use a radio device to give back a signal that the monster was lurking. The answer surprised and intrigued me beyond measure. The most likely area in which these submarines would operate would be in the Northwestern Approaches. Here the wrecks of two wars cluttered the seabed, more than a million tons had been sunk and no radar signal could tell which was a wreck and which a submarine. "Why," said the Prime Minister, "do we not send down divers to mark the wrecks with a device which would say 'I'm a wreck. I'm a wreck'?" It was agreed that these were the measures which would probably prove necessary. The war ended before they were put into use.

The second attribute, not always a welcome one to his colleagues, was the pressure that he exerted on all the principal Departments of State. It is quite true that this was sometimes carried to excessive lengths. At times I even became a little petulant myself about interference from No. 10.

There is no doubt, however, that the general effect of the pressure, whether applied to essential or to trivial details, was good. At the back of a Minister's mind would be the vision of one of those short notes, beginning, "Pray let me know why . . ." or some such phrase.

It would be out of place, in a personal portrait, to attempt a full description of Mr. Churchill as a statesman. It does seem appropriate, however, to mention shortly some of the sources of his inspiration in politics.

First, ceaseless thought about politics—they are never far from his mind.

Next, experience: an experience which has taught him, until the lesson has become an instinct, where the dangers lie, both at home and abroad. He knows when small things are likely to become big. Early the red light starts winking in the control room. Judgement must be exercised. This is not to say that his judgement is the strongest part of his equipment; it can never be in a man whose greatest quality is his power of leadership. That power in anyone resides mainly in the ability to dull man's logical faculty, not to stimulate it. The point, however, is that he knows when to look out for a storm.

Thirdly, there is his imagination. Sometimes it appears prophetic. The following is a passage from a tactical appreciation, written in 1913:

> A prudent survey of chances from the British point of view ought to contemplate that, when the German advance decisively begins, it will be backed by sufficient preponderance for force, and developed on a sufficiently wide front to compel the French armies to retreat from their positions behind the Belgian frontier, even though they may hold the gaps between the fortresses on the Verdun-Belfort front. . . . The balance of probability is that by the twentieth day the French armies will have been driven from the line of the Meuse and will be falling back on Paris and the south. All plans based upon the opposite assumption ask too much of fortune. . . . This is not to exclude the plan of using four or six British divisions in these great initial operations. Such a force is a material factor of significance. . . . France will not be strong enough to invade Germany. Her only chance is to conquer Germany in France. It is this problem which should be studied before any final decision is taken. . . . By the fortieth day Germany should be extended at full strain both internally and on her war fronts, and this strain will become daily more severe and ultimately overwhelming, unless it is relieved by decisive victories in France. If the French army has not been squandered by precipitate or desperate action, the balance of forces should be favourable after the fortieth day, and will improve steadily as time passes.[16]

That passage is uncanny to anyone familiar with the military history of 1914.[17] Some of his telegrams to President Roosevelt towards the end of the war again show a prophetic vision. He foretold the future.

Lastly I turn to his oratory and his writing. Both his speech and his prose give you the feeling that you are witnessing the great panorama of human struggle and success and failure unfolding before you.

If you are concerned yourself, if you are being offered a post or set a task, you swell in your own estimation as he speaks. You feel yourself to be an actor in a great scene.

[16] W. S. Churchill, *World Crisis* (London: Odhams Press Ltd.), Vol. I.
[17] On September 4th, 1914, the Kaiser said: "It is the 35th day, we invest Rheims, we are thirty miles from Paris. . . ." Helfferich, *Der Weltkrieg* (Berlin, 1919), II, 279. The tide of the battle turned on September 7th.

I confess that I slightly prefer his style of oratory to his style of writing. I am a great admirer of both, but my classical education inclines my taste towards the more restrained and less florid type of writing, towards something derived more from Tacitus than from Macaulay.

As an orator Winston strictly rationed his powers of improvisation, and hardly ever set sail upon uncharted seas. He trusted himself with no more than a few impromptu remarks at the beginning of a speech, or some bridges to link his arguments with those that had preceded them. Every word of his main speeches was written, even "R.H.G." (Right Honourable Gentleman) appeared in his notes as an abbreviation; yet such was his art, that he did not give the impression of reading from a script, and if the speech did not always appear spontaneous, it at least did not smell of the lamp.

He had two pairs of spectacles; stood back from the box or the rostrum and read through the longer-range glasses. When he came to a quotation or to a recital of figures, the other pair of shorter range came out from his pocket; they were carefully adjusted, then he openly read.

I have known him take six or eight or more hours to prepare a speech of forty minutes. The labour and the perseverance were no doubt sustained by his feeling that his words might be destined for posterity.

His effects were procured with all the artfulness and artifice which a lifetime of public speaking had given him. He began usually, and of course on purpose, with a few rather stumbling sentences; his audience was surprised that the phrases did not seem to run easily off his tongue. The tempo was slow and hesitant. Then gradually the Grand Swell and the Vox Humana were pulled out and the full glory of his words began to roll forth, set off by the low tones and tempo of the first few bars which had preceded them. The humorous passages were timed with the greatest care, and often used to relax the House of Commons into conceding the doubtful point without interruption, while Members of both parties were either chuckling over a joke or purring over a compliment.

Flattery is the infantry of negotiation, and certainly a large audience is as susceptible to it as a single negotiator. "All through these convulsions, the House of Commons has stood unshaken and unafraid. . . ." he would say. They swallowed it whole, and felt that they had been in a battle and had just been decorated.

At one moment, an old brother officer of mine in the Brigade of

Guards, who was commanding an Officers' Training Unit, wrote an ill-judged letter to *The Times* saying that entries from the public schools made far the best officers. This of course gave offence to the Labour Party. About this time the Prime Minister was announcing to the House of Commons the formation of two bodies, one to be called the Production Executive, and the other the Import Executive. These were the first gropings towards a Ministry of Production, and I have reason to remember them because, as President of the Board of Trade, I was a member of both. The announcement was not going well and the House was a trifle restive, because they thought, and as it turned out rightly, that the instruments were unequal to the task. Referring to the Chairman of one of these bodies, the Prime Minister, apparently rather searching for words, said, "As to the Chairman of this Committee, he is not *facile princeps,* but *primus inter pares,* which for the benefit of any—" he paused almost imperceptibly and several members of the Labour Party seemed about to rise from their seats and protest about the insult on their lack of a classical education that was about to follow. However, he completed the sentence, "for the benefit of any Old Etonians present, I should, if very severely pressed, venture to translate." [18] This delighted everyone, and was more than ever felicitous coming from an Old Harrovian, whose knowledge of Latin was of the slightest. The roof nearly came off, and in the few minutes of hilarity he put the most contentious points and rode off with them in his saddle-bags without as much as an interruption.

Before he was quite so famous, the highly prepared nature of his speeches sometimes came under fire.

One day Arthur Balfour, who had come late into the House, and who was to reply for the Government, asked my father, then Colonial Secretary, what Winston had been saying. My father told him that the line of argument developed by the Government, which was unexpected, had somewhat thrown Winston's speech out of gear and that it had not gone well. Uncoiling himself at the box, A.J.B. began in something of this style: "We have all listened"—which he had not done—"to the speech of the Rt. Hon. Gentleman who has just resumed his seat, we have all listened with interest, and I might even say with admiration. Unfortunately he has trained his guns up a road along which the enemy has—er—along which the enemy has *not* come. Might I suggest that in future he makes his heavy pieces a little more mobile?"

[18] Hansard: January 22nd, 1941.

This inflicted a wound which I have been told took a little time to heal.

I often wondered to what the inflexibility of his large-scale speeches was due. I believe it to be from fastidiousness over the English language, and from the desire not to leave to history some phrase or sentence unworthy of him, or less than his best. It limited his powers of improvisation in making big speeches. This was not due to a lack of the power of repartee or an inflexible mind. This is proved when, for example, he was answering questions in the House: there he improvised readily and turned other men's swords to reeds. It would be fair to say, however, that some of the answers to supplementaries had been previously recruited, and drilled ready to go into action should the occasion for them ever arise.

I do not propose to write of the Prime Minister's most famous speeches. Nothing can be added to the record. These speeches are as immortal as the orations of Demosthenes, Cicero or Chatham. When they were uttered, they brought back to us in our menaced islands the very spirit and the message of Nelson, and when read again the ringing words still stir the blood. I felt at that time, and so I believe did everyone, a positive relief that we were alone, alone but one under his leadership. "For he today that sheds his blood with me shall be my brother" were our profound feelings.

No writer describing these times should, however, refrain from quoting some of the less-well-known speeches.

In the House of Commons of our day, in face of the highly organised political machines of the principal parties, speeches are not often delivered in the hopes of turning the whole House but are more usually directed to unite the speaker's own party, or, if delivered from the Opposition benches, are made to secure modifications in the policy of a Government, rather than seeking to change it entirely. In short, it is rare that a speaker can turn the whole sentiment of the House.

Consequently, I would rate Mr. Churchill's speech on the Darlan episode as amongst the greatest, the most adroit and persuasive of Parliamentary performances that have been heard in this century. I can remember clearly the sentiment of the House before he began; Members were troubled and uneasy; they were asking themselves what the sentiments of the Free French would be, and whether our fair purposes had been tainted by bargaining with traitors. When he had finished, the House was persuaded, satisfied and united. After the speech, no division was called. Incidentally, the speech had been one of the most profound, as it is one of the most sympathetic, explanations of the dilemma which faced the conscience of French officers in those tangled times.

I now turn to examine a peculiar form of French mentality, or rather of the mentality of a large proportion of Frenchmen in the terrible defeat and ruin which has overtaken their country. I am not at all defending or still less eulogising this French mentality. But it would be very foolish not to try to understand what is passing in other people's minds and what are the secret springs of action to which they respond. The Almighty in his infinite wisdom did not see fit to create Frenchmen in the image of Englishmen. In a State like France which has experienced so many convulsions—Monarchy, Convention, Directory, Consulate, Empire, Monarchy, Empire, and finally Republic—there has grown up a principle founded on the *droit administratif* which undoubtedly governs the action of many French officers and officials in times of revolution and change. It is a highly legalistic habit of mind and it arises from a subconscious sense of national self-preservation against the dangers of sheer anarchy. For instance any officer who obeys the command of his lawful superior or of one whom he believes to be his lawful superior is absolutely immune from subsequent punishment. Much therefore turns in the minds of French officers upon whether there is a direct unbroken chain of lawful command, and this is held to be more important by many Frenchmen than moral, national or international considerations. From this point of view many Frenchmen who admire General de Gaulle and envy him in his role, nevertheless regard him as a man who has rebelled against the authority of the French State, which in their prostration they conceive to be vested in the person of the antique defeatist who to them is the illustrious and venerable Marshal Pétain, the hero of Verdun and the sole hope of France.[19]

I end this account of his oratory by quoting a passage from a speech delivered to a meeting of High Commissioners in June 1941. He who does not find that the passage is amongst the highest flights of oratory and, in Macaulay's phrase, is one which will "leave to posterity memorials which can perish only with the English language," is a man without either heart or patriotism, or is some crabbed critic who has fallen into the habit of thinking that praise should not be one of the ingredients of modern criticism.

Hitler may turn and trample this way and that through tortured Europe. He may spread his course far and wide, and carry his curse with him: he may break into Africa or into Asia. But it is here, in this island fortress, that he will have to reckon in the end. We shall strive to resist by land and sea. We shall be on his track wherever he goes. Our air-

[19] A speech to the House of Commons in Secret Session, December 10th, 1942, released for publication February 1946. *The War Speeches of Winston S. Churchill* (London: Cassell & Co., 1952), II, 379.

power will continue to teach the German homeland that war is not all loot and triumph.

We shall aid and stir the people of every conquered country to resistance and revolt. We shall break up and derange every effort which Hitler makes to systematise and consolidate his subjugation. He will find no peace, no rest, no halting-place, no parley. And if, driven to desperate hazards, he attempts the invasion of the British Isles, as well he may, we shall not flinch from the supreme trial. With the help of God, of which we must all feel daily conscious, we shall continue steadfast in faith and duty till our task is done.

This, then, is the message which we send forth today to all the States and nations bond or free, to all the men in all the lands who care for freedom's cause, to our allies and well-wishers in Europe, to our American friends and helpers drawing ever closer in their might across the ocean: this is the message— Lift up your hearts. All will come right. Out of the depths of sorrow and sacrifice will be born again the glory of mankind.[20]

This then is my portrait of Mr. Churchill. Standing back and looking at it from a distance it falls far short of being a likeness.

Some of his engaging weaknesses have not been touched on: his love of uniforms and medals long after his figure or his fame had outgrown them; his worldly inclinations towards cigars and champagne, race-horses, black swans, the company of millionaires and other tinsel decorations of life.

His versatility has not been fully drawn. It is shown now by his pen, now by his brush, now by the flashing phrase or flowing peroration. For thirty years of his life the holder of the highest offices of state, twice Prime Minister at a turning point in history, an honorary Royal Academician, a Fellow of the Royal Society, a member of the Jockey Club and a Knight of Garter, his record attests to the variety of his talents, of his interests and of his experience.

No words can convey the beat of his great heart, his deep and aggressive patriotism, his affection and loyalty to his friends, shaken sometimes but never overthrown by prejudice and anger, his innate humanity, his puckish humour, his courage in defeat, his magnanimity in victory.

He spread round him warmth and colour, and when he spoke it was as if the footlights in a darkened theatre had suddenly been turned up. I could ask no more of life than to have been close to him, to have enjoyed his friendship always and his confidence

---

[20] A speech to a conference of Dominion High Commissioners and Allied countries' Ministers at St. James's Palace, June 12th, 1941. *The War Speeches of Winston S. Churchill* (London: Cassell & Co., 1951), I, 446.

often. Those who worked near him and who saw him in defeat and victory, and had a glimpse of his prophetic inspiration and statesmanship, can look back and truly say, "We few, we happy few." He has lived far beyond the span of ordinary men, and upon his shield we can proudly inscribe the device: *"That casque which never stoop'd except to Time."* [21]

[21] Byron, *Don Juan*, Canto X.

CHAPTER XI

PRESIDENT OF THE BOARD
OF TRADE

O NE DAY in July 1940, when I was still Controller of Metals, I was summoned to see the Prime Minister and went to the underground citadel where he used occasionally to spend the night.

He was dressing. He greeted me smilingly. "I want you to stand for Parliament. I am now leader of the Tory Party and must have more old faces in the ranks, people I know and who know me." I was dismayed by this invitation and said, "Oh, I am ineligible, because I have an office of profit under the Crown. Although my official salary doesn't exist because I continue to be paid by my company, that is my legal standing. I am doing something which I really understand and I think I am making a contribution. The job is not yet by any means routine and the Metal Control is not yet perfected. I have to work day and night. I shouldn't be any good anyway in the House."

"Well, I want you and I am shortly going to sweep away these disabilities under which you and others are suffering.[1] When that's done, we will talk about it again."

At that moment he began to turn to the affairs of the day and I left rather disturbed but hoping that nothing would come of it.

About this time, Moira and I decided that our family should leave our country house, which was at Wittersham, on the borders of Kent and Sussex, because it had become a prohibited area and in my opinion was likely to be on the main axis of an invasion by the Germans. The German history of the war shows that this was a correct appreciation. As the news got worse and when it became

[1] House of Commons Disqualification (Temporary Provisions) Act, 1941.

clear that France would be knocked cut, our search for a house became almost feverish. However, I soon found one, belonging to Sir Frederick Freake, which he wished to let, and I leased it from him for a year.

It seemed well placed, even ideally placed for my purposes: it was under twenty miles from my headcuarters in Rugby and about eleven from Stratford-upon-Avon, to which the part of the Ministry of Supply which dealt with materials, and consequently with my Control, had been moved. It was in the very centre of England and was a pleasant, well-found house, with some pictures on the walls from which you could have guessed that my landlord was a well-known rider and sportsman.

A fortnight after moving in I was asked to go and shoot by Eric Dudley,[2] a life-long friend, at Himley. It was an easy journey from Rugby and I accepted.

At midday, whilst we were out shooting, I got a summons to spend that night and the next at Chequers. At the end of a golden autumn day I left in my car with six brace of partridges in the boot for the Prime Minister from Eric. As I threaded my way through the Buckinghamshire lanes in the gathering dusk, I hoped that the reason for my invitation was rot concerned with a seat in the House of Commons, but I felt sure that it was. I arrived in time to dress for dinner.

"Pug" Ismay and I were the only guests. We were alone with the Prime Minister, Mrs. Churchill and Mary and his private secretary, and spent a most agreeable evening. The Prime Minister was in his best form. After dinner a big air-raid on London began and we could see the flicker of A.A. fire and bursting bombs. "Bomber" Harris[3] arrived from near by in a plum-coloured velveteen dinner jacket, hardly up to my Grenadier standard as "good order" for an Air Marshal visiting the Prime Minister, but he talked clearly and with command of his subject. We went to bed about 3 A.M.

I was alone with "Pug" the next morning at breakfast; the day was dry but sullen. "Pug" suggested a long walk and off we started. I did not realise it at the time but "Pug" intentionally drew me into some military discussion. I have always been a student of military history, and I suppose once you have followed any profession, and especially the profession of arms, you like to go back to your original love. We discussed the German campaign in East Prussia in 1914, of which I have a detailed knowledge. Later on I told him

2 The Earl of Dudley.
3 Marshal of the Royal Air Force Sir Arthur Harris.

that in the last war some young officers, including young Colonel Alexander[4] and myself, had thought the positional battles of those days should be fought on a new model. Our idea was that all the reserves to be used in the battle should be on the march at zero hour; junior staff officers should be pushed out with the leading waves in the attack, and should be empowered to stop the reserves being committed on a divisional front where little progress had been made. Unless stopped in this way, they were to be committed without further orders. In our experience there had always been three or four hours after a successful initial assault when fresh troops, if they had been at hand, could have secured important tactical successes and dominating ground without much difficulty.

The idea of keeping troops under Corps or Army orders for employment in the opening phases of a modern battle was out of date. The senior commanders could not expect to gauge the tactical situation quickly enough. I myself had some experience of these fleeting opportunities. On September 15th, 1916, I had got into the outskirts of Lesboeufs with about a hundred men, had remained there for four or five hours, and had then been hustled out of the position by an overwhelming counter-attack by two companies, or more, of Germans. Lesboeufs had to be captured a few days later, with very heavy casualties, and the graves of many of my brother officers around the village are a tragic evidence of what loss of time means in loss of life.

At another time in September 1916, the imperturbable Fryer, a company commander in my regiment, had patrolled the Le Transloy ridge, a local tactical feature of much importance. Because no fresh troops were available, he could do no more than patrol the ridge; he could not hold it. Two divisions were afterwards cut to pieces in taking it.

"Always exploit success" was our theory, "never failure."

These were our youthful but veteran and professional views. It would be altogether an exaggeration to describe them as the beginning of the theory of deep penetration on a narrow front, of the iron finger thrust into the very entrails of the enemy, but it at least showed how we who were concerned only with the tactical battle had begun to see the answer. This was a method of battle used occasionally by the Germans in the first war, and afterwards adapted, improved and exploited by commanders like Guderian with his Panzers, not only for tactical but for grand tactical objectives.

[4] Field-Marshal Earl Alexander of Tunis.

I enjoyed this talk with "Pug" greatly, and he asked me many questions of a military nature, more it seemed to me to learn the opinions of a regimental officer in the last war than from any feeling that these theories had any particular significance in 1940.

We had an amusing luncheon; the Prime Minister was again in coruscating form, and Mary and Clemmie spurred him on. However, after luncheon the ladies disappeared. Winston went off to sleep for an hour, and then to work, and did not re-emerge. I finished my book and could not find just what I wanted to replace it. I tried one of the works of Philip Guedalla but found too many plums and not quite enough cake. I started on a memorandum about lead supplies; it was short and occupied no more than half an hour. At about 7:15 P.M. I thought I would take a long bath, dress very leisurely and thus fill in the gap before dinner.

I was going up to my bedroom and had reached the first landing of the staircase when Winston, in a boiler-suit, suddenly burst out of a room on the ground floor, and said, "Oliver, come here, I want to talk to you." "Curse," thought I, "this is that seat in the House come to life again," and followed him into his room. He was pacing up and down like a caged tiger, cigar in hand. "Sit down, sit down," and, after the slightest pause, "Neville Chamberlain is dying. His loyalty and magnanimity have been wonderful; I understand his depth of character. He has more than once given in his resignation. I have refused to accept it, but now I must. I cannot ask him to go into the shelters twice and three times a day, suffering as he does. Yes, he is dying. Now my plan is to move Anthony Eden from the War Office to the Foreign Office, and to move Edward Halifax[5] from the Foreign Office to be Lord President of the Council in place of Neville."

I thought that here was an instance of a great man wishing to air his thoughts before a discreet friend. After all, a friendly audience is always a help. "It may be," he went on, "that Edward doesn't wish to move at this conjuncture. If that is so I shall move Anthony Eden to be Lord President. You will see that in either case this means the War Office is open and," speaking a little more slowly, "I want you to be Secretary of State for War." I could not believe my ears. No sentence spoken to me in my life has been such a surprise; my sails were fairly taken aback. I was delighted but incredulous. Had I heard him aright?

Seeing this he rapped out, "Do you think you can do it?" and fixed me with something like a glare. "Well," I replied, having

[5] The Earl of Halifax.

partly recovered from the shock, "I am going to quote you some words of a friend of yours." He didn't like the sound of this and asked which friend. "F.E.," [6] said I. "Well?" "He once began a speech, 'Undeterred as I am by any morbid sense of self-distrust . . .' You can guess what I mean, Prime Minister." The slight tension relaxed. He went on: "Well, at the War Office I want a man with these qualifications. He must have seen a lot of hard fighting at some time in his life. You fulfil that. I must have some-one accustomed to administration on a large scale. You fulfil that. And I must have a gentleman to get on with the generals and," with a twinkle, "I suppose you could train on to be one. I want the administration at the War Office overhauled. Now about the House of Commons; you will take to that; you come of a political family; we'll find you a seat," and much else in the same vein. I then realised that "Pug" had been pumping me in the morning, and had found that I was at least a student of war. I have little doubt that Brendan, who thought my metal control had been well done, had also been at work.

It was an exquisite thrill for me; the surprise was complete; the office one which, if I had ever thought of it for myself, I should have coveted the most. I dressed in a haze and a hurry, and had to tie my tie three times. I was late for dinner, and in the seventh heaven.

After dinner the Chiefs of Staff appeared and I was drawn into the sitting-room and listened to what is inelegantly known as a top-level discussion. It began to look as if I hadn't been dreaming. So to bed at two but not, of course, to sleep. By five I was in an uneasy doze, through which my reason poked its head and told me it was after all a dream.

I had to return to work the next day, so I got up early and had some breakfast. A message arrived that the Prime Minister wanted me to drive up with him to London—doubtless to tell me that he had had second thoughts. However, at this moment Clemmie appeared in her dressing-gown on the gallery above the hall, leaned over the balustrade, smiled and in a Shakespearean whisper breathed, "Congratulations," and then I knew it was true. What a change, and what a chance.

We swept up to London with an escort and the bell mounted on the car cleared the way with an occasional clang. The saddling bell, I thought.

I went straight back to Rugby to some pressing problems of

[6] F. E. Smith, Lord Birkenhead.

Non-Ferrous Metal Control and Diamond Die Control. I had obviously to see the Chairman of the British Metal Corporation, Mr. C. V. Sale, and make some financial arrangements.

Handing over the job was not difficult. I had associated with me as colleagues William Mure, Alfred Baer, Jack Budd, Fred Burgess and my cousin Dick Talbot. I believe that I had contributed something decisive at the beginning, when I framed and negotiated the great long-term contracts, but I was sure that afterwards they would run the control as well and probably better without me.

So to my pangs at leaving a business in which I was expert, and old friends upon whom I relied so implicitly, were not added pangs of conscience.

That Monday evening I motored over from Rugby in high feather to Halford, in order to tell Moira and the family. Antony, my eldest son, was already serving in the Army, but Rosemary, Julian and the three-year-old Adrian were at home. Except the cadet, they were in the drawing-room drinking coffee after dinner. When I broke the news Moira was obviously delighted and Julian exclaimed, "Small-town boy makes good." Rosemary said, "How lovely," and I said, "Champagne! I must get it on the ice quick." So there were general rejoicings and some suggestions from the family of how pompous my maiden speech needed to be. Julian's sample, if it had got past the Speaker, would have given me a permanent footing in the House.

Tuesday dawned, and I thought I had better be on hand in London to await the Prime Minister's summons. This very week I started an acute neuralgia. It came on like clockwork after luncheon and after dinner, and lasted an hour each time. A nerve in my head jangled like a piano string and completely stopped thought and almost sanity during the attack. I supposed the attacks would pass or diminish. I was mistaken.

On Wednesday no message. Yes, I had been dreaming. What had happened? And then on Thursday the summons came. I had the hunch that something had gone wrong; perhaps it was the delay, perhaps the feeling that nothing so unexpected and so thrilling could really happen. I was shown into the Cabinet Room at No. 10 Downing Street.

The Prime Minister disclosed that Edward Halifax did not wish to leave the Foreign Office and Anthony Eden did not relish leaving the War Office, an office with a portfolio and near the war, for one without a portfolio concerned with home affairs. In his position I would have felt the same. Andrew Duncan, however, was being moved from the Board of Trade to the Ministry of Supply, and I was offered the Board of Trade.

I confess to have had an acute sense of disappointment. I was not to escape from the old figures, imports and exports, conversion factors, bank advances, statistical trade data and the like. I accepted the office, however, as a matter of course. The Prime Minister said a seat must be found for me; I had better go and see Lord Windlesham, the Vice-Chairman of the Conservative Party. I was not to disclose that I had a portfolio in my pocket but merely that the Prime Minister wanted me in the House.

I accordingly arranged to see Lord Windlesham at Sunningdale on Saturday; and since the new appointment would not be announced until the following week, I could go on to Halford for the weekend.

It was a warm, cloudless day, and I put on a pair of flannel trousers, a short blue coat, a Zingari tie and brown-and-white shoes, sometimes described as Monte Carlo strollers. As it turned out, I could not have been worse dressed for the occasion, because I arrived in the middle of an air-raid. A few sticks of light bombs had fallen near Sunningdale station. I expect they had been jettisoned. As I drove up to the small red-brick villa then occupied by Lord Windlesham, I heard the drone of aircraft and another stick fell a few hundred yards away. Of course my chauffeur, Ferguson—an ex-sailor—and I got out and gazed into the sky. I then observed that the porch of the villa was heavily sandbagged and that Lord Windlesham, who was inside it, had on a steel helmet, a gas mask, and was carrying a gas rattle. He was evidently the head of the Air Raid Wardens, and was very properly setting an example. I was hastily drawn into the porch and told to put on my gas mask. Neither my chauffeur nor I had one. Disastrous impression. There was another warden, I believe, Lord Windlesham's son-in-law, even more highly equipped to repel raiders. I could not repress a smile, or conceal the levity of my character when faced by the possibility that Sunningdale was to become another Guernica. However, the All Clear sounded in a few minutes, and I was summoned into the drawing-room.

The conversation went something like this. Lord Windlesham: "I understand your candidature is backed by Winston?" "Yes." "A great mistake, but it can't be helped. Have you been through the Divorce Court lately?" "No." "Well, that's something; quite a lot of candidates have, you know. Not lately bankrupt? No? Forgive my asking, did you marry a lady?" I thought I had. With a smile, "Great help, great help in the constituency."

After some other interrogation I was told I might get on to the short list for the Wrekin, and there I had to let the matter rest. I shuffled my flannels into my Jaguar, and left the front for the peace of Rugby and Halford.

I emphasise that it was the situation that brought the element of farce, and that Lord Windlesham's attitude was natural. He had to take the air-raid seriously and both in that and in his questioning of an unknown and most unsuitably dressed candidate for a seat, he did his duty in a friendly and dignified manner.

The following Thursday, October 3rd, 1940, the changes in the Government were announced and on Friday I was sworn in as a Member of the Privy Council and kissed hands on my appointment as President of the Board of Trade and Foreign Plantations. There were two other Privy Councillors sworn in on the same day. First, "Bobbety" Cranborne, and then Moore-Brabazon.[7]

"Bobbety" and I went to Eton on the same day; he went to Oxford and I to Cambridge, but we joined his father's militia regiment on the same day in 1914, and the Grenadiers on the same day, went to war on the same day in January 1915. Although we met occasionally, our ways parted between the wars and by the strangest conjuncture here we were, joining the Government and the Privy Council on the same day. Since "Bobbety" is my ideal of an Englishman I felt for the first time a glow of satisfaction at my new office.

A little later, I was attending the Privy Council when Lord Oaksey was sworn in. His father was Mr. Justice Lawrence, afterwards Lord Trevethin, one of my father's greatest friends and the man who had given me advice about my career in 1919. The sons of the two old friends were proud of this happy coincidence.

So in the afternoon to the Board of Trade, to take over from Andrew Duncan, whom I knew well, because he had been Controller of Iron and Steel, and Chairman of the Controller's Committee. Andrew, when something delicate had to be negotiated, used to exaggerate a trifle his Scottish accent, so I thought something was coming when his greeting was in broad Scottish. It was. Andrew: "I must tell you that I am taking 'Billy' Brown,[8] the Perrmanent Secretary of the Board of Trade with me. I only accepted

[7] Now Lord Brabazon of Tara.
[8] Sir William Brown.

Supply on that condition." "Oh well," says I, "I must do without him, but I shall miss him sadly in taking over. Who succeeds him?" "Sir Arnold Overton temporarily, but W. B. will come back in six or eight months. He doesn't like being translated to Supply."

Then Andrew explained the one or two things likely to give trouble in the next few days. They did not appear to me to be very alarming, and I said, "Oh, well, the private secretary will tell me about them." "Well," said Andrew, "I am taking Harry Beer with me too." This, I thought, is getting a bit thick: the two big men in a Minister's life are being removed at once. So I said, "You are leaving this desk, I hope?" "Oh yes, oh yes." At that moment Sherrington, the President's messenger, came in, carrying two boxes of my cigarettes. "These are for your desk, Sir," he said, and tried to put them into the top right-hand drawer. Both its wooden handles came off. "I now see why you're leaving the desk," I said.

So there I was, President. My first interview was clearly to be with "Billy" Brown, and then his replacement, Sir Arnold Overton. The latter had been what is known in the Board of Trade as a C.R. & T. man, the initials standing for Commercial Relations and Treaties. He was a Wykehamist, and when I first saw him I knew I would like him. He had a fine, intellectual head, thoughtful and kindly eyes, and a figure and appearance of distinction.

The Parliamentary Secretary to the Board of Trade was Gil Lloyd George.[9] He had great Parliamentary experience, a broad and kindly sense of humour, and was popular with all parties. He had a particular way with him with deputations: they used to arrive in indignation and go away satisfied with nothing. We became fast friends and remain so.

One evening he urged me to come and have a drink at the Park Lane Hotel, where he was living, on my way home to the Dorchester, and promised he would show me something amusing. We set out about 7:15 and after a drink he took me down to the ballroom. It was already thronged with people carrying lilos, thermos flasks, blankets, shawls; some had already pegged out their claims and were lying down.

"This is the underground ballroom and I will now show you the head-cover," said Gil, an old Gunner. It turned out that only an inch of ground glass protected the inhabitants from bombs, but it served the purpose of giving a number of people a quiet night in the bliss of ignorance.

[9] Now Viscount Tenby.

Under the President of the Board of Trade at that time was the Mines Department, which was responsible to the President but not to the Department of the Board of Trade. The Secretary was Dai Grenfell,[10] a Welsh miner, a sweet character, and afterwards Father of the House. Geoffrey Lloyd, as a junior Minister, was in charge of the Petroleum Department and brought to his task political experience and administrative ability. He did not consult me very often and went his own way until the signature of the President was unavoidable. We only had one sharp difference of opinion, and that was upon a deal with the oil companies which he had negotiated. I took the view that he had got the worst of the bargain, and secured some substantial savings with his help.

Finally, there was the Department of Overseas Trade, again presided over by a junior Minister, but jointly responsible to the President and to the Foreign Secretary. It was a happy chance that the incumbent was "Crinks" Harcourt Johnstone, a life-long friend. He had devoted much of his private fortune to support the Liberal Party; he was at once very greedy and nicely discerning about his food; he was a connoisseur of wine, with real knowledge; he was highly educated, well-read, fond of racing, and a first-rate bridge player. He gave the impression—and intended to give it—that he was idle and disinterested. It was a piece of protective colouring. I saw a number of pages and memoranda which he wrote when Secretary of the Department. No one was ever able to convict him of putting on paper either an unwise or a slipshod sentence. His conclusions were supported by a thorough investigation of the facts, and informed by sound and logical sequences. He had very few intimate friends, but to them he gave an affection and loyalty which he strove to conceal by an astringent and critical manner. I was one of these friends.

The second day after I was installed, he strolled into my room in a fawn overcoat, and with his bowler hat on. "Well, Ugly," he said, "are you coming to luncheon?" The officials were as shocked as I was delighted by this incursion.

My parliamentary private secretary was Charles Peat, an eminent chartered accountant, much liked in the House. He had the difficult task of coaching me in how to reply to parliamentary questions, and how to behave like a Minister. I became much devoted to him.

The then Board of Trade covered a very wide administrative

[10] The Rt. Hon. D. R. Grenfell.

field. It was responsible for trade at home, including such industries as cotton and wool textiles, chemicals and leather, and for
exports abroad. It looked after commercial treaties and relations
with foreign powers, the Insurance Act and the Gas Act, the Mines
Department and the Department of Overseas Trade (*vide* above).
The Department had recruited a number of temporary civil servants, who were of great value, and, including them, there were
6,000 civil servants at Headquarters. In my considered judgement
they formed a highly skilful, knowledgeable and experienced body,
and I have never wavered in this opinion. They were, however,
brought up and trained—as civil servants should be—to carry
out policy, not to decide it. I had never dreamed of having at my
command such a magnificent instrument of administration.

It was important not to be lodged too far away from Whitehall,
and I took a room on the top floor of the Dorchester. During air-
raids I had the uncomfortable sensation that there was nothing
between me and the Luftwaffe, but consoled myself by remembering that I was in a steel-framed building. When some bombs fell
near Londonderry House, the whip of the steel frame made the
top floor spring an inch or two before returning to the perpendicular, the looking-glasses and prints swung out from the walls, as if
in an earthquake.

One night, soon after taking office, I was bidden to dinner by
the Prime Minister at No. 10 Downing Street. It was a party of four,
and besides myself the other guests were Archie Sinclair,[11] the
Air Minister, and Moore-Brabazon, the Minister of Transport. We
dined in the little room on the ground floor, underneath the Cabinet room. It was trussed up by a few substantial wooden piles.
Knowing what I now do about the foundation and structure of
No. 10, I can only regard these precautions as a token.

We had hardly reached the fish when a stick of bombs fell all
round Downing Street and the Treasury. The Prime Minister
jumped up from the table, and muttering to Sayers the butler
that we would serve ourselves, plunged into the back regions. He
soon came back. "I've ordered the cook, and the beautiful kitchen
maid and the other servants into the dug-out. I'm very afraid of
their getting hurt; there's too much glass about."

We went on with our dinner, and another bomb fell, which blew
in the large kitchen window but did no other damage to us. Three
men were killed in the Treasury, and several wounded. I thought

[11] Now Viscount Thurso.

that all this was getting rather like my old life as a soldier, except
that the office work was now more strenuous.

We had a long and amusing dinner, and though no All Clear had
sounded by 1 A.M., no more bombs fell near us. Archie went off to
the Air Ministry. The Prime Minister offered Brab and me an
armoured car, but we refused and said we would walk. Soon after
we had set out, the All Clear sounded, and Brab became reflective.
"It's always amusing to have just lived through an evening which
one will always remember until the day of one's death." "Oh yes," I
said, "the memories of some putts one has holed or missed, but I
know how you will describe this evening in your memoirs; it will
be something like this. 'I was dining with the Prime Minister one
night, and there were two or three other guests, whom I do not
remember . . .'" Time passes quickly in Brab's company, and
the Dorchester seemed quite near.

There is no doubt that the air-raids slowed down the work of
Whitehall. Sometimes we had to send the staff into the shelters;
sometimes messages were not delivered very quickly. The other
nuisance to me was that I was sometimes woken by bombs and,
more often, by the barrage fired from Hyde Park.

The raids began with German punctuality. One night my messenger, Sherrington, arrived in my room at the Board of Trade
with some tea. "Hello," I said, "you're very early." "Well, Sir," he
answered rather indignantly, "the air-raid warning has just gone,"
and sure enough it was five o'clock.

One great relief to me was that my neuralgia had been traced to
a wisdom tooth, and when it had been pulled out I became a new
man. During an attack of toothache I had said something a trifle
staccato to the press, and they had fastened on to me a guardsman's
voice, and a very military or summary way of dealing with them.

Gil Lloyd George, "Crinks" Johnstone and I were holding a meet-
one afternoon with an export group, when there was a whistle and
a small bomb nearly hit Abraham Lincoln's statue just outside
the office. We looked round; the heads of our visitors were under
the substantial mahogany table, and all they presented were six or
seven pin-striped behinds.

One of the first things I was asked to do at the Board of Trade
was to prohibit the sale of silk stockings. The Department foresaw that if Japan came into the war, we should be short of silk
for parachutes and the like; moreover, there were millions of
pairs of silk stockings in stock which might be turned into dollars
or hard currency, of which we were critically short. I approved the

order and asked how the stockings in stock were to be sold. Sir Arnold Overton said that the plan was to form a corporation which would sell them and in which the owners of the stock would have shares. I said that I thought that sounded sensible, but that I would like to see the scheme when it had been worked out.

Shortly afterwards Overton told me that the representative of the Board of Trade who had been sent to explain the scheme in Leicester had had a disastrous reception. The Department had wished to try the scheme out first without bothering me.

I asked to see it; it was at least simple. A corporation was to be formed under the chairmanship of Cecil Weir[12] and the hosiery companies were to receive one share in the corporation for each pair of silk stockings which they had in stock. I was amazed at the amateurish nature of such proposals and said, with some asperity, that a bad reception for it had been a certainty. A pair of silk stockings was a quick asset. No doubt some of the companies would have borrowed money from the banks on the security of these assets. They were now to be asked—or ordered—to exchange these quick assets for a bit of paper representing a share in a Government-sponsored company without a quotation on the Stock Exchange, presided over by a Government nominee never before identified with the hosiery trade.

I asked for the services of Mr. Hector Leak, then Assistant Secretary and later Director of Statistics at the Board of Trade, and asked him to give me an estimate of the average factory cost of a pair of silk stockings. He soon produced a figure of between 3s. 9d. and 4s. 6d. per pair. I then recast the scheme: each company was to receive 4s. 6d. in cash and one share in the corporation for each pair of stockings, and the Leicester Chamber of Commerce were to nominate the Chairman. When the whole stock had been realised the corporation was to be wound up, and its assets distributed to the shareholders. I think the Department was more surprised than it should have been when the revised scheme was received with acclamation.

Government Departments when faced with practical business sometimes make elementary mistakes, of which the Silk Stocking Corporation was an example.

Another was the constitution of the Colonial Development Corporation, which bore all the marks of the amateur. It should have been made clear from the outset that the role of the Corporation was not to manage a whole jumble of projects, but to do explora-

12 The late Sir Cecil Weir.

tory work. No board of directors sitting in London can manage at once a rubber plantation in Borneo, a coal mine in Tanganyika, a poultry farm in the Gambia, a ranch in Swaziland, an hotel in Belize, a cement factory in Kenya, a shark fishery off the coast of West Africa and an abattoir in the Falkland Islands.

The right system would probably have been to form three or four development corporations, confined to specialist fields, each with a modest capital only partly called up. When one of these corporations had thoroughly explored and examined a proposition, then they should have tried to sell it to a private enterprise company, taking shares in payment for their work and risk. Neglect of these elementary principles cost the taxpayer £9 million and did a disservice to colonial development. The Labour Ministers were badly advised, and themselves had neither the knowledge nor the experience to perceive the unsoundness of the structure. After the war, when I was Secretary of State for the Colonies, I had to wrestle —with the help of Lord Reith—with what he described as "this *damnosa hereditas.*"

I began to find my feet as a Minister. At first it seems unusual that all your letters should be drafted by one of your private secretaries and that he should tap all your telephone calls. It is also rather frightening to find the weight which is attached to any minute of your own. When a file comes back, you will notice a red flag and phrases like "But see the President's minute at 32A," or, "This would not seem to carry out the President's wishes in full; consultation with the Law Officers of the Crown appears desirable," and so forth.

You soon learn not to throw pebbles into the Government pond casually or for fun; the widening circle which follows may give a lot of people a lot of work for nothing.

Civil servants start from the premise that a Minister knows nothing, and I used to be a little impatient when the A.B.C. of some financial or trading subject was spelt out, and not always in a way which my twenty years of experience would have endorsed. I can remember the stricken looks of astonishment when, in front of several of my officials, I suddenly said to some visitor who was trying to do a little log-rolling: "If those are your reasons, they are not sound ones. The whole of the charges which you say are not deductible items against your tax are in fact always so deductible. Don't come here with these complaints until you have consulted your auditors or lawyers, and have your facts right."

Panic in the Department. Great relief and some humiliating

surprise when it is confirmed that the President was correct in what he said. Any trained business man, I may add, would have known the answer.

Another worth-while rule is to ensure that the number of people whom you are to see on a deputation is closely estimated. A few days after taking office I had to receive a deputation from the Institute of Chartered Accountants. The subject to be raised was only known in outline, and because I was familiar with it, I said that I should not require a brief; moreover, I knew the two leaders of the deputation, and could handle them.

On the appointed day, one of the private secretaries came in to say that the deputation was ready in the big conference room. I walked in to find that the room was packed, that there were more than a hundred and fifty people waiting and that I was to begin by addressing them.

A week later, after I had learnt, or so I thought, by this experience, a deputation from the T.U.C.[13] was coming to see me at noon. I accordingly prepared an address in which erudition and eloquence struggled to be first, only to find that Walter Citrine[14] and Edgar Harries were the whole audience at which I could launch it.

It was soon clear to Arnold Overton and me that more could and should be squeezed out of civilian consumption, and that more production and distributive services could be released for the war. He tentatively suggested that we should ration clothes. To which I replied, "Let me know what it would save in men and materials, and if it is substantial, ration clothes we certainly will." "But don't you think it would be politically very difficult? Can you ever hope to get it through the Cabinet?" "I don't know," said I, "but if it is a sound measure, I expect we can."

We then laid out the main lines. It was, on the advice of the Department, to be the first points-rationing scheme to be introduced into this country and it had great and ingenious advantages in administration. The Board of Trade would only be concerned to ration the wholesalers, of whom there were a few hundred. The retailers, of whom there were thousands, would ration themselves.

This was brought about by imposing on the wholesalers the rule that they could only replenish their stocks by surrendering the cancelled coupons which they had obtained from their retailers. Thus if a retail shop supplied clothes without coupons, it could not get the wholesalers to re-stock its shelves, because the whole-

[13] Trades Union Congress.
[14] Now Lord Citrine.

saler himself would not have in his turn the necessary number of cancelled coupons to support his claim for further supplies.

The most difficult part of the scheme on which to form a judgement was, of course, the total number of coupons which each person should have and, within this, the weighting to be given to each coupon. If one for a handkerchief, how many for a pair of socks, or a shirt or a skirt? This in turn posed the question how much, in terms of our tentative numbers of coupons, did the lowest-paid people in the country spend each year on clothes and shoes? They should in principle be able to buy rather more than they were accustomed to, because they had no stocks to come and go on.

Mr. Leak came to see me. I asked him if he could answer the question. He said, "No." I emphasised that we must if possible avoid guessing at the number of coupons and their weighting. "I'm afraid that is inevitable," said Leak, "because I could only give you an estimate on a margin of error of about 10 per cent." I said this was quite near enough. I asked him how he was able to do even this, and it came out that for eleven years he and a lady in the Statistical Department of the Bank of England had been compiling and exchanging statistics on this very subject. Their researches proved invaluable, and we could count on our scheme resting on a sure foundation.

This incident shows how civil servants will work devotedly for years on something which they could hardly expect to be of great importance, and also what high standards of accuracy they set themselves. The scheme was perfected and polished by Watkinson, the head of the Clothing Department, and was ready for its first trial run. This meant that it had to be sponsored by me before the Lord President's Committee, the most formidable and powerful body on home affairs, and presided over by Sir John Anderson.[15]

For two long sessions of several hours he and his colleagues frisked the scheme, took it apart, fitted it together again and asked every sort of question. In the end they only made one or two minor improvements and pronounced it sound and workable.

Sir John himself showed an encyclopaedic knowledge and grasp of each and every aspect, and when he said he was satisfied and would recommend the scheme to the Cabinet, I felt a greatly renewed confidence that all was well with it.

Winston, however, would have none of it; the war, he said, would be won by the civilian population whose morale held out

[15] Afterwards Viscount Waverley.

the longest. Poor people, in rags and tatters on the bureaucratic orders of a new Minister! "Why can't you dress them like me?" meaning in boiler-suits made of the best vicuña wool, which would have taken up most of the Australian wool clip. I replied that the scheme saved 450,000 workers, either for the armed forces or for the munition factories, and that ever since Dunkirk the public were eager to make sacrifices and to be given a chance to back up the Services. "Who are you," he said, "to tell me what the public want? Why, I only picked you up out of some bucket shop in the City a few weeks ago, and what can you know about politics and public opinion? Why, you have got more stocks of cotton than when we began the war." He then reeled off some figures from a paper which had been supplied to him by the Prof. "We haven't; those figures are wrong." "Well, what are the right ones? Oh, you haven't got them with you? The Prof has given me these."

In the end the Prime Minister's figures were shown to be six months old, and it was established that we had far lower stocks than we started with. All the same, he would have none of it. "Clothing rationing! What next? Office has gone to your head. Please, please go back and look after trade, and don't try and strip the poor people to the buff."

However, I had by now powerful allies in the Lord President and Kingsley Wood, the Chancellor of the Exchequer. Even they could not move him.

The day when I wanted to launch the scheme was not far off when the hunt for the *Bismarck* began. Anderson and Kingsley Wood were waiting to see Winston on my business, and eventually got into his room at Church House. It was covered with charts, duty officers from the Admiralty were handing him reports, and he was in close touch with the First Sea Lord.

"Clothing rationing?" he rasped to these two senior Ministers. "Can't you see I'm busy? Do what you like, but please don't worry me now." John Anderson came out and said, "You can go ahead," so I rushed back to the Board of Trade and pressed the button.

When the *Bismarck* was caught and sunk, Winston wanted to return to the attack on clothes rationing, but was told that it was now too late, the machinery had begun to turn. He was not pleased, but could hardly be very angry with me; he had to round on John Anderson and the Chancellor.

We kept knowledge of the scheme to very few, not more than half a dozen until the very last moment. Then a few days before the launch I asked Lady Reading[16] and Miss Frances Farrer,[17] representatives of the two largest women's organisations, to come and see me separately, as it was upon these two women's organisations that I was relying to explain the scheme to the public.

Lady Reading, a very able administrator, came first, looked intently over the scheme and said, "It's splendid, and about time too." She then asked some rather detailed questions about the effect of the coupons upon a woman's wardrobe, which amused me and embarrassed my officials, and then pronounced herself satisfied. Miss Farrer also blessed the scheme.

I announced it in a broadcast on Whit Sunday. The advice from my Public Relations Officers was on no account to use certain phrases, one being, "It will be smart to be shabby," but I overruled them. The public response was favourable and enthusiastic.

At the eleventh hour some smart traders must have got wind of something, because on Whit Saturday there was a free market in Petticoat Lane in clothing; they thought that they had beaten the gun. In fact they had only damaged themselves, because they could not replace the stock which they had sold on Saturday without producing coupons.

About a week after I had launched the scheme I was asked to Ditchley. I came down to dinner a little late and found a party of about a dozen, including the Prime Minister, gathered in the drawing-room. "Ah," said the Prime Minister, with unconcealed satisfaction, "here's Oliver, who knows nothing of politics, who rejects the Prime Minister's views on public opinion about clothes rationing, and turns out to be right. It's been very well done, my dear, a most successful performance, and we will have an extra glass of champagne to celebrate."

This was a minor example of a major virtue, but there are very few people in my experience who have the magnanimity to be so obviously delighted when their predictions have been proved wrong and worse still when those of other people have been proved right. To Winston a success, however small, by one of the Ministers in his Government was a source of undisguised pleasure and satisfaction.

My successor at the Board of Trade eventually reduced the number of coupons and made some refinements which, as the orig-

[16] The Dowager Marchioness of Reading, head of the Women's Voluntary Services.
[17] The Hon. Frances Farrer, now the Hon. Dame Frances Farrer, General Secretary of the National Federation of Women's Institutes.

inal author of the scheme, I thought ineffective and vexatious. For instance, he did not allow men's trousers to have a turn-up; so the tailors made them a little longer, and let you turn them up yourself. "If Lyttelton chastised you with whips, I will chastise you with scorpions," was his motto. I doubt whether this was good socialism; it certainly was not good sense.

The next and even more difficult problem to be tackled concerned the waste of factory space. Severe restrictions had been imposed on such things as the manufacture of sports goods and soft drinks by withholding licences for raw materials, and now there was clothes rationing. The result was that of all the factories supplying these needs each would be working at 30% or 40% of their capacity.

Efficiency demanded that production should be concentrated in a small number of factories, and that they should be fully loaded, thus releasing whole factories for other production.

But what of the lucky company or firm whose factory was chosen? Would it not short-haul on its competitor, and get its own brand so widely accepted that it would be difficult after the war to dislodge it from its undeserved monopoly? Soft drinks afford an example of how this was overcome.

Production was concentrated in a very small number of plants, and the bottles were marked with numbers rather than with the makers' names or brands. This concentration of industry sounds simple, but in practice the administrative difficulties were great. I doubt if in any other country the scheme could have been carried through, but the manufacturers put their own interests into the background and co-operated manfully.

The Board of Trade, as I have described earlier, covered a great range, and for the President this meant many distractions from his main tasks.

Should the papers concerning this insolvent company be sent on the recommendation of the President to the Law Officers and to the Director of Public Prosecutions? A Member had raised a Motion for the Adjournment on cotton supplies. Was a Court of Inquiry into the fire and explosion at a colliery to be set on foot, although no one had been killed or injured?

All this made it hard and distracting work. My own method was to relegate to week-end reading everything that did not require action, to concentrate from Monday to Friday on execution, and to leave the week-end for general reading.

I left the Board of Trade invariably on Friday night, spent two

urs walking at Halford on Saturday and Sunday, and worked
arly all the rest of the time.

At this time Max Beaverbrook was tackling with his usual
speed and energy the task of dispersing the production of aircraft.
The Board of Trade worked itself into a great lather about the
requisitioning of factories and a rumour even gained some currency that officials of the Ministry of Aircraft Production were
requisitioning the first factories which they saw in the Birmingham area. The rumour was born of fear and not of fact. Max was
asking "very much in order to get a little" and was threatening to
requisition the B.B.C. and to store aircraft in Winchester Cathedral. There were some departmental clashes but my dynamic colleague achieved his object and fulfilled his dictums that "organisation is the enemy of improvisation," and "Committees take the
punch out of war."

He succeeded in a short time in making the aircraft industry
much less vulnerable to air attack, and the departmental difficulties were soon sorted out by the establishment, under the Board of
Trade, of the Factory and Storage Control with Philip Warter[18] as
its head.

I have described shortly the administrative and office side of my
life. I began to feel at home. I did not, however, become a Member
of Parliament for nearly a month, and dreaded the day when I
should have to answer questions in the House and make a maiden
speech.

Brendan Bracken, hearing that Lord Windlesham had put me
no higher than the short list at the Wrekin, intervened with Winston. The Member for Aldershot at this time was Lord Wolmer,
and his father, Lord Selborne, was old and in failing health. It
was felt in any case that he would succeed his father before long,
and be translated to the House of Lords. Winston made "Top"
Wolmer a peer in his own right and he thus vacated the safe seat
at Aldershot.

I was duly grateful, but not as grateful as I should have been.
The possession of a safe seat is not merely a comfort to a Minister
which enables him to pursue his duties without anxiety, but it is
also the very bed-rock of a political career. When judging between
two candidates for office, a Prime Minister in the old days would
select the one with a safe seat, with less qualifications, than the
one with greater qualifications but with a small majority. This was
because appointment to Ministerial rank involved an immediate

[18] Now Sir Philip Warter.

by-election. Today, the safe seat has less importance because the new Minister has not to seek re-election, but it has some since a Prime Minister does not wish his senior colleagues to be defeated at a General Election, and if they were, be obliged to select his Ministers from the depleted ranks of those who have survived.

It is also much easier to kick a man upstairs to the House of Lords when the resulting by-election seems likely to be marked "No change."

I was in due course returned unopposed for Aldershot, and held the seat without difficulty, and with increasing majorities throughout my political life. It was an ideal seat, and reachable from London in a little over an hour. My constituents did not expect or exact regular attendance at many meetings. Whenever I went there, I could be sure of being entertained by kindly and agreeable hosts.

As President of the Board of Trade, and now Member for Aldershot, I had joined the small and select club of those who made their maiden speeches from the Front Bench. In those days it included Anderson, Duncan, Bevin, Grigg and me in the Commons, and Woolton, Leathers and Cherwell in the Lords.

I had had no experience whatever of public speaking, had never been inside the Union at Cambridge and had never made anything but an after-dinner speech, which is quite a separate art.

My first speeches as a member of the Government could not, as I was assured by my friends at the time, have been worse. Some of my early failures and deficiencies as a speaker were due to the mistaken idea that writing and speaking in public are allied arts. It is true that sometimes both, though increasingly seldom, make use of the English language, but there the similarity ends.

If an author dictates to a secretary, he is nearly always astonished to hear the result read back to him. A passage which seemed terse, cogent, forceful in conversation sounds slipshod, discursive and repetitive when it is committed to paper. Equally, read out a written passage to a large audience, and you will quickly get the feeling that they have not grasped it, and as likely as not are thoroughly bored.

Soon after joining the Government I had to go and make a speech to three or four hundred people at the L.C.C.; a luncheon-time address by a Minister to tired office workers. There was a distinguished "platform," and when I had finished I saw Lord Bennett beckoning to me. "I was a friend of your father," he said, "and, Oliver, you may have, I believe you will have, a political future, but you should know that in all my life, and after all I have been a

Prime Minister for quite a time, that is the worst public speech I have ever heard. You must do something about it."

I was genuinely grateful for the trouble which he had taken to discharge this painful duty. So I said, "I will. What do I do?" "Well, you must take lessons in elocution. You must make a speech almost every day, and you must study the technique."

I did all these, and I was given some tips about the art which helped me greatly, though certainly not quickly. Some of them Winston told me himself:

"Lloyd George said: 'The art of public speaking is the art of dilution.' Mr. Gladstone said: 'Say what you are going to say, then say it, and then say that you have said it.' The House is not particularly interested in argument; it is nearly always interested in narrative. Lord Hugh Cecil[19] said: 'Begin at the beginning and end at the end.' Figures must never be used as an argument, only to illustrate one. Gestures must precede the point to be emphasised, never follow it. Point a threatening finger and say, 'Those are the guilty men,' and not 'Those are the guilty men' and then point the finger."

The most useful of all these tips are those of Lloyd George and Mr. Gladstone: the larger the audience, the greater must be the dilution. I experimented to prove it. I tried out a phrase. "I now turn to wider subjects. Peace is not a thing like sleep. It won't come to you by lying down and shutting your eyes." I fired this without much "lead in" or preparation at two thousand people. The reaction was nothing. The next night I tried it again to as large an audience, but this time with dilution. "I now turn away from the home scene to world affairs. These are anxious times, ladies and gentlemen. Many of us have anxieties. Many housewives and mothers are anxious lest the rations are not enough to keep their children fully nourished. I am anxious myself, as the head of a great Department. I expect some of you get, at times, so anxious that you can't sleep; it happens to me; it may get so bad that you send for the doctor. He says to you, 'Now, dear patient, relax; lie down, shut your eyes.' If you take his advice perhaps one of God's greatest gifts, sleep that 'knits up the ravell'd sleave of care,' will come to you, and you will awake refreshed to face the trials of the morrow. But let me tell you, ladies and gentlemen, that peace is not a thing like sleep. It won't come to you by lying down and shutting your eyes; it will only come if you make your sacrifices, stand up and fight your corner, and if you never give in."

[19] Afterwards Lord Quickswood.

The difference in the impact can hardly be exaggerated.

Of course, there are natural speakers, who know these things instinctively, like Violet Bonham Carter, whose skill—through the perversity of selection committees or the electorate—the House of Commons has never been privileged to enjoy. Others have developed their inherent gifts; some, I suspect, by addressing themselves as if they were public meetings even in their morning bath; others by treating their friends as if they were public meetings. I have even known Winston on occasions to adopt the second of these methods.

As I have said, it was only slowly that I began to learn the rudiments of public speaking. In addition to this handicap, I was new to the House. A year or two's experience of it is almost essential to a Minister; this experience must extend to acquaintance or friendship with individual members, some knowledge of those whom the House respects, however bizarre their views may be on a particular subject or on a particular afternoon: those who can be put down firmly and those who must be put down gently if you wish to have the House with you.

Above all, it is necessary to grow the antennae which enable you to guess the mood of this changeable and chameleon-like assembly. One day it will take a joke, on another the slightest levity will be greeted with a snarl. I remember much later in my Ministerial life a day when the Government Whips thought the debate on a particular clause was going to be prolonged. They estimated that we should be lucky "to get the clause" by 9:30, and accordingly let some Members leave for an early dinner. However, during Question Time a lady Member phrased an innocent supplementary in words which the House quickly realised to have a highly improper second meaning. An atmosphere of hilarity continued for some time. It was said that that afternoon the House would have passed a resolution to reduce Members' salaries, and the Government "got the clause" much earlier than the embarrassed Whips had calculated.

I believe I was an unusual, perhaps a unique, example of a Member whose maiden speech was received with interruption and obvious dislike. This oration was during the Committee stage of the War Damage Bill. The Bill was in two parts, the first relating to the insurance of property against war damage, the second to that of chattels. The Chancellor of the Exchequer had introduced the second reading, and had been in charge of the Committee stages of the first part. I was in charge of the second.

It was a complicated measure, of a kind never before dreamed of, with all sorts of technical and actuarial difficulties. When I rose to move that the first clause of the second section "stand part," I hardly thought that I could claim, as a Minister, the indulgence of the House, and did not do so. However, I was interrupted on an actuarial point to which I had no immediate answer. I accordingly replied that I would look at the point before the Report stage and try to meet the Hon. Member who had raised it. I did not know, or had not remembered, that the Chancellor had given more than two dozen such assurances on his part of the Bill, and the House was not having any more of it. So I had a rough passage, there was no lady Member to come to my rescue, and my confidence as a Parliamentarian was hardly reinforced by this experience.

On another occasion I had to address a committee of the Conservative Party on coal, and had had no time to prepare a speech, indeed I had hardly realised that an introductory speech was expected. I stumbled along for ten minutes or so, and then the meeting was open to questions.

Almost the first Member to rise was General Jeffreys,[20] the Member for Petersfield, whose Adjutant I had been in the first war. I felt my knees stiffen to the reflex of Grenadier discipline, and only just remembered that I was a Minister. He asked whether it was fair that miners should receive wages so far in excess of those of a fighting soldier. This was, I suppose, a half-volley, but I only took a single off it out of respect to the questioner.

However, this apologia for my shortcomings may be tempered by my claim to have had the most arresting supplementary question asked of me during the life of that Parliament. Some shortage of india-rubber teats to put on babies' milk bottles had been reported, and Mr. J. D. Murray, the Labour Member for Spennymoor, a burly miner and a good fellow, had a Question on the Paper[21]: "To ask the President of the Board of Trade when mothers in the Spennymoor Division will be able to purchase babies' soothers; is he aware that some months ago Hon. Members were assured that supplies would be available in the shops and up to the present time none has been available to retailers or the general public."

Mr. Lyttelton: The Hon. Member is perhaps under a misapprehension and is confusing soothers with teats. I have every sympathy with him. Soothers, however, are a means of deception to which, in view of the

[20] Afterwards Lord Jeffreys.
[21] Hansard: June 5th, 1945.

imminence of the General Election and the present scarcity of rubber, His Majesty's Government cannot lend themselves. The assurances that he, no doubt, has in mind were given in respect of teats, and have been carried out.

Mr. Murray: Is the Minister aware that his answer makes the position still more ridiculous? It does happen to be a question of teats. I have a letter saying that a woman has given birth to twins, and that she is unable to feed these two children with one teat.

In all the offices of state which I have held, and in the companies which I have managed, I have carried on a campaign against official English, periphrasis and genteel synonyms. I have nearly always been defeated. It is curious that young men, fresh from the university with first-class honours in the humanities, after they enter the Civil Service often become infected with some blight, which attacks the bloom of their English and turns the English rose into a fly-blown weed.

Some words and phrases assume the character of an occupational disease, or rather of an epidemic. An example which will occur to many is the word "basis." This wretched old jade is brought out to pull vehicles for which it was never intended: "Society is founded on the family basis." "The negotiations were carried on on the basis that if they were not successfully concluded, a new conference would be called." Why not: "Society is founded on the family," and "If the conference failed, a new conference was to be called." "Basis" is now threadbare and worn out and, together with "viable," should be given a rest.

"When due consideration has been given to the fact that" is not an eloquent periphrasis for "because"; it is merely foul and prolix.

Once a man gets his cheque, he will probably forgive you if you say that he has been "paid" and not "remunerated."

"It may well be" has been debased into an insurance policy to guard against the impossible turning up. It adds something to the security of the writer, but seldom anything to the sense.

We are all offenders; we are all guilty of adding to the mass of verbiage. In 1940, in a spirit of some levity, I addressed a Christmas message to the Board of Trade on this subject. It ended: "While it would be indeed startling and inappropriate to find amongst the correspondence a sentence like: 'Consider the lilies of the field how they grow; they toil not neither do they spin; . . . yet even Solomon in all his glory was not arrayed like one of these,' on the other hand, I think without incurring a charge of being precious, we might avoid this sort of thing: 'When due consideration has been given to the fact that the target programme of the Lily Group has been achieved with virtually no drain upon the manual labour pool and without taxing in any way even the surplus spindle situation, it is noteworthy that the natural product may be said, without qualification, to surpass both in saleability and export-ability the highest grade woven textiles as supplied to the Jewish Royal Family.'

"As a postscript I should like to add that the word 'file' has more than one meaning. Files are not only the sepulchres of our past writings, but are also instruments which can be used to pare away and to eliminate what is superfluous. In the last sense they should form part of our mental equipment."

CHAPTER XII

THE MIDDLE EAST: I

A FURTHER CHANGE was about to take place in my life. I was shortly to become a member of the War Cabinet and Minister of State in Cairo.

Some review of the war and the political situation in the Middle East which led to my appointment is necessary before the reasons for it can be understood.

In February 1941, for the first time in a land battle, the gleam of victory had touched and burnished British arms.

We were to learn later in the year that "the wings of Opportunity are fledged with the feathers of Death." [1]

General Wavell's[2] brilliant campaign in the Western Desert, culminating with the coup at Beda Fomm, had crushed the Italians. A week after the 130,000 prisoners had been herded into the cages, a decision was reached to "secure the flank" in Cyrenaica, and to build up forces in Egypt for a campaign in Greece and the Dodecanese.[3] I believed at that time, and I still believe, that this decision was mistaken. It violated one of my dearly held military tenets that in war you should rarely whip hounds off a hunted fox.

It is significant that at this very moment a new actor appeared on the scene. General Rommel arrived in Tripoli on February 12th. Soon much larger forces would clearly be needed to meet the new threat, which would be backed up by German formations. On the other hand reinforcements could probably be released before long

[1] Drake to Queen Elizabeth I.
[2] Afterwards Field-Marshal Earl Wavell.
[3] Major-General I. S. O. Playfair, *History of the Second World War, Mediterranean and the Middle East* (London: H.M.S.O., 1954), Vol. I.

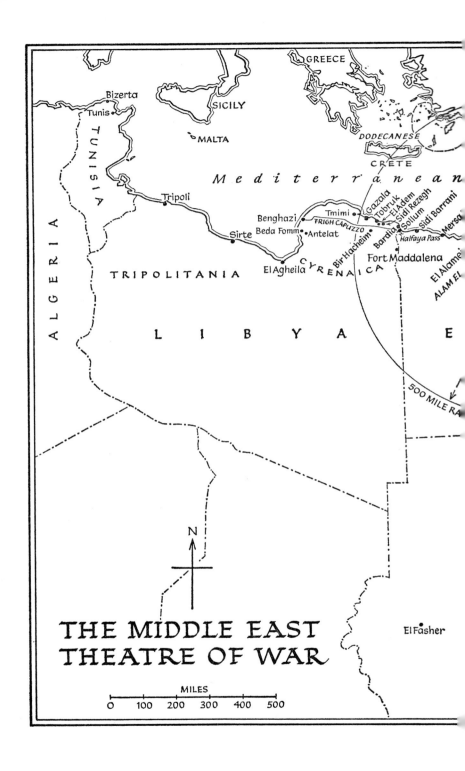

GREECE

SICILY

MALTA

DODECANESE

CRETE

Mediterranean

Bizerta
Tunis

TUNISIA

Tripoli

Gazala
Tobruk
ElAdem
Benghazi   Tmimi   Sidi Rezegh
TRIGH CAPUZZO   Solium   Sidi Barrani
Sirte   Beda Fomm   Antelat   Bardia   Mersa
ALGERIA   Halfaya Pass

Bir Hacheim   Fort Maddalena

El Agheila   CYRENAICA   El Alame
ALAM EL

TRIPOLITANIA

L   I   B   Y   A   E

500 MILE RA

N

THE MIDDLE EAST
THEATRE OF WAR   El Fasher

MILES

0   100   200   300   400   500

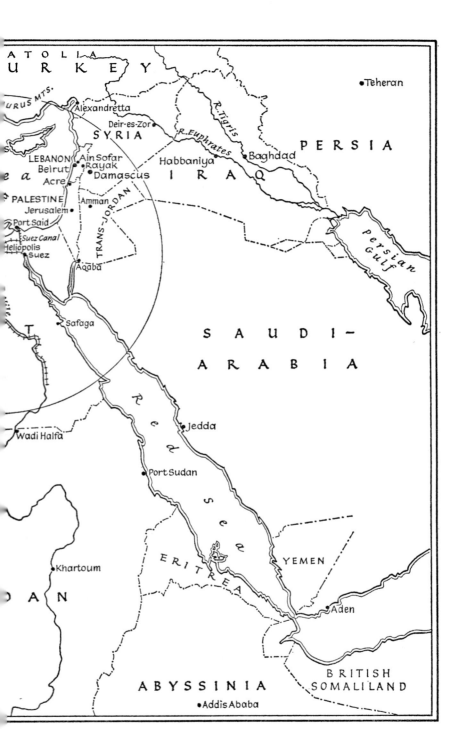

from Ethiopia and Kenya, where General Cunningham[4] and the guerilla leader, Colonel Wingate,[5] were gaining some striking successes.

The Emperor entered Ethiopia on February 23rd. Mogadishu in Somaliland fell to us on the 25th.

The reasons for supporting Greece and not sitting by and letting the Balkans be swallowed up piecemeal, with the consequent reaction upon Turkey, were powerful, but to my mind they should have been discarded. Moreover, the order to secure a flank in Cyrenaica was easier to give than to carry out. It is pertinent to remember that General Wavell's victory had been won by a mere two divisions, that his supply lines were already stretched to the limit and that his mechanical equipment was in need of overhaul.

After the decision about the Greek campaign, no more than a screen could be spared to protect the western flank.[6] General Gariboldi, the successor of Marshal Graziani, had chosen the Sirte position upon which to rebuild his army and to await German reinforcements; his dispositions had been endorsed by General Rommel.

If our defensive strength was no more than a screen, it followed that we could not advance to threaten Sirte.

It thus seemed to me that we were about to throw to the winds the fruits of our victory in Cyrenaica, where, temporarily at least, the odds were in our favour, and to commit ourselves to the mainland of Europe, where the odds were overwhelmingly against us. At this time the Germans disposed of about 180 divisions which had just overrun the whole of Western Europe. They were flushed with victory, and had confidence that their tactics and armaments were invincible; they were led and served by commanders and staff of high professional skill, who had tested their theories in battle and turned them into one of the greatest victories in the history of arms.

The 180 divisions were uncommitted, poised for offensive warfare and seeking something to destroy. No immediate enemy confronted them, though their leaders were soon to create one. To land about 80,000 men, barely two effective divisions, on the Continent of Europe in face of this towering strength, however good a defensive position could be found, appeared to me to flout every military principle and to court disaster. Admittedly the Olympus or Aliakmon position, well known to students of strategy, was a

---

[4] General Sir Alan Cunningham.
[5] Afterwards Major-General Orde Wingate.
[6] *Vide* General Wavell's instructions to General Neame, *op. cit.*, Vol. II.

strong one, but apart from the three gaps through which an enemy might debouch, it could always be turned by the Monastir-Florina valley.

If the campaign did not prove a miracle but the certain disaster which I expected, would the effect upon Greece and Turkey be any better than if we had not intervened? No wonder that Mr. Churchill and Mr. Eden were perplexed and hesitant.

General Wilson,[7] who had been appointed to the Command, was told at the outset of the campaign that we were too far committed by our promises to withdraw from Greece altogether. He rated the chances of holding the Aliakmon position as low, and at once called for a reconnaissance of the Thermopylae line, which he judged could be defended without Greek assistance.[8]

It has afterwards been claimed that the diversion to Greece delayed the launching of the German offensive against Russia by a month.

It seems clear that three factors in order of importance caused the delay: first the *coup d'état* in Belgrade, secondly our intervention in Greece and thirdly the weather. On the last of the three, General Müller-Hillebrand, former adjutant to the Chief of the German General Staff, has written: "Operation Barbarossa could not possibly have started on 15th May because spring came late in 1941. As late as the beginning of June, the Polish-Russian river valleys were still flooded and partly impassable as a result of exceptionally heavy rains." [9]

It is also claimed (although I have been unable to trace any evidence) that Rashid Ali received no German help, because our unexpected intervention in the Balkans had confused German plans.

Even if our adventure was a contributing cause of the German delay, would not further victories in the Western Desert have served us better and produced a greater diversion of enemy troops? This point of view is supported if we remember Hitler's subsequent reaction to our successes in Tripolitania and Tunisia at a time when he was more strained than in June 1941.

In the event, the Greeks suffered all the penalties of their courage.

At this time, from the backwater of the Board of Trade, I used

[7] General Sir Henry Maitland Wilson, now Field Marshal Lord Wilson.
  [8] Letter to the author.
  [9] *The German Campaign in the Balkans,* a study written by General Müller-Hillebrand for the Office of the Chief of Military History, Department of the Army. (Published in the U.S., 1950.)

idly to wonder what would have been my duty if I had been Secretary of State for War.

Certainly it would have been to oppose the Greek adventure, in which I could not bring myself to believe, but seeing that I should have been in a subordinate position, how far should this opposition have been carried? To the point of resignation? Resignation would certainly have been ineffective.

I now ceased to regret the chance of being at the War Office, a chance which would probably have seen the end of me as a Minister.

The finger moved on. In April we were thrown out of Greece and had to abandon the Greeks to the full wrath and reprisals of the Germans.

A month later we suffered an even more bitter defeat in Crete. Our troops were almost entirely New Zealanders, led by my friend and brother officer, Bernard Freyberg, V.C.[10] The only fruits of their gallantry were that the Germans rated the cost of the conquest of Crete as too high and this induced doubts about whether airborne operations against Malta would succeed.

To us in London, the loss of Crete appeared grievous. It deprived us of a naval refuelling point between Alexandria and Malta, but, worse still, it brought the Nile Delta within the effective range of enemy bombers. Benghazi is more than 650 miles from Cairo; the nearest enemy airfields in Tripolitania were 750 or 800 miles away. Crete was a little over 400.

The Navy had also been hard hit and had suffered grave losses from bombs and torpedoes in evacuating the troops from Greece and Crete.

Rommel started to probe the western flank. He "appreciated," to use the technical term, that the British had no offensive intentions for the present and indeed seemed to be thinning out their front. He was soon urging upon the Italians an offensive to clear Cyrenaica and throw the British back to the frontiers of Egypt.

He struck in April. We abandoned Benghazi on April 3rd, 1941, Generals Neame and O'Connor were unluckily captured on the 7th, and on May 27th the Germans recaptured the Halfaya Pass. By a grim coincidence, this was the very day when it was decided to evacuate Crete.

Finally a word is necessary about the situation that had developed on our northern flank. At the beginning of March a political convulsion shook Iraq. On March 31st the Regent fled from Bagh-

[10] Now General Lord Freyberg, V.C.

dad, and Rashid Ali, in the pay of the Axis, seized power on April 3rd. At the end of April, Habbaniya, our air force base, was besieged, but owing to quick action and some audacious bluff by Air Vice-Marshal Smart the danger was quickly under control. Habforce entered Iraq and an armistice was signed on May 31st.

In May, too, the Germans had begun to use Syria for supporting the revolt in Iraq, and we suspected, and rightly, their intention of making Syria and Iraq into a running sore.[11] It was accordingly decided on the 19th to prepare a force for the invasion of Syria with the aid of the Free French.

The soldiers and General Wavell had demurred, but on this occasion, as on some others, they were overruled, and in the event Mr. Churchill's strategical and political judgement was to prove correct.

General Wilson was appointed to command these operations. He found himself once again with insufficient troops to be able to guarantee success. The campaign which he directed, however, was crowned with victory.

Such, in broad terms, was the military situation at the time of my appointment. Disaster in Greece and Crete; the Delta within range of German bombers and the army thrown back behind the Halfaya Pass; military success in Iraq; the campaign against the Vichy French in the balance.

Some account of political events and the political outlook must be added.

The Middle East at this time presented political problems of great complexity. Our allies, the Free French, under General de Gaulle, were still smarting under the humiliation of Dakar. They thought, with some justification, that they were not being treated with the frank confidence which should flow between allies. The reason for our reserve was partly because their "security" over Dakar had proved fragile.

The Free French also feared a pan-Arab policy by the British and suspected that we had designs upon Syria and the Lebanon. The Vichy French appeared ready to offer facilities to the Germans in Syria and the Lebanon. French rule in these countries was hated, as it always had been, but was no longer so much feared.

[11] Hitler's directive No. 30 on the Middle East, e.g. Propaganda will be based on the following fundamental idea: "Victory by the Axis powers will liberate the lands of the Middle East from the British yoke and give them the right of self-determination (except Syria)." Playfair, *op. cit.,* Vol. II, Appendix 2.

The attitude of all the Arab states was doubtful. They were united in their hatred of British-protected Zionism.

Our dealings with the Jewish Agency were uneasy and our general security in Palestine rested more upon military strength than upon any consent of the inhabitants to the existing régime.

The great controversies about the extent and nature of the Zionist state were always hanging over us, though kept in the background. Zionist terrorism was being matured; it led to the murder of Lord Moyne, the Deputy Minister of State, in Cairo on November 6th, 1944.

Iraq was still unstable. Egypt was, it is true, calm. King Farouk, however, was unpopular with his fellow rulers and the Palace Government under Hussein Sirry Pasha, the King's uncle by marriage and a true friend of Great Britain, was far from commanding any popular support. Persia and the Persian Gulf were insecure. As a vital source of oil supplies they were a particularly tender spot. Finally the occupation, after some brilliant military operations conducted by General Cunningham, of Italian Eritrea and the liberation of Ethiopia, both of which territories after victory had come under British military government, were likely to throw up some acute political dilemmas. Our relations with the Emperor were strained. His word at this time did not run further than about forty miles from Addis Ababa. He was suspicious and remained aloof until he became convinced that we were determined to fulfil our promises.

It can be seen from this broad survey that the political, no less than the military, scene was confused. The C.-in-C. Middle East, General Wavell, who had to conduct a campaign in the Western Desert as well as to secure himself from an incursion from the north, was harassed by a host of political conundrums for the solution of which he had neither the experience nor, for that matter, the inclination.

The Cabinet, moreover, was dissatisfied with the supply services of the Army: the Egyptian ports were becoming acutely congested; mountains of motor vehicles in wooden crates were piling up on the quays; insufficient use appeared to be made of resources which could be obtained or improvised locally. The strain on our shipping was at breaking point. In face of these manifold problems, many of which were outside the military field, General Wavell had already asked for the appointment of a Minister to bring him some relief.

Randolph Churchill, the Prime Minister's son, had freely expressed his view on these subjects to the Ambassador. To say that Randolph is no respecter of persons would be a flaccid understatement; he is by nature critical of authority and vociferous in denouncing its mistakes. On June 7th, 1941, Randolph sent his father a short telegram suggesting that a Minister of Cabinet rank should be sent out to relieve the C.-in-C. of a number of responsibilities. Averell Harriman,[12] who had been in the theatre, and the Ambassador supported the idea.

At the time I knew little of this, and was immersed, as President of the Board of Trade, in the administration of clothes rationing, in organising the concentration of production and civilian supplies in general.

One day—it was a Tuesday—the Prime Minister asked me to go and dine alone with him in his flat in the War Cabinet offices, overlooking St. James's Park. I looked forward keenly to this dinner because I knew I should be given some information about our fortunes in the war and some insight into the Prime Minister's views and plans.

The setting for our *tête-à-tête* was as usual. A small dinner table; a bottle of champagne; one servant; the Prime Minister himself in a boiler-suit fresh from his bath, hungry and relaxed. A marine or two guarded the passage outside.

Almost at once he started to develop the theme of the Middle East. He ended up reading me Randolph's telegram and informed me that he destined me for the job of Minister of State with membership of the War Cabinet. Was I prepared to go? And Moira? This hardly needed a reply, but I said that if offered the post I should eagerly accept.

He chaffed me about my prospects as Satrap of the Middle East, of "holding the gorgeous East in fee," and said that he would consult his colleagues in the War Cabinet on the next day. At this time they were Eden and Beaverbrook on the Conservative side, Attlee, Bevin and Morrison[13] on the Labour side, and John Anderson, who was an Independent M.P.

When I learned that the matter had not yet been before the Cabinet, I was not unduly exhilarated by my prospects of being given the post. In the last few months, I had already been told

[12] Special representative of the President of the United States in Great Britain.
[13] Now Lord Morrison of Lambeth.

twice, once categorically, that I was to be Secretary of State for War, and had been disappointed. I had been also seriously considered as Ambassador in Washington. Nothing had come of either of these proposed appointments. I thought that the War Cabinet would not be in favour of Winston's scheme, and as I stumbled off in the black-out to my flat in Park Lane I determined not to set my hopes too high. However, on the next day, June 28th, 1941, I was again asked to dinner and told that the War Cabinet had warmly approved of my appointment and that I therefore sat down to dinner as a member of the War Cabinet and Minister of State in the Middle East.

"When do I start?" I asked.

"Tomorrow, or the day after," he rapped out.

"That," I said, "is impossible. The Board of Trade is a big department. I must be there to hand it over to my successor. Moreover, I must have some staff with me in the Middle East. I shall clearly need a *chef de cabinet* to organise my office, and someone from the Foreign Office on the political front, and of course a private secretary."

After some discussions and admonitions about blowing up my office into a great Nile bull-frog, he granted me a short delay.

The next morning, I discussed with Edward Bridges[14] head of the Treasury and of the Civil Service, my needs for staff and the possible candidates. I shall always be deeply grateful to Anthony Eden and Alec Cadogan that they gave me Henry Hopkinson[15] to be my Foreign Office man. He was at that time Alec Cadogan's private secretary, and was charged with a number of special and secret duties. I dare say that the pain of parting with him from the office was partly mitigated by the feeling that they gained a trained Foreign Office man with full professional qualifications to be at the side of the new Minister of State. Be that as it may, they were both most co-operative and helpful and did not even go through the customary drill, beloved of Government departments and, for that matter, of military formations, of offering the man whom they could most readily spare.

The *chef de cabinet* was a more difficult matter. Eventually I saw and liked greatly Mr. A. N. Rucker,[16] the Deputy Secretary to the Ministry of Health. It was true that he had no experience of foreign affairs, was not widely travelled and was more of an

[14] Now Lord Bridges.
[15] Now Lord Colyton.
[16] Now Sir Arthur Rucker.

administrator than a political adviser. He was, however, a man of saint-like character and of great ability. He was calm and conscientious. I learnt later that when he put his foot down, he trod on no one's toes, and his decisions did not lead to discussion and resentment.

Lastly, I decided to take with me Harry Lintott,[17] who was my private secretary at the Board of Trade. I had got to know him and like him. He was rapid and clever, knew my prejudices and methods of working, and had a happy sense of humour allied to a certain disenchantment with his fellow-men.

Physically these three differed greatly. Arthur Rucker was small and spare with strong spectacles. Henry Hopkinson, with Eton and Foreign Office written all over him, had beautiful manners and faultless clothes; he was calm and balanced. He, too, was fond of a joke, even at solemn moments. He became, and remains, a great friend.

Harry Lintott in earlier life had been described by a gushing Chelsea lady in these terms:

"My dear, I've got a a *wonderful* new friend: he looks like the drowned Shelley and is something in the Customs."

Anyway, I was devoted to him, and if I sometimes thought that he inclined towards Bloomsbury I hardly thought that this predilection would survive in face of our task and of the earthy nature of his chief.

Parting with the children was a searing moment. Moira and I left Halford Manor and Warwickshire with the feelings, shared at that time by so many of our compatriots, that everything was uncertain beyond the passing minute. Exciting though the new appointment and the new scene might be, we should be cut off, perhaps for the whole war, from our own family; we should not feel the heartbeat of our country at the time of its greatest danger and of its greatest hour.

Action to me is the only anodyne of anxiety and strain and we were to get much of it.

We motored over at dusk to dine with the Prime Minister at Chequers. After dinner we saw, not for the first time, the film of Nelson and Emma Hamilton. It was the Prime Minister's favourite film, and he himself must have seen it half a dozen times. At midnight he turned on the news and my appointment was mentioned.[18] He thought the announcement put Moira and me in more

[17] Now Sir Henry Lintott.
[18] The official date of my appointment was July 1st, 1941.

danger on our journey. He was extremely angry, and vowed he would visit his rage on someone. He regarded risk to himself as something to be entirely ignored, but showed deep anxiety about the risks to which he exposed others.

"I may be sending you to your death," he said.

We left the next day for Plymouth by train; my mother saw us off, and with us were Arthur Rucker, Henry Hopkinson and Harry Lintott. One of the pleasures of travelling is often forgotten in retrospect. As a train clanks out of the station, or when you unfasten your seat belt in an aeroplane, or when a ship starts to live and creak as she gets under way, you feel that you are in suspension, that for a while you have time at bay. I had this restful and disembodied sensation as we drew out of Waterloo. I put my feet up and, while green England started to slip by, turned to review my task with at least the consolation that I had a few days in which to find the first answers and to plan the opening gambits.

Elsewhere, I have described how the Prime Minister could clothe in glamour the task for which he destined you and how he made you feel that you were to be one of the leading actors on the great stage. His anaesthetics did not wear off quickly at any time; and in the feverish rush and hustle of collecting a staff and making my preparations I was still drugged and had had little time to think of the problems confronting me, much less of any working method by which they might be overcome. I was a member of the War Cabinet, its representative and projection, so to speak, in the Middle East, although my duties extended far beyond the geographical limits of such a term. I was the highest authority on the spot, but the emphasis and the limitations lay in the words "on the spot."

The Middle Eastern theatre embraced a huge area. It extended to the frontiers of Turkey in the north, to East Africa and Kenya in the south, to Persia and the Persian Gulf in the east and to the borders of Cyrenaica in the west. It thus included Iraq, Syria and Lebanon, Palestine, Egypt, the Sudan, Saudi Arabia, Eritrea, Ethiopia, British and Italian Somaliland and Cyprus.

A number of different Ministers were answerable to Parliament either for a particular country or a particular function which covered them all. Each Minister at home was backed by a department staffed by large numbers of skilled and trained civil servants. My staff was three. The principal Minister involved other than the Prime Minister was, of course, the Foreign Secretary. He was responsible for foreign policy generally, and in the Middle East for our relations with the sovereign powers of Egypt, Iraq and Persia, with the Free French and with the Arab world in general. He would shortly be concerned with the Vichy French in Syria and the Lebanon and, as soon as military government ended, with Eritrea and Ethiopia. Ambassadors answerable to him were entrenched in Egypt, Persia and Iraq; Ministers or Residents reported to him from Jedda and Amman, the Spears Mission acted for him in some of our relations with the Free French. Similarly, the Colonial Office was responsible for Kenya, Palestine and Cyprus. The Ministry of Transport was charged with the over-all control of shipping and ports, the Ministry of Economic Warfare with the denial of supplies to the enemy, the Ministry of Information with propaganda, the Board of Trade with certain trade matters, such as the purchase of Egyptian cotton.

Finally, the three Commanders-in-Chief were responsible to the three Service Ministers and through them to the Minister of Defence, the Prime Minister himself.

How was I to work? How, with a staff of three, could I join issue with the least important of these Ministries? How was I to fulfil my duties without cutting across the manifold responsibilities of my Cabinet colleagues at home? Yet I was the highest authority on the spot, and even if I remained passive, questions would be asked, guidance and decisions sought.

I summed up to myself by thinking, "If I am the highest authority on the spot, in the strict interpretation of these words, I am no authority at all." After a lot of thought I reached the conclusion that I must work on the plan or system of trying to persuade the various representatives of the various Ministries to send home a single, agreed recommendation on all the subjects with which I was concerned and with the oversight of which I was charged. I should stand in a favourable posture, unless challenged, to obtain the agreement of their local representatives, who would remain in some uncertainty about how my relations stood with, say, the Colonial Office or the War Office. It would be difficult for Ministers to set aside from London what their own representatives had recommended in concert with others in Cairo. Without instructions from home they might think it impolitic to oppose or obstruct a Minister who, on paper, appeared to have an overriding mandate.

In fact, this was how I worked. No one on the spot ever really challenged my authority. Ministers at home found some comfort in receiving agreed recommendations which, from their nature, could easily be cleared with other Ministers. Above all, it was war, and we were all members of the same Government. Finally, when

Ministers held appointments junior to my own, they hesitated to pull the nose of one who, from his office, was a member of the body in which ultimate authority lay, and before which they could be held to account. There was no other Cabinet except the War Cabinet; no collective responsibility was engaged for others, who were only Ministers of Cabinet rank, a constitutional point which is often forgotten.

Towards the end of my eight months in the Middle East it was quite clear that my relations with the Foreign Office were bearing the greatest strain or, in other words, the constitutional anomalies created by the office of Minister of State were more patent and more embarrassing in the field of foreign affairs than in others. Anthony Eden was patient and forbearing, but he must at times have been inclined to send me a telegram to keep off his grass altogether.

Arrived at Plymouth, we were greeted with surprise by the Admiral, Sir Charles Forbes, who had been given to understand that the V.I.P. who was arriving was the Empress of Ethiopia, and Moira did not appear to him at first sight to answer the description. The Admiral gave us dinner. About nine o'clock, the Prime Minister rang me up on the scrambler. He only wanted to say some warm words about the confidence which he reposed in me and to wish us a safe passage.

We went on board our Sunderland flying-boat, which was equipped for war and not for passengers. The seats were hard and upright, but the cabin was roomy and you could stretch out on the floor. The crew were entirely Australian and they would have given confidence to a neurotic.

We took off about 10 P.M., and the crew fired a few bursts into the sea from the seven machine-gun positions to see that all was in order, and as an old machine-gun officer I was glad to note the precaution. The crew then turned to the important matter of a meal; they needed it, we did not. They brewed some very strong tea, peeled a whole clutch of onions and made a stew which would have fed a platoon.

We got some sleep on the floor and as soon as dawn touched the windows and turned them from black to silver I went into the pilot's cabin to see the coast of Spain and Gibraltar coming up ahead as the silver turned to gold. At first an apparently limitless expanse of grey laminated clouds with white peaks here and there stretched below us. Then the rays of the rising sun struck them and a majestic view of cloud and sea and rock was revealed.

We landed and went to Government House. Lord Gort, V.C., a brother officer and "Fat Boy" Gort to every Grenadier, was the Governor. He had thrown himself wholeheartedly into his new work and was engaged with boundless energy in improving the galleries and defences of the Rock. After breakfast, I clambered round after him on his tour of inspection. Besides being the bravest of leaders in battle he was a highly professional soldier, an ex-instructor at the Staff College and ex-Commander of the B.E.F. We afterwards found time for a long talk about the German Army, the tank battle, tactics, equipment and other military subjects.

At luncheon, he told us that two Spanish duchesses of his acquaintance were coming to tea. They were charming ladies, he explained, but we must be guarded in what we said in front of them. Ladies of fashion were apt to talk and they might even stand well enough in the eyes of the Spanish Government to be asked to pass on anything of interest. They turned out to be pretty and vivacious, asked us how long we were staying and, when we untruthfully replied "a few days," arranged a picnic for the Governor and us at Algeciras, which I am sure would have been enchanting. They both said they were much pressed for time and must leave almost at once. They hurried away. Arthur Rucker went back much later to the hotel in the town where he was living and returned, his hair standing on end, to say that one of the duchesses was still locked in the telephone booth. I feel sure that her call was to her chef about the *béarnaise*.

The next evening we took off for Malta and arrived without incident at Government House. The Governor was General Sir William Dobbie. He was of the stamp of the Covenanter: the Bible in one hand, the sword in the other. Our party had the feeling of being a little too secular for our surroundings, although the beautiful palace and its garden were a gentle and luxuriant background. At dinner the Governor expressed his dislike of left-handed batsmen and bowlers, and said that he would beat a son of his who tried to bowl with the wrong arm. We shivered, but we were all right-handed.

In the afternoon of the next day he showed me some of the defences and particularly the ground defences of the aerodrome. A Sapper by trade, he had mounted some old 18-pounders in emplacements which had been cut into the rock. They were intended to fire over open sights at any parachutists who might land. "I cannot help wishing," said the Governor grimly, "that they would try an airborne landing," and, raising his voice, "We would blast them off the ground, sweep them away." And then, recovering himself, he added, "With God's help, of course." The glint of battle was in his eyes. He was a man you could not help admiring, but not one that I should have chosen for a companion on a holiday.

I had a drink in the R.A.F. mess, and found these unconquerable young men were having a bad time: they were constantly bombed; the two airfields were frequently pitted with craters which had to be filled in; they spent overlong periods in their flying kit, at the ready, yet they were in a cheerful though blasphemous mood; the only thing which they seemed to mind was that their mail was late and irregular. I promised to try to help.

In the evening we took off for Cairo, and climbed to our usual cruising altitude of between five and six thousand feet. I determined to get a good sleep, took off some of my clothes and lay down on the coats in the rear part of the fuselage. After a few hours of which I remember nothing, I was suddenly woken up by the bell for Acting Stations clanging in my ears and by feeling the aircraft dive steeply to the sound of the plates and mugs sliding off the table in the cabin. I looked out of the porthole and saw we were in the beam of a small searchlight from another aircraft. I could not find my trousers in the dark, and sought frantically to restore the necessary dignity to the Minister of State. It took me some minutes to succeed. The Sunderland lurched down sickeningly to about 500 feet above the sea. At that height it is a nasty customer, with its seven machine-gun positions, and the enemy did not press home his attack. When we had shaken him off, the pilot told me that we were somewhere off Bardia. Moira remained unmoved throughout the incident.

Dawn;[19] and there were the Delta and the Pyramids and the Nile. We touched down on the Nile itself; the great bow-wave of the flying-boat subsided, the roar of the engines ceased. The sun was only just up, and the sky was turning from translucent gold to the shell yellow which is the forerunner of a burning noon. "Forty centuries look down," said Napoleon to his troops at the foot of the Pyramids, and even a statistician must have thought of the liquid history of the great river. My pulse was stirred. There was the Embassy launch, pipe-clay and polish from stem to stern, and in it, standing erect, the tall and massive figure of Sir Miles Lampson,[20] the Ambassador.

He said he was more than glad to see me, and apparently meant

[19] July 5th, 1941.
[20] Now Lord Killearn.

it, although the descent of a War Cabinet Minister into his territory might have made him wonder whether our lines would get crossed. That they did not was partly due to his relief that there was now a political figure by his side who might be used to back up his views with the Cabinet at home and partly because he knew that I admired his single-mindedness and rugged patriotism. He had an intimate knowledge of the country, gained by the experience of fourteen years as High Commissioner or Ambassador.

It became a popular criticism that Lampson was too rough with the King of Egypt, that the velvet glove was threadbare, that he was dictatorial and still saw himself as High Commissioner.

It was easy to make such charges, but equally easy to defend him and to describe him, as I would, as a jealous guardian of his country's name and obligations, forceful and rigid only about essentials. Those who subscribe to this remember the sinuosities of some other British diplomatists in other countries, and whither they led us. The great holders of these posts must at times follow the example of Sir Edward Goschen[21] and make clear where lie the inviolable frontiers.

Sir Miles looked quite unlike the urbane, cynical and detached ambassadors of the films. At this time, the military regarded him with suspicion, and thought that he talked too freely; he in his turn regarded them with a quizzical eye, and might easily have been provoked into repeating Talleyrand's famous saying: "*La guerre est une chose beaucoup trop grave pour être laissée aux militaires.*" [22]

The retiring Commander-in-Chief, Sir Archibald Wavell, was an unusual soldier who wrote the fastidious and pellucid English of a scholar, but who rarely communicated his thoughts by speech. He was taciturn to a degree that concealed from anyone but his intimates his warm sympathy with his fellow-men, his love of poetry, and the selfless and self-critical balance with which he discharged the awful weight of his responsibilities.

Thus to the difficulties unavoidable between the Commander-in-Chief of a large army in a foreign and sovereign state, and the Ambassador—the principal representative of the King—charged with the highest political duties, was added a difference, almost an incompatibility, between two temperaments each in themselves worthy of admiration. Sir Archibald Wavell had just been ap-

[21] British Ambassador to Berlin 1908-14.
[22] Attributed to Talleyrand and quoted by Briand to Lloyd George during the First World War.

pointed C.-in-C. in India and was due to leave Cairo within a day or two. Sir Claude Auchinleck, his successor, was expected the next morning.

I had barely time to drive round the streets and renew my acquaintance with the city. Cairo, except for the crowds of British officers and soldiers, looked much the same. It is a drab and dusty city, redeemed only by the Nile and the Citadel; its brown-grey colour contrasts dimly with the patches of fertile green of the Delta; it cannot make up its mind whether it is Western or Oriental.

It is commonplace to describe its variety: here a narrow street with overhanging houses, the brouhaha of the market and the clink of very small change, there a boulevard looking as if it had been transported from Lille or the outskirts of Brussels; Rolls-Royces and Cadillacs honking their way past the disdainful camels, riches and poverty jostling along together, several octaves of smells, at one moment the nursery smell of cheap carpets and blankets and cottons put out for sale in the sun, at another a stench of open drains of Venetian intensity, at yet another the aroma of coffee roasting, or again just the acrid smell of human sweat and dirty clothes.

You have the feeling that nothing much is ever cleared right away, but rather that another layer has been added, like geological strata, one layer on top of the other. Everything seems to be for sale, baksheesh and corruption are everywhere, pimps pluck you by the sleeve, and a poster of "King Kong" invites you to its wholesome Brooklyn accents; the night clubs and tummy dancers offer a brash contrasting attraction. "Outside the Kasr el Nil Barracks stood a poster advertising whisky. It showed a hearty British sportsman returning from the moors and making for his bottle, while two dogs (most unclean of beasts), one white and one black, greeted him in his cosy parlour. I often wondered how this looked to a pious Moslem: rather like an Egyptian advertisement for hashish, depicting a hopeless addict with his pet snakes, might look to Londoners." [23]

Counterespionage in such a city is baffling, but the British, who are supposed to be unsubtle and simple by their own countrymen, knew, through the intelligence services, most of what went on from palace to bar and hovel. They could not, it is true, control the indiscretions—often unintentionally committed—of officers or men, but they were generally able to confuse and often to confound the enemy intelligence.

[23] Christopher Sykes in a letter to the author.

Following the general system upon which I had determined to
work, I was sure that my first task was to form a Middle Eastern
War Council, with a sub-committee to be called the Middle East
Defence Committee. The founder members, so to speak, of the
second body under my chairmanship must be the three Commanders-in-Chief, the Intendant General and the Ambassador. Its
objects would be twofold: first, to improve the relations and to
foster the unity of the three Services; secondly, to bring into the
closer knowledge of the soldiers the intricate political problems of
the Ambassador, and other political problems in other parts of the
theatre in which I was concerned, and to the Ambassador the
difficulties and needs of the military. In any event, the difference
between strategy and politics in war cannot be nicely defined.

The larger body was further to co-ordinate some of the services
of supply which, if they were to be properly organised and nourished, must include the use of local resources, in order to effect an
economy of money and shipping, and must pay due regard to
the needs of all three Services.

A word is necessary here concerning the post of Intendant General. It is not hard to guess who invented the title, but the nice
Peninsular ring of the name was, in my opinion, the best thing
about it.

General Sir Robert Haining, formerly C.-in-C. in Palestine, and
lately V.C.I.G.S., had been given the appointment. Curiously
enough, and as I think mistakenly, the Prime Minister had left
to Haining the choice of being either an Intendant General with
an independent command in charge of supplies in the "back areas,"
or of being the chief administrative officer under the orders of the
Commander-in-Chief.

I was not able to see how the first of these alternatives could
work. If supplies were inadequate, or failed on the battlefield and
led to some reverse, how could the C.-in-C. be divorced from the
causes, how could he say, "The Intendant General let me down: I
had no control of him"? It is, to my mind, elementary that a
Commander-in-Chief must control all his administrative branches,
forward as well as rearward, just as a manufacturer must control
his materials once they are delivered into the factory.

I saw Sir Robert Haining and put these points to him as forcibly
as I could. I pressed him to decide that he would come under the
direct orders of the C.-in-C. He told me that he had already made
up his mind to have an independent command, and I answered
that I was sure that this would lead eventually to his post being

abolished. Haining was an able and clever man, but ingrained Service prejudices won over his rational faculties. He was a full general, senior to Sir Claude Auchinleck; he had just vacated the second position in the Army and could not see himself under a junior from the Indian Army List. The decision proved fatal to him in a few months.

The Prime Minister was fond of applying to organisation in general the dictum of Napoleon that constitutions should be vague.[24] I am, myself, an advocate of defining areas of responsibility as clearly as possible. Just as the boundaries between armies and army corps must be clear-cut, and just as these junctions have long been thought by soldiers to be the most vulnerable, so in the field of administration as precise a division of duty as is possible is to my mind the root of success, and their ill definition the most frequent cause of failure.

I had been given as my office a sitting-room in the Embassy looking out over the Nile. I next saw, and for the first time, the new C.-in-C., Sir Claude Auchinleck. I looked at him closely: an Indian complexion, blue eyes and a determined chin. He had the indefinable qualities of charm, humour and frankness, and I have remained under their spell ever since. We talked for more than an hour; he accepted, but not very readily, my idea of a Defence Committee. He had obviously the reservation that this body might get between him and his duties, and when I told him that he had my word that it would not, he said that experience would soon show and that he would give it a trial.

He also put his finger on the anomalies of the post of Intendant General, and asked how an independent command of the back areas could be expected to work. I answered that he must rely upon me. I could see that that was not a great reassurance.

I had no difficulty in winning the support of both the Ambassador and Air Marshal Sir Arthur Tedder,[25] C.-in-C. of the R.A.F. in the Middle East, to the scheme of a Middle East Defence Committee. Sir Arthur Tedder, a man of middle height, smoked a pipe with a very large bowl and liked to express himself in a rather banal and colloquial vocabulary. I was to learn later that he was no mere airman, that he knew far more about war than most, and

---

[24] Napoleon began a long speech during his first year as a Consul with the words: *"Une Constitution doit être courte et obscure."* *Napoléon: Pensées pour l'Action*, ed. Driault (Paris, 1943).
[25] Now Marshal of the Royal Air Force Lord Tedder.

that he was a good administrator. If his lack of the dignity of his rank was a fault, it was made up for by a lack of conceit.

The Admiral, Sir Andrew Cunningham,[23] I saw later. He was a great man of war; his ruddy, wind-swept countenance was surmounted by a pair of piercing blue eyes, one of which used to droop in a menacing manner when he was angry or provoked. He had two bars to his D.S.O. You could see he was pugnacious to his fingertips, and that "Keep closer to the enemy" would be his favourite signal. He felt, with some justification, that the Navy was the most professional of the three Services, and he obviously disliked the system of an independent air force. He slept aboard his flagship in Alexandria harbour, and would not think of being away from his command for a single night. He was transparently straight and forthright, a master of his profession, beloved and respected by his subordinates. He could say things of wounding frankness, but nobody was wounded. "Just like the Admiral," they would say. My heart warmed to this great man. He agreed to the Defence Council, but said he would fly back and forth from Alexandria for the meetings. I do not think that he rated its usefulness as high.

The foundation laid, I held the first meeting and easily persuaded the members of the Defence Committee that we should add to the numbers of the Middle East War Council, that is the larger body, when they were in Cairo, the Ambassador in Baghdad, the High Commissioner for Palestine, the Governors of Cyprus and Aden. A representative of the Government of India was also to be added. Field-Marshal Smuts was always intended to come and give us his advice when he was in Cairo.

I chose for my office a small, modern building not far from G.H.Q., No. 10 Sharia Tolumbat, and installed myself on the first floor. I covered the wall behind my desk with the largest-scale map of the theatre which it would accommodate. The wags often called this office No. 10.

I had been offered by Chester Beatty, an old friend, his villa near the Pyramids. I gladly accepted his generosity and determined to live there. Though it had been built to catch the sun in the early spring, and was drenched in heat in the summer, it was near the Pyramids and four miles away from the noise and bustle of Cairo. The villa compromised between the Oriental and the Western. It had an Arab courtyard and fountain, Cambridge-blue tiles from the ground to a man's height, which gave it its name of Beit

[26] Now Admiral of the Fleet Viscount Cunningham of Hyndhope.

el Azrak—the Blue (or azure) House—and some features which owed much to the influence of Sunningdale.

There were some Oriental works of art of great beauty, collected by the owner, who is no dilettante but a world authority on Oriental manuscripts and art.

It is said that when the Nile rises in September, it brings with it some of the sewage of forty centuries. It is certainly the most unhealthy time of year, and when I asked Abdul, my Arab butler, one hot day why he had not turned the fountain on in the courtyard, he replied, "The Nile is rising, Excellency; very bad smell from fountain."

CHAPTER XIII

THE MIDDLE EAST: II

A WEEK OR TWO had to be spent in staffing the villa, and in the meantime I stayed at the Embassy.

I had a talk with the Egyptian Prime Minister, Hussein Sirry Pasha, and paid my official call with the Ambassador upon the King. The King, educated in England, spoke perfect English and when he wished—which was not always—could be charming and courteous. He sometimes called upon me dressed in an English tweed suit, even on a hot evening, unannounced and incognito, drank copiously of very sweet orangeade and talked of his days at Woolwich.

The King kept himself well informed on politics and the movement of opinion, and was shrewder and more serious than is usually supposed. I should judge that he was far from sure that we would win, and that he kept open some line of retreat to Mussolini and the Axis.

At this time I started to reorganise and animate the Middle East Supply Centre; it worked closely with the Eastern Supply Group in Delhi. A little later I appointed Paymaster Lieutenant Commander Jackson,[1] R.A.N.,[2] to manage it, and under him it soon became an effective instrument in obtaining and distributing local supplies and in making use of local manufacturing plants, particularly for repairs. The M.E.S.C. saved us money but more important, it saved us shipping.

The history of the oranges illustrates how easy it is to waste

---

[1] Now Sir Robert Jackson, Chairman of the Development Commission, Ghana.
[2] Royal Australian Navy.

shipping space. The Jewish fruit farmers in Palestine were short
of labour to pick the Jaffa oranges, and asked and obtained help
from the Army. Soldiers in their spare time or on short furlough
became orange pickers and earned a little extra pay. The oranges
were then shipped to England and Scotland to be turned into marmalade. The tinned marmalade returned to the Middle East for the
troops. But that was not all; with the tins arrived letters from soldiers' wives complaining of the shortage of marmalade in England.
So the soldiers bought in the N.A.A.F.I. in Tel Aviv or Jerusalem
some marmalade to send home.

It is not difficult to see how, with a little ingenuity, at the
worst three voyages were turned into one, and at the best no voyage from Palestine took place at all.

I also found chaos in the field of subversive activities and propaganda. I was disturbed, in particular, by the lack of security,
waste of public funds and ineffectiveness of S.O.E. (Special Operations Executive), a body largely staffed by Army officers. It came
within the jurisdiction of Dr. Dalton,[3] the Minister of Economic
Warfare, with whom I was on friendly terms. I frankly exposed
to him by telegram the deplorable conditions of this service, of
which I had incontestable proof, and urged him to clean it up. I
received the rather tart reply that he was not accustomed to accept
allegations against his staff unsupported by evidence, and so forth.
I replied at once that there would be no difficulty in having some
of these officers tried by court martial, which would confirm my
charges, but this was not a course that I recommended. The
answer to this was that Sir Frank Nelson, the head of S.O.E. in
London, would be sent to Cairo forthwith. Several dismissals were
the result, and Nelson was able to assure me that he had swept the
organisation clean, and that he would see that it was kept so.

Propaganda and press relations are, of course, separate subjects, but they are apt to become intermixed and in the Middle East
there was no co-ordinating body. In a theatre of war the relations
between the fighting forces and the press will aways be subject to
severe strains. The press in Cairo were certainly resentful about
the lack of news from the Services, and complained that when
they were given information, it was unreliable and tendentious.
Army Intelligence Service, being well aware of the value to themselves of newspaper articles and paragraphs in the enemy press,
are determined to deny similar advantages to the enemy. This is
natural and sound in principle, but if it leads to over-caution and

[3] Afterwards Lord Dalton.

to starving the press of news, evils almost as great follow: the public at home becomes uneasy, morale is affected and, when reverses can no longer be concealed, sudden shocks are inflicted on an unprepared public.

Propaganda in war, where it relates only to military operations, is largely ineffective. Phrases like "strategic readjustment," "planned withdrawal," "straightening the line," "regrouping our forces," spell to the public the one word—defeat. Conversely, victory is the best propaganda and requires little boosting by jubilant articles or purple patches.

It is rather in the political or economic field that propaganda has its part to play. It is possible, if it is used properly and soberly, to reassure neutrals about your intentions, to underline the consequences to them of an enemy victory, to make them feel that their interests will not be neglected, and that they will be guarded by your strong arm. Its role is also to counter enemy propaganda. At this time, German policy was to frighten the Arab states into believing that their independence was at stake, and that we intended to annex them or place them under our tutelage if we were victorious.

It was clear that all the activities connected with the press and propaganda required central direction and guidance; we must strive to satisfy the press in a reasonable manner, even if it involved some risks. When the press is properly treated they respond by being discreet and careful; when they are starved of news they are apt to succumb to the temptation of guessing it, or even of creating it.

I therefore set up a Propaganda Department, staffed by men with a press training or background, and charged it with the task of co-ordinating the activities of various propaganda bodies carrying on political warfare and other propaganda in my sphere. News of the fighting itself must, in principle, be in the hands of the Services, since commanders cannot divest themselves of the responsibility for the security of their forces. Nevertheless, I hoped that my new department would also help to improve press relations and give some guidance. I was prepared, after consultation with the Service concerned, to hold an occasional press conference myself. About this time, Walter Monckton[4] came to join me as Director General of British Propaganda and Information Services.

I asked him to stay at Beit el Azrak and he added greatly to our small society. Few people that I have known have been more per-

[4] Now Viscount Monckton of Brenchley.

suasive, and his flexible mind and musical voice, so often used to advantage in the courts, were now turned either to the public business of propaganda or to embellishing the gaiety and conversation at Headquarters.

I spent many hours on many days in studying the strategical, tactical and supply problems that confronted us in this theatre of war. The first part of any such exercise must be to "absorb the map," and to know without reference the approximate distances to all points of the compass between the key places.

Some of the problems, and particularly those of supply, can be understood more readily if it is remembered that Benghazi is nearly 700 miles, Crete 400 miles, the Turkish frontier 600 miles, Khartoum 1,000 miles, Port Sudan 800 miles from Cairo.

The first salient fact that struck me was how vulnerable to air-attack were the Delta and our communications. The Germans now held Crete, and if at any time they were disposed to spare some air squadrons from the Russian front they could attack the nexus Alexandria–Port Said–Cairo–Port Suez and the Canal Zone and make things hot for us.

I judged that it was in their power to reduce the capacity of these ports perhaps by more than a half for short periods, and by more than a third for extended periods. All three Services were well aware of this, but did not seem to have considered as an urgent matter how to meet the threat.

Perhaps coming from London and from the Board of Trade, where I had been responsible for certain civilian supplies after air-raids, I was too much impressed by the danger.

There was no black-out to speak of in Cairo or its environs. I was certainly surprised to notice that at dinner parties at the Embassy, a double row of Chinese lanterns stretched across the hundred yards of lawn from the verandah to the edge of the Nile, and very gay and pretty they looked. I called it the Ambassador's flare path, and after a bomb or two had fallen in Cairo, he took the hint.

I started to enquire how to make our communications less vulnerable, and soon unearthed a scheme which appeared practicable and which did not involve an impossible diversion of effort and material.

The Nile Delta is served from the south by the Nile Valley Railway which, as its name implies, strikes northwards from the Sudan by the valley route. About 450 miles north of Port Sudan a knuckle of land projects into the Red Sea, at a small place called

Safaga. There was the possibility of making a port, or at least a lighterage port, at this point, and the Nile Valley Railway passed only sixty miles to the west of it. I was determined that a spur line should be built to link Safaga with the main line. We should then have a new supply route and since it was out of the bombing range of the enemy, we should be able to unload and turn our ships round without interruption. It is true that when the valley railway approaches the Delta itself it becomes vulnerable, but a railway is more difficult to hit and much easier to clear than a port. New railheads can be improvised, and new and flexible lines of supply established. I shall refer to this scheme again.

The Commanders-in-Chief were not only concerned with the offensive in the Western Desert, but also charged with the defence of the Delta. Therefore, the second strategical subject which I studied closely was the chances of invasion from the north. How great was the potential threat?

At that time the appreciation of the General Staff presupposed that the Germans would not be allowed to pass troops through Turkey unmolested. If they tried to do so, the Turks would declare war. The Turks, as we have reason to know, are fine fighters, but their army was ill-equipped and served by horse transport; they had almost no modern aeroplanes or warning system, the artillery was old-fashioned, and the supplies of ammunition precarious. They could not, however, be brushed aside in a few days; they would fight stubbornly and, considering that the communications in southern Turkey, both by rail and road, were primitive, it seemed likely that they would delay in invading army by guerilla tactics for some invaluable time.

We still had to consider what would happen if, with the handicaps of their obsolete equipment, the Turks were eventually brought to their knees. Even then the supply of a German army directed, south of the Taurus mountains, upon Syria and ultimately Palestine and the Delta, would pass through hostile country and could only be supplied by primitive roads and railways.

The General Staff accordingly put the maximum size of any army likely to debouch south of the Taurus at five divisions, with supporting arms, and estimated that the threat would take more than a month or two to develop, provided that Turkey did not join the Axis. If it did develop, our ability to transfer troops quickly from the Western Desert to the northern front in Syria was of great if not decisive importance.

It seemed to me necessary to link the Delta with Palestine by a coastal railway, with railheads within reach of Alexandretta and the Turkish frontier. General Auchinleck was strongly in favour of the project.

Between the wars I had studied closely how the Germans had used their strategic railways in East Prussia in 1914. General von Prittwitz had fought an indecisive battle with the Vilna army of Rennenkampf at Gumbinnen, on his eastern flank. Sooner than expected, a threat by Samsonoff's army began to develop on the southern front between Soldau and Ortelsburg, directed on the general axis Warsaw–Allenstein. Von Prittwitz' nerve failed and he was superseded. Colonel Hoffmann, Chief of the German Operations Section in East Prussia, had no difficulty in planning the disengagement of the whole of the necessary forces in the east, and transferring them by use of the strategical railways to stave off and defeat this southern attack. When Hindenburg and Ludendorff arrived to take over from von Prittwitz, they made no significant alterations to Hoffmann's plans, which were already in motion. The Battle of Tannenberg was fought upon them, and it was thus the dispositions of Hoffmann and not those of Hindenburg and Ludendorff which led to this resounding victory. These dispositions depended upon the use of the strategic railways which had been built in anticipation of the very dangers which threatened East Prussia at this time.

Bearing these lessons in mind, I was determined that a strategic railway to link the northern front with the Delta must be built as soon as the labour and resources could be spared. It was not immediately started because of the more urgent need for the Safaga spur of sixty miles. Haining, whilst he agreed that the spur was desirable, was immersed in other plans and said he was opposed to diverting the resources.

I was at something of a deadlock when, early in August, Field Marshal Smuts arrived in Cairo to inspect the South African Division and study the course of the campaign. He was *ex officio* a member of the Defence Committee, which was to meet on a certain morning at 10 A.M.

The night before, at dinner, I asked the Field Marshal if he could possibly see me half an hour before the meeting, because I wanted his help. He said he could not promise half an hour, but certainly would arrive early. In the event, he reached my office only seven minutes before the meeting. I could only give him the sketchiest outline of the problem and of my proposals; he nodded, and we joined the others round the table. When we reached this particular item on the agenda, the Field Marshal spoke for about a quarter of an hour upon the supply problem of the Middle East. It was a masterly statement. I had been studying the subject for weeks, and I could judge that no aspect of it had escaped him.

He came down strongly in favour of my railway, and then Haining intervened to say that we could not build it at this time. "Then," retorted Smuts, "I am sure the Minister must find someone who can." That clinched it.

I had been introduced to Smuts by my father in 1910, and had seen him once or twice since that date. He always seemed to be even more interested in military than in political subjects. His blue eyes sparkled when he surveyed a strategical or tactical plan. These were clearly subjects upon which he had reflected deeply all through his life and which he held in his grasp. His political vision was, of course, also wide and he ranged over the whole convulsive scene of world politics with a clearness, a simplicity and a penetration which are the stamp of superior intellects: he was one of the great men that I have met.

That night, the Field Marshal and Mrs. Smuts came to dinner at my villa. Mrs. Smuts was an example of unself-conscious simplicity and sweetness of character, which could be read in her face. She had never before been outside the boundaries of South Africa.

Dinner is late in Cairo, and the ladies did not leave the dining-room until 10:30. They went out on to the roof in the hot velvety Egyptian night, and Mrs. Smuts said to my wife, "This is past my usual bed-time, and if you don't mind, I shall put my feet up on this long chair and have a few minutes' sleep until Oubaas arrives." In a moment or two she was in a tranquil sleep, in which the Field Marshal discovered her half an hour later. He was amused and delighted, and teased her about her disregard of conventions.

On July 11th, six days after my arrival, an event of great importance occurred. The Vichy French in Syria capitulated and asked for an armistice. The news arrived in the middle of the night, and the Ambassador and I met in our dressing-gowns in the Chancery. He was an impressive figure and in his robes looked like Sarastro in *The Magic Flute*. Michael Wright,[5] the Head of Chancery, was working late. He is surely one of the ablest men the Foreign Office ever produced. He had been particularly charged with our relations with the Free French; he had won their confidence, and his perfect French had no doubt contributed to his influence.

[5] Now Sir Michael Wright.

An Armistice Commission was to meet at St. Jean d'Acre, *anglice* Acre, on the coast, sixty miles north-west of Jerusalem. General Dentz and his second-in-command, General de Verdilhac, were the delegates of the Vichy French. The Commander-in-Chief, Sir Henry Maitland Wilson, was of course our representative, and General Catroux that of the Free French.

We telegraphed some broad instructions that very night, and spent the next day in settling some further details of our requirements; we kept in touch as far as possible with the Free French, through Michael. Telegrams started to arrive from London, confirming the general lines which we were following. The Ambassador and I also had some matters of our own which we wished to safeguard.

The task of getting the Armistice terms into proper order and of satisfying the War Cabinet was made much more difficult and baffling because I had to stay in Cairo, to be in touch hour by hour with London, and my only quick means of communication with Wilson in St. Jean d'Acre was by the Army telephone via Jerusalem. It was difficult to hear or be heard on this line.

At one point in the negotiations, General Wilson telegraphed to me that the Vichy French boggled at certain clauses, and refused to sign. I telegraphed that he could tell them that we should accordingly resume hostilities at 10 A.M. the following morning. I have an unshakable belief that when once a commander has asked for an armistice it is impossible for him to persuade his troops to resume fighting.

Just after the telegram had left my office to be coded, I got a personal telegram from the Prime Minister saying that on no account was I to permit any resumption of hostilities. I think such a telegram unfair to the man on the spot, because it removes from him his principal strength which the victory of the troops has given him, and absolves the sender from any consequences. In this case it was perhaps excusable, because the Prime Minister was under a great pressure of work.

I am no Nelson, and see well with both eyes, but I decided to let my telegram ride, on the grounds that I was not risking a resumption of hostilities. I confess to having passed an uneasy night. Ten A.M. the next morning arrived and no news; midday, no news. I was getting nervous. By 4 P.M. I could not restrain myself from telephoning to "Jumbo" Wilson. "What is happening?" I asked. "Oh, sorry," he answered, "didn't I tell you? The French signed early this morning."

A few arduous days passed, during which my staff, and in par-ticular Henry Hopkinson and I, got little sleep. We had to get the terms just right, and it is easy to imagine our satisfaction when all was settled and when the wishes of the Government at home and my own appeared to have been met in full.

The Armistice was dated July 14th, 1941. A much abridged ver-sion of the terms is:

> The Allied forces to occupy Syro-Lebanese territory and French forces to be concentrated in certain areas; full honours of war to be granted to the French forces, who will be allowed to retain their arms (this related to personal arms and did not apply to ammunition or artillery); prisoners of the Allied forces to be set free; French troops to be offered the alternative of rallying to the Allied cause or of being repatriated; amnesty to native Syrians and Lebanese.[6]

Under its terms, the British authorities reserved the right to hold a number of French officers as prisoners of war until those prisoners captured by the Vichy French and transported to France were returned.

I freely admit, looking back on the wording of the Armistice, that we should have brought the Free French into its terms in a way which we did not. British policy was firmly established, and for all that General de Gaulle says, it had never been our intention to supplant France in Syria and the Lebanon, but rather to press for these countries to be given independence. On rereading the Armistice terms, I can understand the General's point of view. As he says in his book, they do not even mention the Free French. We wished to imply, he says, that these two countries were liberated solely by British arms whereas, of course, the Free French had played an important role. We never realised—as we should have—how suspicious the Free French had become, and when the Armis-tice terms were settled, we thought that we had covered all the points. These matters having been settled, I went to bed before midnight, easy in my mind.

I was in a deep sleep, about 4 A.M., when the Duty Officer called me to say that General Spears was on the telephone from Jerusalem. "You should know," he said, "that General Wilson has signed a secret protocol with General Dentz, under which it is agreed that no contact should be permitted between the Free French and the Vichy French."

I knew, of course, that General de Gaulle was determined—and rightly—to persuade as many of the Vichy troops as possible to

[6] Playfair, *op. cit.,* Vol. III, Appendix 3.

rally to the cause of the Free French, and had doubtless planned to send his officers and agents into the prisoners' cages on this mission. I was greatly incensed that no reference had been made to me about this secret clause. The only crumb of comfort was that General Catroux was a member of the Armistice Commission, representing the Free French, and must have been a party to this maladroit arrangement. I returned wearily to bed, and with my morning coffee received a telegram to say that General de Gaulle was leaving Brazzaville at once for Cairo.

The next day, July 21st, and it was very hot, General de Gaulle arrived in my office at about 11 o'clock. General Spears had come down from Jerusalem to help and was to give, as always, invaluable support.

General de Gaulle was white with suppressed passion. He strode into my room with his staff, greeted me frigidly and launched the most violent complaint about the British attitude, not only concerning the secret protocol, but also concerning all our actions in the "French territory of Syria and the Lebanon," action which had been taken either without his knowledge or without his consent.

He then handed me a typewritten document in which he formally withdrew all French troops in the Levant from under the command of the British C.-in-C. I was somewhat taken aback, but from some remote recess of my memory the diplomatic phrase "Non Avenu" came to the surface. I said, "General, I must regard this document as not received, and I cannot accept it." I then tore it up.

His reaction was violent, but considering that the Free French had to rely for all their military equipment and stores and for their pay upon the Army or the British Exchequer, I thought the General's position was weaker than his words. However, there was nothing for it but what women call "a scene," and a scene was certainly had.

I felt, however, a hidden sympathy for some parts of his philippic, as well as an admiration for one who stood up so manfully for the interests of his own country. Behind all his complaints lay, of course, the deep-seated French belief that we were pursuing a pan-Arab policy and intended to annex or place under British protection both Syria and the Lebanon, and put an end to French rule.

General de Gaulle continued in a violent tirade until about half past twelve, at which time I said, "General, this is the hour when I go home to luncheon, and my office does not reopen until 4:30 P.M. It is a very hot day and I recommend that we should reflect on this situation during the hour of the siesta and meet again at, say, five o'clock, when both the day—and we—will be cooler." He bowed stiffly, and agreed.

This was my first meeting with General de Gaulle; I had many dealings with him afterwards. I have never seen him, even when he was at his most difficult, other than as a true Frenchman and a true patriot. It was evident that he thought that he alone had the burning flame and *mystique* which could restore to France her respect and her rightful place in the world, but I believe and I still believe him to be devoid of personal ambition.

To his spiritual gifts he added high intellectual capacity; he expressed himself in beautiful and scholarly French and his command over the language, both spoken and written, was as good as that of General Wavell over written English. It was not difficult even then to prove his stature beyond a doubt. At the time when he first raised the Cross of Lorraine—an unbending figure, unbending to foe and friend alike—there were 140,000 French troops in Great Britian, many of whom had been evacuated from Dunkirk by the Royal Navy. Only 8,000—mostly marines—rallied to the cause of Free France. The rest—and I am imputing no blame—elected to return to their own country.

It is hardly possible to imagine a more unpromising beginning for a resistance leader. Yet within a few months this lonely figure had translated himself into an international position almost within sight of the statesmen at the summit, Roosevelt, Stalin and Churchill. Such an ascent from such a start cannot come about by chance; it can be made only by courage, spiritual integrity and brains.

General de Gaulle, moreover, understood how to deal with Anglo-Saxons and the English-speaking races. He took offence upon the slightest pretext.

It is undeniable, but requires no excuse, that when French power was at a low ebb, decisions were and indeed had to be taken without consultation or agreement with our friend and ally. He never let this pass; he pointed with passion to anything ham-fisted or maladroit or impolite which we had done. By these means, and not by *souplesse* or urbanity, he became respected and, since the English-speaking races hate scenes, and hate being exposed as clumsy, inconsiderate or disloyal, he built up a position which no amount of emollient diplomacy could have gained.

His attitude was no pose. He was seared by the wounds which the defeat of France had inflicted upon his pride and patriotism. I really believe that when he got up in the morning he said to himself, "France is dishonoured. Where and when am I going to be insulted today?"

With all this, I could not help reflecting, and with some amusement, how completely different he was from the British idea of a Frenchman. He is a devout Catholic and at times of stress in argument showed a tendency to put his long, artistic and finely modelled fingers into his sleeves, which I thought showed that his family had long been close to the priesthood.

In society he showed little *esprit;* his manners were stiff, he had no small talk or conversation. One night, at dinner at my villa, Moira asked him what his interests were when he was not preoccupied with war or politics and he replied, with the merest ghost of a smile, *"Madame, je regarde le système solaire."* Aloof, affronted, ready—even eager—to take offence, but towering over his compatriots, and with his burning patriotism, he stirred my respect, my admiration and my sympathy.

I do not suppose that I have seen him for more than a few moments since 1942, but he had the great kindness and charming thought to send me a copy of his memoirs, with a graceful inscription on the title page.

I have already described the stormy nature of our first meeting. At 5 o'clock he returned in a different mood. It is possible that his staff had pointed out to him the dangers of being too intransigent with the British and, for that matter, with a Minister whose influence was unknown.

Suffice it to say that after protracted negotiations a document emerged a few days later which, of course, had been agreed by the Foreign Secretary and endorsed by the War Cabinet, known afterwards as the Lyttelton/de Gaulle Agreement. The main purport was to disclaim any intention by the British of adding Syria and the Lebanon to their sphere of influence. As in most diplomatic documents, chinks began to appear later under stress, but it stood at least as a broad statement of our policy and did something to close the breach which had opened between the Allies.

At the moment, however, nothing could get over the fact that a secret protocol had been signed. It had obviously to be honoured, but only if the Vichy French on their side honoured the other terms with an equal punctiliousness. I accordingly issued instructions to the military that the terms of the armistice must be interpreted rigidly and respected in full by the other side; if there was any deviation from them, I should denounce it and make such revisions, and notably to the secret protocol, as seemed desirable.

Soon reports began to arrive that the Vichy French were taking liberties. A large amount of paper had been sold to the Jesuits, a bridge had been blown up, fifty-two British officers who had fallen into the hands of the French during the campaign had been shipped out of Beirut harbour and sent to France only two days before General Dentz had asked for an armistice. There were other irregularities. However, the armistice had not been denounced, as I had wished, and I decided I must fly to Beirut and control events on the spot.

I had been given a Lockheed by the R.A.F. for my use, and Tedder asked to come with me. We were to land at Damascus, the nearest operational aerodrome to Beirut at the time. Our R.A.F. pilot had not been there before, and after circling over the hills to the north of it, he descended in a sharp dive to land. As we were about to touch down, I saw a large guard of honour of British and Foreign Legion troops drawn up, and as the wheels hit the strip I noticed that they had been called to attention. The pilot, however, had come down too steeply, and we shot along the runway at an unconventional speed and were obliged to take off again. The flaps were still down and we cleared the orange grove at the end of the runway without much to spare. Tedder afterwards said jokingly that he had found an orange stuck to the tail-wheel. The guard of honour stood easy. Our second attempt was successful and dignified.

General Legentilhomme, a splendid type of French soldier, who had commanded the French contingent with skill and had recently been wounded, greeted me and I inspected the guard. I noticed one or two *beau sabreur* types in the rear rank of the Legion, talked to the officers, and left a little later for Sofar, on the slopes of the Lebanon a few miles above steamy Beirut. Another guard of honour, entirely French, was mounted, and I was surprised to see in the ranks some of the same legionnaires that I had inspected at Damascus; they had been flown up.

The hotel is a holiday resort, with a shady outdoor restaurant, and I had been given some comfortable quarters next to those of the C.-in-C. The manager of the hotel came upstairs with me, presumably to show me my rooms, but he shut the door of the sitting-room behind him and, in a hoarse whisper, muttered, "Excellency, you will not bring back the French to the Lebanon, I hope?" I recount this ludicrous incident because it shows how charged the Levantine atmosphere is with politics.

The next morning in Beirut I had a memorable interview with General Wilson and General Chrystall,[7] the latter having been appointed—and I think mistakenly—head of the Armistice Commission. I became incensed at the apparent sympathy and complacence with which the breaches of the armistice were regarded. "Blowing up a bridge, General Chrystall: a childish prank, I suppose? Selling paper to the Jesuits: the blunder of some junior official? Shipping British officers to Marseilles a few hours before asking for an armistice: well within the rules of war?" and much else in the same strain.

From these instances, and others, it became clear that General Dentz took a light-hearted view of the terms. The most unpardonable was, to my mind, the sending of the British officers to France. I was determined that if severity would bring them back, it should be applied.

I gave orders that General Dentz was to be arrested; he was to be treated with every courtesy and, since he was ill, was to have the best medical treatment and diet which we could provide, but he was to be kept under surveillance. On his arrest, General de Verdilhac, his second-in-command, succeeded him automatically. One result of these measures was that the fifty-two officers were shipped back to Beirut; one died on the voyage.

The Vichy French, under the terms of the armistice, were to be accorded the honours of war; that is, they were to parade with colours flying before laying down their arms; officers were to keep their swords.

The British seemed at the time to be more in sympathy with the regular Vichy officers, who had respected their oath at the expense of their country, than with the Free French, who had, with deep heart-searchings, set it aside for the greater good and glory of France. The honours of war were interpreted by the military in a far wider sense than the words can ordinarily be made to bear.

The arrest of General Dentz had led to a better understanding between General de Gaulle and myself. There still remained, however, a number of inflamed questions, and I was engaged in some delicate negotiations with him in his office, which was at sea level and was, in the summer solstice, airless and at furnace heat. Things were going smoothly. Suddenly the unmistakable strains of the *"Marseillaise"* came welling up from the streets and reverberated dully through the room. The general stopped dead in the

[7] Brigadier, acting Major-General J. I. Chrystall.

middle of a sentence. He rang the bell and told the A.D.C. to find out at once the reason for the national anthem.

After about a quarter of an hour, the A.D.C. returned to say that the *"Marseillaise"* had been played by the Australian band when the ship carrying the Vichy soldiers who had not rallied to Free France was leaving the harbour, and that an Australian guard of honour had been mounted on the quay and had been inspected by General de Verdilhac. This was the honours of war with a vengeance.

"But I thought you told me that General Dentz had been arrested?" said General de Gaulle, severely. "He has been," I replied. "The British are incomprehensible!" he exclaimed, and I could only say that I thought that on this occasion perhaps they were. I sent orders that this flummery must cease, and we got to work again. Hardly had we begun than the fainter strains of the *"Marseillaise"* re-echoed through the streets, but the general either did not notice the sounds of *"Aux armes, citoyens,"* or ignored them.

Before I left Beirut, I decided to visit the commanders and see something of the troops in Syria. I was also anxious to discover whether our relations with the Free French could be improved, and drop some hints if need be. Just as I was going on board my Lockheed to take off from the airfield at Rayak, two news-reel men asked to come with me, and I agreed.

Our first call was to be Deir-ez-Zor on the Euphrates, in the area of the 10th Indian Division. It was a very hot day, and since we had no oxygen we had to fly below 10,000 feet to be able to breathe in any comfort. At this altitude or below, it was the bumpiest day that I ever remember in all my million miles of flying. The aircraft was thrown about in every direction and it was impossible to unfasten the safety belts for a moment. I heard some groans from behind me, and saw that one of the news-reel men was nearly out. I asked the pilot to come down a thousand feet or so, but when he did so the turbulence was even worse.

After about an hour we saw the desert strip, and as we came in to land there was some dust swirling round, but as yet no dust storm. I saw that a general was waiting for me. He was of middle height, and looked as fit and tough as any man I have seen. His unwavering gaze and humorous smile made me wish I was a soldier again in his command, and not a civilian on a rather delicate mission.

The general's H.Q. was in the Residency in the town itself, and the Union Jack was flying from the flagstaff outside it. By the time we got there we were very dusty and the general asked me if I would like to wash in his room on the first floor. The first thing that caught my eye was the usual japanned tin box which regular officers used to carry with them. On it was inscribed in very faded letters "Major W. Slim," crossed through with a white line, then "Colonel" and "Brigadier W. Slim," also crossed out with much fresher lines, and finally "Major-General W. Slim" in brand-new white characters. For the commander of the 10th Indian Division was none other than he. He was to paint higher and higher ranks on his box until be became a field marshal.[8]

Slim had seized Deir-ez-Zor by a bold coup, with his last drop of petrol, and had barely missed capturing the commander and the whole of the staff of the Vichy French in the town. When he entered the Residency, the table was set for luncheon, and one or two kepis were lying scattered about as evidence of the haste with which their owners had had to get out. A little later the intelligence officer saw a locked file, heavily bound in brass, lying on the table. Here, he thought, is a real find; it will probably give us the orders and dispositions of the Vichy troops. It proved, however, a disappointment, because it only contained the letters of some officer to six different ladies in Paris. A photograph preceded each of the six, and in one case, as a final precaution, the lady's black lace pants had been added to her file of correspondence.

At this time, one of the Free French officers gave us a sight of the instructions which had been issued to guide them in their relations with the British officers. British officers were divided into three categories. First *"les* gentlemen," who were entirely reliable (and Slim was delighted to see that he had made the grade). Secondly, *"les* good fellows," with whom a simple camaraderie was suggested; and thirdly *"les gens de l'*intelligence service," who were described as legion, and who were to be treated with the utmost reserve.

After luncheon, I was introduced to Colonel Reyniers, a splendid type of French colonial soldier, who was to be the new Resident. Slim and his staff liked him and treated him in the most friendly way. He looked pleased enough, but a little bewildered by the brick-red faces around him. I told the general that I feared he would have to move out of the Residency before long, and hoist the French rather than the British flag. He looked a little grim, but saw the point.

[8] Now Field-Marshal Viscount Slim.

I then flew down the Euphrates, heading to the northwest. Most of the way the desert comes to the very lip of the river, but from the air you can see a faint, grey-green discoloration stretching for a few miles on both banks. I believe this is the last vestige of the irrigation schemes of the ancient city of Babylon, and of the lands on which cattle were raised. We landed at Aleppo, and I paid several visits to the troops and enquired about mails and the like.

Then back to Rayak. It was as rough as ever; both the news-reel men were very sick, and one looked so white and exhausted that I thought he was going to die. He had to be helped out of the aircraft, but recovered after a day or two. The two of them, however, had 2,000 feet of film to show for their pains. Unfortunately, the Minister of State's shirt had come out of his shorts at the back, and the whole 2,000 feet had to be destroyed. If I had been consulted I would have let the film be shown, if only as a peppercorn compensation for their sufferings.

The reasons for my next journey, which was to Transjordania, require some explanation; they were twofold. First, the Emir Abdullah, our loyal friend for more than thirty years and a staunch ally through all the vagaries of fortune, was known to aspire to the kingskip of Syria. If we had helped him to attain it, the consequences would, however, have been grievous. He would have been regarded by the French as a British puppet, and as playing his part in our deep design to supplant French power in Syria and neighbouring countries. The Emir would have to be told that we could not fulfil his dearest wish.

Secondly, Glubb Pasha,[9] the Commander of the Arab Legion in Transjordania, had a unique prestige amongst the Arabs, not only in the country where he was employed, but in Syria and Palestine. He had been cut off from some of his friends amongst the sheiks, and very naturally went to visit them again as soon as the armistice was signed. Unfortunately, when he arrived in any district his reception was so tumultuous that the ordinary administration almost ceased. So suspicious were the Free French that they thought he was yet another British agent carrying out the pan-Arab policy of the British Government.

Complaints poured in of French authority being flouted, and barely concealed accusations of bad faith were levelled at us. I therefore decided to fly to Amman and explain, both to the ruler and his C.-in-C., our difficulties.

[9] Lieutenant-General Sir John Glubb.

I had an appointment with Glubb in the morning, and felt rather sheepish about what I had to tell him. When he was shown in, I was surprised both by his appearance and by his diction. He was small in stature, and spoke English in the rather mincing tones usually associated with the clergy or with schoolmasters. First of all, we talked about a memorandum which he had written upon war in the desert. He had likened it to war at sea. I told him I thought that such a comparison was quite wrong. It was true that there were never flanks at sea, and only seldom in the desert, but the great difference lay in the fact that warships can steam about for some days, fully armed and ready for battle, whereas tanks could only operate for a few hours without petrol supplies. Ships, unlike tanks, did not require continual maintenance. Officers and men lived in their equipment at sea, they did not on land.

He seemed slightly pained by my criticism, and I passed on to the delicate subject of his visits to Syria. I told him that I must ask him not to go into Syria or the Lebanon for a little while. I hoped it would not be embarrassing to him. He replied at once that it would be, but that he entirely understood. "You have other fish to fry," dwelling on the alliteration for a moment, "and you are looking to opinion in Metropolitan France. I understand, of course." He then talked with great knowledge and obvious understanding of the tangled politics of Palestine and Arabia.

My next appointment was at the palace. I was received by the Emir with every mark of courtesy, consideration and friendship. He took me by the hand and led me into the drawing room, which was an incongruous compromise between East and West. Some imitation French furniture and European bric-a-brac was mixed with the Oriental pieces and rugs. One or two coloured photographs and daguerrotypes hung on the walls.

The Emir himself was clothed in a shapeless robe of drab yellow, which smelt of musk. He was a short man, with a fringe of beard and kindly, rather disenchanted eyes. He made me sit beside him on a French-looking sofa of Levantine origin, and still held me by the hand. Some other dignitaries and my own staff were grouped around us. It is not overeasy to say something disagreeable to an elderly and very friendly royal personage who is holding your hand, when it is clear that members of your own staff might easily allow their sense of the ridiculous to gain upon them. However, it had to be gone through and I began with what I took to be Oriental subtlety. I brought the Emir messages from the King. I elaborated, some would say that I embroidered, upon the message which I brought from the Prime Minister, Mr. Churchill. I said that both His Majesty's Government and, in particular, I myself were ever mindful of His Highness's unwavering support, and that whenever a suitable occasion arose, he could be assured that we should not forget and would serve him in any way we could.

I had got no further when he turned to me, still holding my hand, and, with a rather wan smile, said, "Say no more, Excellency. I know what you are trying to convey. It is that the British have no intention of making me King of Syria." This was not the first nor the last occasion when I have been grateful for the understanding and good manners which are often the attributes of hereditary rulers. I do not think that those who have been elected by popular suffrage would be less democratic if they paid more regard to politeness, even to those from whom they differed.

Moira and I were bidden to luncheon with the Emir. We were waited on by more than a dozen Arab servants, and the dishes in our honour followed the example of the French cuisine, though at some distance. It could not have been said of the cooks, "*Ils ont apporté toute la pharmacie de la nature au secours de la cuisine.*" Glubb Pasha, being in the Emir's service, followed the Arab custom of wearing his forage cap at the table. The Emir's son had been married the day before, and in the middle of luncheon the Emir turned to Glubb with a smile and said, "Do you think I shall soon be the grandfather of a son?" Glubb replied in very different tones from those in which he spoke English. It was the voice of authority; either the authority of a leader or of a prophet. I saw the gleam of white teeth in the dark faces of all the Arab servants as they smiled. I asked the interpreter what Glubb had said, and he replied, "Glubb Pasha says that the bucket does not go into the well and bring up water every time." I suppose this has the ring of the prophet. The next day we flew to Damascus; the saying had already preceded us, and was quoted to me by some Arab dignitary.

In the evening I had tea with Kirkbride[10] in the Residency, which had been darkened against the sun. In his grey flannel suit and heavy boots he did not look the famous Arabist that he was. More than one prince of the dynasty told me that he would ride hundreds of miles for the pleasure of talking with him the classical Arabic now so rarely used.

I once told Mr. Churchill with some hyperbole that if he wished, I could present a whole platoon of Arabists to him, each one of whom knew far more about Arabs than Lawrence ever did. I would

[10] Sir Alec Kirkbride.

start with Clayton and de Gaury, Buss, Kirkbride, Glubb, Smart, and could go on with many more, less well-known. The Prime Minister, with his strong Zionist inclinations, did not take me up on this point, but retorted that every Briton in the Middle East, especially British officers, ended up by being partisans of the Arabs.

Looking back today, it is curious to reflect how true this seemed to be at the time. There appeared to be some affinity between many Arabs and ourselves; their courtesy and dignified bearing, their splendid looks, their laws of hospitality and respect for tradition, their loyalty to friends, their chivalry and spirit of romance are high virtues. It is sad to think that much of this sympathy has been overborne.

The word Arab of course conceals rather more than it tells. The popular idea of an Arab remains the Bedouin, a swarthy tribesman living in a skin tent, riding a camel, driving his flocks to new pastures in spring, and into the sheltered valleys in the winter. The Arab farmer, the princes of the royal blood, the highly educated Arab of the Levant, the Egyptian scholars and antiquarians, are often forgotten.

I remember a dinner party in my house at Mena when George Antonius and an American general were amongst my guests. Antonius was a man of great cultivation, spoke perfect English, was the author of a well-known work, and had the ease and urbanity of a true man of the world. He talked brilliantly, and with wit, humour and understanding.

When he left, the general asked me who he was: was he perhaps a Britisher or, more likely, an American? When I said, "Oh no, an Arab," the general nearly fainted. There were no tent, no goats, no camel and no robes, which alone conjured up for him the true Arab.

CHAPTER XIV

THE MIDDLE EAST: III

MANY PROBLEMS were involved by the Allied occupation of Syria and the Lebanon and not a few of them were caused by the Allies.

We were lucky that the Spears Mission was in charge of our interests.

Sir Edward Spears, bilingual in French, was a representative who missed nothing. It was often said that he suspected things which never existed, but how small a defect this is when compared with the occupational disease which sometimes assails diplomatists of not suspecting enough. Foreigners have been known to play to a different set of rules.

Soon after the armistice, Spears found that there were several Vichy officials still retained in the Grand Sérail. Many of them had long service and one or two were married to Syrians. To deport them back to France was probably to inflict serious personal injury and Catroux, the new High Commissioner, was loth to act.

Edward Spears pressed for their dismissal with every right on his side, but the two of them got on less happily than they would have if Spears had not spoken French and had not understood too well some aspects of the French mentality.

Spears rang me up and I agreed that some action must be taken. I suggested asking Catroux to Cairo for a dinner party and broaching the subject to him the next day. Catroux accepted. He is one of the few men whom I have known who sets great store upon politeness, that is to say politeness in personal conversation. This inclination does not unfortunately extend to the written word and he has written a few passages about Spears and myself which are certainly rude and almost as certainly inaccurate. In doing so he has not shown himself to be an unusual type of general.

Whatever he may be as an author, as a guest he is charming, light in hand, fond of female company and with the polished manners of a man of the world.

My interview with him looked likely to be painful. I was sure that we should only get our way by displaying more than the usual diplomatic courtesies, especially as Edward Spears had become so exasperated that he had come to employ rather less.

Henry Hopkinson and I furbished up a formula, and when the general came to my office, I said:

"We have become friends, General, and one advantage, indeed one necessity, of friendship is to be able to speak on occasions with a frankness that hardly stops short of brutality."

At this point he looked deprecating and distressed and clearly feared the worst. I went on, "I hope you won't think me either an impertinent or an intrusive ally when I refer to the Vichy officials —and here, please forgive frankness—but as I say, if we can't be frank we can't be friends. Well, here it is—I have to say it—if those Vichy officials are not dismissed at once, you might as well be setting your foot on a road which might ultimately lead to a sharp disagreement with His Majesty's Government."

He took this terrible prospect with some equanimity, but the Vichy officials were at once dismissed. I believe he said to himself, "At least this is the way that two people should comport themselves in a delicate matter."

I got to know Edward Spears very well at this time and to this day few weeks pass without our meeting. He has a restless and enquiring mind; his views are not only well informed but generally original and imaginative. He has the gift of laughter and delights in touching in the ridiculous to any likeness which he may be portraying.

Soon after the armistice, the supply of grain in Syria gave me great anxiety. The crop was being hoarded and speculation in grain prices was widespread. I could see serious troubles arising in Syria unless supplies could be increased and it would have been most embarrassing to have to send troops to police the country.

With some difficulty, I obtained Treasury consent to buy a considerable tonnage of wheat which was to be offered for sale below black market prices, in sufficient quantities to prevent speculators buying it up.

The scheme had a good start, but the entry of Japan into the war both increased the difficulties in shipment of wheat from Australia and destroyed the confidence on which the scheme depended for success. In any case, I probably underrated the age-long skill of the Syrian merchants and should have known better than to take them on.

Later Edward Spears wrote that at first there was some jealousy on the part of the French concerning the plan and everything possible was done to give it the appearance of being an Anglo-French scheme, although it was purely British, since all the wheat imported was ours. When, however, it became evident that the scheme was a failure, it was proclaimed by the French to be a purely British affair. "Curiously enough," Spears said, "this did us no harm. The fact that we had imported 80,000 tons of wheat into the country and thus prevented starvation was widely appreciated and if there were some who criticised our lack of business acumen there were none who questioned our practical interest in the welfare of the people of the Levant States."

These are generous words from someone who was left with the scheme on his hands at a bad time and turned it afterwards to good account; they are even more generous when it is remembered that after I had left Cairo some of Spears' critics were not slow to fasten upon him the parentage of the scheme and its initial failure.

In fact, he worked out and administered a better plan than mine and collected wheat on the threshing floors by buying it direct for cash from the wheat growers.

In the event, the work of the Wheat Office was an outstanding success, and, in Spears' own words, "powerfully contributed towards maintaining British prestige in the Levant, since the people inhabiting this great area have had tangible proof of British interest in their welfare and of British fair play."

By the autumn our anxieties in the Middle East had lessened, and the outlook had begun to improve. The Iraq rebellion had been contained; the Vichy French had capitulated in Syria; the Italian Fleet had been crippled at the Battle of Cape Matapan; we had won overwhelming victories in East Africa, and U.S. ships were able to reach Suez unmolested; the strain on British shipping was less; men and the munitions of war were flowing more readily into the Delta. Above all, the Germans were now concentrating their attention on the war with Russia and had relegated the Middle East and the Mediterranean to a secondary front.

It was time to strike a blow at Rommel. General Auchinleck had for some time been preparing for an offensive in the Western

Desert, with the object of defeating the German and Italian forces, and clearing them out of Cyrenaica. Rommel was credited with similar intentions to clear us out of the Delta, and one of our objects was to forestall him. General Auchinleck was chiefly concerned with two weaknesses which might deny us success. He was not sure, first, whether we should have a large enough air force to secure air superiority, and secondly, whether our tanks were reliable enough and well enough armed, even though in superior numbers, to face the German armour and beat it.

I watched every development of the plan with the greatest attention. Already, by the middle of August, the Prime Minister was becoming impatient to launch the attack, and the C.-in-C. was equally determined to have superiority and to be trained and ready and poised. I asked General Auchinleck to let me see telegrams which he sent direct to the Prime Minister. I did not think that the terse and staccato style which he adopted would produce the necessary results or promote his objects. I felt that any Minister of Defence, and in particular Mr. Churchill himself, would resent their tone and would easily condemn as obstinacy what he might have condoned as patience.

Direct telegrams from the Prime Minister that had not previously been seen by the C.I.G.S. often presented the C.-in-C. with a delicate problem. These telegrams went far beyond general directions or advice; they sometimes descended to the particular, such as the desirable balance between "teeth and tail"—the Prime Minister's phrase for the balance between fighting men and the transport, services, staff, medical services and supernumeraries necessary to sustain them; the use of artillery in the encounter battle; expenditure of ammunition; repair of tanks and the like. These might well have come through the usual administrative machine of the army, and they would have assured the C.I.G.S. that nothing was urged upon subordinate commanders without consultation with him. Auchinleck was not familiar with the workings of Whitehall, nor had he any knowledge of the appropriate presentation of an argument to Mr. Churchill. I believe I was of help over some of these drafts, but it is undeniable that the delays increasingly angered the Prime Minister.

My judgement is that the timing of an offensive must, within reason, be left in the hands of the local commander, and that whilst no doubt a few days, a very few days, could have been knocked off the timetable, the C.-in-C. was right in not moving before he did. The course of the battle when it was joined supports this view.

Towards the end of September I was asked to go home to England for a few days for consultations. I had to leave Moira behind and she was deprived, to her great distress, of this opportunity of seeing the children.

I arrived, after a more or less uneventful flight. I went to a Cabinet Meeting and on October 2nd made a statement in the House. It was well received because I was able to say that my total staff did not exceed twenty-five. I also tried to convince Mr. Churchill that Auchinleck was not obstinate or supine, but I found him restive and impatient.

I spent a day and a night in the country with my children.

During my brief stay in London, my great friends Gilbert and Maud Russell asked me to luncheon at the Ritz, and I found myself sitting next to Ava Wigram,[1] whom I had known for many years. In the hubbub of conversation, I suddenly realised that Ava was talking to me in French, although I understand English as well as most. I only just caught what she said. She was asking my advice about whether she should *"épouser le Président du Conseil."* Not knowing what kind of joke this was, I said I thought it most unlikely that Winston would consent, and that anyway Clemmie might be rather annoyed. It then dawned upon me that she was not referring to the Prime Minister, which of course is what the French words mean, but to the Lord President of the Council, at that time Sir John Anderson. I said that I had too much knowledge of the world to give any advice on such a subject; it was the surest way of losing your friends; anyway it was obvious she had already made up her mind.

The next day, I was sitting on the front bench in the House of Commons when a note was passed down to me from John Anderson himself. He had written: "I understand a certain person has violated the Official Secrets Act. Do come and see me when the House rises."

When we met, he asked me whether he was too old or too set in his ways to marry the lady. I was much touched by this confidence, and broke my rule by advising him that he certainly was not, and to put all to the test.

The marriage was a happy one. It changed and mellowed John Anderson. He was introduced to a world with which he was un-

[1] Mrs. Ralph Wigram, now Viscountess Waverley.

familiar, and he found it agreeable. The food at Lord North Street was famous (the only place in London, said "Crinks" Johnstone, where you could rely on the *bavaroise*), the company never dull, the conversation rippling and usually provocative, and the hostess spreading all sorts of nets and lime for the unwary bird. At first John was slightly shocked by fashionable hyperbole. "Oh," I remember Ava exclaiming, "I've been there thousands of times!" "No, Ava," said John, with a twinkle, "that would mean that you had been there every day for nearly three years, or once a month for thirty-six years." "Oh well, hundreds of times, then!" "That would be almost equally improbable," he answered.

On my return to Cairo, the Commander-in-Chief explained to me his plans: he had two tactical alternatives, but had not finally decided which to adopt; there was no need to do so in a hurry.

The first involved a wide outflanking movement directed on Gazala—it appeared vulnerable to a counter-stroke by the enemy. The second was, after crossing the frontier, to turn north and east more quickly and execute a "left hook" directed roughly on Tobruk. The C.-in-C. informed me later that he had decided on the second alternative.

The Prime Minister was becoming increasingly impatient that we should strike. An October date for the attack had first been mentioned and deferred, and he had accepted with ill grace a further postponement until November 11th. When I was told that there was to be yet another delay and that it had been decided not to attack before the 18th, I feared an explosion from Whitehall. Though it was clearly too late for the command to be changed, I thought that strained relations with the Minister of Defence would add to the hazards and distract the C.-in-C. from his task of winning the battle. I sent some apologetic telegrams to the Prime Minister, and told the general that victory would soon wipe out any distrust of him that might be expressed. The Prime Minister, I said, never carried over his resentment or his impatience to the next account; he was even tolerant of failure, if it had been brought about by taking too many risks. There is no denying, however, that these were uneasy days, and I dreaded the appearance of irascible telegrams and exhortations.

At last, on November 18th, the attack of the Eighth Army, commanded by General Cunningham, was launched. I could not unfortunately go anywhere near the front myself, least of all on to the battlefield, but I was determined to get an eye-witness account of it and to transmit it unexpurgated to the Prime Minister.

I accordingly instructed my Military Liaison Officer, Major C. H. F. Fuller (his official title was G.S.O. II to the Minister of State) to go and report on the battle and get as close to the fighting as he was allowed.

I confess that after the first two days I had the feeling that Rommel was outflanked, and would have to draw back on his haunches. I had not yet really got into my system the mobility of the modern battle: tanks going back and sometimes forward from the battle front to pick up petrol from dumps previously prepared and hidden in the desert, an apparently surrounded force slipping away in the night without difficulty and without fighting, columns appearing a hundred miles behind the main battle and attacking even such sacred places as Army H.Q. In fact, the very term "flanks" was a dangerous one, and red and green arrows on the map represented very little other than the general axis upon which forces were directed.

Chris Fuller sent me back some admirable reports, and enabled me to understand the nature of the battle by bringing a visual picture to my mind.

The Ambassador had arranged a christening party for his newly born son in the big ballroom at the Embassy. He had not, of course, been informed of the date of the offensive and the party took place while the battle of Sidi Rezegh was still in the balance. Although I did not like to, I thought I must go for a few minutes, if only because rumours of defeat were already being spread in Cairo. There were some hundreds of guests. When I arrived, I was amused to hear the band strike up a tune from a German operetta, well-known in pre-war days, *"Adieu, Mein Kleine Gardeoffizier."* I took the hint and left, not without reflecting that on occasions the English are indeed incomprehensible.

The C.-in-C. began to be disquieted by the course which the battle was taking. We had not yet succeeded in joining up with the Tobruk garrison; some formations had been overrun, others defeated, only here and there had we been successful. Our losses of tanks were high; reports gave a confused and certainly not a reassuring picture. In particular, the battle of Sidi Rezegh seemed to have gone against us. Auchinleck told me that he and Tedder were going at once to the front, and that he would be back shortly. The news was a shock to me, and I felt the grip of anxiety.

Two days later I was told that Auchinleck and Tedder were on their way back, and would be at the conference at G.H.Q. in the evening.

At the usual time I went round, and in the corridor leading to the map room I ran into Tedder. He stopped, and in the most marked and significant tones, spacing his words with care, said, "It is most unfortunate—a great mistake—that the Auk has come back to Cairo." "Please don't talk to me in riddles," I said. "You mean that Cunningham is not confident of winning the battle?" "Yes." "Then he must be relieved tonight." I hurried into the C.-in-C.'s room, and asked him the obvious question outright.

He said he was more than glad that I had asked it and had expressed myself forcibly; the command of the Eighth Army was a War Office appointment, and he would have had to ask me to support any action upon which he determined. I said, "You must not give this aspect of your authority a moment's consideration. This is a battle, and I will take the full responsibility for what you decide, but you must act tonight." He then told me that Cunningham had talked of withdrawing behind the frontier but that he, Auchinleck, had ordered him to continue the attack. Cunningham's view had been influenced by his losses of tanks and, he thought, also by stray columns of the enemy appearing miles behind his front. Auchinleck took the view that these attacks could not be more than raids designed to disrupt the higher command and to spread confusion.

This was the most distressing evening I spent while I was in Egypt. I had a great admiration for Cunningham. I could not of course be sure that the C.-in-C. was right, I only knew that a battle could not be left in the hands of a general who did not believe that he could win it. In the event, it turned out that Cunningham had fought himself to a standstill, and that his physical resilience had given out.

I sent a telegram to the Prime Minister. I had certainly acted in haste, but I thought I knew what his attitude would be. I could not sleep for thinking of poor Cunningham, the brilliant commander with so many victories to his credit.

In the morning a telegram arrived from the Prime Minister: "Your action and attitude highly approved." [2] Although I was only responsible for the change in command at second hand, so to speak, I was glad to get the telegram, but it did not remove my gnawing pain.

The C.-in-C. decided to appoint General Ritchie,[3] his Deputy

[2] W. S. Churchill, *Second World War* (London: Cassell & Co., 1950), III, 506.
[3] Now General Sir Neil Ritchie.

Chief of Staff, to command the Eighth Army, and to send his Chief of Staff, Lieutenant-General A. F. Smith,[4] up to the front forthwith to make the change. The appointment surprised me. General Ritchie had not yet graduated in high command; he was now to take over a critical, perhaps a compromised battle. The two corps commanders were senior to him, which is apt to create friction. Nevertheless, you had only to look at him to see that he was a man of strong character and resolute purpose. Moreover, he had the greatest knowledge available of the whole battle and of his chief's plans. He rose to the occasion.

When misfortune overcame Ritchie a few months later and he was defeated in the battle of "the Cauldron," it was sometimes asked why the C.-in-C. had persisted in retaining so junior an officer in command of the Eighth Army. The answer is easy. A general who, by courage and tenacity, has restored a doubtful battle and won a victory against a formidable enemy has earned his place. General Ritchie afterwards commanded an army corps with great success and distinction in Normandy.

General Ritchie assumed command on November 26th, 1941. After a few anxious days the Eighth Army regained control of the battlefield. Rommel's dispositions had become disordered, partly because of his tendency to improvise attacks here, there and everywhere, partly because his lines of supply were strained, partly because he was faced by superior forces. At any rate, after being in some danger of being encircled by us near Gazala, a danger from which he escaped by night without fighting, he decided to evacuate Cyrenaica, to retreat at least to the position at El Agheila, which is the gateway to the invasion of Cyrenaica, and which he judged it would be difficult for us to threaten without some delay. He had made Benghazi useless for some weeks as a port by demolitions, and the weather was bad.

He had retreated, and hastily, leaving behind across the cord of Cyrenaica much material and other signs of defeat. As he had "appreciated," we could only follow him with light forces, because our forward troops were no less than 400 miles from the railhead, and no substantial supplies could as yet be unloaded at Benghazi.

Rommel had disengaged to shorten his lines of communication, to collect his reinforcements and some new tanks and to supplement his supplies of oil. That he had suffered a tactical defeat is undoubted, but so mobile is the modern battle that it is easy to interpret the abandonment of so much territory as a disaster rather

[4] Now General Sir Arthur Smith.

than as a reverse. A hundred miles given up in a day can be re-gained as quickly tomorrow. Whatever interpretation was put on his movement—and ours was over-sanguine—he had left us in command of the battlefield.

Every evening I went to the conference at G.H.Q. and studied carefully the very optimistic reports from military intelligence which I was given, and which I believed. The Commander-in-Chief, although he was in an aggressive mood, was unhappy about his power to strike another blow before Rommel regained his poise.

One night, when the conference at G.H.Q. was about to disperse, he turned to me and asked me what I thought of the dispositions. I said that it was unfair to ask me, but when pressed I replied jok-ingly that I thought our dispositions were too strong for recon-naissance, too weak for attack, and too dispersed for defence. I could see that this was not far off what he thought himself, but he did not judge that my third objection had much force: he certainly did not expect that Rommel would have the necessary resilience to strike back before several weeks had passed, nor—for what it was worth, and that was little—did I.

I suppose, looking back with hindsight, and if we had not been misled by our intelligence reports that the enemy could not quickly recover, that we should have made a *place d'armes* somewhere south of Benghazi, protected by extensive minefields, and concen-trated a well-knit force within it. We should have held back our armour on the eastern flank and prepared a powerful and mobile antitank force to support it. Behind this defence we should have cleared the port of Benghazi and got it working and should have established a forward base. In fact before any such scheme could be put into effect, we were caught whilst our dispositions were much dispersed. Rommel was quick to exploit our weakness; he was presented with just the kind of tactical opportunity upon which he thrived.

No doubt our bad dispositions were partly due to faulty intelli-gence, but I still believe that they could have been bettered.

This phase of the campaign always comes to my mind when Montgomery is accused of being slow and over-cautious. There is no doubt some justification for the charge in one or two of his oper-ations, but few remember the vast distances in the Western Desert, and few remember the penalties that can be paid if lines of com-munication are over-stretched.

Early in December, I got a telegram from the Prime Minister to say that Mr. William Bullitt, who had been American Ambassador in Paris until the German occupation, had been appointed as President Roosevelt's special representative in the Near East and would shortly arrive in Cairo to study the Middle Eastern theatre of war. I was to show him everything and treat him with complete confidence.

It was during the course of his flight to Cairo that the Japanese attacked Pearl Harbour and that the United States declared war on Japan. He arrived one evening at Heliopolis. I had arranged that the Commanders-in-Chief—Admiral Cunningham, Sir Claude Auchinleck and Air Marshal Tedder—and I should meet him. He stepped out of a Liberator bomber, shook hands and said, "Can I go to Bethlehem on Christmas Eve?" "Of course." Then, "Can I see the King of Egypt?" I said this was a matter for the American Ambassador, Mr. Kirk, but I happened to know that it had already been arranged.

Bill Bullitt radiates energy; he is interested in everything and wants to see everything; he likes to probe beneath the surface, and forms the most clear-cut opinions. At the same time he is an enthusiast, and some of his hard-boiled statements are self-protection against being carried away by enthusiasm.

He showed me over the Liberator, which he described as the finest four-engined bomber in the world; it certainly was not, at that time. Its rear armament consisted of two automatic guns, which were not mounted, but lying on the seats, and were supposed to be fired from the shoulder through the rear windows.

On the way from the aerodrome to Cairo I asked him to come to dinner with us at Beit el Azrak after he had seen the King; the earlier he arrived the more time I should have for a survey of the political and military scene, including the supply problems and the flow of men and munitions into the Delta.

He arrived the next evening, fresh from an interview with King Farouk. He plunged straight into the subject of our attitude towards the King. "He's a nice boy," he said. "Your Ambassador treats him too rough. His heart is in the right place, he is very pro us, and even rather pro you at heart. He should be trusted more and treated more kindly." This was too much for me, and I asked him if he would like to see what the palace radio had transmitted to Rome the day before. He read the transcript, which included some unflattering references to himself. This was his last mention of the strong inclinations shown by the King towards the Allied cause; thereafter, Bullitt's democratic and republican beliefs easily survived any monarchical tendencies.

I like Bill Bullitt, and he has remained a friend since those days. He has his critics, like all public figures, but I have not listened to them, and I take him as I find him, eager, receptive, energetic, fearless, almost boyish in his enthusiasm and disarmingly outspoken about his dislikes, which unfortunately included at that time the Secretary of State, Mr. Cordell Hull.

A little later I took him up to the front, and I am sure he enjoyed every moment of the trip, including the discomforts. We visited General Godwin-Austen,[5] commanding the 13th Corps, and spent a night at his headquarters at Antelat (about seventy miles south of Benghazi). Antelat is a small group of mud huts huddled together near a well on the caravan route, and Godwin-Austen's headquarters followed the usual pattern. They consisted of a group of command and wireless vehicles, a few troops in bivouacs to act as a guard, and a small tent rigged up as a mess. It was the usual desolate scene as we arrived at dusk: the enigmatic desert faded into the dim, dust-coloured rim, the only discernible feature at a slight distance was the officers' latrine; the wind was blowing and the canvas all round the little camp was bellying and flapping. The B.G.G.S. of the Corps was John Harding,[6] equally good as a commander or as a staff officer, and proved as both on many a battlefield. He was destined to be a Field Marshal, and Chief of the Imperial General Staff.

We were most kindly entertained, and talked late into the night. Godwin-Austen thought that Rommel was far from done for, and that we should hear from him again. "We'll be back," the German troops had shouted, when they evacuated Benghazi.

It was bitterly cold, and the desert wind found out the gaps in the canvas. Nothing, however, would induce Bill Bullitt to sleep in a caravan or a command vehicle; he insisted on a tent, and I think regretted it.

It still gives me a slight shudder to remember that the following evening Rommel was at Antelat and may well have pitched his camp on the very site of Godwin-Austen's H.Q. I hardly think that the President or the Prime Minister would have been pleased with my arrangements if Bill Bullitt and I had been captured.

We visited Benghazi; the mole was breached in several places, and heavy seas were breaking over it; a number of wrecks lay in the harbour, and the Royal Navy was engaged in blowing them up,

[5] Now General Sir Alfred Godwin-Austen.
[6] Now Field Marshal Lord Harding of Petherton.

or towing them out to be sunk. It was clearly a matter of a week or two before the port could be used on any scale.

We motored along the Trigh Capuzzo and saw some of the troops; they gave a splendid impression of a fit, aggressive and veteran force.

We were to return to Cairo in a Blenheim bomber from El Adem, south of Tobruk. However, by the expected hour of our take-off, a sand-storm was raging and we could not see ten yards. Our very young but obviously competent pilot was not deterred and said he would take off, but only after a car had motored along the strip to see if there was anything on the ground in our way.

The Blenheim is not a commodious machine for passengers, and we were very cramped and had to huddle close together. Bullitt regarded the experience as the greatest fun. We took off, and could not see the wing-tips. Soon the altimeter read 1,000 feet, then 2,000 feet, 4,000 feet, 5,000 feet, and still no wing-tips. Just over 6,000 feet we suddenly broke through the whirling sand and emerged into a cloudless and brilliant blue sky, and set our course for the Delta. The whole panorama of the coast, Bardia and Sollum and Mersa Matruh and the coastal road, began to unroll itself. I had always imagined that a sand-storm would not reach more than a few hundred feet from ground level, and the pilot smiled at my ignorance.

Some years after this, Bullitt told me of an experience contrasting sharply with our sand-storm. In 1944 Bullitt, who speaks fluent French, was the American liaison officer with General de Lattre de Tassigny.[7] In the winter of that year de Lattre's H.Q. was in the Vosges. It was snowing. One day in November soon after midday a car drew up and out of it stepped "Pug" Ismay and Winston.

Winston wanted to go up to the front at once and asked for an officer to accompany him. The French demurred and said that he must wait at least until after luncheon because the roads were impassable. The officers at de Lattre's H.Q., as might be expected, were drawn from the best of the French Army; they were hard-bitten, professional types. An excellent meal was laid on and, when the coffee and old brandy had been put on the table, de Lattre rose to his feet and made a short speech of welcome. The French make these little speeches better than anyone, and not a word was out of place. When he sat down, Winston got up and replied also in French. As a linguist he has only one quality—courage. He does

[7] Posthumously Marshal of France.

not translate English into French, he transposes it and pays little heed to grammar or gender, and little more to accent.

As the snow fell outside, he told this little hushed company of his love of France and of the comradeship of arms which bound us together. According to Bill Bullitt, the only other foreigner present, the French officers in the room were so moved as hardly to be able to choke back their tears.

The incident is worth recording because it shows that true oratory can survive even the medium in which it is expressed and that the quality of emotion breaks through the barrier of language.

But to return from the Vosges and the snow to Cairo in 1941. I was soon to learn more about the variety of my tasks.

In Persia there was a currency problem of some intricacy, which it was clearly necessary to resolve, and quickly. I did not think that our Embassy were being very skilful, and I therefore decided to fly to Teheran.

On my way to the aerodrome in my official car, which flew the Union Jack and was escorted by military police on motor-bicycles, I complained to Peter Laycock,[8] my A.D.C., about the nauseating smell in the inside. He told me that the leather had just been treated with some chemical. I implored him to get rid either of the smell or the car before I got back.

The flight to Jerusalem and then across the folded and twisted country of Palestine and Syria was restful. I had never been in Persia before and longed to explore the enchanting hinterland of Teheran, but for a few days I had to be at grips with the currency problem, which centred round the shortage of reals, the currency of Persia.

The first day after my arrival, I was entertained to luncheon by the Persian Cabinet. The food showed a strong French influ- ence and the room and the linen were in Western style. Some of the Ministers wore shirts with neckbands and without collars, as unbecoming a habit to men as flat ballet shoes are to women. Per- sians often wear a collar without a tie or a tie without a collar from the mistaken belief that a collar and tie are a Christian symbol denoting the Cross.[9]

I was a trifle surprised when the first question which the Prime Minister asked me was how many overcoats were required by the British forces in the Middle East. Not wishing to give anything away, I replied rather airily, "Oh, about a million, I suppose."

[8] Lieutenant-Colonel Peter Laycock.
[9] Christopher Sykes—in a letter to the author.

Now corruption, even amongst Ministers, is not unknown in Persia, and it was clearly thought that if I had my wits about me, a moderate trade-off of say a shilling apiece on the overcoats alone, without counting rifles, guns or ammunition, would provide a satisfactory cushion for my early retirement.

After my answer, I was treated with profound respect, and evidently regarded as a mixture of J. P. Morgan and Machiavelli.

At that time the story was current that one of the half-holidays granted to the Persian civil service had been cancelled and two educational films substituted. The second of these depicted a Persian official in his office, to whom enters a Western trader. A concession is discussed, terms suggested and indignantly refused. At this moment the Westerner produces a bag, from which he draws a few gold bars and says, "Will this help to persuade you?" In the film the Persian official drew himself up to his full height and said haughtily, "Do you know that no Persian official would sell his country's interest for gold?" At this point the audience of civil servants, who had become rather bored, suddenly grasped that the film was intended to be a comic, and greeted the sentence with roars of delighted laughter. Afterwards each appearance of the official was the signal for cat-calls. He was clearly looked upon as the Charlie Chaplin of the Middle East.

The authenticity of this story is rather more supported by evidence than might be generally supposed. It is a fact that when I had occasion to explain that a Ministerial post in Great Britain entailed severe financial sacrifices, I was greeted with polite incredulity.

After a few days of intensive work, a solution of the currency problem was found and I composed a memorandum in which I outlined the measures to be taken. It was a technical study and not perhaps of general interest.

During my stay I was received very kindly by the Shah. He has great charm, talks impeccable French, and gives the impression of an enlightened and civilised ruler. Our Ambassador was Sir Reader Bullard, a scholar who shocked some officers and civil servants by reading Greek and discussing the Greek tragedies, with plentiful quotations, with Sir Archibald Wavell. I could not find it in my heart to regard this as wholly reprehensible, and indeed stepped far enough from the stern path of duty to exchange some views with him myself on these enervating subjects.

I began to receive some disquieting telegrams from Cairo; a political crisis was said to be imminent and it was desirable that I should return quickly. In fact we started a little too quickly, because shortly after taking off I saw fuel oil pouring over the starboard wing. When I told the pilot, we turned back with indecent haste for Teheran, where it was found that the cap on the petrol tank had not been securely fastened and had worked loose.

On landing at Heliopolis I was greeted by an Egyptian guard of honour and one or two Ministers, with whom I exchanged some courtesies. I inspected the guard, and when the two military police on motor-bicycles had started up their engines, I bowed ceremoniously and got into my car. The smell was far, far worse than when I had left, and as we made our way towards the Pyramids I had to sit with clenched teeth and tight lips to prevent being overcome by the fumes. By a long tradition of discipline I did not disgrace the British flag, or the escort or the ceremonial, but on getting out of the car I said to the young corporal who drove it, "Never let me see this car again until it is as sweet as new-mown hay; it smells as if there was a dead duck under the seat."

A few minutes later he asked to see me, and with a barely suppressed grin broke the news that a teal, part of a large bag of several days before, had got lodged between the hinge of the boot and the back axle. The picture of the Minister of State riding ceremoniously behind the escort, with a putrefying duck under his seat, restored my equilibrium, although not until I had drunk a strong whisky and soda.

The political tension in Cairo was acute. The Prime Minister, Hussein Sirry Pasha, and his Cabinet, were a Palace Government, nominated by the King. They enjoyed no popular support, but they worked harmoniously with us and as long as discontent was not active, there was no compelling reason for us to make any intervention. Nevertheless, we regarded the Government as a potential source of danger. The party which had the backing of the large majority of the people of Egypt was the popular party called the Wafd, under the leadership of Nahas Pasha.

At this time a dispute broke out between the King and the Prime Minister about some comparatively trifling matter. After two or three days of to-ing and fro-ing the Government resigned and the King proposed to nominate another Palace Government. The Ambassador believed that if he did there would be a popular outburst and serious riots. He advised the King that we feared for the security of our base in the Delta and pressed him strongly to send for Nahas Pasha. The King flatly refused.

I called the Defence Committee together. The Ambassador favoured strong action. It was clear that words would be futile and that a show of force would be necessary if we were to get our way. The C.-in-C. and the military demurred, but I asked that at least the necessary measures should be concerted so that if an ultimatum from us became necessary, we could enforce its terms. The abdication and removal of the King might be involved. They reluctantly consented to make a plan, but at the same time pointed out that we should probably have tumult in Cairo and a sit-down strike of all the civilian labour upon which we relied. I retorted that the disturbances which would follow the flouting of the popular party were likely to be much more severe because backed, and rightly, by the mass of the people.

The Army rapidly began to formulate a plan in great detail, and as it developed, their objections and queasiness seemed to fade away.

The King, calling to his side two or three ex-Prime Ministers, locked himself up in the palace and sent a strong letter of protest —and not unnaturally—about foreign intervention. After consulting me, Sir Miles Lampson repeated our demands for a government enjoying popular support, adding that if the terms of this letter were not met by five o'clock, the King must take the consequences. Five P.M. passed. We surrounded the palace with tanks. It was decided that the Ambassador should demand an audience.

The Ambassador and I then had a long and earnest discussion in the Embassy. The principal question to be resolved was whether, if the King was at last willing to sign, we should still depose him, because the ultimatum had expired.

I said I was strongly of the view that if the King signed we should rest content. The Ambassador agreed. At about 9 P.M., accompanied by a strong escort of officers, the Ambassador went to the palace, marched impressively up the stairs, was ushered into the drawing-room, bowed and restated our demands. He told the King that the ultimatum had expired and that he must sign an instrument of abdication.

The King took up his pen to sign. His Chamberlain, Hussanein Pasha, struck in with a few urgent words in Arabic, imploring the King to think what he was doing. The King put down his pen and, looking up at the towering form of the Ambassador, said, "Will you give me another chance, Sir Miles?" In accordance with the agreed policy, the Ambassador said, "Of course, if you send for Nahas."

The King agreed. A messenger was accordingly despatched to summon Nahas to the palace. Comedy here intervened. He was waiting in readiness for the call, hurried to obey His Majesty's commands, but was unable to get through the cordon of tanks which surrounded the palace. Half an hour elapsed before he was admitted and told to form a government.

Of course, our action was afterwards criticised, but for two opposite reasons. Some said that our demands were too severe and our action too drastic. They might well seem so in the Westminster of 1962 but this was war and Cairo in 1942. My first duty was to keep our base secure in this life-and-death struggle. Weakness and vacillation might easily have made the maintenance of our armies in the field, which were there to protect Egypt, highly precarious. Moreover, we were only pressing for a government backed by the people to replace one nominated by the King.

The other critics claim that we were mistaken in not having deposed the King. It is true that the history of Egypt might well have been less troubled if at that time his power had been finally overthrown, but the reasons which made us hold our hand still appear to me unanswerable—namely, that he had agreed to our terms only a few hours after the time demanded.

It is impossible to say what would have occurred at the time of our defeat in the desert battles if a puppet government and a partially disaffected and hedging King had ruled in Cairo. It is only possible to put the positive rather than the hypothetical alternative. The positive fact is that when the invasion and occupation of the Delta by the Germans seemed imminent, the base on the whole remained stable, and as calm as could be expected in an Oriental country.

Faced by the same circumstances, I have no hesitation in saying that I should have reached the same decisions and backed the Ambassador in the way which I did.

As described elsewhere, I had just had an acrimonious exchange of telegrams with Mr. Churchill. My last telegram demanding a withdrawal of his strictures upon me had remained unanswered. There was a good reason for this, because it was in fact unanswerable, but unanswerable facts are not always the most endearing way of dealing with your superiors.

When, therefore, I got a message from the Cabinet Office in London that the Prime Minister wished to speak to me on the telephone, I supposed that our quarrel was either to be continued or that I was to be removed. This feeling was made the stronger because the telephone to London was hardly ever used.

I was relieved when a friendly voice said, "Is that you, Oliver? I hope you are not vexed with me." I answered, "Oh, well, I've got over it, but why no answer to my last telegram?"

"It was a very good telegram," said the voice. "Now I want you to come home, still of course as a Member of the War Cabinet, to be Minister of Production in charge of the whole of the production of munitions of war. The job has proved necessary; your appointment has the support of all my colleagues and will certainly be strongly backed by the House of Commons. Do you accept?"

"Yes."

"Start as soon as you can."

I confess that on the whole I was pleased. The prospect for both Moira and me of being once again with the family was uppermost in our thoughts to the exclusion of most others. Nevertheless, no other office but the one which I then held could present the same opportunities for usefulness, the same independence, the same authority, or, for that matter, the same interest and challenge. I was absorbed in my work. I had built up the office from being an experiment with a staff of three into a useful, almost essential instrument of government. I was far enough away from my colleagues to be able to make up my own mind upon many critical occasions. My powers were wide and unchallenged and I had to spend little time in clearing subjects with other Ministers. Moreover, I was very close to the Services and deeply in their confidence.

With my military background, and as a student of military history, my duties towards them were to me the most interesting of all my varied tasks. I was, too, physically closer to the war itself than any civilian Minister; it was on my very door-step. I could go to the front when I liked. I could see generals and regimental officers fresh from the battle. No other political office has ever been so enthralling to me, but my days as the Satrap of the Middle East were ended.

I felt in my bones that I had been successful in Egypt and was unfeignedly proud when I was shown a telegram which Field Marshal Smuts had sent to the Prime Minister, in which he had used the words: "Lyttelton's work has been outstanding."

Perhaps I may be forgiven for quoting a passage from the official history of the war, regarding the discharge of my duties:

Mr. Oliver Lyttelton, the Minister of State in the Middle East, left to become Minister of Production and the Commanders-in-Chief thought it right to put forward their views on the importance of the post based on their experience. . . . They regarded the Minister of State as a link with His Majesty's Government which was indispensable to the successful prosecution of the war in the Middle East. His guidance and advice on military policy from the political and governmental point of view had been invaluable. He had been able to relieve the Commanders-in-Chief of innumerable political and economic problems connected with Persia, Iraq, Syria, Palestine, Egypt, the Sudan, North and East Africa and the Arab world generally—apart from helping in their dealings with the Americans and with numerous allies. They could not cope with all this work, and, at the same time, exercise their primary functions as Commanders-in-Chief. Moreover, the office of the Minister of State had become a focus for the co-ordination of the views of the Services and of the other authorities in the Middle East: this made it easy to concert action and was to the general advantage.

In short, they were convinced of the need to have in the Middle East a Member of the War Cabinet who possessed the confidence of the Government at home. He should be served by an adequate staff qualified to deal with the many and varied political, financial, economic and propaganda problems which were constantly arising.[10]

I am content to rest upon these words.

[10] Playfair, *op. cit.,* Vol. III.

CHAPTER XV

THE MINISTRY OF PRODUCTION
AND THE WAR CABINET: I

W E MADE rapid arrangements for our journey and said
good-bye to most of the friends whom we could find.

Walter Monckton was to act as Minister of State until a new appointment was made. He had been staying as my guest at Beit el
Azrak, and it would have been hard to find a more delightful one.
After consulting Chester Beatty, I told him to make use of the villa
as he wished.

Moira and I had to start soon after dawn on February 26th from
Heliopolis in the R.A.F. Lockheed which I had used during my term
of office. The three Commanders-in-Chief and the Ambassador came
to see us off. I felt sad at saying good-bye to men whom I had liked
so greatly and with whom I had worked so closely.

The sun, magnificently red, had just risen. It was a warm and
clear morning, and except that Moira had a cold and a slight temperature, everything seemed set for a good flight. Our route was
to be Wadi-Halfa/Khartoum/El Fasher on the first day; El Fasher/
Brazzaville/Kano/Lagos on the second. At Lagos we were to leave
our Lockheed and, on the third day, take the Boeing Clipper, a
flying-boat, to Bathurst; there we had a wait of a few hours and
then on to Lisbon. After a day at the Embassy, we were to fly on the
fifth night to Poole and London. The distance by this route is about
10,000 miles.

We took off from Heliopolis and climbed rapidly to 12,000 feet.
Cairo and the Delta and my satrapy faded into the distance. The
higher we got, the hotter got the cabin. I could not understand
why, until the pilot came back and explained that the valve
which controlled the heating system was stuck. He feared that we

should have to swelter until we landed at Wadi-Halfa. Twelve thousand feet in an unpressurised machine is a most uncomfortable height at the best, but with the central heating full on it is almost unbearable. Your feet swell even more than usual, your heart pumps, and you become breathless and exhausted. What Moira with a temperature must have felt I can hardly guess. It was very hot on the ground at Wadi-Halfa. We spent almost an hour in a room wired in against mosquitoes while the machine was refuelled; then we took off again and climbed to nearly 14,000 feet. We were at last cool for the moment but even more breathless. As we came down at Khartoum the heat flowed up at us as if from a furnace; even Government House seemed airless and stifling and we were both so deaf from flying that we could hardly hear what the Governor-General was saying.

We left soon after luncheon. The seemingly endless panorama of Central Africa unfolded itself below us, the earth rufous in the sunlight, an occasional coffee-coloured river winding its way sluggishly to the horizon, some herds of antelopes galloping away from the sound of our engines—these are the fleeting impressions of a traveller by air. Down again to refuel and then in the cool of the evening we reached the mud houses of El Fasher and were hospitably received by the Resident. We were too tired to take in the full picturesqueness of this African town, the beauty of the sunset, the glow that turns everything to soft gold, and then the velvet night with its stars, and the farmyard noises and sounds of men and beasts settling for their rest.

The next morning we took off at dawn; our first stop was Brazzaville on the 27th. The aerodrome and buildings were primitive and fly-blown; most of the types to be seen sucking warm beer or Coca-Cola were straight from the pages of Somerset Maugham. Then to Kano on the Nigerian plateau. We were too tired to do more than drive round the walled city and look at the seething market, and too hot to relish the stew which was set before us for luncheon.

We took off again and soon began to descend gradually from the arid plateau and cactus towards the lush vegetation and dense trees to Lagos and its humid coastal heat, and so to Government House. Sir Alan Burns was the Governor and he (unfortunately as we thought) had a dinner party that night, which entailed unpacking our clothes. I was later to stay often in this house when I was Colonial Secretary and I found it cool and comfortable, but that night the suit cases showed all the malice of inanimate objects and in spite of repeated shower baths we felt intolerably hot and travel-stained. At one moment we despaired of ever being able to pack up again, and sat staring hopelessly at the confusion of clothes and the obviously inadequate spaces into which they had to be fitted.

We boarded the Boeing at about 2 A.M. The cabin was like a Turkish bath. After a long wait the engines were started; the heat rose a little more as we taxied on the water down wind. At last we turned into it, the engines roared on the boost and a breath of air and blessed coolness was wafted upon us.

By this time Moira was completely exhausted and I was anxious about the further fatigue which she would have to face. We got some sleep in the rear cabin and landed at Bathurst. We spent most of the day there, during which we walked a few hundred yards amongst the mosquitoes. It was an unattractive drab-coloured town; ten or more years later it had been so much improved that I could hardly recognise it.

Our next flight was to Lisbon through the night. The Tagus, as we swept in the next morning, looked enchanting; at least it was Europe and we knew that the hospitable Campbells and the Embassy and beds and sheets awaited us. Moira had developed a raging cough and her temperature was about 101. After two or three hours' sleep, we motored to Estoril and had luncheon—and a very good one—in the fashionable restaurant. The Ambassador pointed out some Nazi officials and a German agent or two who were also taking their luncheon at adjoining tables. If Brazzaville was Somerset Maugham, Lisbon at this time was Phillips Oppenheim. Diplomatists of powers at war with one another, secret service agents, military attachés trying to pick up some crumbs for their diplomatic bags, refugee cocottes from Paris and Brussels, were all jostling along in a peace-time setting: the *délices de sole*, the *tournedos*, the *béarnaise*, the *macedoine* and the *babu au rhum* all brought a nostalgic message and seemed to flaunt themselves in defiance of war.

We took off after midnight, and landed about 3 P.M. on March 2nd at Poole, where the War Cabinet plane was waiting. Green England at last, and a biting March wind to keep our joy in control.

Then London, and there were the children, Antony and Rosemary and Julian and Adrian, in a high state of excitement, waving at us. A secretary from the Cabinet Office came up. "The Prime Minister's compliments and he would be delighted if you could make it convenient to dine with him tonight." I could have shot

him; this was the only thoroughly unwelcome invitation I have
ever received from Mr. Churchill.

I am very strong and healthy and in the first war could keep
going for a week or two with no more than three or four hours'
sleep a night. A journey by air, however, in an unpressurised machine across Africa when you have to fly at ten, twelve or even
fourteen thousand feet to avoid the turbulence and then have to
come down three or four times in a day to a burning heat produces
a fatigue, and for that matter a deafness, unequalled by anything
in my experience.

There was nothing for it but to change for dinner and hope for
an early bed. These hopes were not realised and I crawled home to
the Dorchester at 2 A.M.

The next day, I went to my so-called Ministry; it was housed in
the Cabinet Offices in Great George Street, not far from the scene
of my first Ministerial experience as President of the Board of
Trade. Lord Beaverbrook had held the office of Minister of War
Production[1] for a fortnight. The fire and energy that he threw by
day and night into his task, and the frustrations of Ministerial life
had brought on an attack of asthma, to which he was intermit-
tently subject. On the 26th February, 1942, he wrote a letter to the
Prime Minister in his vivid and muscular English, resigning his
office. The letter shows the depth of his feelings and concludes:

I owe my reputation to you. The confidence of the public really comes
from you. And my courage was sustained by you.

These benefits give me a right to a place in your list of lieutenants
who served you when you brought salvation to our people in the hour of
disaster.

In leaving then, I send this letter of gratitude and devotion to the
leader of the nation, the savour of our people and the symbol of resistance in the free world.

The Prime Minister's reply held language no less generous to
his friend:

We have lived and fought side by side through terrible days, and I
am sure our comradeship and public work will undergo no break.

All I want you to do now is to recover your strength and poise, so
as to be able to come to my aid when I shall very greatly need you.

Your work during the crisis at M.A.P.[2] in 1940 played a decisive part
in our salvation. You shaped the Russian policy upon munitions, which
is all we can do for them. The figures of the Ministry of Supplies speak
for themselves. You are one of our very few fighting men of genius.

1 When I was appointed, "War" was dropped from the title.
2 Ministry of Aircraft Production.

At the Ministry he had not had time to get started and the staff which I inherited consisted of Sir Walter Layton,[3] the economist and writer, a private secretary, Hilton Poynton,[4] an assistant, Robbie Burns, and a typist or two.

That morning I was reminded that the Production Executive and the Import Executive, set up a year before,[5] had proved inadequate to the task of central co-ordination and planning in their respective fields and that the Ministry of Production had been formed under pressure from the House of Commons.

It was true that I was the only Minister of War Cabinet rank concerned with munitions, but the Ministry of Supply, the Ministry of Aircraft Production and certain sections of the Admiralty could hardly be expected to welcome my appointment. They would not take readily to interference. Moreover, I should have to invade the territory and affect the supplies of other Ministries, such as the Board of Trade, responsible for civilian needs, which could not be regarded as merely residual.

I had been away from Whitehall for nearly a year and had acquired a reputation often conferred on the absent which set the expectation and speed of success above what seemed humanly possible.

Once again I was called upon to forge an entirely new instrument to meet the needs of war. My two previous tasks had been first, the organisation from the "grass-roots" of the Non-Ferrous Metal Control and, secondly, that of the Minister of State's office in Cairo, also from nothing. Here, for the third time, I had to start off again with a staff of under five upon a task of much greater complexity and scope than the first, and with much less authority than I had wielded in the second.

The role assigned to me was expressed in simple terms.

The Minister of Production is the War Cabinet Minister charged with prime responsibility for all the business of war production. . . .

Notwithstanding anything in this paper, the responsibilities to Parliament of the Ministers in charge of Departments concerned with production for the administration of their Departments remain unaltered, and any Ministerial Head of a Department has the right to appeal either to the Minister of Defence or to the War Cabinet in respect of the proper discharge of such responsibilities.

The Minister of Production will also be the Minister responsible for

---

[3] Now Lord Layton.
[4] Now Sir Hilton Poynton.
[5] The Production and Import Executives were set up in January 1941.

handling, on behalf of the War Cabinet, discussions on the Combined Bodies set up here and in the United States to deal with Munitions Assignments and Raw Materials as between the Allies.[6]

My first prop was Sir Walter Layton. He could give the best background information, drawn from experience on war production in the first war. A man of saintly character and charm and of high intellectual calibre, he clearly had to be supported by a team of executives.

It is not my intention to discuss the administrative problems which towered above me. One of them had been impressed upon me by the battles in the Western Desert—namely to bring the tactical needs of commanders in the field much more into correlation with potential production, and vice versa. It was a curious fact that none of the Ministers of Supply, since the beginning of the office, Burgin, Morrison, Duncan, had ever taken part in a battle or had even served in the forces. One of these Ministers once asked me whether a Bofors gun was a howitzer.

In modern war it is easy to build up a race of generals, admirals and air marshals who can win battles with weapons that cannot be produced. "Give us for example a tank with a 25-pounder high-velocity gun, with six inches of front armour and capable of a speed of 30 to 40 m.p.h. and we shall be on the road to victory." Such an animal was beyond the practical bounds of engineering at that time.

It is equally easy for civilian Ministers to inveigh against the constant changes and modifications which appear desirable to meet the changing tactical needs of war, and for them to point out that the full volume of production cannot be attained unless there is some reasonable continuity of design. A synthesis of the tactical and production plans is essential to successful production for war.

Again, one of the compelling reasons for my appointment was the need for a Minister who could speak with one voice to the Americans on the combined requirements of the diverse departments concerned.

Given that the U.S. could and would give us much direct help in the supply of munitions, it was also obvious that the pattern of production between the two countries should be rearranged to prevent the worst overlapping and waste.

For example, the U.S. had designed their fighter aircraft mainly with an eye to war in the Pacific. Their fighters were of much

[6] White Paper Cmd. 6337, Office of the Minister of Production, February 1942.

longer endurance and consequently less manœvrable than the Hurricanes and Spitfires, which had been designed for the metropolitan battle. Endurance was of less importance to us since only twenty miles separated us from our main theatre of war.

Again, we pursued a policy of bombing by night without fighter escort, and designed the Lancaster and similar machines to fulfil this role. The Americans founded their tactics upon daylight bombing by heavily armed bombers protected by massive formations of fighters. I would therefore have been mistaken to have asked the Americans for fighters or four-engined bombers. Their own were unsuited to our needs and tactics, and to have asked them to manufacture some to our designs would have caused waste and delay. The two-engined reconnaissance machines and shorter-range bombers were common to both tactical plans, and in the event we were given and used predominantly American machines of this type, whilst we manufactured our own fighters and four-engined bombers. Other needs and other developments of weapons were also common to the tactics of both countries; the tank is the obvious example.

Thus the size of my task in Great Britain would have given anyone pause. It appeared all the more daunting when negotiations and arrangements with the United States were to be undertaken. All would depend there upon my powers of persuasion.

The prospect was bleak. Physically I reacted to it, to the cold climate and the fatigues of my journey by getting a sharp attack of influenza. I had to take to my bed at the Dorchester.

Sweating and aching, I planned my first moves and, by way of convalescence, started to think out my first speech to the House as Minister of Production.

It would be tedious to trace the development of my Ministry and the gradual expansion both of its usefulness and my powers. The intricate nature of the problems are described with great lucidity by Professor Postan in the Official History of the War (*British War Production*) and for those who are interested in this piece of large-scale administration his book will remain at once the most readable and the most reliable.

In part of his summing up he uses these words:

Thus, in the closing years of the war the growth of the Ministry of Production completed the administrative structure of war production. The old and much discussed "gap" between strategic and industrial plans was at last filled, and so were the more recent gaps between American supplies and British production, between central plans and regional action, between declining employment and rising demands from the field of battle, and, finally, between military and civilian requirements in the period of conversion. These gaps might not have been filled equally well or equally quickly by the alternative means of interdepartmental consultation. For, although the habits and the machinery of co-ordination had been well developed before the Ministry of Production came into existence, there was bound to be greater expedition and efficiency under a prominent member of the War Cabinet served by the administrative facilities of a fully-fledged department of state.[7]

The Ministerial function in the more remote past was confined to forming policy and much of the machinery of Whitehall has been fashioned on this assumption. My Ministry, however, almost more than any other, demanded that a large amount of data should be sifted and a mass of figures studied before any course could be plotted or decisions taken. This departmental work done, as a War Cabinet Minister I, like my colleagues, had to turn to other responsibilities and read all the papers for discussion at Cabinet Meetings. I was also a member of the Defence Committee, of the Anti-Submarine Committee and the Man-power Committee.

The work was killing; I calculated that a War Cabinet Minister at that time had to read the equivalent of one full-scale novel a day every day of the year. The Prime Minister's own régime did not help. He started work very early in bed, got up in time to go to the House of Commons, which met at 11 A.M., had a good luncheon, talked to his guests with brilliance and animation and then, putting a black bandage over his eyes, slept from about 3 P.M. until 5:30 P.M. and sometimes to 6 P.M. or 6:30 P.M. He worked very long hours, but they were not the hours of his colleagues.

After the end of our departmental day—around six o'clock—we usually had to attend a Cabinet, and these meetings often lasted until nearly nine. Dinner in an hotel or a club was difficult to get at this hour, especially when an air-raid was in progress. The Defence Committee often met at 10:30 P.M., at which hour the Prime Minister was fresh and ready to tackle anything.

At 2 or 2:30 A.M. the Prime Minister often called his Conservative colleagues on the Defence Committee, that is Anthony Eden and myself, into his private sitting-room to take a whisky and soda and talk about some military event or plan. In the middle of these discussions, I sometimes used sadly to think of the meeting of, say, the Man-power Committee at 10 A.M. the next morning, and the massive schedules that wanted more study. I wondered if the

[7] Official History of the War. M. M. Postan, *British War Production*, (London: H.M.S.O., 1952).

habits of a Montgomery—no alcohol, bed at 10 P.M., rise at 6:30 A.M.—would have been preferable. I add that my answer was invariably that they would not have been.

My work was so exacting that I had to have a flat prepared for me in Great George Street. Although I moved some of my own furniture and pictures into it, it was a grim and cheerless place. I started to build up my staff. I added another assistant private secretary, Garrett Moore.[8] As a gunner officer, he had fought in the battles before Dunkirk. Before the war, I had marked him down as a man of great ability. He was not only thorough and lucid but, what is almost as important, extremely rapid, and I decided to put his talents to the best use. His wife was in the United States, and I persuaded him to live in the flat. This helped the work along but it also gave me the solace of talking to a friend with many common tastes.

I later added to my personal staff Lord Strathallan.[9] He, too, was a friend of great ability. He had married a charming American lady and had the great advantage of being much liked in the United States. He was a very hard worker and his sober judgement was only formed upon careful study.

Sir Henry Self became the Permanent Secretary of the Department. He had a computer-like brain. I believe that in a few months he could have passed an examination in anything. At least he had collected two degrees in divinity whilst permanent head of the Air Ministry.

He started to build the organisation. Afterwards he went to represent the Ministry in the United States. In this role he was most successful, and gained the respect and admiration of the Americans, and even more important their friendship.

He was succeeded in the Ministry of Production by "John Henry" Woods[10] as the permanent Civil Service Head. Sir Robert Sinclair,[11] afterwards Chairman of the Imperial Tobacco Company, became Chief Executive. What I owe these two men could never be written, because whatever success the Ministry achieved was due almost entirely to them. It was on Rab Sinclair's advice that I prised John Henry out of the Treasury. We three became the greatest of friends. John Henry has a particularly happy turn of wit, and is liked by everyone. He smoothed our path with other

[8] Now the Earl of Drogheda.
[9] Now the Earl of Perth.
[10] John Harold Edmund Woods, now Sir John Woods.
[11] Now Lord Sinclair of Cleeve.

Ministers. Rab and I kept sane largely because of John Henry's gaiety and sense of the ridiculous.

Rab had one fault: he worked too hard. In my opinion he had no others. His integrity, keen Scottish judgement, humanity and humour single him out. Nothing ever appeared above the signature of these two men that had not been thought through and carefully matured.

At the Ministerial level, Garro Jones,[12] a member of the Labour Party, was appointed at my request Parliamentary Secretary, and be served until the end of the Coalition Government in 1945. He was succeeded by Jock Maclay, who was previously the Head of the British Merchant Shipping Mission in Washington.

My private secretary, Hilton Poynton, to whom I pay tribute elsewhere, was promoted in 1943, and was succeeded by Denis Rickett.[13] Denis, a Fellow of All Souls and devoted to the arts, had at once a lively and attractive mind and sober judgement. It is rare that so refined a scholarship should be found allied to such unforced and engaging social gifts. I leant upon him greatly; he was with me at a time of very great personal sorrow, and over the years our friendship has deepened and endured.

For the last year, George Blaker was my private secretary. He was another example of a civil servant of ability and charm. He is now Treasury Representative in New Delhi.

I have touched upon these various men to show how exceptional were those who served with me. I should add to the roll Thomas Chegwidden[14] and Eaton Griffith from the Civil Service, and Norman Kipping,[15] David Eccles,[16] Geoffrey Crowther,[17] Ivan Spens, Hugh Weeks, Bill Edwards[18] and Julian Piggot, all of whom joined the Department from outside. My debt of gratitude to them and to the many others can never be discharged.

Being a member of the War Cabinet, I now found myself for the first time near the centre of affairs at home.

In March 1942, the members of the War Cabinet were the Prime Minister, Mr. Anthony Eden, Foreign Secretary, and myself from the Conservative benches, Mr. Attlee, Deputy Prime Minister, Mr.

[12] Later Lord Trefgarne.
[13] Now Sir Denis Rickett.
[14] Now Sir Thomas Chegwidden.
[15] Now Sir Norman Kipping.
[16] Now Lord Eccles.
[17] Now Sir Geoffrey Crowther.
[18] W. P. N. Edwards.

Bevin, Minister of Labour, and Mr. Morrison, Home Secretary, from the Labour Benches, and Sir John Anderson, Lord President of the Council, a self-designated National Liberal and without party affiliations. Lord Woolton did not join the War Cabinet until 1943.

The daily lives of these seven, and later eight, were locked together; upon them fell the main impact of the multitudinous events, dangers and problems; from them the first impulses to counteract, balance or originate had to spring. Whatever political differences were to emerge after the war, these seven or eight men are bound together by the indelible experience of those times.

It does not appear to me out of place to essay some impressions of my colleagues.

Elsewhere, I have devoted a chapter to my portrait of the Prime Minister; it is generally supposed that he loomed so large that the other members of the War Cabinet were merely his lieutenants, and that he overrode them whenever he wished. This is not the truth, because for one thing Mr. Churchill's respect for constitutional propriety extended as much to the collective responsibility of his Cabinet as to the ultimate power and dominance of the House of Commons.

I can think of a number of highly important matters upon which Mr. Churchill did not get his own way or had his first wishes greatly modified. He fought hard on these occasions, but when a changed or modified policy was agreed, he rarely looked over his shoulder or bore resentment.

Anthony Eden I had known on and off since our Eton days and between the wars we sometimes met at dinner parties or country houses. We were now the only two Conservatives, apart from the Prime Minister, in the War Cabinet, and though Anthony Eden's duties covered by far the most important field other than that of the Prime Minister himself, and mine were limited and pedestrian, we were naturally thrown much together.

He was a mature and experienced politician and statesman. He was highly trained in foreign affairs; he could have stepped down to be the Permanent Under Secretary of State at the Foreign Office as a civil servant, without shaking the organisation. I was a mere novice.

Anthony Eden is not an easy man to know. Added to a natural reserve, he sets high store upon good manners and they sometimes concealed the depth of his convictions. His elegant appearance and ease of manner, his disregard of men's clubs, his appreciation of painting, his liking of female society and his hobby of gardening perhaps concealed from the superficial observer the inflexible nature of his principles on high matters of state.

We have lived together through some of the most testing experiences which fall to men; sometimes it was his duty, if possible with the support of his only other Conservative colleague, to disagree with his chief. In all the many years in which I have served in the same Cabinet, I can never recall an occasion when he abandoned for expediency a principle in which he believed. Sometimes he fought his corner with impatience and even petulance but rarely, if ever, gave any rein to anger.

Physically, his slim figure gave some impression that his constitution was delicate. The impression at that time was false. Few of my colleagues showed less signs of fatigue; he appeared to carry the burdens of the Foreign Office as easily as he fell in at times with the diet and régime of his leader. He could smoke a long cigar after midnight without flinching, and his digestion was robust.

The effect upon the House of Commons of his sober and unexaggerated mode and of his sense of balance, which led him away from phrase-making, often as far as undistinguished language, was cumulative. Until the crisis of Suez, I can think of no occasion when he was not listened to with the deepest attention and respect.

He had in my opinion a greater hold upon the House—day by day—than even the Prime Minister himself. The words "day by day" are necessary because on the very greatest occasions, Mr. Churchill dominated the assembly by his stature and by his eloquence, but on some others his combative nature and love of argument aroused the House to anger, even to bitterness.

Anthony never overstated a case; his reproofs were always concealed by apparent mildness and by impeccable Parliamentary manners. "I hope I didn't put so-and-so down too hard," he said to me one day. "My dear," I replied, "I thought that your commination was more like a caress." He smiled and saw no harm in that.

John McGovern, the Clydesider and a friend of mind, once said to me in the smoking-room: "Anthony is our idea of a gentleman. We respect him, but we shan't ever match him."

Politics are, of course, Anthony Eden's dominant interest, and when his health broke down and the Opposition, on a great national occasion in the debates on Suez, fell far short of the standards which he himself had always set, I felt the grief of a personal tragedy. He has sustained it with an unflinching fortitude which springs from his belief in the rightness of his policy and of the ultimate verdict of history upon his actions.

His wife has helped him immeasurably to enjoy for the first time in his life the peace of inaction which his illness has imposed upon him.

The title of his first volume, *Full Circle*, is at once the epitome and solace of this bitter period of a life devoted and spent for his country.

The Deputy Prime Minister—although formally there is no such title or position—was Mr. Attlee.

Just after I had joined the Government in 1940 and was waiting outside the Cabinet Room to sponsor an item on behalf of my Department, Clem Attlee came up and shook my hand and gave me a warm, almost an affectionate welcome. He said he had been a boy at Haileybury when my Uncle Edward was Headmaster, and asked me to keep in close touch with him and seek his help when I needed it.

From that day to this my personal affection for him has grown. His was a true modesty, and first as the leader of his party, and then as Prime Minister, he never had a good conceit of himself. At the same time he maintained a rigid and somewhat aloof control of his party, and was feared as well as respected by its members.

His intellectual equipment is of a high order, but he appeared to lack the slightest interest in the future, and never to project his mind or his imagination further than the immediate problem. If you said, "Won't this lead to great difficulties in a year or two?" he abstracted himself and started to doodle.

This does not mean that he had no general line of thought about the future. He adhered consistently to his socialist principles, and was informed by a social conscience. The goal was clear; the methods and the means could be left for that moment when action was needed.

He approached most daily problems without any preconceived judgement, and this made him one of the best chairmen of a committee that I have ever sat under. His keen mind missed no points; he was curt and businesslike, and he knew the exact moment when his colleagues were nearing agreement. His interventions were perfectly timed, and he used to say, "I think we are agreed . . ." and then sum up with great lucidity and adroitness. We thus got through a great deal more day-to-day business than we did under Winston. Winston regarded committees as an opportunity for ventilating his own views, or even for giving his speeches a trial run;

he was frequently irrelevant and often impatient. Attlee was a chairman and Winston a leader; different qualities are needed.

Attlee had a pungent sense of humour and used occasionally to push notes across to me when some argument appeared to him to be insubstantial or plainly ridiculous.

At the same time, there was something waspish about him. I remember drafting a memorandum concerning national air lines and how they should be financed. I suppose I had drafted it badly, for he clearly did not understand it. He poured out a good deal of acid and vituperation upon it.

Although he did not merit the caustic comment "A sheep in sheep's clothing," he was not, it must be confessed, from the mould of greatness. Clever, cogent, humorous, of absolute integrity, with the inherent modesty of a truly educated man, he was not an inspiring leader. Nevertheless any country that could command his services could count itself lucky.

I have not forgotten, though I have not been able to repay, his kindness to me when I was a new Minister.

During the whole of my service in the War Cabinet as Minister of Production, Mr. Ernest Bevin was Minister of Labour. Production and labour are inextricably linked and we had to work in close harness; we had some disagreements but no rows.

Perhaps I was too close to him to feel the unbounded admiration which he earned from the foreign service when he was Foreign Secretary, but my affection for him was warm and permanent. He was first a patriot, next a Minister and, some way behind, a Labour leader. Once his word was given, nothing would shake it; it had the cachet of a guarantee by the Bank of England. It is perhaps a small defect that he had the overweening confidence of many self-made men. To him the solution of many tangled problems appeared simple and his approach to them sometimes naïve. His lack of education and superficial knowledge of European history were, however, offset by his rugged perception of where British interests lay.

One day, my permanent officials at the Ministry of Production persuaded me that the necessary co-ordination of one important matter concerned with munitions could not be achieved unless my Ministry made some inroads into the authority and the responsibility of the Ministry of Labour. They said that Mr. Bevin would never agree. I replied that I would not be so sure, and that I would go and see him myself in St. James's Square. It was not a common practice to visit a colleague in his Ministry; we usually cleared our business in a Committee or at No. 10 Downing Street. To my chagrin, I was told that Mr. Bevin was ill. I asked if he was well enough to see me at his home, and got the answer that he was better and could see me the next day.

I went to Fortnum and Mason and bought him some Muscat grapes, and went off to his flat. Mrs. Bevin,[19] who was jealously standing guard over him, looked me severely in the eye and begged me not to be too long. I was shown into his bedroom.

He was in bed wearing some very loud pyjamas which seemed to tickle his skin. He scratched himself from time to time, and the memory of his pyjamas still makes me itch.

"Ernie, I hope you are better." "Well, Oliver, I have been poorly, but I am all right." "Do you like grapes?" "Well, I don't know that I do give much for them," he said. "Oh," I answered, "I'm sorry, because I have brought you some," and put the open box on the bedside table. He took one or two and was apparently soon able to overcome his distaste.

He plunged straight into the subject on his mind. "Look here, Oliver, I know you've come on business, but I have been very queer. Do you think any of my Labour colleagues have made any enquiries or come to see me? Not a word, not a telephone call. I got an enquiry and these flowers from Mrs. Churchill, and Winston has been on the telephone, and now you're 'ere"—spitting out a grape stone—"but nothing from the others. When I was a farm boy," he went on, and at this point I relaxed and sat back, for it would be true to say that I was familiar with his life story from his own lips, and it was not unduly abbreviated. After he had finished one of the episodes, I said, "Ernie, I have got to go in ten minutes, and I have a paper here which affects you and your Ministry. I think it is a piece of impertinence to ask you to agree, but perhaps you would think of it." I put the point in three sentences.

He did not do more than glance at the paper and then said, "You do what you think best. I'll help. As I was saying, the Trade Unions in 1935 . . ."

Soon afterwards I left, ushered out by some searing remarks about Herbert Morrison, with whom he was in conflict. I pretended not to hear.

The Ministry of Labour did not like the arrangement to which we had come, but Ernie never budged from his undertaking. "I said so, didn't I?" was his only comment to his officials.

At another time, Ernie Bevin and I were opposing together any

[19] Now Dame Florence Bevin.

further increase in the "extraction" of wheat. For every one per cent rise in this extraction, 100,000 tons of offals, which are used as animal feeding stuffs, are lost, making it necessary to import and pay for a corresponding amount from abroad. In peace time, the extraction of wheat for the ordinary loaf is 70% –72% ; it had already been raised to between 80% and 90% .[20]

Our contention was that the extra husk put into the bread made the centre of the loaf uneatable and indigestible, and that the centre was generally thrown away.

At a committee meeting, Ernie Bevin was backing me up and exclaimed, "I say, Deputy Prime Minister, that the loaf is indigestible. I can't digest this stuff in the middle. I throw it away; it's just waste." At this point, he belched undisguisedly. "There you are, you see. What did I tell you?" In spite of this persuasive demonstration, we did not wholly succeed, though we prevented any further rise in the rate of extraction.

Ernest Bevin had warmth and humanity and loyalty: high qualities, and even if I thought that buying him at my valuation and selling him at his own would have resulted in an appreciable profit, he never appeared to be a small man either in purpose or in action. Until the day of his death our relations were unclouded.

My other Labour colleague, with whom I was less often in close contact, was Herbert Morrison.

He is a typical cockney, very quick in the uptake, who sees a point coming a long way off. He has some of the caustic and disenchanted humour of the Londoner and his company is refreshing. He is through and through a politician, adroit and mobile in debate, but in ordinary life he was less reliable round the corners and up the hills than was Ernie Bevin. He is a sound administrator and had a proper regard for the public purse. He does not like waste, a dislike which I have known to transcend party advantage.

Late in the war, Lord Woolton (Fred to us all) used to preside over a committee concerned with some post-war problems. Morrison and I were both members. Fred was wont to preface the meetings with a bland exordium, not always of startling originality. We, the other Ministers, were generally hard-pressed and became a little restless over these prologues. On day, Fred was embarking upon one of them when Herbert Morrison, who was sitting next to me, leant over and a tendril of his quiff of hair brushed lightly across my forehead: "Call me after prayers, Oliver," he said, and

[20] Source: Ministry of Agriculture, Fisheries and Food.

resumed his study of the Home Office papers. I forgave him much for this remark.

The best speech which I heard him make was when he decided, and rightly, to release Oswald Mosley from detention imposed under the wartime regulations. It was at that time an unpopular decision with his own party. They were restless and fractious. It was therefore a brave decision and the speech was both adroit and courageous and at a high level. Nevertheless, I had the sensation that his courage was not without political objectives and that he thought he would benefit by taking a strong line.

Morrison's undoubted gifts as a parliamentarian led him after the war to believe that he could make a good speech without profound study and one or two careless or carefree speeches damaged his reputation at a critical moment.

If the Labour Party had made him their leader, his flexibility of mind and his address would, in my opinion, have patched up many of the rents in its fabric and would have given it a better chance electorally. On the other hand, his leadership would hardly have animated a party which existed to right wrongs, most of which were no longer there.

He was deeply, and naturally, wounded when he was passed over, but faced his political demise with dignity. His misfortune has mellowed and not embittered him. I admire him for that; he and I have remained friends and still exchange quips at one another's expense which leave no rancour behind them.

I have left Sir John Anderson to the last because he did not belong to either of the great parties.

In 1940, when I had been a Minister no more than a few days, I was nominated as Chairman of a Committee on the Supplies and Transport of Coal, both of which had been disrupted and disorganised by the heavy bombing of London and the railway network. Someone had mercy upon me and substituted John Anderson as Chairman. Moore Brabazon, the Minister of Transport, and I were members from the Government. Fred Leathers, not at that time a Minister, was the expert member.

I barely knew John Anderson, and in those days sitting on this committee gave me some of the sensation of being back at school under a strict master. From fear, I did my homework with great thoroughness.

Moore Brabazon had a good grasp of the transport problems involved, but he has never been avid of detail. One day John Anderson turned to Brab, who was smoking a cigarette in a long holder, and asked, "Minister of Transport, how many wagons at this moment are immobilised south of the exchange points?" (The exchange points are the crossings of the Thames through which the coal traffic has to be directed to the southern counties.)

Brab, stifling an incipient yawn, said, "I've no idea but can easily get you the figures from my Ministry in a few minutes."

"On future occasions," said John with a frown, "you will please come to the Committee armed with the necessary information."

Brab smiled and was delighted at the rebuke of the dominie, which he thought was unusual between Ministers of the Crown.

John Anderson was Lord President of the Council and presided over the Lord President's Committee on Home Affairs. From his knowledge of the Service, he had unerringly picked Norman Brook,[21] the ablest of the younger civil servants, to be its Secretary.

Under John's direction, and with Brook as lieutenant, the Committee became famous as the principal instrument of government outside the military and foreign spheres. Its contribution to the Government can hardly be over-estimated, for it relieved the War Cabinet of a mass of administrative work. Moreover, once the initials "J. A." had been appended to a Cabinet paper, everyone knew that the subject had been thrashed out by an expert mind and that no one was likely to improve upon its findings.

His expertise was only matched by his scrupulous fairness. I came as President of the Board of Trade to know him well. His manner, it is true, was ponderous, but those who have an insight into the qualities of the Scottish race could detect the gleam of humour that flitted across the deep waters of his character.

He was one of the few men whom I have known who never expressed an opinion on a matter upon which he was not fully informed. For example, he never spoke about strategy or tactics and seldom upon purely political issues. This self-denying habit is not usually counted as a social grace. When, however, he turned to administration in other spheres, his guns were unmatched.

In 1940 he was a lonely man, and I judged that some of the austerity of his manner was due to his loneliness. After his marriage he started, at first rather heavily, to make his way amongst a more butterfly society. His wife encouraged controversy and hyperbole amongst her guests and, once accustomed to the mode, John enjoyed the banter. When it became too outrageous he used to sink it with a broadside of reason and fact.

[21] Now Sir Norman Brook.

After the war when he was an Opposition politician and Chairman of the Port of London Authority, a Russian Trade Delegation arrived in England. Their first official visit was to the Port of London, and they were entertained in the official yacht by John and Ava, who pointed out the features of the landscape: Greenwich Hospital, the Docks and the Flour Mills. It caused much surprise to the Russians that this huge port should be under the control of a political opponent of the Government.

About three o'clock the Russian Delegation asked to be put ashore, as they had a meeting which they had to attend. They were in fact bound for the Committee charged with the oversight of nuclear fission and atomic energy. Their astonishment may be imagined when they found that the Chairman was this very same politician, John Anderson.

One night, they were invited to see *Swan Lake* at Covent Garden as official guests. John and Ava Anderson waited in the Royal Box to greet them: they were dumbfounded.

I would have dearly loved to see their analysis of the British Constitution and how it worked.

John had the highest and most unshakable principles that I have ever known in any man. Nothing would ever make him deviate from them and as a sort of dividend on these capital virtues, no one asked him to bend them; it was known to be useless.

I am proud to have enjoyed his unbroken friendship. We remained on intimate terms for the rest of his life. His untimely death deprived the State of one of its greatest servants.

Lord Woolton, who joined the War Cabinet much later, in 1943, had made his reputation as Minister of Food. He had in that office quickly collected around him an able team of experts in food and in distribution. He himself paid particular attention to the relations of his Ministry with the public. It was clearly the key to success.

In his dealings with the public he had a sure touch; his training and experience, first as a social worker and then as the head of Lewis's, had kept his finger on the pulse of ordinary people. He had, too, the grasp of the obvious which is necessary in dealing with mass opinion and mass psychology, and he had a warm and sympathetic knowledge of the tribulations and struggles of the poorest classes.

He was a man of transparent honesty. I can recall no instance of him saying an unkind word about anyone. It was because of these great qualities that his associates worked happily under him.

With his Cabinet colleagues he affected an urbanity and polish which might have passed unnoticed in Lord Chesterfield, but appeared slightly out of harmony with our times. You could almost see him holding a snuff box, and taking a pinch of snuff to emphasize his point.

Sometimes he overdid the oxymoron, and when he wished to put before his colleagues a pellucid drop of distilled wisdom, it sometimes became too distilled. "I have come to the conclusion that the key to the housing problem is to build more houses," he once said to the Reconstruction Committee. He no doubt meant that in essence housing policy is simple, but for once his words were unsuited to his audience.

He used to make good after-dinner speeches, and they were illuminated by a delightful and natural sense of humour. His nickname was "Uncle Fred."

At one time, in October 1941, when he was leading the House of Lords during the temporary absence of Lord Salisbury, a debate was raised by the Bishop of Winchester on the motion: "To call attention to the grave increase in the number of fatal accidents on the roads; to ask His Majesty's Government what steps they propose to take to reduce unnecessary loss and suffering caused by these casualties, and to move for papers."

Fred Leathers was the Minister concerned. He believes and excels in action rather than in exposition, and he galloped through the Ministry brief, and treated the punctuation with disrespect. He had misjudged the temper of the House. There was as near an uproar as their Lordships permit themselves. Some angry protests were heard, and one or two peers rose in their places.

At this moment Fred Woolton entered the House and gazed about him with bland surprise. He looked like a man who had opened the window only to find that the wind was blowing all the papers off his desk. "What's all this about?" he said to Leathers. "What *do* they want?" Leathers replied, "Dear boy, the Government is going to be defeated." "Yes," said Woolton, "but what do they want?" "They are asking for papers." "Well," said Fred Woolton, "we will give them papers." Fred Leathers accordingly agreed and, rising to his feet, said he would be pleased to grant papers to the Right Reverend Prelate.

This ended the debate, and their Lordships' proceedings came to an abrupt stop. The wigs of the clerks at the table seemed to rise from their heads in astonishment. In Parliamentary practice, to grant papers in the House of Lords is not far removed from accepting a Motion of Censure. The clerks hurried to the Ministry of Transport, where that earthy and sensible character Jay Llewellin was the Parliamentary Under Secretary. "What are we to do?" they cried. "Well," replied Jay, calling in the Permanent Secretary, "didn't we have a committee on road accidents?" "Yes." "Well, make up a bundle of the minutes. You had better look through them and tick the right ones, put some white ribbon round them and send them to the Bishop." No more was heard of the incident.

CHAPTER XVI

THE MINISTRY OF PRODUCTION
AND THE WAR CABINET: II

I MUST RETURN to my narrative and to my own Ministry. I have already made it clear that a close integration of the programme of production on both sides of the Atlantic was desirable, if not imperative. My Ministry was the responsible body in Great Britain, and it was decided to ask the American administration to receive a mission headed by me. The objects of this mission were twofold: the first, which no doubt was the most important, was to "procure"—for that is the technical term—a large number and a wide range of weapons, and secondly, to negotiate the foundation of a Joint War Production Board, on which would sit representatives of both countries.

In June 1942, my mission flew to Washington. My opposite number in the United States was Don Nelson, the Chairman of the War Production Board. He had been an executive in Sears Roebuck, the great mail-order store, and his selection for this important post had surprised some of the leading industrialists in the United States, and even incurred their hostility. Nelson was a tall and heavy man, his face was kindly but did not carry the mark of intellectual distinction. His speech was not incisive. He smoked a pipe with a very large bowl, and gave the impression of being easy-going and somewhat on the defensive.

His task was made even more difficult by the intricacies of the Washington maze. A foreigner took many weeks to find his way about, and even with experience he could never be certain that he was negotiating with the right body or, when bargains were struck, whether the American signatories had the authority to conclude them.

The President, Mr. Roosevelt, shared with Mr. Churchill a belief that the structure of organisations should follow Napoleon's dictum about constitutions, and should be vague and not too closely defined. The overwhelming and comprehensive power which resides in the President made it easy for Roosevelt to indulge in his fancy for improvisation. It was commonly said in Washington at this time, by both American and British, that a compass and an iron ration were necessary for anyone about to hack his way through the jungle of Government agencies in his search for an answer.

It is my belief that other causes more profound than the character and fancies of the President were at work, although I found few Americans other than my friend Jim Forrestal[1] to agree with me.

A Minister or Secretary of State in Great Britain, once he has kissed hands upon his appointment, derives his authority direct from the Sovereign, a permanent head of the State above change or politics; his powers are not delegated to him by the Prime Minister. All that he has to do, and it is much, is to ensure that his powers are exercised in accordance with the policy of his colleagues and of the Prime Minister as head of the Government. He has not from time to time to ask himself, "Can I do this?" but rather, "Should I do this without consulting the Cabinet?"

In contrast to our own system, all the members of an American Government except the Secretary of State, who has some special powers under the Constitution, are Secretaries to the President, and derive their powers from the Head of the Government, who is also the impermanent Head of the State. The doctrine of Cabinet or corporate responsibility is absent. In Great Britain the Government falls if it fails to command a majority from day to day in the House of Commons. The Executive in the United States is not dependent upon a daily majority in Congress.

Given this system, and the character and predilections of Mr. Roosevelt, there is no doubt that many agencies or sub-agencies were created without it being precisely determined whether they had been given appropriate powers, or whether those powers overlapped or overrode those of other agencies or Government departments.

[1] James V. Forrestal, Secretary of the Navy.

At a later stage in the war, in April 1945, I was head of a Food Mission to the United States, and was accompanied by the Minister of Food, Jay Llewellin.[2] We paid a courtesy call upon Senator James Byrnes, who was at that time Director of War Mobilization, and outlined our task. I remember him saying, "I have great sympathy with any Britisher trying to do business in this city. The Administration is cuckoo." This coming from a high officer of state struck us as a little unconventional, but we better understood the reason for his frankness when we read the next morning that he had resigned that afternoon.

This is, however, anticipating the course of my narrative. The lack of system in the war-time administration which I have described was partly the cause of the unending difficulties of the War Production Board and of its leader, Don Nelson. It should also be borne in mind that the Services were headed by the Secretary of the Navy and the Secretary of the War Department, and that Nelson was not a Minister or a member of the Government as we know the terms in Great Britain.

We had this in common, that just as the Ministry of Production had been improvised to meet the special needs of war, so had the War Production Board.

I arrived at the Embassy in Washington one afternoon, after a flight of some vicissitudes, and had a short talk with Dorothy and Edward Halifax, and Angus McDonnell.[3] Angus had the gift of friendship; his humour would salt the stiffest official function. He knew everyone in Washington from Senator to jockey, and was prepared to sit up all night and talk with either. He gave parties at which he cooked the chipolata and delicacies himself, and its other ingredients were as skilfully mixed and blended. His urbane influence has never been sufficiently recognised.

At this time, Americans had got to know the Ambassador, and his reputation had steadily grown. At the beginning of his mission some mistaken publicity—for which he was not responsible—had given the public an image of a fox-hunting Tory peer, inclined to formality and even to stiffness. When he left, I should guess that he was the most liked and respected British Ambassador who has ever been accredited to the United States. His manners owed something to the traditions of the English nobility but they were natural and unforced. He listened with the most courteous attention, and

[2] Afterwards Lord Llewellin.
[3] Colonel the Hon. Angus McDonnell, Attaché to the British Embassy, Washington.

his liking for Americans and the American scene was genuine and evident. His great piety never descended into bigotry or censoriousness. He maintained, in spite of the tragic personal losses which he had sustained, a delicate sense of humour. He loved to gossip and laugh over some incongruous experience. It is true that he remained ignorant and incredulous about some of the seamier side of American politics, and refused to believe in the existence of this or that commercial lobby in time of war. Dorothy Halifax was an Ambassador in herself, and we all felt proud of her beautiful manners, shining goodness and warm sympathy.

I found the life and society of Washington highly agreeable. It was at that time the most cosmopolitan of cities and the visiting foreigner was much welcomed and widely entertained. A reputation as a conversationalist and a companion was accorded, particularly by American ladies, to many foreigners who hardly deserved it but who liked it all the more for that.

The reasons seemed to be that the conversation and outlook of the foreigner were new and different from those of most American men and were perhaps more concerned with ideas and abstractions than is usual in American society. Moreover, Americans and more particularly American ladies were cut off from foreign travel, a pastime to which they are much addicted, and though a Frenchman or an Englishman was doubtless a poor substitute for Paris, London or Venice, they brought with them a whiff of Europe.

Eugene Meyer, the proprietor and inspiration of the *Washington Post*, used to give parties to visiting Ministers and the like. First of all, a dozen guests were given an excellent dinner, cooked it seemed by a French chef. Conversation flowed readily and tongues were loosened by some well selected Krug or Bollinger. After dinner, about fifty guests assembled in his magnificent library; the panelling and bookcases, if I remember rightly, had been brought over from Europe. The visitor was put into a conspicuous chair, was assured that nothing of what was said was ever repeated, and was then asked to answer questions. I was invited to one of these parties.

At the time of my visit, British policy in India was widely discussed—and universally condemned. India was a burning and dangerous topic.

As soon as I was led to the chair I was therefore hardly surprised when a lady, though in the friendliest tones, asked me if there was anything in Anglo-American relations which caused me anxiety at the moment.

I hesitated and looked embarrassed, and said that there was but that I was far from home and would prefer not to speak about it. Several people said, "Oh, come on, you can say what you like here: no one will mind."

I still demurred, and was further pressed. I then said, "Well, if you really want to hear it, it is that . . . but it does sound rather silly two or three thousand miles from London, so I had better hold my tongue." Loud protestations that I was among friends, and more pressure—to which I yielded with simulated reluctance.

"If you must know," said I, "there is indeed something very disturbing in Anglo-American relations at the moment. I'm afraid it will sound rather silly; I think I had better not go on." There were more friendly protests, so I said, "Here goes—please forgive me in advance. There is a rumour going round Liberal and left-wing circles in England that when the war is over, the United States does not intend to hand back Hawaii to the Hawaiian kings but may even try to incorporate it in the Union. I know the rumour is absurd, but you did ask me and now I have told you."

There was an awkward pause, when I wondered whether I had gone too far, but the company gave unmistakable evidence that they were delighted by the quip. Americans will take almost anything from a friend. I heard a Senator explaining to his wife that this was a naughty counter-blast to accusations of imperialism which were being levelled at the British at this time. Afterwards the party went with a swing, and I was as indiscreet as discretion permitted, and not a word was ever repeated.

My first duty after arriving in Washington was to meet Don Nelson and the American press. It was an alarming ordeal, because it was thought by our hosts that if the press photographers were given a free rein for an hour, they would not want us to pose again. It was a hot and humid day, and we sat sweltering whilst we were photographed from every angle by men some of whom were in shirt-sleeves, some smoking and some chewing the ends of cigars, some from a yard or less away, some reinforced by incandescent screens. Don Nelson had soon sweated through his shirt and showed signs of distress.

I found on this and on subsequent occasions that the American press gave me a fair deal. They did not, of course, attempt to cover up mistakes which I made from inexperience, but they were friendly and did not indulge in inferential journalism such as, "Minister fails to mention . . ." and so forth. In my experience, once the press guess that you like Americans and America, and are not in their image of a high-hatted, stand-offish, contumacious, goddam Britisher, they give you fair treatment.

On one of my visits towards the end of the War, I was finishing an arduous week's work in Washington when my old friend and colleague, H. B. van Sinderen of Charles Tennant Sons & Co., called me from New York to suggest that I should spend Saturday and Sunday there as a break. I agreed with alacrity. When I got to the Waldorf Astoria in New York, I found a group of press men and press ladies waiting for me in the foyer near the elevators. "Hallo, Captain, what are you doing in New York? A breakdown in your job? Who's to blame?" And then, "How do you like the U.S., Captain?" I answered thoughtfully, "There is one small something that I hate like hell about the U.S., and hate like hell about Americans"—at this point they all took out their pencils and looked hopeful—"but I've been trying to think what in Heaven's name it is for the last six months, and I can't remember." With that, I got into the elevator. Halfway up I thought this joke might have been a little unwise, and could easily be distorted, so I asked the whole of the press representatives up to my apartment, where I had liberal supplies of gin and whisky for just such an emergency. The guests gave a remarkably efficient performance in dealing with the drinks, and we parted on cordial terms. They treated my joke just right, although one tabloid began on these lines: "Arms Czar Wise-cracks Press. Mr. Lyttelton, balding, whose middle-aged spread is ill concealed by a double-breasted vest, wise-cracked our representative in New York's leading luxury hotel," and so on.

To return to Washington and my first mission. After the press conference, I had been invited to luncheon with the President at the White House. He generally did not leave his office for luncheon, but had it brought to his desk. If you were invited to the "desk lunch," there were never more than one or two other guests to share it. At this time I did not know Mr. Roosevelt, and had had only a fleeting glimpse of him at some party in London many years before. I felt some constraint as I was shown into his room. He was sitting at his desk, against the background of the Stars and Stripes arranged in a stand against the wall; the desk was covered with papers in some disorder; there were photographs of a yacht and of members of his family. I noticed a hare's foot, obviously given him as a charm.

He greeted me with the utmost cordiality. "Hullo there," he exclaimed in ringing tones. "Come in, Oliver, come in. I am going to call you Oliver, if you don't mind, and may I say you look just what I expected? How's Winston? He has written to me about you, and I've also heard about you from Harry Hopkins, who is coming to this desk lunch."

This kindness I found disarming. In all my relations with him, he treated me with almost paternal affection, and exhibited at times an indiscretion in talking to me which is one of the most flattering ways by which a man can show friendship and trust. After a short exchange about the situation of the war, Harry Hopkins walked in. At this time the relations between the President and H. H. were of the closest. I believe that one of the reasons for this was because Harry was a very sick man, and the President, being himself the victim of a dreadful disease, took a particular delight in looking after him and treating him as far frailer than he was himself.

The President rang the bell, and a tall, chromium-plated cabinet, not unlike a refrigerator, was wheeled in by a coloured servant. "Oliver, I am now about to offer you a verry rare American delicacy." A pause. "It is known as cold lobster." The President opened his mouth very wide when he made this quip. It was a habit of his, and it was almost as if he had said, "Don't miss the joke."

An astonishing quantity of lobster was extricated from the cabinet, and he then exclaimed, "With this verry rare American delicacy, I am about to offer you another verry rare American delicacy." Pause. "It is known as mayonnaise sauce." Wide-open mouth. Flaps were opened at each end of the desk, and Harry and I sat down. Soon there were lobster shells all over the desk, and not a little mayonnaise had found its way on to the papers, the commissions, the reprieves and the reports which littered it.

This was my first introduction to one of the most powerful, if not the most powerful, man in the world. He was an incongruous mixture of an aristocrat and a demagogue. He once said to me, "I find it much easier to negotiate with a gentleman. I understand them better than the others." At the same time, he had an uncanny instinct for popular politics, listened to every rustle in the leaves and built up his own position with unending care and subtlety.

Much of the bitterness and almost hatred with which he was regarded by American "society" and by leading Republicans was because they regarded him as a traitor to his own class, a Knickerbocker with a *bonnet rouge*. His brain seemed to me to be imaginative, even fanciful. He allowed his thoughts and conversation to flit across the tumultuous and troubled scene with a lightness and an inconsequence which were truly frightening in one wielding such power. He appeared to me to be the least methodical of men, and to rely overmuch on intuition.

Very late one night I was drinking whisky and soda with him in his room at the White House when he said to me, "You know, Oliver, in Belgium there are two communities which can't live together; one are called Walloons, and they speak a kind of low Dutch—you know I am Dutch in origin—and the others are called Flemings, and they speak . . . NO, NO STOP. Go back. One are called Walloons and they speak French, and the other are called Flemings, and they speak this kind of low Dutch. They can't live together." I was a trifle taken aback by this preface, and I thought it unlucky that the President had chosen me as his audience on this theme, because I had an unusually wide experience of Belgian politics and politicians. I had had close relations with the Société Générale de Belgique and had known Jadot, General Blaise, Fernand Pisart, Camille Gutt, Edgar Sengier and other leading Belgian figures. However, the President continued, "After the war, we should make two states, one known as Walloonia and one as Flamingia, and we should amalgamate Luxembourg with Flamingia. What do you say to that?"

I gasped, and said I thought the proposition required a good deal of study, the two populations were much intermixed in Belgium. Whether Flamingia or Walloonia should control the Scheldt and the port of Antwerp would be another point, and the complex of iron ore, steel and coal, markets and ports posed some grave economic problems. The President sheered off on to another subject.

When I made my report on my mission I followed the practice of British Ministers and diplomatists by reporting what I had heard in unofficial as well as in official conversations, and touched upon the future of Belgium as sketched in by the President. Anthony Eden was surprised that I had allowed myself to venture into fields of foreign policy, and wondered if the President was not merely joking. I replied that he and not I had raised the topic, and that, though I could not be sure, I had the strong impression that this was a serious idea, of which the last had not been heard. Anthony was incredulous. However, he happened to go to the United States a few weeks later, and when he got back he told me with a laugh that I had been quite right, that the idea was a serious one, and that the President had given it another airing. It was not heard of again.

At this time no two men in their positions can ever have worked so closely together as the Prime Minister and the President, though separated by 3,000 miles of ocean. Yet the President held and retained some of the innate suspicions of the British which are a pathological tradition of Americans. He believed to the end of his life that we intended to use American power, if we could, to pull chestnuts out of the Balkans and out of Europe for ourselves. He had once been stung by a mosquito in Bathurst which, it must be admitted, at that time was not a showpiece as a colonial capital, and this added to his American prejudices against our colonies. Bathurst was always known as "that hell-hole of yours." He believed that we levied taxes upon our colonies and battened upon their riches whilst oppressing the people and refusing to allow them any sort of progress. On the other hand, he unfeignedly admired the courage and stubbornness of the British race, and at this time regarded Winston as the epitome of the British character.

Towards the end of the war, when he was an ailing man, he became intensely jealous of Winston, and could not help a derogatory and ironical tone from creeping in, even when talking to a devoted lieutenant like myself. "Poor old Winston keeps on thinking . . ." he said to me once, and I felt it necessary to say that I profoundly believed that poor old Winston was right.

I should judge that Mr. Roosevelt's brains were not of the calibre of either Stalin's or Mr. Churchill's, but there is another side to this picture.

His achievements in bringing a united nation into the war, his consummate handling of Lend-Lease, his generous impulses in the defence of freedom, his sympathy with the under-dog in his own country, his trust in the courage and steadfastness of Great Britain, by themselves would give him a high place amongst great statesmen. To these beliefs he gave expression through the massive authority of one who ruled and governed the most powerful industrial nation in the world, a nation scarred and roused by Pearl Harbour.

To this day, sneers directed against his memory rouse my anger. I believe that he had as large a hand in winning victory as anyone. No doubt he also had the largest responsibility for misjudging Russia and for advocating a peace in Europe on terms and boundaries which have brought untold difficulties in their train.

I was supported in my mission by most able colleagues. They included General Sir Ronald Weeks,[4] then D.C.I.G.S., Air Marshal

[4] Afterwards Lord Weeks.

Slessor,[5] who was at that time Assistant Chief of the Air Staff. The Service chiefs negotiated the procurement of the weapons for their various Services, and we co-ordinated our work through a Steering Committee, which met daily under my chairmanship. I carried on some direct negotiations with Generals Marshall and Somervell and Admiral King, and applied myself also to the formation and terms of reference of the Joint War Production Board. It was set up during my visit[6] and it had only two permanent members, Nelson and myself. Though at times its machinery creaked, and though the strongly individual tendencies of both countries and their Service chiefs sometimes impeded and even halted its working, I believe that it fulfilled a useful role.

When it was formed, I had the ordeal of addressing its first meeting, which was attended by the Vice-President, Mr. Wallace,[7] by Don Nelson, Sidney Goldberg and other members of the War Production Board, Service chiefs, including "Hap" Arnold,[8] commanding the U.S. Air Forces, and General Somervell, who was head of the supply and procurement services under General Marshall.

At times, when the Services had reached some deadlock, I had to invoke the aid of Harry Hopkins. If the President himself was the greatest maker of bottle-necks, Harry was the main force in breaking them down. He had an uncanny instinct for the essential. He added to this gift a great influence with the President, and a considerable hold over Generals Marshall and Arnold and Admiral King. Without Harry Hopkins we should not have got very far, and his help cemented my friendship and affection for him.

For a sick man, or perhaps because he was a sick man, he liked to drink more whisky when the sun went down than was good for his health. It probably kept him alive, but it also impelled him to sit up very late and make a round of the night clubs in Washington. Many a time I returned home to the Embassy at 3 A.M. or 4 A.M. after a night out with Leon Henderson, the Price Administrator, and Harry. One very late night, I forgot to shut the lift door at the Embassy, and Angus McDonnell, who came in later from an equally dedicated evening, had to climb two long flights of stairs. The next day a notice was pinned up in the lift: "Night hawks returning late are reminded that other night hawks may be

---

[5] Now Marshal of the Royal Air Force, Sir John Slessor.
[6] The Joint War Production Board was set up on June 9th, 1942.
[7] Henry Wallace.
[8] General H. H. Arnold.

later and are asked to SHUT THE LIFT DOORS." This notice was still in the lift many years later, and I believe survived to the days of Sir Oliver Franks.

The other American who gave us untold help was Averell Harriman. He and I had spent much time together in London and were already friends. He had inherited a vast fortune in early life, had enjoyed himself and had been better known on the polo field, where he represented the United States, than in the councils of the nation. He had put aside a life of pleasure and was now devoted whole-heartedly to making his contribution to the war. He was a Democrat and the President had made him a peripatetic Ambassador. In this capacity he had been in the Middle East and in England on several occasions.

He now brought to bear administrative powers and a grasp of detail of a high order. He was in touch with the ebb and flow of world trade. He was no doubt ambitious for high political office, but at this time seemed determined to gain power and influence through the more humdrum merits of competence and administrative ability, rather than by spreading his wings into wider skies. His character and methods were thus in sharp contrast to those of the President and Harry Hopkins, and he supplied many qualities which would otherwise have been lacking. I have not forgotten the help we received and the part that Hopkins and Harriman played, nor has my gratitude been dimmed by time.

In the end we received generous treatment from our Allies; the massive schedules setting out in detail the aircraft, the spares, the guns and tanks, the armaments and the stores which the United States had undertaken to supply were signed.

The Mission returned to London, and I made a statement on its work in the House of Commons.[9] After paying tribute to the helpfulness and courtesy of the American authorities and tracing the history of the British Supply Missions, I concluded by saying that a Combined Production and Resources Board had been formed and was now at work. The British would have the same share of components and finished munitions produced in the United States as the American forces, provided they were engaged upon operations of equal strategical importance.

The Board would be charged with saving shipping, and with the greatest standardisation of weapons possible. The Combined Munitions Assignment Board, set up in Washington and London, would give flexibility to the scheme to meet changed operational

[9] June 24th, 1942.

requirements or emergencies. Except for this, the supply of components and munitions was to become a "firm contract."

Just before this statement, we met with a grievous reverse in the Western Desert. Tobruk fell on June 21st. The Eighth Army was in full retreat. It was uncertain what defensive position covering the Delta would be taken up, and uncertain whether it would hold.

One evening, Stafford Cripps, then the Leader of the House of Commons, came into my flat in the Ministry in Great George Street, and said that a Vote of Censure had been put on the paper. It was to be moved by Sir John Wardlaw Milne, and seconded by Admiral Sir Roger Keyes.[10] He thought that I should reply first for the Government, after the opening speeches. The Prime Minister would wind up. I was chosen partly because I was lately back from the Middle East, and partly because criticism would surely be directed against our arms and equipment, for which I had recently assumed responsibility. I said I would, of course, do what I was told.

On July 1st, 1942, the motion of censure was moved by Sir John Wardlaw Milne. The only substantial part of his speech attacked the Prime Minister for being also Minister of Defence and for interfering with the Chiefs of Staff. He went on to suggest that H.R.H. the Duke of Gloucester should be made Commander-in-Chief.[11]

H.R.H. was a splendid officer, but had not commanded any large body of troops and had been prevented by official duties from passing the Staff College. It is not disrespect to H.R.H. to recall that the House literally gasped at this suggestion. Wardlaw Milne's reputation as a parlementarian, and as a critic of the Government, which never rested upon very solid foundations, disappeared in a sentence and was never again recovered.

The Admiral, in seconding the motion, criticised the Chiefs of Staff, and in particular the First Sea Lord, for moving too slowly in support of the Prime Minister. "It is hard," he said, "that three times in the Prime Minister's career he should have been thwarted —in Gallipoli, in Norway and in the Mediterranean, in carrying out strategical strokes which might have altered the course of two wars, each time because his . . . naval adviser declined to share the responsibility with him if it entailed any risk." [12]

Thus the mover complained that the Prime Minister had too

[10] Afterwards Lord Keyes.
[11] Hansard: Vol. 381, Col. 228-29.
[12] *Ibid.*, Col. 242.

much power and thwarted the Chiefs of Staff, and the seconder that the Chiefs of Staff thwarted the Prime Minister.

It was the first really large-scale debate in which I spoke for the Government to a full house, and it must be confessed that my speech was a disastrous failure. I began by "getting the House wrong," by pointing out the inconsistency between the mover and the seconder. The seconder, I said, has conceived his role as that of answering the arguments of the mover. The House did not like it. When interrupted by Sir Herbert Williams, I said that Hon. Members supporting the motion had permitted themselves the indulgence of approaching the battlefield with flying colours, and then faded out when the actual issue was joined.[13]

I was very quickly aware that I had "lost the House," at least those Members facing the Government. I was frequently interrupted, did not give way to Maxton,[14] a serious mistake, and the age-long complaint which is always made about new Ministers that I was reading all my speech, though not true, made things worse.

I have recently re-read the debate, and my own speech. Although I should be far from claiming that it was a good speech, it appears in print to be perhaps over-frank, but more or less adequate. Yet at that moment, and in that House, it was clearly not.

I suppose all parliamentarians get the House wrong at times, but it was certainly a pity for me that I had so far misjudged its temper on my first voyage in a storm.

Sir Herbert Williams, whose record as a junior Minister had not been impressive, enjoyed himself with a particularly offensive speech, and I certainly had the feeling that I had let down my colleagues.

Reading the subsequent debate, any historian would be surprised at the acerbity of the attack upon the Government and the Prime Minister and, for that matter, the liberty that was taken with many of the facts. This bitterness reached its zenith in a speech by Mr. Aneurin Bevan. It would only be kind to assume that he was carried away by his own Celtic oratory, and said things that he did not mean. Everyone, however, who was there still remembers the malice with which he picked his phrases. It was an eloquent speech, but he too lost the ear of the House when he suggested that we should replace British generals with Russians or Poles or Frenchmen. When he went on to urge that he and

---

[13] *Ibid.*, Col. 248-49.
[14] James Maxton, M.P. for the Bridgeton Division of Glasgow.

other Members of Parliament should be sent to the front—and it became clear that he did not mean to fight, but to make speeches —the House hardly regarded his philippic as serious.

The most virulent speeches seemed to be made by those who thought either that they should have been in the Government, or that they should not have been dropped from it.

When he came to wind up, the Prime Minister did not spare the critics.

> Everything [he said] that could be thought of or raked up has been used to weaken confidence in the Government, has been used to prove that Ministers are incompetent and to weaken their confidence in themselves, to make the Army distrust the backing it is getting from the civil power, to make the workmen lose confidence in the weapons they are striving so hard to make, to represent the Government as a set of nonentities over whom the Prime Minister towers, and then to undermine him in his own heart, and, if possible, before the eyes of the nation.

Later,

> I have found it very difficult, even during the bitter animosity of the diatribe of Mr. Bevan, with all its carefully aimed and calculated hostility, to concentrate my thought upon this Debate.

He ended with an eloquent passage about the intensity of the battle then raging, dismissed Wardlaw Milne's proposals in a few contemptuous phrases, finally claimed the right to divide the House and called upon it to give the Government a great majority and carry this message to the world. We got it. Four hundred seventy-five Members rejected the Vote of Censure, 25 supported it. Amongst this small band were included Hore Belisha, Clement Davies and Sir Herbert Williams. Some Members, including a handful of Conservatives, abstained.

On this day, July 2nd, the national fortunes and the credit of the Government reached, it seems, their lowest point. It was not long before the critics were confounded by events and discredited by victory.

My own speech hung round my neck like a tin can; it did not increase my own confidence, and though I continued to be fully supported by my colleagues and by the Coalition members, I was written down as an almost irretrievable parliamentarian. I thought I had deserved it; it was not until my last year or two in office as Colonial Secretary that, in my own opinion at least, I began to live it down.

In September 1943, Sir Kingsley Wood, the Chancellor of the

Exchequer, suddenly died. Winston suggested to me that I should succeed him and still remain in the War Cabinet, of which Kingsley Wood had not been a member. I welcomed a change, if only because my work at the Ministry of Production, though no less exacting, was becoming more stereotyped.

It so happened that, on the day on which Winston had spoken to me, Anthony Eden and I were guests at dinner of the First Lord of the Admiralty at Greenwich to entertain Colonel Frank Knox, the Secretary of the U.S. Navy Department. We drove home together and Anthony said that my appointment had been decided. I was pleased with the news.

The next night I was entertaining a party of Americans at Claridges when I was called to the telephone to speak to the Prime Minister. He told me that he thought John Anderson would be much distressed if he did not become Chancellor. Having started life as a civil servant, it would crown his career to be the head of the Treasury.

I at once told Winston that in my view he could not find anyone better suited for the post and as for myself I felt that the Treasury was further away from the war than the Ministry of Production and I was perfectly happy to stay where I was. I went on, "You must do exactly as you think best or as suits your needs. Never regard my personal position; it counts for nothing."

It amused me to remember that this incident brought up the toll of offices to which I had been nominated or appointed to eight: Secretary of State for War (1940), President of the Board of Trade (1940), Ambassador to Washington (1940), Secretary of State for War (announcement printed) (1941), Minister of State in the Middle East (1941), Minister of Production (1942), Viceroy of India (1943) and Chancellor of the Exchequer (1943). I had held three of these offices. I was later given a ninth appointment which was also cancelled.

Rab Sinclair and I made two journeys to Normandy. The first in June 1944, and to see the artificial harbour, Mulberry, at Arromanches. My Ministry had had the overall responsibility for the plan, but the execution of it was in the hands of Sir Andrew Duncan and the Ministry of Supply. I was more than once grilled by the Prime Minister, and told that I was about to let the country down, but I relied on Andrew and he did not fail. We two had some anxious moments, and had to use the instruments and powers of Government ruthlessly to bring home this priority on time.

As Rab and I flew in, the whole port looked as active as an ant-heap; thousands of tons of ammunition and stores were being unloaded and driven off daily; the handling capacity of the port was still rising.

At the Ministry of Production our chief Parliamentary troubles concerned the design and production of tanks. The most persistent critic was Dick Stokes,[15] the Labour Member of Ipswich. Himself a successful industrialist, he had become interested in a very heavy tank of which a prototype had been built by private enterprise. The fact that the Army did not want a tank of this type, which was too cumbersome and too slow, did not weigh much with Dick. Even when it proved unreliable he still persisted in pressing for its adoption.

It is, of course, true that we did not produce a really good tank until the end of the war, but the reasons are not far to seek. A tank is a mechanical headache, and just as no operational or, for that matter, civil aircraft has ever been delivered in under four years from its conception, so we, who did not seriously begin the design of modern tanks until after the war had begun, could hardly expect success before the end of 1944.

The Americans fell back on the huge automotive industry of their country and certainly came nearer to producing a satisfactory weapon in a shorter time than we did. By 1943 they had a serviceable tank. Considering that we were the original inventors of tanks, this was a sobering fact.

When we began to advance rapidly in the west, but when it was still uncertain how long the war would last, I determined to pay a visit to the front, and if possible seek some advice from Field Marshal Montgomery upon weapons in general, and tanks in particular.

Rab and I set off for Normandy again at the beginning of September. From the situation reports we thought that we could just about fly to Amiens, and that if we succeeded we might have the chance of asking the C.-in-C. at his advanced H.Q. a few questions.

We had a Lockheed machine and an excellent Polish pilot, and landed at an aerodrome near Amiens. The field was almost deserted and we were told, but did not believe, that there were still some German snipers in the neighbourhood. Amiens itself was *en fête*. We got in touch with the rear echelon of Montgomery's H.Q., and with Major-General "Freddy" de Guingand,[16] his Chief of Staff. The

[15] The late R. R. Stokes.
[16] Major-General Sir Francis de Guingand.

rear H.Q. were just moving in to some buildings in the outskirts and, being obviously in the way, we could not expect the information for which we sought. We therefore determined to try flying to Brussels.

In fact we landed there simultaneously with the first squadron of the R.A.F. to fly in. The city had been liberated that very day,[17] and had gone wild with excitement. Even we civilians, because we drove in an R.A.F. tender, came in for a tumultuous welcome. Most of the women in the streets were dressed in red, white and blue, which, though hardly becoming, was a touching tribute to the occasion. The soldiers and airmen were fêted everywhere; they were given drinks and meals and kisses, entertained in every café or brasserie on the boulevards, and often invited to the family board.

Rab and I walked the streets for some hours, but we never saw a drunken or rowdy British soldier or airman. Their manners were impeccable and gave yet further evidence of how different they were from the veterans of the Peninsular, or even of later armies.

The military anxiously asked where Rab and I were going to stay. I answered, "We shall go to the nearest hotel."

In my experience of war, and of the occasional revolution which I have seen, ordinary life and the momentum of ordinary life stand a lot before they are stopped. This proved true once again. The nearest hotel was the Palace. We went in and booked two bedrooms and a sitting-room. Everything was normal except that there was no hot water.

We then made for the Chapon Fin in the Rue Grétry, a restaurant which I used to frequent in peacetime. The proprietor nearly fainted when he saw me, but prepared the most delicious meal and dug out a bottle of the finest burgundy. Our pleasure was a little damped when we saw the bill for something over £25 at the current rate of exchange. The proprietor would not accept sterling, and I had to promise to pay him later in Belgian francs—enemy propaganda had worked in this instance.

The next morning when paying our bill, the hotel seemed deserted. The clerk said that three floors had been the H.Q. of the Gestapo and the hotel was supposed to be mined. He clearly did not believe this rumour himself.

We made our way in the morning to General Horrocks's[18] Corps

[17] September 3rd, 1944.
[18] Now General Sir Brian Horrocks.

H.Q. near Laeken, and met General "Boy" Browning,[19] a brother officer and friend of mine, who was commanding the Parachute Division. We heard some of their experiences of the campaign. Our advance through Belgium had been as quick as that of General Patton's army on the right flank, and we were told that our new tanks had acquitted themselves well.

The armies were still advancing and we decided that we should be an embarrassment if we stayed on and had better fly home. On reaching the airport, we found that our aeroplane and pilot were missing but, seeing an American bomber with the engines running, we asked whether it was bound for England and if we could get a lift. "Sure, get in," said the captain.

A moment later, a tall, rangy-looking American pilot accosted me and asked if he, too, could get to England in this machine. He explained that he had been shot down in flames over Brussels a year or more ago and had just been liberated by the Irish Guards. He too asked the captain and got the same answer: "Sure, get in."

I found myself sitting next to this young American, and he proved a delightful character. He showed me his hands, which had been terribly burnt, and said that the German surgeons and doctors had effected a wonderful cure.

We took off; the weather was appalling; the machine shuddered and lurched and dived and screwed its way into a gale of wind. A grinning G.I. dumped a galvanised pail on the floor and said, "Folks, you all know what that's for, I reckon."

My neighbour, however, was in an ecstasy. "Gee, six thousand feet; it's great. Gee, it's great to be flying again." A large lurch. "Gee, ain't it wonderful?" He told me that he had been posted as missing and was not sure whether his father and mother knew that he was still alive. I told him I was a Minister, and if he gave me their address I would send a cable from London direct; it would reach them that very day.

"My granddad was a minister too," he said. "His church was near my home." I was delighted that my appearance and conversation seemed so godly, but had to explain.

I duly sent the cable; his father in reply wrote me one of the most touching letters of gratitude that I can remember.

Shortly after this expedition, I paid a visit to General Alexander's H.Q. in Italy.

Alex was kind enough to get a few days' leave for my eldest son,

[19] Now General Sir Frederick Browning.

Antony, and my second son, Julian, who was serving in the Grenadier Guards. We were housed in the same billet. It was an indescribable joy to me, and I would have given anything in the world to have had Moira with us. I cannot write of this reunion because it was the last time that I was destined to see Julian[20] and the memory even today is too poignant to share with anybody but her.

I went up to the front with Alex and General Mark Clark. Both these commanders had impressed themselves on the troops. As we passed I could hear them say; "Look, Alex, or Mark," and Americans and British were alike in this.

Alex wore a powder-blue sweat shirt, riding breeches and jack boots and a flat-fronted cap; he too showed that some eccentricities in dress help men to recognise a leader.

We had long and fascinating talks about his Tunisian campaign, which he described to me in some detail. We reminded ourselves of how holes made in the enemy line by the infantry, especially when fighting Germans, are no more than jagged and that forces to tear the holes wide apart must be at hand before the momentum is lost. These tactics were used in his final assult on Tunis; the two armoured divisions had rumbled up, shattered the enemy line and crowned with victory one of the great battles in the history of arms. Two hundred and forty-eight thousand prisoners were captured.

Alex owes his fame and success to his complete dedication to the military profession. "I've spent more than fifteen years of my life on the battlefield," he once said to me.

His role is that of a commander more that that of a planner, and he needed a high-grade Chief of Staff to work out the details. At this time John Harding held that position and was an outstanding success. Partly from his concentration upon the military art and partly from his experience, Alex's judgements were always simple, lucid and convincing.

In December 1944, the Prime Minister, somewhat against the wishes of the military, had insisted upon intervening in Greece to prevent its being dominated by Communist partisans. Winston, joined by Harold Macmillan, went to Athens on a political reconnaissance. They were soon cooped up in the British Embassy, which, much to Winston's delight, was under fire. Bullets were thwacking against the walls in obvious disregard of diplomatic propriety. The whole situation was confused.

[20] Died of wounds received in Italy on October 11th, 1944.

In Italy, Alex received some alarming reports, and soon arrived in person. He drove from the Piraeus in a tank with the hatch open. He immediately went round the lines and inspected the troops. Everything seemed to fall into place and confidence was at once restored. He did not like the dispositions and, on returning to the Embassy, said; "Prime Minister, you are in considerable danger. There are not enough troops here, and I am getting some more at once—a whole division. They will begin to arrive from Italy tomorrow. In the meanwhile, I think you will be all right, but I can't be sure until we are reinforced."

"On ne règne sur les âmes que par le calme," say the French, and Alex has the gift of calm. It is one of the greatest of military assets because it not only inspires the troops but enables sober decisions to be made, even under fire and stress. Alex's presence on the battlefield—and I saw it more than once in the first war— is worth a great many troops. When he came to the highest command, I used to think of Napoleon's words:

"La présence du général est indispensable; c'est la tête, c'est le tout d'une armée; ce n'est pas l'armée romaine qui a soumis la Gaule, mais César; ce n'est pas l'armée carthaginoise qui faisait trembler l'armée républicaine aux portes de Rome mais Annibal; ce n'est pas l'armée macédonienne qui a été sur l'Indus, mais Alexandre; ce n'est pas l'armée française qui a porté la guerre sur le Wéser et sur l'Inn, mais Turenne; ce n'est pas l'armée prussienne qui a défendu sept ans la Prusse contre les trois plus grandes puissances de l'Europe, mais Frédéric le Grand." [21]

Alex's simplicity of manner, absence of conceit or of nationalist prejudices made him loved by the Americans. "They are splendid comrades," he said, "splendid." He added, reflectively, "You see, at times a soldier's duty is to obey and to die. We all have to remember that." This remark was made from the depths of his heart and was without a hint of pretension.

I flew with him to the front. Alex took the controls himself and piloted us through the mountains. "I'm no good at landing," he said, as he handed over to the regular pilot.

I went up the line to take a meal with the 1st Guards Brigade, commanded by my great friend Andrew Scott.[22] When the war broke out he had long been retired from the army and had rejoined the Irish Guards as a junior captain. He had climbed to a brigade

[21] N. Tomiche, *Napoléon écrivain*, (Paris: Armand Colin, 1952).
[22] Colonel C. A. Montagu Douglas Scott.

and his high spirits and dash made him one of the best of his rank in the whole army.

It was exhilarating to be back amongst my brother officers and when a few shells fell a hundred yards or so from Andrew's H.Q., I recaptured the sensation of my youth and hoped the next salvo would not be any nearer.

As soon as victory began to look assured, the War Cabinet ceased to be a united or indeed an effective body. Disputes and disagreements began to paralyse action. Defeat knits together, victory opens the seams. The Labour Ministers were preparing for a general election and would not let anything pass that had a bearing on their prospects. The Prime Minister tried hard to keep the Coalition together and brought all his unique powers of persuasion to bear. His efforts were in vain; our Labour colleagues had decided to leave. I felt sad at the farewell party in the Cabinet Room at No. 10 Downing Street. The departing Labour members looked rather gloomy and sheepish and I could not help remembering all that we had been through together. Clem Attlee adopted a very correct but rather chilly attitude. He did not allow his humour off the chain that afternoon. Ernie Bevin looked shaken and anxious, Morrison expectant and Albert Alexander[23] made some remarks about "my Navy," which raised a smile.

Winston set about forming a new Government. He sent for me late one afternoon, and I found him in bed. He began very tentatively by saying that the War Cabinet was a thing of the past; a new Cabinet of sixteen Ministers would be formed.

"You, Oliver, of course are assured of a place, but what place? You could, if you wish, continue as Minister of Production, but would have to combine it I think with being again President of the Board of Trade. This would take you some way from the war but has some advantages. It had occurred to me to ask you what you would think of the Admiralty; if you like it, you would still be one of the sixteen."

I answered, "I should like it above all else. A Service department has always been my dearest wish. The war with Japan is still on; the Fleet has got to be deployed in the Far East. I shall remain close to you and, for that matter, I shall move into that lovely house." Winston, who thought that I should regard the Admiralty as demotion, was much moved by my answer. Tears coursed down his cheeks. "My dear First Lord," he said, wringing my hand, "that's

[23] Viscount Alexander of Hillsborough, First Lord of the Admiralty, 1940–45.

splendid; we shall still be together: I thought you would like it. All the arrangements should be completed by tomorrow. By the way, I shall now send Brendan to the Board of Trade."

I was quite delighted, but when I told Wyndham Portal [24] in confidence what was toward, he was much shocked. "You have been put down a grade, Oliver," he said. "Winston will run the war against Japan for Great Britain and you will only be a lieutenant or chief of staff. He will try to run the Admiralty over your head."

Though I was a little disturbed by the remarks of this shrewd observer, I said that I was completely indifferent to matters of grade; that I was sick of figures and production, industrialists, trades union leaders, exports and imports, exchange crises, gold standards, velocity of circulation, employers' federations, chambers of commerce, bankers, merchant houses, commercial Members of Parliament, deputations, price levels, Ottawa duties, Imperial preference, statistics and statisticians, and looked forward to drinking port with admirals in their cabins and going on deck with them to get a breath of fresh air in my lungs. And Admiralty House: what a home, and the Board Room with those jolly wind-swept faces around me and the wind-vane swinging above one's head, and those marble dolphins adorning the fireplace. I inhabited Admiralty House in my imagination all that afternoon and evening, and went to bed happily. I threw down a volume of statistics about trade and slept as a First Lord should.

About 10 A.M., the Prime Minister rang me up. A weary voice said, "I'm so sorry, it has all had to be changed. Brendan and Max, I don't know which, have persuaded themselves that Brendan can't accept Bretton Woods, so you are back where you were as Minister of Production and President of the Board of Trade. I'm sorry."

I recovered my book of statistics from the waste-paper basket and sadly set myself to study the figures.

The new Cabinet met. Looking round, I was interested to see how hardy is the political tradition of many families. I suppose that today this Cabinet would have been described as one of the grey cells of the Establishment. It is easy to poke fun at the Establishment, but in politics it brings a certain continuity, a tradition of disinterested service, and I would hazard at least as high intellectual equipment as could be found elsewhere. Tradition it certainly had.

The Prime Minister was the son of a Chancellor of the Excheq-

[24] Afterwards Viscount Portal.

uer; Anthony Eden a descendant of a Governor-General and Viceroy of India, who later became First Lord of the Admiralty; Lord Salisbury the son of a distinguished Minister and grandson of a Prime Minister; Lord Rosebery and Dick Law[25] were both sons of a Prime Minister; James Stuart [26] a descendant of James V of Scotland; Oliver Stanley the son of a Minister and descended from a Prime Minister; "Rab" Butler[27] the son of one of the most distinguished Colonial Governors; Harold Macmillan was allied by marriage to the Cavendish family, his father-in-law had been a Minister and Governor-General of Canada; I was the son of a Secretary of State for the Colonies.

The whole atmosphere had changed overnight; tension had relaxed. No one amongst the sixteen, other than perhaps the Prime Minister and the Foreign Secretary, was particularly anxious to remain in office, although the majority of us thought that we should be condemned to a further four years. Above all, there were no intrigues, no finessing for position. We all felt that if any of us was in difficulties he could rely upon the unstinted help of his colleagues. The Government became known as the Caretaker Government.

I judged at this time that one of the principal tasks which faced the country was the reorganisation of the cotton industry. I formulated a plan.

One day, I was to go to Manchester to negotiate part of it with the employers and unions. Together with my Parliamentary private secretary, Norman Hulbert, and several senior officials of the Board of Trade, we were to fly up in a Dakota from Hendon.

When we got on board, we noticed that the wind was blowing across the main road from the west. We accordingly taxied out and turned our tail to the road and our nose towards Hendon, one of the densest of built-up areas.

At 200 feet on the take-off, first one and then both the engines failed. This usually means death. We missed a row of houses by a foot or two and we saw a motor-bus just below the starboard wing. Norman Hulbert, who was a wing commander, gave it a look in which a sense of outrage could be discerned. A small recreation field called Camrose Park appeared a few feet below us; there was a path with a few saplings along its verge. The experienced Czech pilot belly-landed the machine. The wings broke off one or two of

[25] Now Lord Coleraine (his father was Mr. Bonar Law).
[26] Now Viscount Stuart of Findhorn.
[27] The Rt. Hon. R. A. Butler.

the saplings, and we skidded along the ground and came to rest in some allotments, fifty feet from a row of houses.

"I think we get out now," said the Czech pilot. We obeyed. Only the second pilot, who had put his knee out, was hurt.

Soon after, whilst we were standing round our wrecked machine, an old man, looking like Strube's tax-payer with steel-rimmed spectacles on the end of his nose, came up to me and said, "Are you the Minister?" "Yes." "May I dig up my pumpkin?" "You can dig up any bloody thing you like."

Thus reassured, he produced a spade and a wheelbarrow and set to work under one of the wings. He soon unearthed a large pumpkin and, putting it under his arm, said "Thank you, gentlemen. I am exhibiting this at the flower show. Good-morning," and walked off. *Le flegme anglais.*

The first people to arrive, after the gardener, were the police, and about thirty minutes later an R.A.F. tender. It was soon after noon when we motored back to the aerodrome and my party was herded by me into the bar. I ordered a clutch of whisky and sodas. "The bar is not open," said the barman. "It will be, and at once," I answered in unmistakable Ministerial tones.

Another machine was fuelled and we flew off to Manchester without further incident.

It turned out that our crash was due to an empty petrol tank. From the pilot's seat it is impossible to judge which engine has cut out. Our pilot at once realised that it was a fuel failure that had caused an engine to cut out and unluckily switched the other engine, which was drawing on a full tank, on to the empty one. He was in no way to blame. The failure to check the tanks with a stick—the standing order—before the take-off, might have killed fifteen or sixteen people. Those responsible were tried by court martial and severely punished.

The electoral prospects of the Conservative Party were difficult, if not impossible, to assess. No election on party lines had taken place since 1935; a high proportion of the voters were still in the Forces; the electoral registers were more than ten years old and completely out of date. Some of the constituencies in London had shrunk in numbers to a size which would not have been tolerated in peace time. Large numbers of people had migrated into other parts of the country, driven away either by the needs of production or by the destruction or potential destruction of their homes.

The Labour Party machine had been kept in some state of efficiency; the Education Corps was supposed to have penetrated the Army and Air Force with socialist doctrine. The Labour Party had suffered no casualties amongst its members in either House of Parliament, a fact largely due to their high average age.

On the other hand, the Conservative machine had been dismantled; we had suffered some severe casualties amongst both the members and our potential candidates.

The main factor in our favour was the stature and unequalled prestige, national and international, of our leader. Everywhere he was greeted by great multitudes, whose cheering and enthusiasm seemed to proclaim the gratitude of the whole country.

As Ministers, we were uncertain but on the whole confident, and if asked to bet would have put our money on a Conservative victory. Rab Butler alone was pessimistic and would have preferred to delay putting matters to the test. Max Beaverbrook was confident and urged the Prime Minister to seek an immediate dissolution. His views prevailed.

I had a safe seat at Aldershot, but I had never fought an election for myself. I found it the most uncongenial activity. I am very fond of my countrymen and I hate the squabbling and vulgarity and slogans of a popular election.

I was opposed by Tom Wintringham, a member of the Common Wealth Party who had fought in the Spanish Civil War and was an experienced electioneer.

I had one minor success on the platform. I had been followed round by an unpleasant young man who had been deferred upon some grounds or other. He heckled me at several meetings in a highly offensive manner. It had been put about that I had sold lead to the Japanese during the war. This was true, but the sales, which had been directed by the British Government, had been made before Japan was in the war, and the lead was used chiefly in the tea trade.

"The implications of this statement are lies," I said. Up got the young man. "Why don't you prosecute Mr. Wintringham for libel?" he sneered. "Well, I am thinking about it, but everything which is a lie is not necessarily a libel." Uproar. "Answer the question." "A lie is a libel, isn't it?" and so on. I answered:

"I will prove you are wrong: if I said you were a nice, well-spoken young man, who had fought for his country, it would be a lie, but it wouldn't be a libel."

The ex-servicemen liked that one and threw the offender out. My agent said, "That's worth five hundred votes."

The results were not announced for three weeks or so after the close of the poll because the postal votes from the Forces had to be counted. Early one morning I went down to Aldershot for the announcement of the result, and was greeted by my agent, who seemed much shaken. "You're out, Mr. Lyttelton, I am afraid," he said. I had thought that I was indifferent, but I was shocked. "How do you know?" I said.

"Well, I have roughly counted the piles of votes on the tables in the town hall, and Wintringham has a majority."

I did not feel like joining the other candidate for a few minutes and was drumming my fingers on a table in a small waiting-room when my agent came back. "I feel a bit happier," he said. "I hadn't noticed that there were some more tables on the dais and they are mostly for you."

I went in, and Wintringham said to me, "You have a substantial majority, Mr. Lyttelton, and I must congratulate you."

In the event my majority was 5,021. As soon as it was announced I walked over to the Officers' Club to listen to the results. In twenty minutes it was clear that we were out and that something near a landslide had overwhelmed us.

Moira and I went straight back to London and joined Winston in the map room of the Cabinet Office at his invitation. The Prime Minister was surrounded by gloomy faces. He watched the results coming in with some detachment and far more cheerfully than any of those around him. He made no complaints. We stayed with him for two or three hours.

The next morning it was a curious sensation even for me to find myself without an office desk or a typewriter, without a secretary, without a car, without a house in London and without an income.

For Winston, the reaction was of course made more violent: no power, when he had wielded it so comprehensively; a defeated party; no say in the peace settlement; no marines to guard him. Yet even then his resilience was unmistakable; it was not the first, though it was the most important, occasion on which he had suffered electoral defeat.

"They won't last for ever," he said. "Pray God they don't do too much damage before we can get back to them. We shall return. We shall return, as sure as the sun rises tomorrow."

For myself, I confess to having felt a great relief and buoyancy of spirit. I had worked myself almost to a standstill and was stale and tired. The economic problems towered over us, and as a Minister I should probably have been one of those selected to grapple with them. The prospect of earning my living again instead of living on my capital was encouraging. I looked forward to being able to speak without weighing every word.

When Parliament met,[28] I was a little late in reaching my seat on the front Opposition Bench. Some of the House of Commons officials looked stunned and, as I hurried past, muttered, "They're singing the Red Flag."

My complacency melted in a minute. I began to fear for my country.

Any party returned with a large majority[29] usually exhibits bad manners. Back-benchers who have won seats think they are party figures; men who have never administered anything bigger than a bazaar find themselves charged with great offices of state. The members of the victorious party usually jeer and interrupt and think they are as permanent as the benches they sit on. The Liberal Party after their victory in 1906 would not give Arthur Balfour a hearing. In 1945, the socialists greeted Winston with derisive cheers and volleys of rather childish interruptions. Without him they would probably not have been free. Gratitude is not one of the ingredients of democracy.

The House of Commons soon pricks some of these bladders. Since legislation has to be got through the House on a time-table, back-benchers in a party with a large majority are restrained by the Whips from speaking. Arguments to which they have not an immediate answer begin insidiously to enter their heads. It begins to dawn upon them that there may be two sides to most questions. Moreover, so closely knit is the British race that it is impossible to confine more than 600 Britons within the precincts of Westminster without tolerance beginning to spread. Many incongruous friendships are formed and although bitterness and abuse and disorder may come to the surface any day, they certainly do not on most days.

Whilst these adjustments are taking place, an Opposition faced by the hubris of an overwhelming majority has a testing time. After an electoral defeat everyone knows the causes better than the leaders. "You can never get back as long as you stick to the name Conservative." "Winston's Gestapo broadcast cost us the

[28] August 1st, 1945.
[29] Labour majority was 150.

election." "Our propaganda is puerile." "Our organisation is obsolete." "Our policy was never 'put over,' it didn't reach the people." "They are there for twenty years," and so forth.

Faith and confidence are strained at first; if a party is united in the House, it gradually begins to gain confidence, whatever the clatter is from the Government benches or from their own constituencies.

CHAPTER XVII

OPPOSITION

My FIRST OBJECT was to find a secretary. In 1940, when I was President of the Board of Trade, I began dictating my speeches to young ladies drawn from the pool of typists. I was amazed by the paucity of their vocabulary and by the number of blanks left, even when I used words which seemed to me far from recondite. "It looks like 'altruism' in my notes," one of them said, "but that isn't a word, is it?"

When I returned from Cairo to become Minister of Production in 1942, I began to dictate to a Miss Bradshaw, who had been recruited for the secretariat of that newly formed department. I found that she left no blanks, was rapid and was not confused by patching and rephrasing.

When the Labour Ministers left the War Cabinet, Hugh Dalton had asked me to secure the release of his private secretary from the Civil Service. This I did; the difficulties were great, because the bars to the Civil Service zenana are strong, and the locks not easily picked. Having found out that Miss Bradshaw, by then Mrs. Thomas, wished to continue as a secretary and would come to me, I asked Hugh Dalton to repay me for my efforts on his behalf and get her released. He succeeded. Mrs. Thomas has remained my private secretary ever since. She can not only read my handwriting, and rather too many of my thoughts, but knows how to turn away invitations whilst giving the impression that it is duty and not distaste that has led to the refusal.

If I have time I dictate all my speeches to her, revise them and "pot" them. Often I take the typescript as a foundation or as a life-

line to which to cling if I lose my bearings. Mrs. Thomas put
serial number on each speech, except those in the House of C(
mons, which are reported by Hansard. No. 1 was delivered
August 1945, and the last on the list at the end of December 1ᵤᵤₓ
was No. 813, which gives some measure of her benign endurance.

I next had to look around me for an income. I had been away
from the British Metal Corporation for over four years. My colleagues had taken over the management in 1940: and had run the
company to everyone's satisfaction, including that of the Government. Even if the Board invited me, it would hardly have been
fair to them to return.

Another obstacle was that I now had duties as a front-bench
Opposition member. Once back in my old trade I should be quickly
submerged. In the Metal Corporation the directors were themselves
dealers, and were obliged to keep their ears to the telephone all day
long. A number of directorships were also involved. I should not
have been able to attend the House of Commons regularly and thus
fulfil my obligations.

There could be no half-measures, and I decided to seek other
employment, if possible in a large company in which the functions
of direction and of management would be separate. By direction
is meant the decision whether to expand, whether to break into
new markets, what scale of credit to grant, how to train, educate
and select the leaders, how and when to raise capital, and so forth.
Management is different from direction. Of course good direction
is sometimes marred by bad management, but no amount of good
management can stop, although it may lessen, the damage done
by bad direction. The best guides are useless if directed down the
wrong roads.

It so happened that the Chairman of Associated Electrical In-
dustries, Sir Felix Pole, had gone blind. He had gallantly served on
during the last months of the war, but clearly could not continue.
Morgan Grenfell & Co., who had been the merchant bankers of the
British Metal Corporation, were also the merchant bankers of
A.E.I. Lord Bicester, their senior partner, knew me; he was on the
Board of A.E.I., and through his offices and that of his firm, I was
offered the chairmanship.

Before accepting I spent a few days in examining the figures.
They disclosed a large and successful company, of massive financial strength. I accepted the offer, and soon after presented myself
at headquarters and took up my duties.

When I looked round, I found that the head office and its decoration touched the bottom for ugliness. I got a stiff neck looking at the fireplace in my room: it had a chimney-breast on one side and not on the other; heavy mahogany furniture covered with green baize, and some photographs of deceased directors, gave an antique warning to the newcomer. There was not a square room nor a symmetrical angle, nor a decent piece of furniture in the whole building. I have never understood why directors or managers should be asked to spend their lives in surroundings which no one would tolerate in his own house. I determined that all this should be changed.

I started to examine the organisation, and soon found that there was a wide field in which my professional qualifications would be useful. My role was to organise the company on modern lines. In 1945 the market in electrical equipment was a seller's market; the engineering skill and reputation of the two main constituent companies, Metropolitan-Vickers and the British Thomson-Houston Company, stood high.

The central organisation was as antiquated as the office; the constituent companies arranged their own finance; although their records and costings appeared to me to be a model, the information given to the Board was exiguous, the recruitment of staff, the secretarial and legal services, and control of finance fell far below the standards which I expected; above all, there was overlapping and competition between the constituent companies.

I set to work with zest; it was a wonderful company, but it would one day have to face keen competition.

At my first Board meeting I asked each of the directors privately to give me his estimate of the company's reserves. The nearest was £14 million below the correct figure. This confirmed my opinion that the Board was given too little information.

I have an obsession about disclosure, whether to the Board or to the shareholders. I have always said to my colleagues, when Chairman of a Board, "I hope you will take the keenest interest in the company's affairs, but I can't make you. What I can make you do is to share the responsibility. You are entitled to, and will get, all the information that we can give you. Every major decision will be referred to you; when made, it will be in the minutes. If you have agreed you will not be able afterwards to complain that you did not know, or would have acted otherwise." These warnings are often disregarded when things go wrong, and executive directors cannot escape the major blame.

The shareholders are the owners of the business. Disclosure of the state of the company is their due. Many of the scandals that I can recall have begun either by concealment or the glossing over of inconvenient facts. Disclosure, however, is not such a straightforward matter as the layman thinks.

Accountants, partly to protect themselves, love to bring out any unfavourable features, love to bring a dead rabbit, so to speak, out of the garden and deposit it on the drawing-room carpet. They are less given to disclosing good news or favourable prospects. If, however, disclosure gives too gloomy a picture a shareholder may sell his shares when it would be to his advantage to hold them; if it gives too rosy a picture someone may buy shares prematurely. It is perhaps natural that greater weight is given to preventing the second mistake. The duty of directors towards shareholders is to strike the balance. Nearly everything which does not damage the company or give advantage to its competitors should be disclosed, but it is quite easy unwittingly to mislead; the balance in short is a delicate one, and a nice matter of judgement, since it often involves forecasts which events may stultify.

I found my new position well suited to the life I had to lead. I had time to direct and organise. No amount of time would have enabled me to make any contribution to the engineering side of the business as such. I spent every day in the office, and in the main kept the usual office hours, although on occasions I had to leave to be in the House of Commons by 3:30 P.M.

I became Chairman of the Trade & Industry Committee of the Party, and was responsible for formulating the Opposition policy on these matters for submission to the Shadow Cabinet.

I found the House of Commons of 1945 uncongenial. We had too small a party for the Whips to give us any indulgences. The Government could, of course, allow their supporters time out of the House; we could not. The manners of our opponents made life harsh and disagreeable. When the House was sitting my day was a long one. After I left the office I was generally in my place in the House from 5 o'clock till 10 o'clock or later. Much of this time had to be spent hanging about or listening to debates. Practice in listening grows slowly; familiarity with a subject produces impatience, especially when well-worn arguments of doubtful force are steadily deployed from one side or the other. These hours of listening must be regarded as payment for the pleasure of having a front seat on a great Parliamentary occasion, and for the opportunity of learning how the expert parliamentarians handle their case, or of how the speech of orators like Winston are modulated: first hesitation, then eloquence, then humour, then irony, and finally the climax.

The first time that I began to get the feel of the House, and to be more at home in making parliamentary speeches myself, was when I was charged with leading the opposition to the bill nationalising steel.

I confess that those measures which are aimed at nationalising services such as transport or electricity do not rouse in me political hostility; I question them solely from the practical standpoint. For example, are not the nationalised railways too large and sprawling an undertaking to be efficient? The L.M.S. in itself was the largest railway system under single control in the world; the nationalised system is three or four times as large as the L.M.S. Moreover, it comprises docks, ships, canals, hotels.

When, however, nationalisation is to extend to industry, my political as well as my practical beliefs are outraged. In industrialised countries there must always be a conflict of interest between agriculture and industry; the industrial worker wants cheap food, the countryman wants to see a secure, well-balanced and well-paid agriculture. It is one of the main duties of the Government to hold the balance. If it becomes itself the largest industrialist in the country, it cannot be impartial.

In the steel industry, the line at which steel production becomes engineering or semi-manufacture cannot be drawn. Thus at what point does the manufacture of structural steel become bridge building or engineering?

We tenaciously fought the bill in detail, and on occasions were able to make some of the Government's proposals look a little ridiculous. We forced the Governments to confess that in one of the great works of Stewarts & Lloyds, it would be necessary to build a partition. On one side of the partition, on the same shop floor, would be nationalised steel, on the other private enterprise.

The bill was fought out in the committee stage "upstairs"—in parliamentary terms. This means that only the fifty Members selected to sit on the committee take part in the debate, clause by clause. When a bill is taken "on the floor of the House" any Member can take part. We met on thirty-six occasions, and as I generally led the Opposition, these were strenuous days. The other ex-Ministers concerned were Harold Macmillan, Sir Reginald Manningham-Buller,[1] and amongst the back-benchers Walter Fletcher,

[1] Now Lord Dilhorne, the present Lord Chancellor.

Freddy Erroll [2] and Bill Shepherd.[3] They were a formidable pack.

Walter Fletcher was a man of great versatility, trilingual in French, German and English, an accomplished painter, at once a gourmand and a gourmet, who matched his wine and food with a pretty wit. He had few pretensions to good looks, a porridge-like complexion and a monumental bulk. He weighed, I should judge, nearer twenty stone than fifteen.

At this time there was a sensational murder case at sea, and the body of the young woman who was the victim had been thrown out of a port-hole. Walter Fletcher had occasion to go to New York and sent me a telegram when he arrived. It read: "Owing small size port-holes flannel nightie and general aversion to my type have arrived safely. Walter."

My greatest friend was Oliver Stanley.[4] As a Minister his reputation was high, but he was thought to be somewhat negative. In Opposition he was unrivalled. He had a great eye for parliamentary weather and kept us, and Winston in particular, out of much trouble. Our leader sometimes plunged into a fight just because it was a fight and he felt like fighting. When in this mood the only man to restrain him was Oliver. His wit was devastating, and he was prepared to use it on his leader, his colleagues or his opponents. He fenced with such skill and brilliance that even the victims bound up their wounds and smiled. The Government benches always filled when he was to speak, and the members of the Labour Party chuckled or laughed unrestrainedly at his sallies.

In an economic debate Alexander,[5] the Minister of Defence, got into some difficulties and when driven into a corner lost his temper and exclaimed, "Piffle and poppycock!" His supporters, who knew he was in the wrong, thought his own speech was more deserving of the phrase.

A second economic debate took place a few weeks later. Alexander was not amongst the Government speakers. Oliver began, "The Rt. Hon. Gentleman, the Minister of Defence, took part in a previous economic debate, in which he characterised the arguments of my Rt. Hon. Friends as piffle and poppycock. We understand that he is not taking part in this one (titters from the Labour benches)." The Government, he implied, having found that

[2] The Rt. Hon. F. J. Erroll, now the President of the Board of Trade.
[3] W. S. Shepherd.
[4] The late Rt. Hon. Oliver Stanley.
[5] A. V. Alexander.

they could not make him strong, had at least been able to keep him silent.

I hardly think I could have endured the six years of opposition without Oliver's society and friendship. We usually drove home together after the debates; his comments made up for hours of boredom. The most mordant were usually preceded by a serpent-like hiss. He used to expose with ruthless wit the pretensions of several of our colleagues to the leadership of the Party "if anything should happen to Winston." As half a dozen of the most powerful of us had unreservedly decided to back Anthony Eden for the succession, the ambitions of others appeared illusory, even ridiculous.

One day Oliver and I were having luncheon with Lady Pamela Berry in Cowley Street, and Mrs. Odgen Reid, the proprietor of *The New York Herald Tribune*, was one of the guests. She asked us what we thought of the lady Members of the House. The two Olivers, according to Pam, gave such a light-hearted and malicious reply that Mrs. Ogden Reid believed that Great Britain was slipping into frivolity and cynicism.

In defence, I must say that during my fourteen years in the House of Commons there was not an effective lady parliamentarian. As a rule, in the House women are too earnest, and seem apologetic and on the defensive. This is hardly surprising when their handicap is weighed up. There are no more than a handful, perhaps twenty-five or thirty in all, out of a House of 630. They do not use the Smoking Room, and necessarily are out of touch with the current opinion of Members. They find it difficult to distinguish between the smart Members, whom no one is willing to listen to, and the solid, sincere bores, who will always get a hearing because the House likes sincerity. One very popular Member, who had a fierce and burning faith in personal liberty, never spoke, as far as I can remember, a word of sense in any debate which I heard. Yet the House would fill up and listen to him with respect. The ladies would not have known his qualities, which were only manifested in private. Smoking-room stories are also bandied about in the House of Commons and usually, from their nature, the lady Members do not hear them.

In short, the lady Members seldom get the tone or mood of the House right. A small number tried to assert the equality of the sexes by being ruder and more unruly than the worst of their masculine colleagues.

Oliver Stanley was clearly destined to be Chancellor of the

Exchequer; he dealt with the financial debates for the first four years of Opposition, and I with trade subjects.

The most difficult position from which to make a speech—especially on economic matters—is second, that is immediately after the Minister. Winston himself almost always avoided it. He liked a few hours in which to survey the enemy dispositions, to bring up his ammunition and train his guns. If you have to follow the Ministers at once, you can only prepare your own speech lightly; you have to try to guess the Government line. Moreover, you have got to absorb, as the Minister's speech proceeds, a lot of figures and arguments, carefully prepared by the Civil Service in support of Government policy. Fortunately we generally had a good idea of the official arguments, and were ready to dispute them. It is a strain to listen to a Ministerial speech, to digest a new argument and its figures, or spot a new slant or a new fallacy, and then reply without more ado.

I remember being nominated as the second speaker in the debate which took place on the devaluation of the pound. I was not overpleased when I heard that Aneurin Bevan was to open for the Government. He was a formidable parliamentarian, perhaps the most formidable since Lloyd George, and never more brilliant than when supported by a large, cheering majority. He was far less effective when the scales were even.

In this particular debate on devaluation I had a piece of luck. Aneurin made the most glittering though meretricious speech. It was clear that he knew very little about the subject; he never even mentioned the word devaluation, although he urged great national effort to increase our exports. He poked a great deal of fun at Winston, who was supposed to have favoured the nationalisation of the railways. He read out some damaging quotations, and after each one he exclaimed with much gusto, in his Welsh accent, "Why read the crystal when you can read the book?"

Before his speech his supporters had been unhappy and uneasy about the failure of their policy, which had led to humiliation. He now had them in transports of delighted laughter. So tumultuous was the applause from the Government benches when he had finished that I could not begin my own speech for more than a minute, and a minute seems a long time.

Expecting that Aneurin would say something about exports, I had brought his book with me, so was able to begin like this:

I find it extremely difficult to take the Rt. Hon. Gentleman seriously upon either economics, devaluation or exports. After all, he is the person who wrote this remarkable passage a mere four years ago:

"By some twist of the Tory mind it is good trade to persuade someone in a remote part of the world to buy our goods but ruinous to allow the same goods to be consumed by our own people."

And that is not all; much more disagreeable things are to come:

"We are now told, by some people who ought to know better, that we shall have to increase our exports after the war by some 50 per cent."

Why read the crystal if you can read the book? [6]

When Oliver Stanley died, I succeeded as Chairman of the Finance Committee of the Party. Selwyn Lloyd was the Secretary. I soon got to know him well. He is able and humorous; his character is of sterling worth, it rings true on the counter; he is brave and combative and modest. When he reached the high offices which he deserved, he was always willing to listen. He knows how to make use of his advisers, and is not too proud to alter his opinion.

We fought two Finance Bills together. Except for the all-night sittings, the task was easier than fighting the Steel Bill. By this time the Labour Party realised that the long shadows were beginning to fall across the ground where they thought that their innings would go on for ever. The economic clouds were darkening, and the jeers and hubris of 1945 were now replaced by a sullen and anxious cast of countenance.

I loathed all-night sittings perhaps more than most, because I had to earn my living, and run my company.

At the next general election I increased my majority at Aldershot to over 6,000. We returned with very different resources from those of 1945. The Labour majority had been reduced to eight, and on three-line Whips the ambulances rolled into the Speaker's Yard to disgorge those Labour Members who, though not able to walk or talk, were still able to vote.

It was clear that the Government was paralysed and that economic disaster was imminent. One morning we heard that the Government had wisely run away, and that the Ministers had resigned. Time alone will show whether they ran away to fight another day. We were returned, and the new House of Commons was 320 Conservatives, six Liberals and 296 Labour, a Conservative majority of sixteen.

[6] Hansard: Volume 486, No. 164, Col. 326, September 29th, 1949.

CHAPTER XVIII

THE COLONIAL OFFICE—
APPOINTMENT AS
SECRETARY OF STATE

D ESPITE THE SMALL MAJORITY, no one had any doubt that Mr. Churchill would wish to form and lead a Government.

It had always been thought that a majority of forty was the minimum on which a Government with any serious programme of legislation could work. Anthony, from his much longer experience, and I had more than once discussed the difficulties of parliamentary life in a Government on anything much below sixty, and here we were with sixteen.

For myself I waited for the formation of the Government with anxiety. Except for my eight months in Cairo as Minister of State, I had been an economic Minister, first as President of the Board of Trade, then as Minister of Production, and finally in the "Caretaker Government" as both. In Opposition I had been Chairman of the party Committee on Trade and Industry and the spokesman of the Opposition on these subjects. Since the death of my greatest friend, Oliver Stanley, I had changed from Chairman of the Trade and Industry Committee to Chairman of the Finance Committee. I had thus been in charge of financial affairs and had fought two finance bills in the House. I did not ask for this position as Chairman and I had never raised a finger to improve my chances of the appointment. I have always believed that one of the greatest misfortunes which can come to a man is to be over-promoted.

If such a thing happens by chance it cannot be helped, but if it should come about by enlisting favour or by personal lobbying, then it often assumes the colour of tragedy.

Happiness in the world of affairs, as in many other worlds, lies in being if not the cock of your own walk, at least in having your crowing respected by the rest of the farmyard.

So my rather trite advice to all political aspirants is the same as that to beginners at golf: don't press.

On some aspects of this subject I often look back on the brilliant career and life of my friend Wyndham Portal.[1] He had the instinct, the very genius of success. Everything he touched was successful. He had an ambition to elevate the family business and to make a million; he did it in his stride and made two millions or more. He wanted to become a peer; he ended as a viscount. In youth he aspired one day to be Chairman of the Great Western Railway Company; he became the Chairman.

He gained his success by personal genius and drive, not by delegated policy. He studied men, made his store of knowledge from conversation, not from books. He was, of course, like everyone worth anything, in some degree ambitious, and he wanted to become a Minister. This spur did not make for his happiness.

The only part of my political life which I regard with unalloyed satisfaction (I hope not complacency) is that I have never intrigued, lobbied, said a word or lifted a finger on my own behalf. I would have to confess, however, that this apparent altruism does not come from virtue, but because high political office is only attractive to me in war or times of crisis.

I had, because of my Chairmanship of the Finance Committee, been tipped to be Chancellor of the Exchequer. I was told at the time of my appointment as Chairman of the Finance Committee that Rab Butler, who was not chairman of any important committee of the party at that time, but who had done such enlightened work as the head of the Conservative Research Department, was worried about his own future position. I did not myself see any department which seemed suited to him unless it were—perhaps—the Treasury. I never, therefore, entertained solid hopes of being given this position myself.

I do not disguise that I should have taken it with zest, and that I thought I could make a contribution, perhaps even a decisive contribution, to the immediate financial and economic problems of the country.

On the other hand, after a life-time of figures, after the desiccated study of applied economics, after having lived with imports and exports, the volume of bank deposits, balance of payments and monetary theory, the prospect of other political employment

[1] Afterwards Viscount Portal.

was seductive. Yet I could hardly see any office likely to be offered to me that was more of a challenge than the Treasury. In this I proved wrong.

So I awaited the Prime Minister's summons with anxiety. It arrived and somewhere about eleven o'clock I went to 28 Hyde Park Gate with my heart in my mouth. I was shown into the downstairs sitting-room: it is a friendly room, panelled in pine, with some harmonious pictures and furniture. There were gleams of sunlight, but a fire was burning in the grate. In front of it sat two of my oldest friends and contemporaries, Salisbury and Macmillan. We discussed the election for a few moments and then the private secretary came in to take me upstairs to the Prime Minister's bedroom. He was in bed, in a quilted flowered bed-jacket, the garment slightly reminiscent of Don Pasquale, and he was smoking a cigar. He had the tired look of a trawler captain who has got into harbour after a buffeting. From time to time he sketched in a point by restrained gestures with one of his rather small, rather pink, well-cared-for hands—gestures that were delivered from the wrist and not from the shoulder.

"Our duty is to form a Government; the tasks facing it are appalling. I have seen a Treasury Minute and already I know that the financial position is almost irretrievable; the country has lost its way. In the worst of the war I could always see how to do it. Today's problems are elusive and intangible, and it would be a bold man who could look forward to certain success. After much talk, and particularly on the House of Commons aspects, I have eventually decided to send Rab to the Treasury and I want you to be Minister of Materials and Rearmament. The sphere is not yet fully defined and will require study. I hope you don't mind and will do it." After a pause, "Are you disappointed?"

"Yes," I said, "I am deeply disappointed. Of course I will do what I'm told but," I added, "only for a short time. This job is not a man's job in peace, and on any scale is misconceived. We controlled materials in the war by the sanction of scarcity and by our comprehensive grip of the world's, yes the world's, shipping by Navicerts; that can't be done now. Again, on the rearmaments aspects, when I was Minister of Production I came to know the difficulties of controlling and co-ordinating the Ministry of Supply, the Ministry of Aircraft Production and parts of the Admiralty. My Ministry creaked. It worked only because my power sprang from scarcity and from the needs of war. In peace the departments will not submit."

"Well, we must see," said the Prime Minister. He seemed to think that my disappointment was at not being Chancellor, but I had long thought that unlikely. My disappointment, and it was deep, was at being consigned to a new Ministry, which had small chance of being useful and which would be perpetually engaged in departmental wrangles. I foresaw its early funeral and I thought there would be few mourners and no flowers at the graveside.

I again said, "Of course I will do what I'm told and I mustn't waste your time by telling you of the difficulties I foresee. You will forgive me if I say again I can only do it for a short time." With that I smiled, waved my hand and made for the door.

"I am sorry you are disappointed. It was touch and go, but the Chief Whip thought the House of Commons stuff was a handicap to you." And then, suddenly, "You wouldn't have preferred the Colonies, would you?"

"Would I have preferred the Colonies?" I cried. "Now there is a job, and there is Malaya, which we are going to lose unless something is done."

So after a few words with Salisbury and Macmillan and after expressing my disenchantment at being Minister of Materials and Rearmament, I left to tell Moira what had happened. She had not liked my remaining in politics after 1945 because she detests anything which savours of partisanship or the *argumentum ad hominem*. She thought I should work too hard and reap only the tares. The news merely confirmed her dislike of politics, and she said, "Of course, I always knew you would be let down." Hardly had we finished talking about it when the telephone rang. The Prime Minister: "I've altered it and offer you the Colonial Office. Do you accept?" "You bet I do," I said with relief and exultation. "Do you want it published tonight with the other five I have appointed, or would you like to wait?" "I should like it published now." "All right. Good-bye, old cock. I'm so glad you prefer it."

"I'm Secretary of State for the Colonies," I exclaimed to Moira. "Now that is something," she said. "It is a splendid office which, incidentally, will take you—and me—into these fascinating countries."

"Well, it is about as tough and challenging a task as you will find," I replied.

At least this was an end to my disappointment. I never regretted the Treasury, and never had the impertinence or the audacity, or for that matter the wish, to grumble.

The next day, so out of touch with colonial affairs had I become that, believing the Colonial Office was still there, I presented myself at the Commonwealth Relations Office in the yard opposite No. 10 Downing Street, or rather to its door. Seeing the name plate, my memory revived and I went on rather sadly to Great Smith Street.

For a few hours I had pictured myself in the stately and dignified room now occupied by the Secretary of State for Commonwealth Relations. I remembered the room from childhood, for I had been taken there in 1904 to see my father soon after he took office as Colonial Secretary. I was eleven, and I can see him sitting there as if it was yesterday. On his desk there were two or three coloured india-rubber bulbs, looking like the bulbs on a scent spray. By squeezing one of them you could summon the appropriate official, but, like Portia's suitors and the caskets, it was a guess which was the right one. My father said that on his first day the room became colder and colder and he was forced to ask for coal to be put on the fire. He plunged for red, but after a pause the leading authority on tropical diseases—or so I remember—came into the room. "Secretary of State," he said, "can I be of help?" My father confessed his difficulties. Amid some laughter the coals were summoned, the fire revived, and a friendship had begun.

A very different room and prospect awaited me. Church House is repugnant to my idea of aesthetic propriety, or even of common comfort. It is pervaded by a faint smell of size, or of some preservative which I associate with the interiors of churches and with the schoolboy faintness which often made the psalms at matins something of a physical test of endurance.

My room had been the Prime Minister's when, in the war, we moved from the old House of Commons to Church House. I remembered him poring over the charts while the Navy hunted the *Bismarck.* Signals kept coming in and he followed every shift and change in the drama. In it I remembered pressing for clothes rationing and being brushed aside. The room was large and L-shaped, furnished in the Cunard tourist style and lit by a number of suspended spittoons in copper which are the modern version of chandeliers. The walls were spattered with some singularly poor paintings by colonial artists. There was, however, one exquisite wooden head by a Nigerian sculptor mounted on a bracket.[2]

One of the pictures, in which the breasts of the dusky women were developed with a ruthless reality, was afterwards taken down at my orders. I found that it distracted the attention of deputa-

[2] By Ben Inonwu.

tions from the niceties of constitutional argument and discussion.

A large buhl clock completed the décor—and there were no maps. The last deficiency was soon remedied. I cannot live without maps and my early training as a soldier has given me a reverence for time and space even in political affairs.

Jim Griffiths,[3] the outgoing Colonial Secretary, came to see me. I had known and liked him in the old days, but his emotional approach to public affairs was to drive me first to boredom and finally to exasperation. It may be a defect to believe that *"pas trop de zèle"* is a good political motto, and that a certain disenchantment about human progress is a necessary ingredient of statesmanship. Conversely, to imagine that universal suffrage, elections and self-government with a few trades unions and co-operative wholesale societies thrown in spell immediate peace, prosperity and happiness outrages my historical sense and affronts my reason.

Our personal relations have remained friendly, though some incidents in which I consider that he acted a shade more for the sake of immediate party advantage than for the interests of the colonies gave, I confess, a slight chill from time to time to our relations.

I then saw Sir Thomas Lloyd, the Permanent Head of the Department. He is not tall, not a forward but a three-quarter, neat and clear, with a twinkle.

I have never prided myself on being able to sum up a man in a few minutes and when I have sought to do so I can recall few instances when I have been right. I have long given up the attempt and secretly believe that those who say they can are either psychic or fools.

I can only form my judgement of people when I have worked with them long and shared with them either the dangers of action or the analysis of baffling problems. So the judgement which I give of the head of my department is the matured opinion of one who lived with him through many trials and discontents.

Tom Lloyd was an example of the best in the Civil Service, wise and salty in his judgements, never in a panic or a hurry, enlightened and broad-minded on colonial policy, a good judge of men, insistent that humour must be among their qualifications. It is certainly amongst his.

Some said that he did not allow his imagination to walk abroad,

[3] The Rt. Hon. James Griffiths, Secretary of State for the Colonies, 1950–51.

but only took it out on a lead for a short time. If this were true I should be far from saying that it was a fault in the permanent head of a department. A little deflation from time to time is as good a thing for Ministers as it is for monetary policy.

With all this, he had perhaps too much loyalty for some of his particular swans who had turned, in the stress of colonial affairs or under the erosive influence of Government Houses, into geese.

Speaking of geese, I remember a tumble with Mr. Churchill on this subject. Telephone: "My dear, have you seen what so-and-so has said in America, a member of your Committee?" "Yes; very silly." "But I wish you would stop him saying this sort of thing; pronouncements on high policy should only be made by front-benchers. You don't know the harm that is done. Why, this will be in the Labour 'Hints to Speakers.'" "Yes, I know," and—rather nettled—"but I can't really be responsible for everything that some ass says. It's a free country, with free speech." "Yes, but he shouldn't have said this." Then I, slightly recovering my poise: "Anyway, Prime Minister, please remember that geese saved the Capitol."

A long and somewhat ominous pause. "Geese? What are geese?" I: "Plural of goose." W. S. C.: "Oh, it's a joke, is it?" And then, to give a more genial end to the conversation, "Well, ta-ta" (an often used valediction, spoken, so to speak, in inverted commas). "See that that idiot doesn't do it again."

These first days in office were spent in seeing old friends as well as new faces. The next senior official I saw was Hilton Poynton, who had been my private secretary in 1942, when I was Minister of Production, and was now a Deputy Under Secretary and the head of the Economic Division of the Colonial Office. He had blossomed into Sir Hilton Poynton. His brilliant brains are allied to a pretty wit and his classical upbringing and scholarship, as well as his many other merits, made me truly thankful to see him again.

I remember an example of his wit. I was reading a report by Lord Reith on a tour that he had made in Africa where, as Chairman of the Colonial Development Corporation, he had been inspecting some of its properties and ventures. Lord Reith had seen many Scotsmen and seemed to have absorbed tea in Africa with an almost Australian frequency. No doubt this willing sacrifice of his digestion enabled him to gain information which otherwise only whisky, with all its moral disadvantages, could have elicited. But each pot was recorded, and I minuted some petulant comment that I was not interested in tea, either in print or in pot. Hilton wrote in the margin: *"Te veniente die te decedente canebat."* [4]

Later I found that Bill Gorell-Barnes,[5] who was away with the mumps, was one of the Assistant Under Secretaries in the Economic Division. I had known him slightly in the Coalition, when he was in the Cabinet Office.

Possessed of good intellectual equipment, a transparent character and deep devotion to the cause of Africa, he had been one of Tom Lloyd's felicitous choices. I became and remain much attached to him. His gifts of negotiation are not, in my jaundiced opinion, outstanding and he used to pass threatening notes to me when I was conducting a particularly delicate negotiation, such as, "You should surely get their agreement to two African members before giving the concession which you mentioned and which I think I can support." To which I generally replied by writing underneath his note, "O. L., Born 1893."

And lastly my private office. The three private secretaries were Angus MacKintosh, Barry Smallman and John Osborne. Angus, whom I hope to be able to keep as a friend for life, suited me as if I had chosen him myself. He had a fine war record, a Scottish humour expressed in rotund prose or in elaborate anecdote, and a classical education. He shared with me a dislike of flaccid and obscure official English.

Barry Smallman was a delightful junior. He brought to his work a natural piety and earnestness. He was soon promoted.

John Osborne was in charge of the parliamentary questions and spent nearly all his time preparing the replies. He knew, too, all the mechanics, whether we should be "reached," which questions by the preceding Minister were to be answered in one, so accelerating the timetable, and how you pronounced the unpronounceable. Since the Colonial Office ship rarely faced anything but the roughest weather at Question Time, the enlistment of so admirable a chief mate often kept us from too much baling. The new rigging was always ready and bent for the next storm.

I have gone at some length into the leading personalities to show the high quality of the advice available. Of course, it takes new Ministers quite a long time to know and understand the Civil Service and what it can do for them if they know how to use it. I was glad I was not a new Minister. It is imperative to be on such terms with your senior officials as to know what is being agreed or

---

[4] He called for "te" at break and close of day.
[5] Sir William Gorell-Barnes.

disputed at lunch in the Reform Club or the Athenaeum by the heads of the Civil Service. An early and unequivocal statement of your own policy often enables your permanent secretary to prepare the ground over the sherry in the club, so that either the money is forthcoming from the Treasury or the complaisance of some other department secured, or at the worst, that the departmental rocks awaiting you can be marked on the chart.

This wonderful machine, the Civil Service, responds to clear-cut decisions if they follow frank discussions and a willingness to face the essential argument and to take a dialectical toss without chagrin.

The Civil Service is not organised for the day-to-day management of affairs. It is at its worst over quick decisions on small matters; the progress of the minutes from an Assistant Principal to Principal, to Assistant Secretary to Under Secretary to Permanent Secretary to Minister, will nearly always disclose the tigers that lie behind every defile which leads to action. On the other hand, because great principles such as the liberty of the subject may be involved in otherwise small affairs, many decisions cannot be delegated to juniors. The dismissal of one schoolmaster from a colony or the prosecution of one newspaper may loom locally as large as the arrest of the five Members.

One of the reasons for the dismal failure of nationalisation is the misuse of this wonderful instrument.

The Civil Service is also too much withdrawn from some parts of the national life. For example, civil servants regard with suspicion and distaste illiterate and vulgar men who have made a lot of money. "If Heaven had looked upon riches to be a valuable thing, it would not have given them to such a scoundrel," is their attitude, and this again is apt to make them over-suspicious of the motives and over-anxious of the methods of business. Strangely, the commercial morality of Government Departments sometimes does not reach the minimum standards which the instinct of survival imposes on the business world.

I can remember senior officials without a smile on their faces saying, "Well, Minister, we have studied the contract with great care and we see no way in which we can get out of it." They do not grasp that in business a reputation for keeping absolutely to the letter and spirit of an agreement, even when it is unfavourable, is the most precious of assets, although it is not entered in the balance sheet.

One day the Colonial Office agreed to buy back from the Anglo-

Iranian Oil Company for about £90,000 a site which they were not going to use. The letter covering this transaction was specific but by an oversight had not been referred to the Finance Committee of the Colony, which had an unofficial majority—that is the number of elected members exceeded the number of officials.

This is what is known as a crisis in a Government Department; either the Governor must use his reserve powers on a subject for which they were clearly not intended, or the Colonial Office must pay. In that event the Public Accounts Committee will doubtless wish to know the reason why. Treasury sanction may have to be sought.

The Finance Committee of the Colony valued the site at about £40,000 and were reluctantly willing to give that price for it.

The teacup in which this storm had been brewed was put on my table. "All right," I grumbled, "I will arrange it for you some day soon." So I asked the private secretary to ring up Sir William Fraser,[6] the Chairman of the Anglo-Iranian Oil Company, and ask him if on any day convenient to him he would look in to the Colonial Office on his way to the City. Willie Fraser was an old friend and of course was a famous name in the hierarchy of business. His Scottish character did not like sloppiness anywhere in his company or in business transactions.

One morning he turned up and we immediately plunged into a long conversation on the intricacies of Persian oil: the prospects of a new agreement, the growth of Anglo-Iranian—which was four times as large in 1953, without Abadan or Persia, as it was in 1938. After about half an hour I mentioned the Colonial Office mistake and described very shortly the circumstances. He paid scant attention to this and said almost in parenthesis, "Put it in at £40,000 if that is right. As I was saying, the refining capacity of the world . . ."

So it was settled and my success was thought by the Department to be a small instance of magic, whereas it was only an example of Willie Fraser following a City tradition that you do not hold people, or rather honest people, to mistakes.

Every wise man must see first that a contract is profitable to the other party; he is sure to see that it is profitable to himself. Contracts where the other party does well seldom come into the courts and in my business life litigation on a commercial contract by companies with which I have been connected has been so rare that I can hardly recall an instance.

[6] Now Lord Strathalmond.

These personal interviews being concluded, I turned to a rough survey of my task and concentrated my attention on two subjects. The first: "What theme to announce or re-announce on colonial policy?" The second: "What immediate action was called for?"

Turning to the first: responsibilities can only be discharged properly in relation to a dominant theme. Empiricism and expediency must be banished from the topmost council chamber, though no doubt they have their part to play in the execution of a policy once it has been formulated.

In war, Montgomery talked of the "Master Plan" and the Joint Chiefs of Staff of the "over-all strategic concept." On a lower plane the theme underlying my policy at the Board of Trade at the beginning of the war had been obvious: it had been to squeeze out of consumption everything that was superfluous and to use the resources thus released for war whilst at the same time arranging that civil life was sustained at a tolerable and humane level.

At the Ministry of Production, the policy was equally simple: to make the most effective use of our capacity to produce munitions and to try to effect a synthesis between military and tactical needs on the one hand, and production, its quality, volume and time-scale, on the other. We had to plan that each side should have a clear idea of what was needed and what part of it was producible.

In contrast to these simple aims, to announce the dominant theme of colonial policy is a wide matter of statesmanship; nevertheless I think any Secretary of State for the Colonies taking office in 1951 would have come to the same decision as we did. The dominant theme of colonial policy had to be the careful and if possible gradual and orderly progress of the colonies towards self-government within the Commonwealth.

Most of us, and amongst them I should certainly be numbered, would regard this as an end in itself; but whether it is enlightened statesmanship or not, it was clearly the only practical course, and still is.

The reasons for this bald statement are not far to seek. The first reason is that we do not have the force to govern without the consent of the governed. The second is that with modern communications, that consent has to be engaged by open and candid discussion of policy.

In the days of Queen Victoria we had the force. British power policed the world and kept it at peace. African potentates sought Her Majesty's protection. A stiff letter and a gunboat, or a small show of force, soon calmed disorder and faction. Above all, the white man was supposed to know the answers. No pan-African movement could be conceived, much less brought to birth, because the communications between one part of Africa and another were primitive and too slow to carry the flame of the nationalist aspirations of one territory and set alight the same fire in another. Today the African no longer lives in a world of his own. The newspapers, now the *Guardian* and the *Mirror*, now the *Daily Telegraph* or *The Times*, or *Life*, tell different stories and propose conflicting policies. If the white man knows the answers, they are not all the same answers.

The radio has penetrated into the villages, and the discordant voices of a world of which the African was ignorant three or four decades ago blare out from the beehive receivers hung in the banyan trees. At one time the aeroplane disgorges the Secretary of State or a colonial expert, or a professor of tropical diseases; at another, Mr. Fenner Brockway, or Mr. Michael Foot. "The isle is full of noises" is what the African must think of Great Britain.

Even if it were desired to rule without engaging the consent of the governed, and in my opinion it certainly should not be, that consent is a plain necessity in the nineteen-fifties in multi-racial societies. If such a policy is enlightened, well and good, but necessary it surely is.

It is also important to grasp, at an early stage, that the constitutional evolution of the colonies should differ greatly from one colony to another. Almost every problem differs. This is because of a great number of varying conditions. In some colonies, notably in Kenya, the white man can make a permanent home; he can bring up his children in a climate which will not undermine their health; in another, he will always be an expatriate, as in the Gold Coast, and must send his children home once they begin to grow up.

In some colonies, like Northern Rhodesia, nature has put into the ground great mineral wealth. Excluding Russian aid, it can only be brought to the surface, at least for many years, by mobilising Western capital and Western skill. The mining itself, the concentration of the mineral, its smelting and refining into metal, can only be achieved through the complex skills of the Western mining industry.

Moreover, power to drive the plants has to be developed, whether from local coal through the heat cycle, or from harnessing the great rivers to produce electric current. Several generations of highly civilised and technically highly educated men and women have patiently developed these skills; they cannot be improvised and cannot be built up in Africa in less than a generation or more.

The proportions between subsistence crops varies greatly amongst the colonies, and in some the standard of life depends chiefly on the sales of cash crops. In one colony the emigration of the Nilotics down the caravan routes has brought the people into some touch, however remote, with the ancient civilisation of Egypt or the Mediterranean; in another, the wheel and the fulcrum were unknown fifty years ago. Sir Philip Mitchell, when he came to take leave of me upon retirement, recalled that when he was a cadet, the tribe amongst which he worked knew neither. In another colony, primitive religions, witchcraft and superstitions sway the people, as in parts of Northern Rhodesia; in another, the Muslim religion, with all its discipline, embraces large masses of people, as in Northern Nigeria. In another, the Creole population of Sierra Leone has spread its culture down the West Coast and into the new universities which the British have promoted and helped to build and endow. In yet another, as in the former Gold Coast, the influence of the slave trade and of Western commerce is still discernible. The very word African is a misnomer, or an oversimplification.

Finally, the differing racial balance between the black indigenous population and the immigrant white gives evidence of the diverse forces that have been at work: climate, accessibility, natural wealth, railways, and sometimes just chance. It is necessary to grasp the figures which tell this story in the territories south of the Sahara. For convenience, I give the figures of the population in 1960. In the Federation there were something over 8,300,000 inhabitants, of whom just over 300,000 were European; in Kenya, out of a total of 6,500,000 there were about 68,000 Europeans; and in the Union of South Africa, out of a total of a little under 16,000,-000 no less than 3,100,000 were Europeans and nearly 2,000,000 were Asians and coloureds.

These figures show that a few words should be devoted to the native problem in the Union (now Republic) of South Africa. Here, if the white man wishes to govern by force, be that a reactionary policy or not, he can do so for many, many years. This is because there are 3 million European, 2 million coloured and 11 million African inhabitants, and if it is rightly assumed that the coloureds are mostly on the side of the Europeans, the ratio is a little more than 2 Africans to 1 European. In comparison, the former Gold Coast had, in 1955, 7,000 European and 4,000,000

African inhabitants, a ratio of nearly 6,000 to 1. Yet quite intelligent people correlate the two problems.

One other salient point emerges from these figures. It was estimated that in 1951–54 the total number of colonial subjects of the crown was about 82,000,000. Of these, no less than 65,000,000 were in the territories south of the Sahara, and of this number nearly half were in Nigeria.

It is necessary to add a few words upon the essential dilemma of native African politicians. At first politics were easy for them. "Freedom," they shouted. "Get rid of the British." "Votes for the people." "Government on the Westminster model," and the parrot cry echoed through every village. I remember visiting the Cocoa Research Station in the Gold Coast with the Governor, Sir Charles Arden Clarke. A few miles short of it, two black boys, whose combined ages could not have been twenty, and who were completely naked, were holding up a large blackboard. On it, in impeccable copperplate, was written in chalk, "Away with the three ex-officios."

These democratic aspirations found sympathy with the people of the U.S.A., still suffering from a pathological hatred of colonialism, reinforced by a profound ignorance of what Great Britain was trying to do, or of the very nature of the difficulties.

A successful party and a successful leader in Africa had to deliver to the people large and visible constitutional gains or he would be swept aside by those who promised more, or who promised it quicker. On the other hand, the wiser leaders—and there were not many—realised that to stay in power, to fulfil a true and not a meretricious mission, the standard of life and education of their peoples must be raised. For this the help of the British and other white men was necessary with capital, powers of organisation, skilled direction, skilled supervision and skilled workmen. If they went too far—or too fast—with freedom and constitutional advances, the sources of this capital and these skills would dry up.

Much later, when I was in the Gold Coast, I thought that Dr. Nkrumah had a lively appreciation of this dilemma. I said to him, "There are two great tragedies in human life on the material plane. One is when you want something with all your heart and cannot get it." "Oh yes," he said, opening wide his expressive eyes, "the other is when you have got it." Today, Dr. Nkrumah's quick intelligence and grasp of affairs seem to have been overborne by the intoxication of power. He has set his sights at targets which will prove out of reach even if his Messianic powers are as high as he believes.

To sum up, it seemed clear that the development of self-government, though at different rates and with different methods, was at once the only enlightened and the only practical theme of a colonial policy in the nineteen-fifties. No difference exists between the two great political parties in Great Britain on the main theme. Policy in its broadest sense appeared to be bi-partisan.

I was, however, to witness with sorrow the complete breakdown of a bi-partisan policy.

In 1951 the Labour Government had left office only just in time. Economically they had brought the country to the verge of disaster. Our adverse balance of payments including invisible exports was running at £419 million a year. Economic retribution was knocking at the door. Their recent political record had undermined their confidence and they feared an inquest on their performance as a Government. The high-flown hubris of 1945 was being stalked by the economic nemesis of 1951.

What more natural than to turn a good deal of attention, under one of the leaders of the party, to an area where there appeared to be endless opportunities of trouble, whether those troubles were spontaneous or fanned into flame by faction; at least Lyttelton seemed to be a weak parliamentarian and a toothsome victim.

I had no more than a suspicion at the time of what to expect, and only the first step was clear. A theme must be announced or reaffirmed. I used almost the very words of Mr. Creech Jones,[7] one of my respected predecessors.

I said that our aims were first to help the colonial territories to attain self-government within the British Commonwealth and, secondly, that we were determined to pursue the economic and social development of the colonial territories so that it kept pace with their political development.[8]

[7] The Rt. Hon. Arthur Creech Jones, Secretary of State for the Colonies 1946–50.
[8] Hansard: Vol. 493, No. 10, Col. 986, November 14th, 1951.

In telling the story of my term of office as Secretary of State, which follows, I have, in the main, written separately about each territory.

To have attempted an over-all chronological sequence would have meant that the narrative would have had to shift from one subject to another, and would have become confused and disjointed.

The reader should understand that some of the dangers which had to be faced took place concurrently in more than one country.

The most acute problems concerned Malaya, the Central African Federation, Kenya, Nigeria, Malta, British Guiana and Uganda. The first two fall naturally into a chronological sequence; the others do not. I have omitted all references to the West Indies and to the Caribbean Federation, for although the opening moves took place during my term of office this Federation was not brought to birth until later. I have equally omitted to describe the course of events in Ghana, Sierra Leone, the Gambia and Tanganyika, and my visits to the first three, because the story only became of general interest after I had resigned.

CHAPTER XIX

THE COLONIAL OFFICE: MALAYA

T HE BROAD LINES of policy having been settled and announced, the next question to be asked was what immediate action
was called for and where. The answer was clear; action in Malaya,
and at once. I must see for myself what ought to be done and then
get it done.

I had had a long connection with the country and had spent
some time there. From early in 1935 I had been a Director of the
London Tin Corporation and its subsidiary the Anglo-Oriental
Company, and had succeeded to the chairmanship of both in
March 1937. These companies owned or managed forty-four
dredges in Malaya. I suppose this was by far the largest dredging
enterprise in the world. It took me to Malaya in 1937, and my love
of the country dates from those days. It was at that time the happiest country which I have ever seen. The sunshine and flowers
and the riotous and exotic vegetation incline men, at least of eastern blood, to smile and not to frown.

The Malays are a happy, easy-going race, endowed with simple
good manners. Their villages were spotlessly clean; the colours of
their clothes show that they love the sunshine. The crowds at a
race-meeting or a feast in Kelantan or Ipoh look like a parterre of
many-coloured flowers.

The Chinese in Malaya also believe in good manners. By their
sophistication they dominate trade and commerce. Their taste for
line and colour further enhance the beauty of the country.

The common labour is provided largely by Tamils, who prosper
modestly and live better than they would in their own country.

I remembered looking out of the window of Adolph Henggeler's house—he ran our Malayan business—in Kuala Lumpur the first morning which I spent there and seeing his syces leading some race-horses round his paddocks, their chestnut flanks gleaming in the early sunshine, and, nearer to me, one of his gardeners cutting away the orchids from his window with a billhook.

In this country Nature is in a lavish and luxuriant mood. Her symphony is in the exuberant manner of Wagner or Brahms at their most rhetorical. The hibiscus, the flame of the forest, the orchids, the bougainvillea, the dense jungle and forest, an iridescent curtain of butterflies hanging across the roads to a height of twenty feet, the sunshine, the smiling inhabitants, made up the picture which the word Malaya evoked in my mind.

Malaya is a small country about the size of England. It is divided by a dorsal ridge which runs from north to south and which rises in places to two thousand feet. Three-quarters of the country is covered with dense jungle into which little light penetrates. Because of this, the few aboriginals who survive are small and stunted, and the Malayan elephant is less than half the size of the African breed. Nearly all the communications run from north to south and few roads cross the spinal barrier from west to east.

There are numerous rivers; their waters are usually pale coffee in colour due to the erosion of the rich soil.

Broadly speaking, there are no seasons; the temperature does not rise at any time much above 90°. It rains a little almost every day, a lot once a week and still more during the monsoon. Humidity is high. At one moment the sky is overcast, at the next, when the sun shines through the showers, it is sparkling. The background of the mountains and the foreground of vivid colours of the nearer vegetation provide a contrast of unsurpassed beauty. The sunsets call for the brush of a master.

Considering that only a quarter of the country is clear of forest the population is dense; at this time there are more than five million inhabitants: two and a half million Malays, two million Chinese and half a million Indians, mostly Tamils.

The Malays are for the most part farmers, growing rice and vegetables and small quantities of pineapple; they produce copra, palm oil and oil seeds and provide some of the labour for the cultivation and tapping of rubber. They are rarely found in industry or commerce. The Chinese on the other hand are engaged in all the activities of the country, as agriculturists and common labourers, as merchants, bankers, contractors, traders and shopkeepers, and the richer Chinese classes are proprietors of tin mines and rubber estates. A fifth of the rubber in small holdings and just short of a fifth of the rubber in large plantations were Chinese owned. Two-fifths of the production of tin came from mines in Chinese ownership. The rich Chinese are sophisticated, shrewd, urbane and politically wide awake. Their hold upon the business life of the community is great and pervasive and becoming greater as time goes on. The Tamils had little cohesion and were politically neither mature nor vocal.

The religious differences between the races are as marked as the economic. The Malays are Mohammedans; they strictly observe Ramadan. There is no fasting at Chinese festivities and the Chinese New Year is celebrated with a continual rattle of fireworks. The Malays do not work on Fridays. The Chinese, with an eye to over-head expenses, work every day. Their favourite diet—pork—is prohibited to the Mohammedans. There was no intermarriage between Malays, Chinese and Tamils. All lived happily together.

Such was the Malaya I remembered. What a change had come over it. Now the country was held in fee by a few thousand terrorists, nourished and supplied partly by willing and fervent partisans, partly by unwilling and fearful neutrals.

Many of the British civil servants administering the country had been interned by the Japanese for four years: some, like Sir Shenton Thomas, the High Commissioner at the time of the Japanese occupation, had yielded nothing under stress, had maintained in servitude and suffering a disdainful pride, and had worked to sustain the weaker.

Some, not unnaturally, had bent and wilted under the dreadful scourge. All inevitably bore the marks, the trauma, of their sufferings.

Prisoners of war, even in tolerable conditions, can hardly escape an introspective and disenchanted outlook on life and their fellows. In captivity, the personality of the human being, if his spiritual or intellectual resources are meagre, can easily break into fragments.

All the inhabitants of Malaya in 1951 felt that perhaps it would prove true that "history repeats itself." This facile old saying only means that human beings faced by the same chain of causes are likely to react in the same way. Government and leaders, when they are good, see that bad causes do not recur.

In Malaya, the memory of the Japanese occupation was strong and recent. Was it not likely that the peninsula would again be invaded by foreigners, this time by the Chinese? It was not to be wondered at that many of the immigrant Chinese looked with surreptitious pride at the renaissance of their country on the mainland, and even if they had been Malayan for a generation or two, it was natural that they should look over their shoulders to Mother China.

I read and talked Malaya for two days. It was evident that we were on the way to losing control of the country, and soon. The repercussions of such a loss on South-east Asia, one of the most troubled and tender parts of the world, were incalculable. Moreover, rubber and tin were amongst the most important exports and dollar earners of the Commonwealth.

My predecessor at the Colonial Office, Mr. James Griffiths, in a short talk when he handed over to me, confessed that the previous Government were baffled by Malaya. Sadly he said, "At this stage it has become a military problem to which we have not been able to find the answer."

This grim and worsening condition of affairs spurred my instinct for action, an instinct developed and perhaps over-developed by my training as a soldier and a business man. It is dangerous, no doubt, to think of action as the sovereign solvent or catalyst of human discontents, but it is deeply ingrained in me that to do something, even if it is not the best, cures much; to put out your hands and grasp the danger is surely less deadly than wringing them.

I have the belief that men more often want to be led than persuaded; if you can do both you are a Churchill; if you can only do the first, you can do much. I saw quite clearly that I must go to Malaya at once. The Department applauded the idea; the Prime Minister, because of our precarious majority, agreed with a little reluctance; the King granted me leave. With greater difficulty I persuaded the Whips to let my parliamentary private secretary, Hugh Fraser,[1] come with me. He proved to be invaluable and gleaned information from a large number of private sources which otherwise would have been shut to me.

I thought of Rab Butler and the Treasury as we made our quick preparations for the journey, and thanked my stars that Malaya and not the balance of payments was my immediate task.

I took with me my private secretary and already trusted friend, Angus MacKintosh, and Paskin,[2] the experienced Under Secretary in charge of the Far East.

[1] The Rt. Hon. Hugh Fraser, M.P.
[2] Sir John Paskin.

On November 29th, we took off in a full plane from Heath Row and climbed to about nine thousand feet. The fuselage was stuffy and airless, and I began to feel the premonitory symptoms of breathlessness and heart flutter. I soon learned that the pressurisation had broken down as we took off; it was hoped to put it right at Rome. We took the southern route to avoid crossing the Alps. At Rome the repairs were unsuccessful; further attempts would be made at Beirut; these were no more successful. By this time the forty passengers who had paid for their tickets were resentful and mutinous and even I, whose ticket had been paid for by the taxpayer, was becoming a trifle outspoken. By Karachi we were more exhausted by lack of air than lack of sleep. I did go frequently to sleep, it is true, only to wake up with a start when the height affected my heart. Nothing could be done at Karachi and we flew down the west coast of India in a sad condition of crumpled exhaustion and pounding veins. At least we were to have a night off at Colombo and were to stay with Lord Soulbury, where I knew that our reception would be civilised.

I determined that we should not continue beyond Colombo until the pressurisation was restored, and said so in decisive terms, but that did not help our present plight. We flew on and never has Ceylon, the pearl of the East, gleamed in more entrancing shape than when we saw it coming up over the port wing, a shining island with a cap of clouds. Gasping for breath, crumpled, dishevelled, ties and collars loosened, sweating and dirty and ill-tempered, we welcomed our cracking ears and aching necks as we descended towards the air-strip.

At the base of the ramp stood the Governor's A.D.C., benignant and immaculate, his newly pressed tussore silk suit crowned by an orchid, his curling moustaches trimmed to perfection, his brown-and-white shoes a masterpiece. I wondered whether he was a little shocked to receive a party which looked more like a number of displaced persons from behind the Iron Curtain than the Secretary of State and staff. If he did, he blandly concealed it, but I fancy it was a conscious effort. In a state of almost complete deafness, I vaguely remember saying something a little staccato and unpolished to the vernacular press, who seized upon this unappetising statement with eagerness and by the morning had blown it up into some leading articles which gave me, if I remember right, a slightly reactionary complexion.

We enjoyed a truly agreeable dinner with Soulbury, and quoted some Horace over the port.

The next day, soon after dawn, came the cheerful news that the pressure was restored, and clean and pressed, we dozed our way happily to Singapore.

Yes, there was Malcolm MacDonald and a guard of honour, and a huge concourse. The concourse was not to greet me but to guard me, for there were more than 2,000 police round the aerodrome.

I stumbled at the foot of the ramp and nearly fell into Malcolm's arms. After reviewing the guard of honour I was introduced to some press men. "What have you come for?" they said. "To see for myself," I answered. "To restore law and order is the first thing. When I know more we will have a press conference and you shall have my views and ask questions." To me these appeared to be innocuous remarks, but they were ill received. Much of the journalism in Malaya is in the inferential or deductive manner, and there is in my experience no press which is more difficult to handle, more unpredictable in its comments, or more speculative in its guesses. Nor are these strictures only applicable to the vernacular press. I was to have an early taste of these defects.

Driving away with Malcolm from the aerodrome, heavily escorted by motor-bicyclists and armoured cars, and catching an occasional glimpse of military patrols watching the side roads, I said to him casually, "Was that all right, what I said to the press?" "Hum, yes," he answered, "but I do wish you hadn't said what you did about law and order; the effect will be bad; I confess I am nervous about that. You see, it is political advancement that will solve these problems, not bullets." "Of course, but it seems to me the merest platitude that you can't have political advancement until you have law and order. It is a mockery to give a man a vote when you can't protect his life. Personally, I should like to keep my head on my shoulders before I thought of the polling booth."

Malcolm was, of course, right in his forecast; the general tone of the press was: "Secretary of State denies constitutional changes," "Continuance of police state forecast," and much in the same vein. A few letters arrived saying, "At last first things first," "A healthy tonic," and so forth.

I had to remain indifferent to the tone of the Malayan papers, but I decided to treat them with the utmost caution and circumspection.

We arrived at Bukit Serene, a palace of the Sultan of Johore, rented to Malcolm MacDonald. It looks like a palace in a Walt Disney film. It has copper-covered minarets and commands a view of the Straits of Johore, which are studded with thickly wooded islands set in waters gleaming like silver.

We were greeted by Mrs. MacDonald, a beautiful and gracious Canadian lady, and the comfort of the East began to lap us round. Dirty and crumpled clothes were whisked away by smiling Chinese servants. "All shirts washed tomorrow, master." A tailor was summoned to make a tropical suit or two and a sharkskin dinner jacket. I used to get these for £2 10s. apiece, and was a little shocked to find that £12 or £15 was now the minimum. The garments, however, arrived in twenty-four hours and were well made and fitted.

The governors of all the South-east Asian territories and colonies, the O.A.G., that is the Acting High Commissioner of the Federation, del Tufo, the governors of North Borneo, Sarawak and Singapore, were in Singapore for the annual conference of United Kingdom representatives in the Far East, presided over by Malcolm. It was a useful chance for me to take part in their discussions and to make acquaintance with the governors.

I sat in at these discussions, but at the end of the day I had a sense of frustration. The discussions covered a broad range of subjects—part of them was concerned with the co-ordination of defence between Singapore, the Borneo territories and the Federation, part of them covered political measures to overcome "the Emergency"—but there was not enough said about action, and nothing clearly proposed to put right the administrative tangle.

The next day I was taken on a tour of inspection. It was a brilliant morning, and the sense of peace was profound. An armoured car rumbled up to the door. I was to ride inside and was to put my head down in the defiles, or where the rubber plantations came down to the edge of the road.

I did not like the orders which had been given for my safety, and which were over-cautious, but on the whole did what was wanted of me. To be in command when the Secretary of State was shot would be a black mark against an officer, and it would not be fair to him to neglect the precautions which he had been told to enforce.

These were, however, carried to some absurd lengths. I am all in favour of preventing people shooting at me from ten or twenty yards, but given that I am moving at a good pace, I am prepared to run some odds of being shot at from 200 yards' range. This is not bravery; I have not been a musketry officer for nothing.

The next morning I began an intensive study of the whole situation, political, military and para-military, police, administrative, legal. I clearly had to receive deputations from the Malays, the Chinese, the King's Chinese, the Tamils and the British and Europeans. I should not at this stage be able to give them many answers, or much encouragement.

The situation was far worse than I had imagined; it was appalling. From a long life spent in administration, I could draw no parallel. I have had experience of the Brigade of Guards, the most highly perfected and disciplined human organisation of which I can think, great joint stock companies and Government Departments, all faced at times with dangers and difficulties in their various spheres, but I had never seen such a tangle as that presented by the Government of Malaya. The last High Commissioner[3] had been murdered five months before my arrival. No successor had been appointed. There was divided and often opposed control at the top. Civil affairs rested in the hands of the O.A.G., military and para-military in those of Lieutenant-General Sir Harold Briggs. The two authorities were apparently co-equal, neither could overrule the other outside his own sphere. But what was each sphere? The frontiers between their responsibilities had not been clearly defined, indeed they were indefinable, because no line could be drawn to show where politics, civil administration, police action, administration of justice and the like end, and where para-military or military operations begin. The civil administration moved at a leisurely, peace-time pace. A rough estimate put the police force at 60,000, and that in a country the size of England with 5,000,000 inhabitants, but no one could tell me how they were disposed. The reason for this extraordinary fact was that the police force had been partially decentralised. There was no central roll and each state had posted and used its officers according to its own ideas.

The police itself was divided by a great schism between the Commissioner of Police and the Head of the Special Branch. Intelligence was scanty and unco-ordinated between the military and the civil authorities. Our weapons were not fitted to the task; there was a serious shortage of armoured or protected cars. Morale amongst planters, tin miners, and amongst Chinese loyalists and Malays was at its lowest. The grip of the terrorists was tightening, and the feelings of the loyalists could be summed up in one word: despair.

The constitutional tangle was no less than the administrative. It had been further bedevilled in April 1951 by the establishment of

[3] Sir Henry Gurney, murdered October 6th, 1951.

the Member System. Under it, the responsibilities for the different departments of Government were divided amongst nine members, of whom six were unofficial, that is to say not of the British Malayan Civil Service. In addition to the two Settlements (Colonies) of Penang and Malacca, there were nine Malay States ruled but not governed by a Malay Ruler. The Chief Minister of each State, the Mentri Besar, was a Malay nominated by the Ruler. The position of the British in Malaya rested upon treaties with the Rulers, and British advisers were attached to their courts. Our influence had to be exercised by persuasion rather than by direction. In short, a political and constitutional pattern had been formed which was ill adapted at any time to the needs of a small country with a delicate racial balance and least of all at a time of emergency and turmoil.

Collaboration between the Chinese in Malaya and the Communists was widespread. Protection money was known to be paid, and some unmistakable signs could be seen. For example, no oil tankers or filling stations were attacked, not because the oil companies paid protection money, but because the drivers and agents were well paid and protected themselves.

I was forcibly urged by the European community to take some drastic measures.

First, I was exhorted to bring down all the severity of the law upon those who could be found to be paying protection money; secondly, I was urged to dispense with the normal courts and speed up the administration of justice. Drumhead courts were to be substituted. I refused both requests point blank. On the first, I said that until the Government could deliver its part of the bargain, which was to protect the citizen on his lawful occasions, it was mere cynicism to prosecute those who were protecting themselves in the only way open to them. "At the point of the gun you would pay rather than be murdered," I said, "and so would I, and you know it." Once we could provide reasonable protection, the collaborators would be treated as traitors, but not before.

I poured scorn upon the second proposal, against which my deepest beliefs were engaged. "We stand for law and order," I said. "It is perhaps the greatest gift and heritage which we can bestow on these peoples, and if we suspend the law because we are too incompetent to secure order, that is the end of us, of our mission and our ideal. Never, while I have anything to do with this territory, will I agree to suspend the processes of law. Speed them up I will, if I can, but their principles must remain intact."

I heard no more of either proposition, and I believe that our fellow-countrymen, when faced with these issues, will in the long run always take the right view. I was to find my belief confirmed in other parts of the colonial territories.

That was the picture. I could only find one bright spot. The imaginative—and I believe correct—scheme of Briggs and the late High Commissioner, Sir Henry Gurney, of picking up the squatters, the isolated farmers and peasants on small and lonely plots of land, and resettling them in new villages and towns, protected by barbed wire, had been brilliantly executed. It had involved moving 400,000 people. One day our task in protecting them would be eased by the Briggs plan.

At the time of which I am writing, however, most of the new villages or towns had already been penetrated by the Communists. Sometimes raiders carried off supplies at night; at others they terrorised the inhabitants at the point of the Tommy-gun and made them pass food or money through the wire to sustain the gangs in the jungle.

My first days in Kuala Lumpur at King's House were spent in receiving deputations from various parts of the community. The most important Malayan political party was U.M.N.O. (United Malays National Organisation). Its President until lately had been Dato Onn, but he had split it and formed the Independence of Malaya Party (I.M.P.). The splinter enjoyed little support.

The corresponding Chinese body was M.C.A. (Malayan Chinese Association.) Its President, Dato Tan Cheng Lock[4], was a man of good intentions which he was wont to clothe in profuse and nebulous words.

The Indians had no comparable organisation. Finally, there were European bodies representing the rubber planters and tin miners. I listened for some hours—and I hope with patience and attention—to all that these deputations had to say. It was a somewhat dehydrating experience. To all of them I said, "I cannot promise you speedy success; I can and do promise you speedy action."

I saw the Chief Commissioner of Police and the Head of the Special Branch. I talked to the Commander-in-Chief at great length. He had a clear grasp of the situation and was incisive and helpful. The outlines of the picture began to be discernible.

I started to move about the country. One of my first visits was to Pahang, a highly disaffected area. I arranged to spend a day talking to the planters and the miners, one of whom was working a gold mine. I flew in an Auster and although in those little two-

---

[4] Afterwards Sir Cheng Lock Tan.

seater machines it is desirable to dodge round any storms that come up, the journey took less than an hour and a half.

On arrival I was told that I was the first person from Kuala Lumpur whom they had seen since the emergency began. The representatives had the usual complaints, most of them well justified, but their isolation from the seat of government, only an hour or so away by air, was the lesson which rankled with me.

I visited one or two rubber plantations. A Chinese was arrested somewhere near my car; he had a Mills bomb on him, but I was too well guarded to have been in much danger.

My headquarters for a few more days were at Kuala Lumpur, then I flew to Perak, Penang, Kelantan and Johore.

My visit to Penang began inauspiciously. We flew there in an R.A.F. Valetta; it was a beautiful, cloudless day; not a breath of wind stirred the glass-like sea as we approached the island. The reflection of the fishing boats in the water was as sharp as the silhouettes of the boats themselves. Hugh Fraser and I were sitting in the rear cabin; the air was inert. As we started to lose height, he said, "This bloody machine is going to crash." I angrily replied, "Don't be so silly." At that very moment we came in to land and the pilot, intending to use every inch of the runway, made a minute error of judgement and hit the drainage ditch with the wheels about a yard from the tarmac. The undercarriage was badly damaged, and we careered off down the runway, out of control, at 150 miles an hour, took to the paddy fields, crashed and caught fire. The sprinklers put the fire out quickly as we scrambled through the doors. The propellers were grotesquely bent and the machine was written off.

The first thing we saw was, of course, a stream of press cars hustling one another down the runway. At least the press had a story for that day.

The first report I read later began: "The Secretary of State appeared unmoved by his experience and said, 'I thought we were going to get fried.' " The second said: "The Secretary of State was clearly much shaken by the crash."

I saw one or two deputations. The first was from the King's Chinese, that is members of a community which had been so long settled in Malaya that they regarded themselves solely as subjects of the British Crown. Few of them could even speak Chinese. They naturally wished to be safeguarded in any new constitution from being swamped by either Malays or Chinese.

When they left, I had a chance once again of driving about

Penang and confirming my memory that it is one of the most beautiful spots on earth.

At sea level the gardens are coruscating. All the tropical trees and flowers gleam with colour in the sunshine and are splashed on the canvas with a lavish hand. The top of the mountain, which rises steeply from the harbour, houses a few Scotsmen, and only Scotsmen, for at that height there are often mists and rain, and often the need of a fire.

I felt shamefaced during my short visit to Kelantan. In the whole State there was a mere handful of terrorists but I was canned, like a sardine, in an armoured car. The town had turned out to have a look at the Secretary of State, perhaps even to greet him. The crowd were dressed in every colour of the rainbow and brought a brilliant pattern of pointillist detail to the landscape. They were all smiling and waving, and for once I disobeyed the soldiers and sat on top of my armoured car and waved back.

During this far-reaching tour I inspected one or two of the Briggs villages, and was able to confirm that the task of moving the squatters and forming the new village communities had been well done.

The state of the Malayan Civil Service gave me acute anxiety. The housing shortage was disastrous. An officer and his wife and two children recently returned from leave had been posted to a new district. The only accommodation they could find was two rooms over a Chinese brothel. Fortunately, the British Adviser was able to crowd them into his own house. The pay code was antiquated and had been enforced by Establishment officers with little regard to the needs of the Service in the emergency. It was not to be wondered at that recruiting was sluggish and that there were 500 unfilled vacancies.

I also studied the subject of education. In this rich country there was no compulsory primary education. I considered that to regard the effect of primary education paid for by the State only as a long-term weapon in the war of ideas was a mistake. Children coming back from school would sometimes convert their parents to our way of thinking and provide some answer to the propaganda being whispered to them from the jungle. It was clear that we had to win the war of ideas if we were ever to look forward to a peaceful country which could be entrusted with self-government within the Commonwealth.

I visited one or two of the new schools. In one, some small boys were learning English. "What's that?" I asked a smiling Chinese child of about four or five, pointing to a picture in his primer. "Peeeg," he replied, and squealed his delight at his first step towards eleven-plus. I studied the primers: they can be useful or dangerous political instruments.

I also insisted on going into one of the "worst" villages, said to be full of terrorists. I was preceded by two or three soldiers or policemen with Tommy-guns, and followed by an escort and the press. These villages were supposed to be the real danger spots. A rather timid press man asked me in tremulous tones what I should do if the villagers opened fire. I answered unwarily, "Oh, don't you know? I should go round and offer them all votes." It took my press officer an hour or two of hard work to get this unguarded remark—and it was the only unguarded thing within sight—suppressed. For all that, it was not an inappropriate, though it was an unwise, comment.

I talked to many officers of the Army and the R.A.F. The war, or near-war, that was being waged in Malaya differed from that to which I had been accustomed because it was difficult to find the enemy, a disability from which I had not suffered when I was a soldier. A few thousand terrorists held the country in fee. The terrain was ideally suited to guerrilla warfare. Jungle and forest cover three-quarters of the area of the country and the Malayan jungle must be one of the densest in the world. I imagine it to be a rival of the Matto Grosso. A man can only hack his way through it at a few miles in a day, and he has to wade through swamps, in the hot and humid semi-darkness, up to his armpits. The field of vision is only a few yards. Ambush was the usual tactical method of the enemy, and it is trying to troops to be always on the alert, their rifles at full-cock, ready to reply instantaneously to a burst of fire.

I saw some of the patrols before they went out; they were heavily, perhaps too heavily, equipped, and one or two of the men had sweated through their shirts before they had even started. The National Servicemen were impressive. They would have given the lie to those who think that the youth of today is unadventurous and tied to the cinema and the dance hall.

I devoted much time to the subject of law and the police. The position was intolerable. The Government had wide emergency powers of mass arrest and detention without trial. It was estimated that perhaps 200,000 persons had been detained for less than twenty-eight days; it was known that 25,000 had been detained for twenty-eight days or more: of those, less than 800 had been prosecuted. Even after deducting the numbers of those who had been released or deported to China, there were at this time still 6,000 persons detained without trial. I judged that a properly trained police force would be able to make a great, even a startling, reduction in these numbers.

At this moment, however, the organisation of the police was in utter disorder. Drastic reorganisation of the force was urgent. Owing to decentralisation into the nine States and two Settlements, after ten days of study no reliable estimate could be given to me of either the numbers or the deployment of the very large force of police.

At this time, in a country the size of Wales, the figures were thought to be 560 Gazetted Officers, 614 Asian Inspectors, 743 European Police Lieutenants, 19,704 Regular Police and 38,466 Special Constables. The ratio of officers to men in the regular force was one to thirty; that in the force of Special Constables approximately one to five hundred and eighty.

Finally, one of the most disturbing features of the emergency was that both the Regular and Special Police Force were overwhelmingly of Malay nationality whilst both the bandits and those whom they were terrorising were overwhelmingly Chinese. Out of the supposed total of 38,466 Special Constables, only 1,860 were Chinese. Since the emergency, 2,578 bandits had been killed; of those 2,409 were Chinese.

I proposed to make a step towards adjusting these proportions by the organisation of a Home Guard.

At the end of my tour I had made up my mind on the main things to be done, and how to do them. I determined that there must be one man in charge of both military and civil affairs, and that he would have to be a general. I judged that he must be supported by a Civilian Deputy High Commissioner to take some of the political and administrative work off his shoulders.

My host at King's House, del Tufo, had been Chief Secretary under Gurney, the previous High Commissioner, was an expert on the country, and spoke first-rate Malay. He had been Acting High Commissioner for five months and had hesitated, not unnaturally, to commit the Government to irreversible lines of action when he expected a new High Commissioner to be appointed any day. Moreover, he had not had any clear direction from home, partly because unsure hands were at the helm, and partly, no doubt, because the general election had intervened.

Despite all the admitted handicaps under which del Tufo had laboured, and the very cogent excuses which could be advanced in his defence, I concluded that he would not exactly fill the position, and that someone else would have to be brought in as the Deputy. It is not a very agreeable task to sit at a man's table and, over his port, tell him that he is to be passed over.

The creation of the post of Deputy High Commissioner, and the proposed appointment to it of a British overseas civil servant, caused an acute difficulty with their Highnesses the Rulers, and with the protagonist of the Malays, Dato Onn. First the consent of their Highnesses was necessary to change the existing constitution, which did not provide for a Deputy; and secondly, the post once created, they all thought that the holder should be a Malay. I knew, however, that only the highest administrative knowledge and experience would serve my purpose. I did not think that a Malay of the necessary calibre was available.

In all ordinary situations del Tufo would have been the man, but these were strange and extraordinary times. He was in the unlucky position of being so to speak a major-general when promotion to an army command not to a corps was all that was offering.

It fell to del Tufo to help me negotiate with their Highnesses for the creation of that very post for which he had been passed over. He helped me to the utmost of his skill and experience, and gained my respect and admiration of his selfless devotion. Their Highnesses, who treated me with the greatest courtesy and politeness, eventually agreed and soon afterwards I appointed MacGillivray,[5] the Colonial Secretary in Jamaica, and the best man of his rank in the Service, to be the Deputy High Commissioner. As I had feared, del Tufo elected to retire. Much to my satisfaction, he was knighted by His Majesty, on my recommendation, as a recognition for his loyal and distinguished service.

Some particularly distasteful action had to be taken. I secured the resignation of the Commissioner of Police, a gallant officer but not a professional policeman, and also of the Head of the Special Branch.

There was much study of details still unfinished. I put various teams to work upon these, and their reports, when endorsed by me, were to be added to my main Cabinet paper as appendices. One of these, on the subject of intelligence, was the work of Hugh Fraser, my parliamentary private secretary, and it showed what a grasp he had of the subject. It proved a useful foundation upon which the High Commissioner afterwards planned these services.

Whilst this work was going forward, I had time to fly to Hong

[5] Now Sir Donald MacGillivray.

Kong, which had not been visited by a Secretary of State for more than fifty years. I also determined that I would not fly straight home, but would return to Kuala Lumpur and stay incognito at the Chief Secretary's house, which was partially empty, in order to write my report for the Cabinet. I should be left in peace, and at the same time have access on the spot to many facts and figures which I wanted to check.

Approaching Hong Kong, everyone experienced in flying used to get a slight tremor when the four-engined machine scraped through the small rocky defile into Kowloon aerodrome, and as often as not had to land down-wind. I was no exception, but once on the ground I could appreciate the beauties of the harbour, which surpass, in my opinion, those of either San Francisco or Sydney, its only two rivals.

I was met by Sir Alexander Grantham, one of the ablest and most successful of all the colonial governors, and we were soon in the Government House launch, speeding across the harbour. The weather was clear and sparkling, and was like a draught of champagne after Malaya.

Lady Grantham, a charming American, had lavished her exquisite taste upon Government House. Everything was perfectly mounted; the scarlet liveries of the Chinese servants, curtains, carpets, furniture, flowers and food all showed what discernment and discrimination can do.

The population of Hong Kong had been just under a million before the war, and considering the physical size of the colony— no more than a few hills rising from the harbour—it must have seemed overcrowded even in those days. After Hong Kong had been liberated, the population rose rapidly and by 1951 had reached the figure of over two million by the influx of refugees from Communist China. Today it is about three million, and one of Hong Kong's cleverest and most successful citizens, Mr. Kadoorie, believes that it will reach seven million in a little more than another decade.

Apart from the enchanting prospect, my most striking impression was of the truly amazing powers of resilience and improvisation that are inherent in the Chinese race. Even the water supplies were inadequate to meet the needs of the people, but somehow or other, with scoops or mackintosh sheets or bamboos, the inhabitants wrung enough water from the hillsides in Hong Kong and Kowloon to support life.

Improvised industries were growing everywhere; some sophisticated products—torches, soap, thermos flasks, textiles—were made in backyards or primitive go-downs. The less desirable counterpart—a large shanty town still rapidly growing—also struck the visitor with great force.

The colony, in my belief, re-established itself and began to prosper on the foundation of two things: first, market and currency freedom, and secondly because it opened a window for Communist China on to the Western world. The Hong Kong dollar rapidly became the free currency of the Far East, and still remains so; it was acceptable as tender to every nation whose ships plied to the harbour, and not least to Communist China. Those who are wedded to pegged exchanges, who cling to inconvertible currencies and who regard a "floating" pound as anathema, would get a salutary lesson by visiting Hong Kong.

I was asked to open the Chinese Manufacturers' Exhibition in Kowloon, and make a speech. When I had finished, I went round the exhibits. The first stall which I saw was clearly in charge of the proprietor, a fat, Chinese merchant. He was affable and smiling. Somehow, his expression conveyed, "Well, if this is what they want, I am here to give it them," and his large stall exhibited a wide range of Christian religious pictures in the vilest taste, and of humiliating crudity. Virgin Marys and St. Josephs and crucifixes aganst crimson-lake sunsets, zinc-white lambs and Cambridge-blue saints outraged the eye. I asked him where he sold them. "All over South America," he said. Considering that the Chinese themselves can hardly sell ginger without putting it into a jar of impeccable line and taste, this traffic seemed to me to have some lessons for British traders and manufacturers, even if they had no wish to compete in these devotional exports.

I spent an afternoon in Kowloon and saw the Communist army at close quarters. In one village only a line of stone posts along the side of the street separated the two ideologies. I was begged not to step even a yard into this forbidden world. We motored along the frontier wire and saw some of their cantonments; we inspected the railhead, from which refugees still poured into the colony. The Chinese Communist soldiers, in greenish uniforms and with a red star in their caps, did not seem ill clothed or ill equipped with personal weapons. They looked impassively and incuriously at the strangers.

I talked officially to the Executive Council of the Colony. Some sensible and gradual developments of the constitution were being discussed, and I found little difficulty in giving the affirmative impression that I felt without committing myself too far upon the details.

The Executive Council of twelve, which was partly Chinese and partly European, invited me and Hugh Fraser to a Chinese dinner party. They had the mah-jongg room of a restaurant cleared of players, and there mounted the dinner, which was to be of more than twenty courses.

All my hosts were in dinner jackets except one, who wore traditional dress, a blue cotton robe, cotton socks, felt slippers and a biretta-like cap. He was a small man, much darker in complexion than Chinese usually are, almost mahogany coloured, wrinkled and inscrutable. I hoped, it must be confessed, that I should not be next to him at dinner for the next four hours but on looking at the list I saw that in fact he was to be my neighbour.

Chinese hostesses stood behind our chairs. Their long and artistic fingers picked out the tit-bits and manipulated the chopsticks with a strict attention to the priorities of their temporary masters. After each course they smilingly wiped our faces with warm, scented towels.

Dinner began. Birds' nest soup. I turned to my inscrutable Chinese neighbour and asked in ordinary tones whether they worked him hard on the Executive Council. Not a flicker of expression crossed his face. This is bad, thought I, worse than I feared, so—a little louder—"Do you like parties?" He started, and then, in perfect public-school English exclaimed, "My dear fellow, I do apologise, I didn't realise you were speaking to me. Parties! Why, I adore parties. I go to one almost every night and," in an undertone, "I sometimes go home a bit whistled. That reminds me, don't touch that gin, it's muck, stick to the Scotch. Here, take away this stuff and give the Secretary of State some of that Johnny Walker." "Your English is perfect," said I. "When were you last in England?" A dreamy look came into his eyes. "Well, it's longer than I like to think of, let me see, let me see, I haven't been there for over eight months. I try to go every year, to keep in touch with my old College at Oxford."

A more charming and entertaining companion for a twenty-five-course dinner would be hard to find. The food was delicious and the evening passed in a flash.

I stayed only a few days in Hong Kong, and then flew back to Singapore and Kuala Lumpur. Arrived at the Chief Secretary's house, I was surprised to find the hall filled with police officers. I learned that the butler at King's House, that is the High Commissioner's house, which was in the same compound, had been found to be a Communist agent. He had handed me my coffee every night after dinner. I had been lucky that he had belonged to the intelligence and not to the operational branch of Red China, for he could have shot me as easily as he gave me the sugar.

As a result of this somewhat overdue discovery, all the servants of both houses had been dismissed, and none would be re-engaged without rigorous screening. The police officers were not only there as guards; they were also to see that the bath water was hot and that some breakfast could be improvised the following morning.

It took me two or three days to write my report and collect the appendices. The moment it was finished we flew back in an Argonaut—slow and reliable but noisy—and reached London on December 21st. This was the first of many times when I landed at Heath Row, after no sleep, tired and deaf, to find the newsreel cameras, television interviewers, the press and the whole apparatus of publicity awaiting me. It is a difficult moment in which to collect yourself and find words to give any coherent account of your recent actions.

The next morning I received an invitation from the Prime Minister to go to Chartwell the following day for luncheon, to discuss Malaya. Shortly after I had accepted, he rang me up to say that he had forgotten that he had already asked Field Marshal Montgomery to luncheon on that day. Would I mind if he too heard my report? I replied that I was only too glad.

The press heard of the composition of this luncheon party, and understandably inferred that Montgomery was to be the new High Commissioner in Malaya, even that he wished keenly for the appointment himself. I did not think this could be true, especially as the political jungle and entanglements loomed even larger than the military. Even if politics had appealed to him, which I took leave to doubt, I hardly thought that the South-eastern brand would tickle his fancy.

At this luncheon I reviewed the Malayan scene as I saw it, and in the broadest terms exposed the course of action which I should recommend to the Cabinet. The key, I said, was that one man should be responsible for both the civil and military sides. Politics and para-military and military operations were inextricably mixed. Two authorities, one political and one military, with responsibilities ill-defined, and each with overriding powers, had been the main reason for the appalling state of the country. The control of the police alone had presented the authorities with an obdurate dilemma. Were they to be under military or civil direction?

I told the Prime Minister that my report was with the printers, and would emerge the following week, and our discussions did not descend far into details.

I summed up by saying that we could not win the war without the help of the population and of the Chinese population in particular; we would not get the support of the population without at least beginning to win the war. Once, so to speak, over the hump, the improvement would be at an increasing rate.

In the event my main paper to the Cabinet was supplemented by appendices on Federal and State Councils, Armoured Vehicles, Arms and Equipment for the Police (obtainable only from the U.S.A.), Earth Shifting Equipment, Chemical Defoliation of the Jungle,[6] Language Teaching, Intelligence Services, Subversive Activities, Deception Tactics, Terms of Employment of British Officers and Other Ranks Posted and Seconded for Service with the Malay Regiment, Detention and Repatriation, Manpower and National Service, Tax Evasion, Finance, Extension of Service beyond Retiring Age. The number and size of these Appendices demonstrated how inadequate were the instruments of our policy at that time.

The next day I got a letter from the Field Marshal—the only one from him which I have ever received—it read:

> Dear Lyttelton,
>   *Malaya*
>   We must have a plan.
>   Secondly, we must have a man.
>   When we have a plan and a man, we
>   shall succeed: not otherwise.
>   Yours sincerely,
>   (signed)
>   Montgomery (F. M.)

I may, perhaps without undue conceit, say that this had occurred to me.

The Field Marshal was, of course, right. I needed a man. My thoughts on the way home had turned to General Sir Brian Robertson,[7] at this time Commander-in-Chief Middle East Land Forces. He was a soldier with an intimate knowledge of politics and of

---

[6] On either side of main roads.
[7] Now Lord Robertson of Oakridge.

strange conjunctures in strange lands, in North Italy, Germany, Egypt. He was an administrator of a high order; his organisation of the services of supply under General Alexander had been a masterpiece. To all his tasks he had brought to bear an acute intelligence, a character of the highest integrity, and a calm resolution, qualities which on any score would have numbered him amongst the great soldier-administrators of our times.

The idea found favour with the Prime Minister. A telegram was despatched, asking Robertson to fly home for consultation. The Prime Minister said that he wished to see him alone for a quarter of an hour, at the end of which I was to join them.

When I entered the Cabinet Room I was dismayed to hear the Prime Minister say, "I have talked over our ideas about the High Commissionership in Malaya, and Sir Brian Robertson feels obliged to decline. He would dislike leaving the Canal Zone at the moment, and when he does he urges that he should not be asked to undertake another long period of foreign service. He has spent twenty-eight years of the last thirty-one abroad, and feels entitled to be excused and to enjoy, at long last, some settled family life."

These appeared to me to be compelling reasons, and clearly no one who did not wish to be entrusted with this most difficult assignment should be overpressed, and I did not attempt to do so. I was sad, however, because Sir Brian seemed the ideal choice.

I had to cable to Malcolm MacDonald that Robertson was not available, and that I was looking for another general with the right qualifications, but a few days must still pass before an appointment could be announced. He replied in terms that annoyed me. He could not be responsible, he said, for the safety of Malaya if there was further delay (this after five months without a High Commissioner), and above all if a general was appointed, with all the implications of military dictatorship which it implied. I sent him rather a tart reply that I and not he was responsible for the security of these territories, which fell to be administered by the Colonial Office. It should be explained that Malcolm was Commissioner-General for the United Kingdom in South-east Asia, and was at once the emanation of the Foreign Office and of the Colonial Office, with a rather vague role to oversee the whole area.

I was somewhat at a loss to find the right man. Bill Slim, one of the greatest of Englishmen, felt himself a little old to go flipping around in an Auster aircraft in the trying climate of Malaya. I consulted my friend Antony Head, the Secretary of State for War. Unlike most departmental Ministers, he determined to give me of his best. I saw one or two officers on the short list, and then Sir Gerald Templer.[8]

He had been Director of Military Intelligence, a Commander of distinction, and was now G.O.C.-in-C. Eastern Command. He had a store of nervous energy such as I have rarely seen. He did not particuarly relish the appointment, though it obviously would fill in the three or four years before he was to be considered for the post of C.I.G.S.

He has a high sense of duty and patriotism. I was sure that he was the man. The appointment, which is of course on the recommendation of the Secretary of State, has to be approved by the Prime Minister, usually a formality, before it is submitted to the King. Winston was in Ottawa, and would not consent to "my general" unless he had seen him himself. Time was pressing, so Templer had to fly out to Ottawa for dinner.

They spent an evening together. The General's sobriety was subjected to some strain; he did not get to bed until very late, but he had won the Prime Minister's confidence. I was permitted to recommend him to the King.

There was one other key post to be filled, that of Commissioner of Police. I persuaded the Corporation of the City of London—and have for ever remained grateful to them—to second Colonel Arthur Young, then the Commissioner of Police, City of London. He was above all a professional, and that was sorely needed. He did outstanding service. His aim was to make the people believe that the police were on their side, and were their friends, not their inquisitors. He called upon the police to give personal help to civilians in trouble or difficulty. He devised a badge for them to wear, in which the clasped hands of friendship symbolised their task. The scheme was known as Operation Service. The idea took hold, and proved a simple and effective measure towards his end. Before long he had a loyal, well-knit and efficient force under his command. Mass arrests were soon unnecessary.

General Sir Gerald Templer's name was submitted to the King, and he was duly appointed.[9] We had a plan and a man. I could only trace the hand of Providence which must have guided us in this appointment. No one could have faced this deadly and critical assignment with greater energy, wisdom or courage than he. In a few months I had almost dismissed Malaya from its place in my

---

[8] Now Field Marshal Sir Gerald Templer.
[9] February 7th, 1952.

mind amongst the danger spots. My role had become simple: it was to back him up and support him.

The Opposition lost no opportunity in making trouble. The questions and arguments seemed directed to show that our countrymen were always wrong, and nearly always wicked. The execution of a terrorist, found with the blood of a British soldier on his hands, raised a storm; any administrative steps that appeared rigorous or severe were attacked without regard to the terrible dangers from which we were trying to protect the country, or for that matter to the state in which the last Government had left the administration and the law.

I had determined not to be moved an inch by all this clatter. The morale of the Army, the Malayan civil service, the police and the inhabitants had to be underpinned by the feeling that support for them from home in the near-war was undeviating and unshakeable.

I began to be an unpopular Minister, and a popular target for attack.

Some incidents that were merely laughable relieved the tension. Irritated and angry beyond measure at some article, Templer called the editor of a vernacular news-sheet a rat. Gerald sent me a private telegram, hoping that he had not embarrassed me. Storm in the House of Commons. I telegraphed him not to worry in the least, and not to give it another thought, and to the Opposition I said that if they expected generals never to employ anything but parliamentary language, they would often be disappointed.

Herbert Morrison, in a kindly way, asked me why I did not make answers that would turn away wrath. I did not reveal that such answers, when telegraphed to a hard-pressed High Commissioner and to his Government, created wrath where it mattered, and that I must ride the storm at home. It would be better to lose my job than for us to lose a country.

Templer soon penetrated to the heart of the political tangle, and with the racial balance so delicately poised, nevertheless gained the confidence of all the races. He recast the military plan, and knit the police into it. He made some wide constitutional changes; he reorganised the intelligence; he travelled tirelessly and visited every part of the territory. In short, he dominated the scene.

He was nobly backed up by Lady Templer, who devoted her energies largely to women's welfare and to the hospitals. She found time, however, to fly in the little Auster aircraft and to visit almost every rubber plantation and tin dredge in the country. MacGillivray also did outstanding service. He relieved Templer of a mass of administrative detail and his advice on the broader issues was wise and informed.

The Templers established a *mystique*. Almost everyone of the five million people knew them by sight, everyone knew them by repute. When their term of office was finished, the farewell which they were accorded was an unbelievable and moving tribute to a great proconsul.

I was proud to have played some part in the restoration of the country. I had only laid out the plan and chosen the instruments; the work and the skill and the success were Templer's. The happiness, progress and prosperity of Malaya today are largely due to his inspiration. He deserves well of his countrymen, and of every citizen, British, Malay, Chinese and Tamil, who is living prosperously today within the British Commonwealth and enjoying, under the enlightened rule of a Malay, an independence which has been gladly given to them by Great Britain, after law and order had been restored by the strength of her arm.

CHAPTER XX

THE COLONIAL OFFICE:
CENTRAL AFRICAN FEDERATION

AFTER THE CABINET had approved my paper on Malaya and General Templer had been appointed as High Commissioner, the next task which confronted us at the Colonial Office was that of Central African Federation.

I shall try to give a true account of how the problem appeared to me at the time and what policy impelled my colleagues and myself to certain courses of action. I remember saying to Alan Lennox-Boyd,[1] then my Minister of State, "Central African Federation is a very difficult matter to get right and we shall have a lot of trouble with European as well as African opinion. It will take us eighteen months or so to negotiate it, and more to get the legislation on the statute book, but at least we ought not to get too much trouble in the House of Commons, because the Labour Party is already committed to federation. The present deadlock and the muted noises in Northern Rhodesia are only because they have fumbled it." We had, in fact, much more trouble in the House of Commons than over the negotiations. We had to face eleven debates, in which the Labour Party attacked the policy with great bitterness.

The opposition of the Labour Party and their *volte-face* was due ostensibly to the premise that federation was against the wishes of the Africans. If, in this context, the word Africans could be construed as a small number of political leaders, it would no doubt have some substance, but the word was soon used to embrace all the inhabitants of the three territories; in that sense it had little or no foundation. Most of the peoples concerned were illiterate; there

[1] Now Lord Boyd of Merton.

is no word for federation in any of the native languages, as far as I can ascertain.

On the other hand if an African leader wished, he could fan public opinion into flame by the simple expedient of saying that federation meant the never-ending domination of the white man. In fact it meant nothing of the kind. If it had meant this then I can at least give the Labour Party the credit of believing that they would never have advocated it. Their changed attitude was in my belief as much dictated by parliamentary expediency as by any belief that a majority of Africans were opposed to federation.

Federation concerned both the Colonial Office and the Commonwealth Relations Office. During the period between 1951 and the birth of the Federal State, the portfolio of Commonwealth Relations was held successively by three Ministers, Lord Ismay, Lord Salisbury and Lord Swinton. It fell out that I was the only Cabinet Minister who was engaged upon these affairs throughout the period. If there were changes in the holders of the office of Commonwealth Relations, there was no change in the policy, nor anything but full agreement between each of these Ministers in turn and myself.

I have said elsewhere that in the twentieth century, if peace and stability are to be gained, the consent of the governed must in some measure be engaged—a platitude if you will. But consent to what? The words must not be construed to mean that a tutelary Power, in this instance Great Britain, can divest itself of responsibility and merely try to find out what policy would cause the least trouble, or would be the most readily acceptable. Such a course is merely *"Nous sommes leurs chefs pourvu que nous les suivons."* If, therefore, we determined that to federate Northern and Southern Rhodesia and Nyasaland would advance their political stature and economic growth and promote the happiness and welfare of their inhabitants, it was our duty to propound the policy, and having negotiated a constitution with the necessary safeguards, and with the necessary checks and balances, to try to make it acceptable to the majority, even against the opposition and maybe the violence of a vocal minority. Nor can constitutions be regarded as static instruments of government; at their beginning they can do no more than lay the foundation on which to build, or provide a starting system from which progressive institutions can be evolved.

It is now necessary to look at both the economic and political advantages of federation.

The economic reasons for federation have never been seriously challenged, although some critics seek to divorce them altogether from politics. This is as absurd as to say that wars or convulsions have never sprung from economic causes. When it suited our opponents, they tried to insist that the origin of the Mau Mau rebellion was economic, and to ignore the lust for power and the black magic of African witchcraft which inspired it. In the debates on federation they used the opposite tactics and tried to relegate economic advantages to the shadows and to ignore the part which they play in the pursuit of happiness and freedom.

Economically, the three territories stood to benefit greatly from federation in their several ways. Southern Rhodesia derives its prosperity and wealth mainly from agriculture. The great coalfield at Wankie, south of Livingstone, adds a variety to the economy, gives it an export potential, and enables local industries to be established and nourished on cheap coal. Tobacco is the principal export, and Rhodesian supplies are now an essential in the world market.

The economy of Northern Rhodesia depends largely upon copper. I can remember vividly when the extent of the deposits was first discovered; it was no longer ago than 1925. One of the pioneers, Mr. Chester Beatty, from his office in London, formed the geological theory that two outcrops of copper, one of which was called Roan Antelope and which had long been known to prospectors, were the outcrops of the same syncline. He sent an eminent mining engineer, Mr. Selkirk, to Rhodesia to explore these possibilities. Selkirk found that the bush was discoloured between the two outcrops, which he ascribed to the leaching of copper by rain. He suggested that £30,000 spent on one or two diamond drill-holes would prove the existence of a mine. That mine today is Roan Antelope. The other great pioneer was the Rhokana Group.

Not only were the discovery and initial opening up of the mines due to Western enterprise, but the sinking of the shafts, the mining itself, the concentration of the ore and its smelting and refining called for all the specialised skills which were available in Great Britain and the United States. Generations must pass before the Africans can acquire the skill and experience to work these deposits and plants themselves.

Nyasaland is the weakest and least prosperous of the three. Its economy is agricultural, and depends mainly upon the cultivation of tea and tobacco; the latter is flue-cured and is consumed as pipe tobacco. Nyasaland, comparatively poor in natural resources, is the reservoir from which Northern and Southern Rhodesia draw a significant amount of their labour.

Of the three territories, Nyasaland stood to benefit the most from federation.

In general, it was also clear that the roads, railways, air links, the telegraph, telephone and wireless networks of the three territories should be developed on a unified system. Finally, and most important of all, the harnessing of the Zambesi and the production of electricity from water power cried aloud for a common plan.

The second and closely allied reasons were political. It is often advanced, and with some justice, that frontiers in Africa have been drawn to delimit the colonial boundaries of European powers, and not upon an ethnographical plan. The African inhabitants of the three territories which we sought to federate do not however differ so greatly as to make unity unattainable; Swahili and English, in a lesser degree, are helpful.

Just as coal and power require to be developed and interchanged by a central administration, so do the advancement and education of men and women and the use and conditions of labour.

Another political reason, now conveniently forgotten, has to be added. Afrikaaner elements had begun to penetrate deeply into Southern, and to a lesser extent into Northern Rhodesia. The Broederbond was the active instrument in this invasion. It was calculated that Afrikaaners would certainly hold political power in Southern Rhodesia within a decade and might, within that time, force a federation of Southern Rhodesia with the Union.

It is quite unnecessary to enter into any controversy, or here to condemn Afrikaaner policy towards the native races; it is enough to say that it ran counter to British conceptions of our responsibilities and our mission.

If our way of leading these nations to self-government and independence was to prevail, federation seemed to us to be essential. It had the effect of immediately diluting Afrikaaner influence.

It is ironical to reflect that many of the most bitter attacks that are levelled against federation today claim their justification on the ground that federation was intended to perpetuate the domination of the white man upon South African principles.

This facile argument lumps all "white" policy together, whereas the aim of federation was the evolution of self-government upon our model, and not upon that of others. Our colonial record in

Africa gives no ground for the assertion that we wished to keep the African races in political bondage.

Our policy was and is one of partnership. The skill and experience, both economic, social and political, of Great Britain must for many years be the foundation, if a free, law-abiding, well-administered and prosperous society is to be built.

On the other hand, all these will be useless unless the African is brought increasingly into the control of affairs. His labour and therefore his goodwill and his consent must be engaged. Only partnership will achieve the common aim.

Opposed to the idea of partnership are the "arithmetical" statesmen: one man, one vote. In a highly educated, literate and sophisticated society, this may well be an ideal, but in Central Africa it would be plainly a disaster if brought about too quickly.

In the Rhodesias and Nyasaland there were more than 8 million Africans and about 300,000 Europeans. Universal suffrage would have handed over to primitive and largely illiterate people the task not only of running but building a modern state. These people have as yet neither the cohesion, the knowledge nor the experience to govern.

It is difficult to see how anyone, however starry-eyed, imagines that the complete swamping of the European vote by 20 to 1 could do other than lead to political disaster, administrative chaos, and the strangling of all the skills and capital which are required to bring these countries to prosperity and sound government. Or are prosperity and sound government things about which we should not concern ourselves? Would it not be better to stand aside and say, "At least we have given them our method of Government: let them try to make their own way on their own resources"? That indeed would be a cynical way to a quiet life. Patience and time, time and patience must be our guides. The only really wicked doctrine to espouse in colonial affairs is that which seeks to impose a rigid timetable to the granting of wide franchises, self-government and independence. Yet this is just what the arithmeticians urge. Every time someone says "independence by next week," it becomes more difficult to persuade the local nationalists that anything slower is not reaction, or hostility, or selfishness. It has not yet occurred either to the orator of the tub in this country, or to some of the African leaders, that it is not reaction or hostility, but sense.

It may be expected, perhaps, that the events in the Congo will throw some of these lessons into relief. If educated Africans soberly study the recent history of the Congo, it will, little by little, be borne in upon them that when the British advocate gradual and progressive evolution to self-government, we are not selfish reactionaries, but realistic statesmen.

It has taken nearly nine hundred years to build a democratic system in our own blessed islands. It has been evolved in later centuries by a literate and sophisticated people. Nevertheless, its growth has been scarred by convulsions and wars, by struggles between the Crown and the aristocracy, between the Crown and the Church, between the Church and the laity, between the Crown and Parliament, and since the English Revolution, between the Executive and Parliament. It has witnessed the Wars of the Roses, the beheading of one king and the expulsion of another. Blood and tears have soaked the pages of its history.

At the end of these nine hundred years, there is much in our democracy which we should be chary of describing as perfection. Yet to listen to some of the more vociferous, Africa should be able to reach these goals by Tuesday week.

It also appears something of a mockery that elections upon any popular franchise can today only be held in these territories if pictures or symbols of the candidates and their policies—for example, the lion, the elephant or the giraffe—are displayed in front of the electorate, because nine out of ten of them cannot read or write.

It appears that the only way to build up democratic institutions is slowly, by evolution. In these countries there is hardly any political class amongst the Africans, the nucleus is often irresponsible and factious, and the political institutions are in their earliest formative stage. No political institutions can be permanently founded without a political class, no political class can be established without political institutions in which to practise the arts of democratic government. The two must patiently be evolved together.

One other aspect of the controversies that rage round the politics of the Rhodesias has an almost bizarre side to it.

I have discussed these subjects many times with undergraduates in our universities, and the most strident of the intelligentsia. I have been struck by the almost frivolous ignorance with which they plunge into the subject. For example, a brilliant and charming young man who had just gained a first in history spoke to me about the failure of British colonial policy as if its failure was an ac-

knowledged axiom. I did not think the remark particulary in-
gratiating, and asked him whether it was a failure in, for example,
Nigeria. He said, "Perhaps not," so I asked him how many people
lived in Nigeria, and he replied, "About six millions." There happen to be thirty-five millions, nearly half the population of British
Africa. He later confessed that he had not read the Constitution of
the Central African Federation, though he was sternly critical of it.

Now this young man would not have dreamed, in a history
paper, of putting down anything not supported either by his own
research or that of scholars. He would have hesitated to criticise,
let us say, many of the dealings of Charles II with the French
without at least a passing survey of the evidence from a book of
reference.

The judgement of Ministers and of the highly trained Colonial
Service, both at home and overseas, may have been wrong, but at
least the motives underlying the policy of federation were enlightened, liberal and unselfish.

The first difficulty was to assemble a constitutional conference
in order to frame the constitution and to see that on the one
hand it did not tend to perpetuate white domination nor on the
other to move too quickly to an African majority and thus dry up
the sources of capital and skill.

Opposition to the conference was fanned by the left-wing press,
as well as by Labour Party leaders; the first conference was consequently boycotted by the Africans. It has been claimed that we
should therefore have dropped the policy in which our opponents
had believed and in which we still believed. Such an abdication of
the responsibilities of government found no favour in the eyes of
the Prime Minister, my colleagues or myself, or, for that matter,
of the experienced and highly trained body of our advisers.

In January 1953, the conference therefore met in the Commonwealth Relations Office under the leadership of the two Secretaries
of State, Lord Swinton and myself. The head of the Southern
Rhodesian delegation was the Prime Minister, Sir Godfrey Hug-
gins,[2] that of Northern Rhodesia Sir Gilbert Rennie, and of Nyasaland Sir Geoffrey Colby, the last two being of the Colonial Service
and Governors of the respective territories.

Mr. Roy Welensky,[3] the leader of the unofficial members of the
legislature in Northern Rhodesia, also attended. I got to know him
and like him. His disarming description of himself as 50 per cent

[2] Now Viscount Malvern.
[3] Now Sir Roy Welensky.

Polish, 50 per cent Jewish and 100 per cent British gives an insight into his character and humour.

The task was long and arduous. Not only had we to strive for the right balance between state and federal powers, always a delicate subject, but in some degree we had to preserve the protectorate status of two of the three territories, conferred upon them by Queen Victoria at their request.

Secondly, we had to devise a system by which Africans were assured of a larger representation in the legislature than either a qualification defined by standards of education or property could have conferred. The flimsiest standards of either would have disfranchised 95 out of every 100 Africans. At the other extreme, universal suffrage with only an age qualification would have swamped the Europeans and led inevitably to consequences upon which I have already dwelt.

The dilemma had to be faced. Our solution, which still appears to me to be the only one, was to secure a predetermined representation for the Africans without engaging the whole machinery of a franchise, and to leave the majority in the hands of the Europeans for the time being. As long as there was to be a limited franchise and not a common roll for the electorate, we set up the African Affairs Board with an absolute veto—to be followed by reference to the Secretary of State—upon any legislation which was discriminating against any of the races within the Federation.

Upon this foundation we expected that a less artificial system could eventually be built. I thought that we should only be able to claim success when constituencies with an African majority elected a European, and when constituencies with a European majority elected an African. Such a consummation may perhaps be fifty years away.

There were to be thirty-five members of the Legislature, of whom twenty-six were to be Europeans, six specially elected African members and three Europeans charged with special responsibilities for African interests.

The Constitution was to be reviewed after seven years. During that time we hoped to see advances made towards the common roll.

It is now alleged, and I confess that I think with some justice, that the Europeans sat still during the seven years and made no progressive, or at least too hesitant, moves to engage Africans in a further share of the Government. If they had gone faster or further, they would today prove to have been wiser and safer.

Many of the troubles of my successors at the Colonial Office no doubt sprang from the rigidity of the white man's attitude. Because the white man may not have advanced quickly enough along the road set for him, that is no excuse for going to the other extreme and at this stage letting the power rest solely in African hands. Go slowly is not an heroic doctrine, but it is the only one in Central Africa. The exercise of patience, the rarest political virtue, may bring home the ideal of a multi-racial society, with all the countless benefits that it would confer upon all. The chance is still there, though it appears more slender today than it did ten years ago.

Finally, the present conflicts and controversies over the Federation should not lead anyone to despair of a multi-racial society being the eventual issue.

It is easy to take too short a view; it is equally clear that many convulsions are likely to shake this adolescent state. Sometimes the metal is refined in the furnace and a useful instrument of government is forged.

CHAPTER XXI

THE COLONIAL OFFICE: KENYA

U P TILL THE AUTUMN of 1952 our work at the Colonial Office had centred largely upon Malaya and Central African Federation. A new and unexpected convulsion now shook Kenya.

I must turn back the page. Shortly before he was to retire after a holiday, Sir Philip Mitchell, the Governor, came to take leave of me. He was an able man, with a long experience of colonial administration, and of Africa and Africans in particular. He recalled some of his earlier service, and ended by saying that he had the satisfaction of handing over to his successor a colony at the height of prosperity and lapped in peace.

This claim was shown, within a few weeks, to be without foundation. There is no doubt that, during the two years' extension of his governorship, Mitchell had got out of touch with his District Commissioners in the field and, like many men at the end of a long term of office, was anxious to discount any possibility of trouble. His complacence could be excused by the weakness of the intelligence service. Nor was Kenya the only territory where this was true of intelligence; it was weak in most colonial territories, and many security and remedial measures could have been taken earlier if the Colonial Office had been kept informed by the local governments.

At first, the extent of the infection by Mau Mau of the Kikuyu tribe was much underrated, and it was thought that the rising would easily be suppressed. I had been sure that Mitchell's successor must, in any event, be the best whom we could find; no colony was more important at that time. We all in the Colonial

Office thought that Sir Evelyn Baring was the man, and I was overjoyed when he accepted the appointment. It was formally announced in April. However, he had nearly chopped off his hand with an axe, while felling a tree at Howick, and wanted three or four months to recover. To this I agreed. In consequence, when the Mau Mau rebellion assumed a much more serious aspect, there was no permanent Governor in Nairobi, and I was bitterly criticised for the interregnum, although in the past there had been nearly always a gap between the retirement of one and the appointment of another Governor. The Opposition exploited this opportunity, the press inflamed opinion by calling it a scandal, and even the Prime Minister was uneasy.

This is the sort of conjuncture when to be a critic and not a Minister is the happier role. It would have been a hard decision to ask Sir Evelyn, whose general health was never very robust, to go out before he had completely recovered and obviously impolitic in the highest degree to appoint someone inferior because the better man was not immediately available. Looking back, I regret that I did not ask him to curtail his leave by a month or two, but I cannot believe that the situation slipped further than it would otherwise have done because of these niceties of time.

The Kikuyu number about a million; they are not a warlike people, and were accustomed to live on their wits. In a moment of irritation I once said that they were like the Irish in politics without their humour, and like the Jews in business without Leviticus, but the description is at once unfair and exaggerated. For generations they had inhabited the fringes of the bamboo forests, which were their refuge in trouble, and for generations the warlike Masai had been wont, from time to time, to raid and burn their villages, and carry off their women. These excursions were no longer permitted under the ruthless British administration. The Kikuyu, a trading and intelligent but somewhat uncongenial people, came under the influence of Kenyatta, a daemonic figure with extreme left-wing views. The driving force of the Mau Mau movement was, nakedly, power, and the expulsion of the white man; its methods of gaining adherents were the methods of African witchcraft. The Mau Mau oath is the most bestial, filthy and nauseating incantation which perverted minds can ever have brewed. I am not unduly squeamish, but when I first read it I was so revolted that it got between me and my appetite. It shocked even lawyers who had prosecuted or defended in cases of ritual murder in Africa. Its political object was simply to outlaw and ostracise from the tribe and tribal customs anyone who had taken it.

I can recall no instance when I have felt the forces of evil to be so near and so strong. As I wrote memoranda or instructions, I would suddenly see a shadow fall across the page—the horned shadow of the Devil himself.

Nevertheless, all through the anxiety and atrocities of the rebellion, the Opposition sought to establish that its causes were essentially economic. This was a convenient but false argument. Just as the massacre of St. Bartholomew's Eve or the cruelties of the Inquisition cannot be ascribed to economic causes, so it can be said that they were not the primary or motive force of the Mau Mau rebellion.

The Opposition also attacked their fellow-countrymen, the "Settlers," for their tenure of the White Highlands, which, so they seemed to imply, had been torn from the indigenous Africans and turned to the profit of the Herrenvolk, the British. Few of them cared to remember, or care even today to remember, that modern Kenya has been made by the British.

In her painstaking life of Lugard, Miss Margery Perham, writing of the year 1890, says:

> And the first step was to find the last point of entry into that great block of country . . . which was then regarded almost with exasperation as an immense obstacle between Mombasa and Lake Victoria and which the Foreign Office referred to as "that sterile region." [1]

Part of that sterile region is now Kenya. Until modern times, the White Highlands were lean grazing lands for nomadic tribes, and not a tithe of their inherent wealth as farming land was discovered or exploited. I suppose that it could be argued that here, as elsewhere in Africa, it would have been best to have left the indigenous Africans to their own devices, in the insubstantial hope that some risorgimento would have enabled them to emerge from the primaeval darkness in which they had lived since the dawn of man and by themselves achieve a more prosperous and civilised future.

I doubt whether, at any time, this would have been an enlightened policy. Today we hear much of our duty to develop and expand the under-developed countries. If this is our duty, it would seem retrograde to withdraw from our responsibilities because nationalist pressure is mounting. Without the foundations of gov-

[1] *Lugard* (London: Collins, 1956), I, 175.

ernment which we have built into African territories, and without the concept of law and order which we have implanted, none of these worthy objects of helping these countries could be attempted, much less attained. Railways, for example, and tribal warfare go ill together. Foreign capital and foreign skill are difficult to graft on to a tribal and sometimes nomadic society which is still in the thrall of primitive superstitions and witchcraft. Agriculture will not thrive if the general system is to take a crop or two of maize from the land, then move on to another strip and leave the original land to lie fallow for seven years. Even today the high standard of African agriculture is attained on small holdings by methods different from those used by Europeans. African agriculture in Kenya owes its advance to the example and help of the European farmers.

Moreover, crops like coffee and pyrethrum, which add much to the wealth of Kenya, were unknown until the advent of the white man. In short, it is one of the ironical anomalies of colonial politics that those who are most vociferous about our duty to help underdeveloped countries are also the most critical of our very presence and of the foundations which the British have laid and without which the very word "development" is meaningless.

The restoration of law and order posed some of the same problems with which we were still grappling in Malaya. In Kenya, as in Malaya, the enemy, for that is what they were, were difficult to find. They swooped suddenly upon the isolated homesteads or tribal villages or police posts, and then vanished into the forests. Many, perhaps the majority, of their passive supporters had been intimidated by threats and murder into giving unwilling succour to the militant Mau Mau.

Concerted operations were rare, but on one occasion a gang pressed home repeated attacks upon a police post, in spite of heavy losses. This was unlike their usual mode of warfare, but was explained when it was found that their fanaticism had been hopped up by smoking hemp.

The white settlers, living generally in isolated farms, gave an example of steady nerves. They did not know whether to trust their Kikuyu boys or overseers. At night they barricaded their farms and kept loaded rifles at their side. They must have waited tensely for the sound of the door or the windows being tried, or for footfalls in the darkness. In the day-time they went about armed, and could never be certain that a gang would not spring upon them. It is true that sometimes the danger was over-dramatised, and I remember a middle-aged lady talking to me after dinner in Government House, and showing me her handbag. A Colt automatic nestled beside her lipstick and handkerchief. She assured me it was fully loaded, and I saw with some alarm that it was fully cocked.

Thirty European civilians were murdered between 1952 and 1954 and two between 1955 and 1959. In this period more than eighteen hundred African civilians were murdered. The facts are grim and they show that the overwhelming weight of the Mau Mau attack fell upon their fellow Africans.

The first measures to be taken were clearly to reinforce and strengthen the police and military, in order to restore order. We at once landed a battalion of Lancashire Fusiliers in Kenya; they were followed (in March 1953) by the Headquarters 39th Infantry Brigade, the 1st Battalion the Buffs, the 1st Battalion the Devonshire Regiment and a flight of Harvard aircraft.

From London the whole situation appeared confused, and worsening. I accordingly set out for Nairobi, at the end of October 1952, to judge for myself and consult Sir Evelyn Baring, upon the military, para-military and political measures which appeared to be called for.

The inescapable facts had also to be faced. There were almost six million Africans in Kenya; over a million of the Kikuyu or neighbouring tribes were either disaffected or living in terror of Mau Mau. There were something over 50,000 white men, and more than 150,000 Asians, the last divided between Indians and followers of the Aga Khan.

As in Malaya, it was first imperative to put down the rebellion, in order that the life of the colony could resume its normal tenor. At long term, however, neither the institutions, political, economic and educational, nor the lives, property nor land of the white man could be secure unless the confidence of the Africans was gained by giving them, gradually, a share in government. The only alternative was government by force.

This second alternative was impossible; on the lowest level of argument we did not have the force, on the highest level we did not believe in it as a method of government. Moreover, to govern by force would have been to do so in face of world opinion, and of prejudiced opinion in the United States in particular.

My first few days I spent in Nairobi, and I found life at Government House congenial under the calm and humorous rule of Molly Baring. She had made the gaunt, impersonal, uniform house liveable and had done up some of the rooms to her own standards of taste and comfort. I count myself lucky to have begun a friendship with both the Governor and his wife upon which I leant much in the discontents and dangers, which were to grow much worse before a glimpse of dawn could be discerned.

I never feel well on the African plateau for the first ten days, and there was much to be done. I travelled widely and talked to men and women representing all shades of opinion, African, European and Asian. I received a number of sectional deputations at Government House. To the "Settlers" I spoke with brutal candour. "Sixty thousand Europeans cannot expect to hold all the political power and to exclude Africans from the legislature and from the Government. The end of that will be to build up pressures which will burst into rebellion and bloodshed. You are suspicious and critical of what you term in a pejorative sense 'Colonial Office rule.' When, as the result of over-conservative or traditional policies you provoke an explosion, you are not slow to ask the British Government and the Colonial Office, which at other times you attack, for troops, aeroplanes and money to suppress a rebellion. I warn you that one day you will be let down, and therefore besides force, which must now be used and which we will furnish, you must turn your minds to political reform, and to measures which will gradually engage the consent and help of the governed. The security of your homes, the security of the money, hard work and skill which you have lavished upon your farms, and upon the industries which you have begun to build, cannot rest upon battalions of British troops; it can only rest upon the building of a multi-racial society. I may or may not have principles or ideals concerning democracy to reinforce these arguments but I am not going to deploy them. I am at this moment confining myself to hard facts and to your material interests."

The constitution of Kenya was no longer adapted to her needs. The Government had an "official majority," that is the majority of the portfolios were held by Colonial civil servants. The head of the Government was the Governor. Almost the only political career thus open to a settler was to be a member of the Opposition.

It was often hurled at the heads of the settlers that they were politically irresponsible; if it had been said that they had few political responsibilities except as critics of the Government, that would have been true, and less offensive.

At this time, one of the leading figures in politics was Michael Blundell,[2] a successful farmer and a man of liberal inclinations.

[2] Now Sir Michael Blundell.

He was in favour of a higher degree of African participation both in the legislature and in the Government, and was set upon trying to build up a multi-racial society. He was then the Leader of the European Members, and he still carries the banner unflinchingly, in face of much abuse and hostility from a large section of his fellow-countrymen.

It was often supposed that Mau Mau had been the creation of Soviet policy, planted and cultivated by the over-large Soviet Embassy at Addis Ababa. I do not think this can be established on the evidence available; it is, however, true that, once the rebellion had broken out, support and money reached the insurgents from Addis Ababa. It is also, I fear, true that large sums of money and other help came from the Congress Party in India, and that the activities of the Indian High Commission went far beyond the bounds of diplomatic propriety.

The Roman Catholic Church is powerful in Kenya. Their missions are close to the people, and combine in an admirable way the duties of practical training and spiritual guidance. I saw many of their settlements and was much impressed.

The Protestant churches, although they also did devoted work, were a little further removed from the daily life of the people, and seemed to be more intent upon their spiritual than upon their terrestrial tasks.

The Catholic Church ascribes most of the evils and distempers in the world to Communism, and so in Kenya they thought that the training which Kenyatta was supposed to have received from Moscow, and the help given to Mau Mau by the Soviet Embassy from Addis Ababa, once again confirmed the justice of their view.

I was talking one day to the Catholic Bishop, Bishop McCarthy,[3] a delightful character, and asked him why he thought everything bad in Kenya was inspired by Communism. There was no evidence whatever to support it. We had now collected much information and knowledge about its origin, why did Catholics persist in their views? He began to be driven into a corner. He extricated himself with honour by saying in his delightful accent, "Well, if you have a back like a duck" (pronounced "dock") "and you have web feet like a dock, and you quack like a dock—it's just as well to call it a dock." He would have been good at answering Parliamentary Questions.

Once again the need for summary justice was urged; it was said that too many safeguards watched over the accused; the or-

[3] He was appointed Archbishop of Nairobi in 1953.

dinary processes of law were too slow and too cumbersome. To those who advanced these views I asked one simple question: "Do you think that a man upon a capital charge should have the right to be represented by counsel?" There was generally a pause of nearly a minute, but at the end the answer was always the same, an unequivocal "Yes." Once this point is conceded, justice cannot be summary. We later were able to speed up the machinery of justice by cancelling or curtailing the proceedings of courts of the first instance.

At one moment a parliamentary storm appeared likely to break out in Westminster on this subject, until I pointed out that it is the normal practice in Scotland for Crown Counsel to bring prisoners charged with a serious offence straight to the High Court without any proceedings in a court of the first instance.

The President of the East African Court of Appeal, Sir Barclay Nihill, was a man of high calibre. He speeded up the administration of justice by some practical measures, without in any way eroding the indefeasible rights of the accused.

I am absolutely rigid about these principles, because the impartial administration of justice, which carries with it the corollary that the judiciary must be insulated and separated from the executive, is in my view the very pillar, the very ark of the covenant of democracy.

The Attorney General, John Whyatt,[4] also incurred great unpopularity because he too conceived that his duties did not end with bringing malefactors to justice, but extended to maintaining the principles of trial by jury and the principle that the accused was innocent until proved guilty.

Once again in a time of danger, when balance and wisdom are imperative, we were blessed with a Governor who was endowed especially with these qualities. He did not always act very quickly, and incurred the usual criticisms of the hotheads, but his slowness sprang from the mature nature of his mind: he wished to be sure before being forceful; the dangerous people are those who are forceful in order to be sure. His eyes, moreover, were always on the future, and he was never diverted from the great objectives by expediency in the face of some unexpected but transitory danger.

Once he had decided, he acted with a bland and unshakeable determination.

It was decided to prosecute Kenyatta. He was to be tried by Mr. Ransley Thacker, formerly a Judge of the Supreme Court,

---

[4] Now Sir John Whyatt.

who had once been the Assistant Secretary of the British Metal Corporation, and whom I knew. The trial was to be conducted at Kapenguria, as far away as possible from the intimidation of Mau Mau and other pressures. Mr. D. N. Pritt, Q.C., a former M.P. and on the extreme left wing of the Labour Party, defended Kenyatta. His methods were to provoke the Judge, and some undignified exchanges were the outcome.

Only the most prejudiced can now claim that the trial was other than fair and impartial. In April 1953 Kenyatta was sentenced to seven years' imprisonment, after which he was further to be detained under the Emergency Security Regulations. He has recently been freed.

I learnt all I could in a short time. My experience throughout my tenure of office was that you could learn all that was possible for a visitor in under a month; two or three months would have been useless; to know more was a matter of a year or two. I flew back to England; another visit would clearly be necessary.

At home, the weight of the Opposition's attacks upon the Colonial Office and myself was now largely transferred from Malayan to Kenyan affairs.

Far be it from me to complain of the workings of the House of Commons, but a certain eye to the public interest in convulsions like that which was shaking the colony is desirable in an Opposition. Loading the Order Paper with questions of every kind certainly puts a strain on the Minister, and no doubt in purely administrative matters does no more than cause him to overwork, but a certain restraint when he has to deal with the deadly problems such as those with which I was confronted, far from weakening an Opposition, in fact strengthens it and gives it the impression of a stern watchdog, rather than a factious and yelping pack of terriers.

It sometimes happens, though rarely, that the whole of Question Time in the House of Commons is taken up by questions to one Minister. Mr. Ernest Brown, when Minister of Health, answered a hundred questions at a sitting; this is likely to remain a record, because the modern mode is to ask more supplementary questions than was previously the custom, or perhaps more than were previously allowed by the Speaker.

On December 16th, 1953, I occupied the whole hour in answering eighty questions (including supplementaries). When I woke up the next day I felt as stiff as if I had made a hundred at cricket, or had been out riding after a long interval. Acute rheumatism at my age, I thought sleepily; this is bad. Then, a little more wakeful, I remembered the previous day. Eighty times in an hour I had had to rise from a sitting to a standing posture. Even if your answers do not please, you at least have the satisfaction that the muscles of your back and loins have been exercised and strengthened.

The office of the Secretary of State for the Colonies was, and will doubtless remain as long as the office persists, a very vulnerable one. He had in my time to be answerable for thirty-seven territories[5] and for the actions of the Governors and administration in them, over which he could not exercise a detailed or day-to-day control. Mistakes are made; within reason authority must be upheld; and the feeling must be engendered that defensible errors will at least be defended.

One or two isolated incidents of atrocities by the British occurred in Kenya; they were due either to the breakdown of the quality of mercy under strain, or to panic in men of low intellectual capacity or low personal courage. The full force of the law must bring such men by fair trial to punishment. They cannot be condemned, either by the local government or by the House of Commons, in advance.

There are other rules which must be enforced. For example, colonial civil servants and educational officers in Kenya undertake as a condition of employment not to be members of political associations or to express their own political views in public. It would be thought that the obvious reasons for such a rule would have the support of all opinion in a democracy.

A schoolmaster in Kenya was found to have attended Kenyatta's meetings, and to have evinced considerable sympathy in public with Mau Mau. The local government dismissed him, because he had broken the terms of his engagement, and went so far as to declare him a prohibited immigrant, which in fact sentenced him to exile. These measures were taken without consulting me, and the second of them should perhaps have been more carefully con-

[5] These territories are: Aden, Bahama Islands, Barbados, Bermuda, British Guiana, British Honduras, Brunei, Cyprus, Falkland Islands and Dependencies, Fiji (and Pitcairn Islands Group), Gambia, Gibraltar, Gold Coast, Hong Kong, Jamaica, Kenya, Leeward Islands, Federation of Malaya, Malta, Mauritius, Nigeria, North Borneo, Northern Rhodesia, Nyasaland, St. Helena (with Ascension and Tristan dà Cunha), Sarawak, Seychelles, Sierra Leone, Singapore, Somaliland, Tanganyika, Tonga, Trinidad and Tobago, Uganda, Western Pacific, Windward Islands, Zanzibar. (The Colonial Office List 1954.)

sidered. The police entered his house after he had left, and there found evidence which in any event showed that he was unfitted to be a schoolmaster.

A storm broke on my head in the House of Commons. I stood fast on the simple facts that the man in question had broken his terms of engagement and must take the consequences. I avoided bringing to light the further evidence in my hands because I did not think it justifiable to use evidence obtained after action had been taken on other grounds.

Under extreme provocation and a spate of leading articles, open letters to the Secretary of State and so forth, I found it necessary to give some private warnings. The agitation in the House of Commons disappeared very quickly, but one highly respected newspaper continued the attack, although they had been apprised of the facts. Free speech should stop short of espousing false causes of this kind when once the truth has been made known, even if privately.

Gradually the Mau Mau rebellion was contained; in February 1954, before it had been stamped out, and before the life of the colony was normal, I returned to Kenya for my third visit to press forward with a new constitution. My staff was different on this occasion; the only veteran of these visits was Hugh Fraser, my parliamentary private secretary. I had used him in the interval to keep in touch with the Governor and the political leaders of all races, and he had made one or two journeys to Kenya. I had complete confidence in him, and he was able to discuss my views and wishes untrammelled by official inhibitions.

Angus MacKintosh, my former private secretary, had been promoted. I was sad to part with him, but I found his successor, Jack Johnston, equally congenial. Jack has gentle and engaging manners, a happy wit and acute brains. His industry and thoroughness are masked by an easy-going appearance. Once again I was thankful for the high quality of the Colonial and home Civil Service upon which I could draw.

The senior member of my staff was Gorell Barnes, whom I have already described. The effect of the high altitude was to make him gayer, though no less useful. He favoured Government House with one or two imitations which many of his old friends would have thought outside his range.

The Governor and I discussed our constitutional policy at length, and decided upon a course of action.

It was the hot weather, and at 5,500 feet above sea level, in a

rarefied air, tempers are friable. Negotiations have to be conducted with the greatest tact. I reduced one leading politician to
tears by some outspoken but well deserved criticism of a speech
which he had made. As some compensation for hair-trigger tempers, negotiators are apt to tire after a few days and concede some
points which they would not have surrendered in a cooler climate
or at a lower altitude.

The Governor and I set to work to obtain agreement on the
new constitution, and we kept up a relentless pressure on European, African and Asian leaders.

At this time I could not neglect the military and para-military
operations which were being conducted by the Army and the Police. The Commander-in-Chief, General Sir George Erskine, was
tackling his task systematically, some thought too systematically.
It is always difficult for those accustomed to handle large formations to adjust themselves to a form of warfare in which even a
brigade is too large an instrument. It was a company commander's
or even a platoon commander's war. I personally did not find General Erskine or his brilliant Chief of Staff, Major General "Slim"
Heyman, adverse to unorthodox methods.

Experience in Malaya had taught us that the frontiers between
military, para-military, police and civil activities cannot be rigidly
drawn, and that some synthesis must be made. With my help,
Erskine and the Governor welded the military, police and civil district officers into a number of emergency and defence committees.
General Erskine was prepared to improvise, and he worked in close
harmony with the Governor. He and I became friends, and he was
kind enough to take me round his troops and their cantonments,
always to me a relief and an encouragement.

With him I witnessed a sweep being conducted across some
farmlands, in the hopes of rounding up a few Mau Mau adherents.
The mesh of the net appeared to us too wide, and the effort out of
proportion to the catch. Two battalions from county regiments
were stationed in this locality, and as so often happens the British
soldier had made himself very popular with the local inhabitants.
Being country boys they knew how to help countrymen: they
drove back to their Kikuyu owners cattle that had strayed, they
helped to mend the fences, they played with the children, milked
the cows and swore genially at everyone.

One day the C.-in-C. and I in full fig were driving in his car,
flanked by military policemen and flying the Union Jack from the
forepeak. We were passing at a sedate and dignified speed through

a large village. The whole population, including hundreds of almost naked children, turned out, chattering and smiling and waving their hands. Most of the children greeted us with delighted cries of "F—— off"—a term of obviously military origin which they clearly thought to be one of endearment, or a variant of cheerio. The dignity proper to a C.-in-C. and a Secretary of State could not be maintained under this treatment.

During our visit to Kenya some strange events seemed likely to change the whole course of the struggle.

A gallant police officer, Ian Henderson, had taken his life in his hands and had frequently gone unarmed into the forest at night to parley with the terrorists. He brought back information that if we would grant a political amnesty, the hard core of Mau Mau—a band of about 1,400—would give themselves up. The question was posed to me. Should we grant the amnesty?

Personally I never considered any answer but "Yes." My views were not shared by many. A political storm arose. Speeches were made condemning my proposed action as "grasping hands stained with blood, parleying with murderers, and letting wild animals go free."

Whilst I well understood the reasons why these emotions were aroused, well understood the strain which gave them birth, whilst I loathed the terror and murder and mutilations, I considered that passion was a bad guide. By refusing to treat with the rebels we could not bring back to life those who had been foully done to death; the refusal might well lead to future tragedies. Peace can be too dearly bought if the embers of war are left smouldering, but here there was reason to think that surrender would stamp them out and leave behind only the cold ashes.

I insisted that Government policy should be to treat. This policy, under the then system of Government, was not to be defended by skilled parliamentarians, but by the official Members, unversed in the arts of debate and accustomed to distrust and discard rhetoric. I outlined the speech which should be made:

"Hon. Members wish to be assured that we shall never make terms with rebels and criminals. Does anyone deny that an opportunity now exists by treating with them to end the terror and to end the strain under which many of our countrymen have been suffering for so long. You want to keep your hands clean; so do I, but I want even more to keep them clean from future bloodshed.

"If from maintaining a rigid refusal to parley it should come about that the emergency is prolonged, what are you going to say to the widow of some poor farmer murdered a month or two hence? 'Yes, your husband was foully murdered. We are deeply sorry. Console yourself, madam, that though your husband is dead, at least our hands are clean,' and so forth."

For once I knew that I would have pulverised the Opposition, but the speech made by the official was not a recognisable copy of what I had suggested.

All was arranged; about 1,400 of the hard core of Mau Mau were ready to surrender, but by a mere mischance whilst they were assembling in a clearing, ready to be marched off, some firing broke out a mile or two away. The terrorists thought they were betrayed, and rapidly dispersed. The opportunity did not recur.

We continued to press on with a new constitution. Agreement seemed to be impossible. I was due to return to England in a few days; time was running short.

I did not leave Government House for ten days, and we redoubled our pressure and eventually, on the very day of my departure, we succeeded in obtaining African, Indian and European agreement. A new pattern of government was formed.

Previously, the Government of Kenya had been carried on by the Governor, the Deputy Governor, six official members—that is colonial civil servants—and two nominated members.

The new constitution provided for six official members, two nominated members and six unofficial members. Two Asians and one African were to be amongst the six unofficial members, and would hold the offices of Works and Community Development, and one Minister (Asian) was to be without portfolio. I also included five under-secretaries amongst the Ministerial posts; two of the new under-secretaries were to be African and one Arab.

I set up a War Council for the emergency, which was to be headed by the Governor and would include the C.-in-C. and Michael Blundell as a civilian member. A Development Committee under the chairmanship of the Minister of Finance to further the economic life of the colony was set up at the same time.

This new constitution was dubbed the Lyttelton Constitution, although much of it had been framed upon the Governor's advice. The constitution was to last until the next general election, which was to take place six months after the Governor had proclaimed that the state of emergency had come to an end, or on June 30th, 1955, whichever was the later.

Thus the new arrangements pointed the way to reform by giving representation in the Government to Asians and Africans for the first time, and by engaging for the first time unofficial members of the Legislature in the Government.

I tried hard to get the other races to accept one more African in the Ministry, but to have insisted would have been to break down the agreement which I had secured. Politics are the art of what is practicable.

CHAPTER XXII

THE COLONIAL OFFICE: NIGERIA, UGANDA, MALTA, BRITISH GUIANA

1 *Nigeria*

I n 1953 the constitution in Nigeria, by far the largest British colony in Africa, appeared to be working ill; there were the familiar signs of unrest; the storm cones were being hoisted; the Central Council of Ministers was hardly more than a debating society, and at that divided into factions; as an instrument of government it was palsied and ineffective.

The general tone of the press in England was that agreement amongst the three or four principal races that made up the thirty-one million inhabitants of Nigeria was nearly impossible, and the left-wing press foretold doom if these delicate balances were to be subjected to the ruthless and clumsy hands of the Secretary of State.

I called a conference; some shadow-boxing by the Opposition made it harder for the principal parties in Nigeria to accept the invitation of Her Majesty's Government, and some irritating exchanges and delay were the result. However, it was eventually arranged that the conference would assemble at No. 10 Carlton House Terrace on July 30th, under my chairmanship.

The date was not a very agreeable one to me. All Ministers and parliamentarians know that the House of Commons is at its worst in July. Members have sat since the end of January, with two very short breaks at Easter and Whitsuntide, tempers are frayed, the very air of the Chamber is stale, Whips find it difficult to "keep a House." Everyone looks forward with relief to the first days of August and the long vacation, which will last till at least the middle of October.

This break in parliamentary duties was to be replaced for me by the responsible and delicate task of steering the Nigerian Conference through the shoals, at a time when the only unity amongst the crew was said to be dislike of the captain.

In the event it turned out to be the most successful of the many negotiations in which I was engaged during my term of office, and I take pride in the result.

The opening days of the Conference were occupied by speeches made by the leaders of the various parties, by Obafemi Awolowo of the Action Group, by Mallam Aminu Kano of the Northern Elements Progressive Union, a splinter party, by Mr. Eyo Ita of the National Independence Party, by Abubakar Tafawa Balewa, the "golden voice of the North" of the Northern Peoples' Congress, by Dr. Endeley of the Cameroons, and by Dr. Azikiwe of the National Council of Nigeria and the Cameroons.

Although most of these speeches were made "for the record" and for local consumption, they demonstrated only too clearly the disunity of Nigeria; hostility to the British was expressed or implied by every speaker except Abubakar Balewa. We were even accused of a cynical policy of "divide and rule." When I replied to this opening debate I did not mince words. I said that the only cement which kept the rickety structure of Nigeria together was the British. Let that be recognised. We drew little if any material gain from our rule in Nigeria; we had for example just made a grant—yes, a grant—of £23 million for development. Anyway, what was the present Conference for? It had been convened by us to try to keep the diverse elements in Nigeria together; left to themselves they would clearly fall apart in a few months.

The speech was frank and brutal, and was not intended to be well received; in this it succeeded.

We got to work; it was clear that Nigeria, if it was to be a nation, must be a federation, with as few subjects reserved for the Central Government as would preserve national unity. In my opinion, the fatal flaw in the existing constitution was that members of the Central Council of Ministers were nominated by the Regions; in this system it was inevitable that they should regard themselves, and act, as delegates and not as national figures.

The first major change should be to secure that the Central Government was elected by a separate vote. Only in this way could a Nigerian policy be formed; otherwise compromises amongst the "delegates" would take the place of decision, and where compromise became impossible the bearings would burn out and the machine of government would grind to a stop.

There was some support for this point of view, but the atmosphere of the Conference was troubled. The black faces round me looked hostile and sullen.

At this moment a member representing a not very important group asked that the Charter of Human Rights should be incorporated in the constitution. I replied by saying that they could put "God is Love" into the constitution if they so wished, but not while I was in the chair. I had the prestige of Nigeria too much at heart to wish that general ethical aspirations should be attached to the laws and constitution. This sally was greeted with the first laughter and applause that I had heard. I called for the Charter of Human Rights. It was produced.

Freedom of speech. Of course, I said, but subject to the law of slander, and if written, of libel. If I were to say that Mr. X had had his hand in the Government till from the very day he became a Minister, I should rightly be sued for slander, and no doubt heavily mulcted for damages. My freedom of speech would be punished. The Mr. X whom I had selected was supposed to be somewhat venal, and again the Conference greeted the example with prolonged laughter.

Freedom of conscience. Putting these words into the constitution would hardly help Nigeria. For example the delegates didn't know for sure what I sincerely thought, and I didn't know what they sincerely thought. I advised against trying to get between a man and his conscience; the area was unsuitable for constitutional checks.

Freedom of assembly. Of course, I went on, subject to the responsibility of the police for keeping order.

I warmed to my theme, and exposed with some ridicule the general but not unusual proposition that in civilised societies freedom can only be exercised by anyone if it did not interfere overmuch or cancel out someone else's freedom. All laws limited in some degree or other the freedom of the individual. You can't have the freedom to bring a cobra into the Legislature, or to park your car in your neighbour's garden. Laws limit your freedom, and if the constitution appeared to subscribe to the idea that freedom was absolute and unlimited it would merely make Nigeria look ridiculous, which I could not stomach.

After about twenty minutes of this, someone amongst the delegates got up and begged that the Conference should hear no more of the Charter. The meeting had obviously enjoyed hearing my work of demolition and the discomfiture of the proposer.

Miraculously the whole atmosphere of the Conference changed; it dawned upon the members that I might be human; they had enjoyed the jokes, as Africans generally do; it even occurred to them that I might be a friend. In this last they were right, because I am deeply fond of Nigerians, and react spontaneously to their gaiety and sense of humour.

I was soon able to steer the Conference in a more direct manner. I said that there were certain constitutional matters upon which Her Majesty's Government was not prepared to negotiate at all. If our advice upon them was neglected, we could not proceed.

These matters were, first, that the Judiciary should be entirely insulated from the Executive. This was one of the first pillars of democracy. Someone immediately interrupted and said that we enshrined no such principle in the constitution of the United Kingdom; the Lord Chancellor, who was a political figure, in fact advised Her Majesty whom she should appoint as judges, and she could not set aside his advice.

I explained that the Lord Chancellor in recommending these appointments did not act in his political capacity but in his legal, and that judges reached the bench irrespective of their politics or political antecedents, and solely on their merits. The Conference accepted these assurances.

The second matter was that the police must not be subject to any political party. When someone demurred, I said that of course I should have no objection if the police was subject to the control of my party (prolonged laughter). No political party could, however, run the risk that another party controlled the police.

Immediately a West Coast lawyer whose shining ebony face and vast form partly concealed an acute intelligence, sprang to his feet and said that the Home Secretary in Great Britain controlled the Metropolitan Police, and he was a political figure. I emphasised once more that he did not act as a politician in these matters; parties came and went, but Scotland Yard and the Metropolitan Police went on just the same, impartial and undisturbed.

Such is the respect with which our knowledge of the arts of government is held, especially by lawyers, that this explanation was also accepted.

Finally, I said, the Civil Service must be recruited, appointed and promoted outside the influence of Ministers. Yet again, a member of the Conference declared that the appointment of Permanent Secretaries in Great Britain had to be countersigned by the Prime Minister. Once more I had to say that notwithstanding this, the appointments were generally, though not always, made on the recommendations of the Head of the Civil Service, that is the Permanent Under Secretary of the Treasury. "I have no influence," I continued, "none whatever, upon the careers of the distinguished civil servants present at this table as my advisers. I could not make or break Sir Thomas Lloyd or Mr. Gorell Barnes if I tried. I should be more likely to break myself." This too was accepted.

These interchanges threw into sharp relief two things. First, the detailed knowledge of British practice displayed by African lawyers and politicians, and secondly, the profound truth of Disraeli's dictum: "Countries are governed by force or by tradition." All these three pillars of democratic government, independence of the judiciary, of the police and of the civil service, are secured in Great Britain in spite of the apparent written system, and rest wholly upon an enlightened tradition.

It would be wearisome to describe the debates upon the division of Federal and Regional powers, the concurrent subjects and the foundation of a federal system. No one could have listened to the debates without gaining a respect for the grasp which the Africans had of the complicated issues, nor of their readiness to accept arrangements which appeared anomalous, but which had been worked successfully and wisely in the United Kingdom.

There was, however, one inflamed subject which was likely to cause a great turmoil and even a breakdown of the Conference, namely the status and position of Lagos.

Lagos at that time was *de facto* the Nigerian capital; in it were situated the Government offices and Government House; it was by far the greatest port; the headquarters of most trading companies were there established; it was thus not only the political but the commercial focus of Nigeria. It had been, in my opinion, a cardinal mistake of my predecessors to incorporate Lagos into the Western Region, and a surgical operation would be necessary to cut it off.

It was quite clear that the Conference itself would never be able to agree; the Western Regions and the able Mr. Awolowo would naturally resist losing from their jurisdiction so important a centre; the other two regions could hardly be expected to treat as a federal capital a city administered under the laws and by the officials of a regional government. After long and bitter debates, in which I did not intervene, there was a deadlock.

To my surprise the delegates referred the matter to the sole decision of the Secretary of State. I regarded this as a vote of confidence in my impartiality. I made it clear that if I accepted this critical task, my decision must be regarded as final, without further debate. This was agreed on August 17th.

The Conference decided to defer the next plenary session to the 19th, to give me time for reflection. I undertook during this pause to study the statements made upon the subject by all the political leaders, and to give the matter the greatest attention.

On the 19th I announced my decision on behalf of Her Majesty's Government. It was that Lagos should be separated from the Western Region and should become the federal capital and its territory federal territory.

At this point the Western Region and their spokesmen, the Oni of Ife and Mr. Awolowo, expressed astonishment at the decision; they could not agree; they had been given a definite mandate by the Yorubas not to accept a compromise. They would have to refer back the whole matter, a course which they had strongly condemned when suggested by others during the Conference.

I pointed out that they had previously agreed to refer the matter to my sole decision, and to abide by it. I asked that they should give the matter further thought, and hoped that they would see that my decision was in the interests of Nigeria as a nation.

The Conference then passed on to consider the subject of self-government in 1956. I was obliged to say that I could not accept 1956 as a fixed and unalterable date. The representatives of the Northern Region, which contained rather more than half the population of Nigeria, did not think that the country would be ready for self-government by so early a date. Further steps along the road to self-government depended not on the running out of a certain number of days, but on the ability of Nigerians to overcome the disruptive forces in Nigeria. I was prepared to agree that a conference similar to the present one should be held in 1956, but that Her Majesty's Government could not be bound in advance to grant self-government in that year. They would have to be satisfied that the necessary unity had been achieved to make it workable. Dr. Azikiwe, in a long statement containing many apposite quotations upon federalism, accepted my proposal of a review of the constitution by 1956.

The controversy concerning the representation of the Western Region on the Central Council of Ministers burst into flames. Ministers from other regions on the Central Council would not accept the two Western nominations. At this point Mr. Awolowo pronounced a violent philippic. The Western Region had suffered a series of humiliations and victimisations, he said; Ministers who enjoyed the confidence of the Western Region were not acceptable to the North; the latest humiliation had been the severance of Lagos from the West. When this decision was known there would be a tumult; the streets of Lagos, he feared, would run with blood. The amended constitution could not be given even the semblance of workable government. He asked for leave to withdraw from the Conference.

I replied with some asperity that having listened in the early part of the Conference to arguments in favour of granting self-government in 1956, I little thought to have been confronted so soon with conclusive proof that Nigeria was unready for it. Mr. Awolowo followed with a provocative speech, in which he threatened direct action to bring the two Ministers into the Central Council. He and the other representatives of the West then formally withdrew from the Conference and marched out of the room.

I believed that their emotion was due more to the outrage upon their feelings caused by my decision upon Lagos than upon the other point. Their other arguments underlined once again the flaw in the constitution which did not provide for direct election to the Central Government.

At the next meeting, and in the absence of the Action Group, the Conference, much to my satisfaction, reversed its previous decision and agreed upon direct election to the Central Government. This at once reduced to size the vexed question of the two Western Ministers, and enabled the Action Group to return and a unanimous report to be presented.

The work of the Conference was not, however, finished; a number of important matters regarding the public service and the repartition of revenues between the constituent elements of the Federation remained to be settled, and it was decided to reconvene the Conference in Lagos in January 1954.

Aminu Kano, who had made many attacks upon the Northern rulers, asked the Sardauna of Sokoto for police protection when he returned to Kano. The Sardauna, drawing himself up to his full height, replied, "He who raises the wind must swallow some dust." Beyond this rebuke, Aminu Kano came to no harm.

I was deeply satisfied with the result of our labours in London; not one of the provisions considered by us necessary for the exercise of a federal government had been set aside; the defective constitution was to be amended. I had done all that was possible to protect the careers of our Civil Service. Many other matters had been settled which are perhaps only of interest to students of colonial affairs and of new constitutions. The Report of the Conference (Command 8934) sets them out succinctly.

Above all, the happiest relations between the Nigerian leaders and myself had been established. I could talk freely and in terms of friendship to the Sardauna of Sokoto, to Abubakar Balewa, to Mr. Awolowo, for whom, in spite of a short period when I thought him intransigent, I had a high regard, and to Dr. Azikiwe.

The date fixed for the final Conference was January 24th, 1954, and the night before I was due to fly out I was discussing affairs with the Prime Minister. At about midnight he gave me a cigar as long as a slide-rule, and suggested I should sit up with him till I had finished it. I said I was starting early, had already smoked one big cigar, but would keep the new one to smoke when I got to Lagos.

I found it on my dressing-table on the morning of the Conference, and put it into my pocket. The first plenary session was to be opened by me in the Legislative Chamber. The dresses of the delegates were as magnificent as they were varied; some of the headgear, for instance an Oxford straw boater with feathers, appeared somewhat incongruous to Western eyes, but the chiefs, and the superb clothes of the Muslims from the North, made an engaging background of colour.

I made the opening speech impromptu. I brought messages from Mr. Churchill. I was with him, I said, the night before I started. He had wished Nigeria well. I went on, I cannot think why: "He gave me this cigar," I held it up, "but I have decided not to smoke it unless the Conference becomes difficult and factious. I am sure it will never be lit." For some reason this statement seemed to tickle the fancy of the delegates.

The work of the Conference went on in an atmosphere of goodwill; the only row that appeared likely to break out concerned the subject of whether museums were to be a central or a regional subject, and one of the chiefs, in whose domain one of the best museums was established, felt deeply, almost passionately, that they must be a regional subject. A confused babble of voices was heard, and one or two provocative speeches were delivered. I held up the cigar: laughter; peace returned: the museums went to the regions.

Earlier, in London, Mr. Awolowo had raised the dangerous topic of whether a state in the Federation should be given the right to secede. By the usual devices of the conferencier I had succeeded in getting this subject deferred to the closing days of the Conference, when all the political leaders would be committed to every other clause of the constitution.

One of the best debates to which I had ever listened in any country ensued. Dr. Azikiwe had primed himself with quotations from statesmen of the Union from Daniel Webster to Abraham Lincoln. The old-fashioned oratory suddenly came to life in the hot council chamber, ringed by black faces.

> Secession! Peaceable secession! Sir, your eyes and mine are never destined to see that miracle. The dismemberment of this vast country without convulsion! The breaking up of the fountains of the great deep without ruffling the surface! Who is so foolish, I beg everybody's pardon, as to expect to see any such thing? Sir, he who sees these states, now revolving in harmony around a common centre, and expects to see them quit their places and fly off without convulsion, may look the next hour to see the heavenly bodies rush from their spheres, and jostle against each other in the realms of space, without causing the wreck of the universe. There can be no such thing as a peaceable secession.[1]

After citing such authorities as Robert Birley and de Malberg, he quoted from Abraham Lincoln:

> If the United States be not a government proper, but an association of states in the nature of contracts merely, can it as a contract be peaceably unmade by less than all the parties who made it? [2]

Abubakar Balewa also made a magnificent and eloquent speech, and Mr. Awolowo was little behind him.

I wound up by a speech which I fear did not reach the same heights. I said that reflection would surely show that the right of secession would paralyse a central government if allowed to one or more of the constituent states of a federation. The Central Government could always be placed in a dilemma. "Either you agree," they would be told, "or we secede." It might even break up—to use a fanciful illustration—the United Kingdom, if the Whitehall Government doubled the excise duty on whisky and Scotland had the right to secede.

At the end, the right of secession was not granted, and our labours at last were done; the constitution in all its clauses had the unanimous support of all the political parties from East to West and North to South. The new Nigeria was born. Farewell speeches of goodwill were made, and I was asked to present my

---

[1] Daniel Webster, March 7th, 1860.
[2] Abraham Lincoln in his inaugural address.

still unsmoked cigar to the Legislature. It was put in a glass case and hung behind the Speaker's Chair.

The next day I left Lagos, and drove through the city on my way to the airport. So far from the streets running with blood, the Lagotians turned out in some strength to give the Secretary of State a send-off. They waved and cheered, and this was particularly gratifying to me, because it so happened that Miss Barbara Ward,[3] a lady not imbued with wholeheartedly Conservative principles, was driving in the same car as I, and saw the demonstration for herself.

11 *Uganda*

For me the year 1953 was not to close before I had to deal with the relations of Her Majesty's Government with the Kabaka of Buganda and, on December 15th, with a Vote of Censure upon the general topic of my conduct of African affairs.

There could be no doubt about the gravity of the first issue. The Kabaka had made it clear that he intended to set aside the treaty under which he enjoyed the protection of Great Britain, and was determined to seek the dismemberment of Uganda by the secession of Buganda, its largest state. The treaty in question had not been imposed, but had been sought by his predecessors and had been freely negotiated.

Sir Andrew Cohen, the Governor of Uganda, had been appointed during Mr. Griffiths' term of office. It was supposed that he would become Permanent Under Secretary at the Colonial Office as soon as the Conservative Government fell, which happy event would harmoniously come about at the end of his governorship. The electorate perversely upset this time-table.

He was a man of obvious integrity and powerful intellectual equipment. Both he and his wife were dedicated perhaps with more enthusiasm than judgement to the swiftest advancement of Africans.

He had repeated meetings with the Kabaka, but failed to move him an inch from his separatist policy.

It is interesting to reflect why a man with such obvious sympathy towards Africans should have made so little impression. It may be that the confidence the Labour Government had in Cohen

[3] Mrs. Robert Jackson, now Lady Jackson.

did not make him the most acceptable advocate at the court of a royal personage; it may be that Cohen's manners to the Kabaka were too censorious or too didactic. From my knowledge of him, I should doubt this. Antipathies are often the children of mere chance. I cannot judge, but the fact remains that the Kabaka remained obdurate.

I myself held the view strongly that if I invited the Kabaka to fly to Great Britain I should be able to persuade him to alter his views. His Highness speaks perfect English, has agreeable manners, was an honorary officer in the Grenadier Guards, my own regiment. He had been a friend of my eldest son, Antony, at Cambridge. He had many other English friends, and under their influence and the congenial atmosphere of London, I felt sure that he would listen to a fellow Grenadier.

I cabled in this sense to Cohen. His reply put me into a vice. He said that he was sure that I should fail to persuade the Kabaka. If after successfully defying the Secretary of State the Kabaka was to return to Uganda, he could not be responsible for the safety of the Colony. The Governor asked whether, if he refused to change, I should detain him in England.

There was only one answer to this question: no. To persuade the Kabaka to come and hold discussions with me, and then to use the opportunity of detaining him, would not be a straight course to steer. Whatever the outcome of our talks he must return. On the other hand, to saddle the Governor with someone who had successfully defied Her Majesty's Government would hardly be fair.

It is easy to sit in Whitehall and cause convulsions in far distant colonies which might endanger law and order, and even threaten the lives of the Governor and the British community. Henry Hopkinson, Lord Munster (the Parliamentary Secretary), Sir Thomas Lloyd and I pondered long and earnestly over this dilemma. I felt in my bones that action to depose the Kabaka might be a wrong decision; reason, however, pulled the other way. In the end, with many misgivings, we decided to support the Governor but told him to make another all-out attempt to persuade the Kabaka to change his mind. Cohen had already seen His Highness on the 6th, 27th and 30th November.

This conjuncture illustrates some of the problems of the relationship between the Secretary of State and Governors. The principle is clear—sack or back—and if the Secretary of State decides to back, the backing must mean that he has overcome his own misgivings and must identify himself with the Governor without reservation. Usually when the man on the spot is put on the spot he should be supported.

I sent Cohen instructions in the following sense. He was to see the Kabaka again; he was not to take no for an answer; he was to allow His Highness two or three days in which to ponder; only when he had exhausted all the methods of persuasion were the consequences, namely the withdrawal of recognition by Her Majesty's Government, to be explained.

In face of this account it is perhaps foolish to say that I still believe that if the Kabaka had come to England I could have persuaded him to alter course. My long experience of negotiations has taught me that atmosphere is everything.

Cohen once again failed; we were obliged to act. The Kabaka was put into an aeroplane and flown to London.

I arranged that a young civil servant from the Uganda department should get into immediate touch with him. The Kabaka might have little ready money with him; he was to be handed £50 in notes and was to be informed that a liberal transfer of his revenues would be arranged to meet his needs in England.

Shortly afterwards the Kabaka came to see me. Our conversation—which did not decrease my embarrassment—began like this, these are His Highness's very words:

"I say, Secretary of State, thanks awfully for that fifty quid you sent me and," with a smile, "I happened to have nothing with me but some small change, and I must buy an overcoat. By the way, how's Antony [my eldest son]?" I told him, and went on to say how deeply sorry I had been to learn of the death of his sister. His Highness was deeply affected, and could hardly hold back his tears.

I assured him that no personal issue between us could arise, but that I had a duty to fulfil from which I could not escape. My unshakeable belief was that the progress of both Uganda and Buganda could not be assured unless the unity of the Protectorate was maintained. "Fair enough," he replied.

Throughout this interview I was struck with His Highness's courtesy and gentleness, and with his apparent goodwill towards myself. I again felt that if the conversation could have been joined before drastic action had been taken, an accommodation could have been reached. It was now too late.

Subsequent events in Uganda showed that whilst our action

clearly maintained the unity of the Protectorate, it unleashed other disruptive forces.

These events formed the subject of a Motion for the Adjournment in the House of Commons. It was moved by Mr. Fenner Brockway, and seconded by Mr. Leslie Hale, that is by two backbenchers.

They both made moderate speeches—or for them moderate speeches—but whether from ignorance or enthusiasm they permitted themselves considerable departures from the facts. My action was described as impetuous and unconsidered, and they both, though vainly, tried to tie the crisis in Uganda to words which I had used in a previous speech. "Nor," I had said, "should we exclude from our minds the *evolution, as time goes on* [my italics], of still larger measures of federation of the whole East African territories."

When I replied, I quoted the words with which I had reassured the Kabaka and public opinion in Uganda, and which he for one had accepted. I had made it clear that unless public opinion changed, no further measures of federation were possible or in contemplation. Uganda was to be essentially an African State.

I was able completely to demolish the charge that Her Majesty's Government had acted hastily and without mature thought, and to underline the persistence with which the Kabaka had declared his intention of seceding from the Protectorate.

When I came to describe my meeting with the Kabaka I could not keep emotion from my voice, and my emotion was deepened by my uncertainty about whether we had acted for the best. Disraeli once said, "Never apologise for showing feeling. Remember that when you do so, you apologise for truth." At least my speech moved the House.

Mr. Griffiths wound up and was in some difficulty. Sir Andrew Cohen had been his nomination as Governor. To be found attacking a Governor whom he had himself appointed and whom he admired, and supporting a feudal ruler who had defied him, did not seem the most becoming posture for the Labour Party to take up, but Mr. Griffiths is an experienced parliamentarian, and made the best of it.

I watched afterwards the course of events in Uganda with anxiety, and in spite of the Governor's protestations remained uneasy about the outcome.

It so happened that in April 1954 I was in attendance upon the

Queen when she visited Uganda in the course of her long tour of the Commonwealth. The Queen and Prince Philip stayed with the Governor at Government House at Entebbe, and my wife and I were also his guests.

The Queen inaugurated the Owen Falls power station (by chance the turbines had been built by my company) at an impressive ceremony.

Sir Philip Mitchell, the retired Governor of Kenya and an African authority, had written a private letter to the Governor to suggest that as an act of clemency upon her first visit to Uganda after her accession the Queen should be advised to restore the Kabaka. When I asked the Governor whether in his opinion the state of the country permitted me so to advise Her Majesty, he was emphatic that the country was settling down and that a restoration was impolitic. I accepted his point of view—perhaps wrongly.

The next event which I shall always remember was the Queen's and Prince Philip's visit to the game reserve. Moira and I and the Governor flew up with them in a small aircraft. After landing they rode in a special Land-Rover, and we followed in another. We had a wonderful day. After inspecting—and that is the right word— a hippopotamus which was taking a siesta in a water-hole just big enough for him, and some way from the river, we came upon a cow elephant with a calf a few days old. The Queen and Prince Philip got within fifty or a hundred yards and took ciné-camera pictures of the couple. The white hunters who were in attendance looked a little anxious and kept their fingers on the trigger in case the cow became infuriated and charged, as cow elephants will sometimes do if disturbed with their calves.

In the course of the day we saw hundreds of elephants and hippopotamuses in their natural state as well as buffaloes, pigs and antelopes.

I must tell the story of the famous pink diamond. This unique stone had been discovered by Dr. Williamson in the Tanganyika diamond field which he owned and developed. Pink diamonds of a few carats are not unknown but this specimen ran to over 30 carats. It was presented to the Queen in its uncut state on the occasion of her wedding to Prince Philip.

Mr. Chopra, an Indian and Dr. Williamson's charming and able man of business, had approached me at the time of the Coronation and asked me whether it would be agreeable to Her Majesty that Dr. Williamson should, as a Coronation gift, have the diamond cut and mounted by any jeweller whom the Queen nominated, and set with any white diamonds which she cared to select.

The Queen accepted this fabulous gift; she would certainly have deeply offended Dr. Williamson if she had not.

It so happened that although I had been the intermediary in the matter, I had never seen the stone.

One night I was sitting next to the Queen at dinner at Government House, and said that I had missed a great opportunity of seeing the pink diamond which I had just heard she had been wearing at the garden party that afternoon. I had of course been walking behind her.

The Queen smiled and said that unfortunately she had taken off the brooch in which the pink diamond was set, and her maid had put it in the safe. I would no doubt see it one day.

When we joined the ladies after dinner, the Queen beckoned to me and pointed to the brooch, which she had again put on. "There it is," she said. To have got hold of her maid and taken the trouble to get the jewel out of the safe in order to show it to one of her Ministers was a charming example of her exquisite manners.

The subsequent history of Uganda shows that our anxieties were not without cause. The country, in spite of the Governor's assurances, remained restless and uneasy.

I resigned from the Government in July 1954, and within a week the Governor advised the new Secretary of State to invite the Kabaka to return to Buganda. I confess that at first I harboured the suspicion that Sir Andrew had awaited my resignation, which had been known of for some time, before taking this step, which was contrary to all his previous advice. I believe these suspicions are groundless, but they rankled in my mind at the time. Legal uncertainties played a larger part in his *volte-face* than is generally known.

Alan Lennox-Boyd, my successor, found his very first task was to take this action. He at once consulted me and asked me if I had any personal objection. I answered that I was entirely indifferent to any reflection that might be cast upon me, or to any suggestion that he had taken the first opportunity of revoking my decision. He must feel free to do whatever he believed right.

The Kabaka returned. I hope that the wounds have now healed, because in 1962 he received the K.B.E.

It is not uncommon for retired Ministers, or for that matter retired officials or directors, to feel how much worse affairs are conducted by their immediate successors; growls from Chislehurst, so to speak, are not uncommon. I had no such feelings, and watched Alan's conduct of the Colonial Office with unfeigned admiration. It was governed by his all-absorbing interest in colonial affairs, and by his sympathy with Africans.

Perhaps the only action which he subsequently took with which I did not entirely agree concerned Archbishop Makarios (that Scotchman Mac Arios that causes all the trouble in Cyprus, as the British soldiers complained).

In the few weeks before my resignation I had become increasingly distressed by the failure of this prelate to condemn, either by bell, book or candle, the murders and atrocities committed by the Cypriots upon the British. If things got to such a pass that he had to be deported, I decided in my own mind to deport him— to Athens. All exiles tend to lose support, and even bonny Prince Charlie soon forfeited his influence at the French court. I thought that this very political prelate would soon weary the Athenians, and after all to deport a man to his country of origin hardly seems to be inhumane.

This was a minor disagreement with Alan Lennox-Boyd. He will always rank as one of the great holders of the high office of Secretary of State for the Colonies.

In December 1953, the Opposition thought the events in Kenya and Uganda, and the uneasy stirring of African nationalism south of the Sahara, provided material for a Vote of Censure upon the Government and upon my conduct of African affairs. Mr. Griffiths opened the debate in familiar—all too familiar—terms. He tried to pin upon my conduct of affairs and my ruthless personality the fact that Africa was stirring. In his day there was trust, there was confidence, there was mutual relationship. "What do we see now?" he exclaimed. "White racialism spreading beyond the Limpopo to the north, and to the east." He foretold a white federation in East Africa, soon to be followed by a West African Federation. He made some grudging references to the Nigerian Conference. He even asserted that the Opposition had supported action to put down terrorism in Kenya.

When I came to reply, I traced the true reasons why Africa was stirring. I felt that I had the House with me.

I hope I am considerate enough or humble enough not to wish to blow upon the old embers of a speech and I will not quote from it.

The Times used these words:

Mr. Lyttelton showed himself completely master of the occasion in a manner which recalled his handling of the Buganda debate. There were the same deadly restraint, the sense of indignation held on leash, and a magnanimity which gave powerful effect by contrast to the searing rebukes he piled on the Opposition for having broken the traditional all-Party approach to Colonial matters.[4]

III *Malta*

The difficulties which arose concerning Malta, the George Cross island, were acute at the time of the Coronation, so I will touch on some of my memories of it in this section.

I well remember the last time I saw the King. When Princess Elizabeth and Prince Philip left Heath Row for Kenya, the King and Queen came to see them take off. The appropriate Ministers were in attendance, and amongst them myself, since the royal journey was to a British Colony.

I was shocked by the King's appearance. I was familiar with his look and mien, but he seemed much altered and strained. I had the feeling of doom, which grew as the minutes before the time of departure ebbed away. The King went on to the roof of the building to wave good-bye. The high wind blew his hair into disorder. I felt with deep foreboding that this would be the last time he was to see his daughter, and that he thought so himself.

Winston asked me to drive back with him to London, and when I told him of my opinion about the King's health he was very angry and told me that I was completely wrong; a not unusual reaction from people who do not want to believe bad news.

As everyone knows, the Princess was in Kenya when she succeeded to the throne. The day after her return, the Privy Council was summoned to St. James's Palace. There must have been nearly two hundred Privy Councillors present in the large room next to the Picture Gallery. The door opened, and the Queen in black came in. Suddenly the members of the Privy Council looked immeasurably old and gnarled and grey. The Queen made one of the most touching speeches to which I have ever listened, and I, like many others, could hardly control my emotions. All the pageantry of the Coronation did not convey so clearly the great burden which the Queen was called upon to carry so early in her life.

A few people fulfil their responsibilities with success; it is not obsequious or insincere to say that the Queen discharges hers as nearly to perfection as a mortal can. Her beautiful manners, her undisguised interest in many subjects are clear to everyone. She

[4] December 17th, 1953.

is moreover a speaker of rare attainment. Like her mother, she has a limpid voice of great charm allied to a faultless enunciation which I have little doubt owes something to study and training.

The Prime Minister was captivated by his Queen. I often recalled the relations between Disraeli and Queen Victoria and here an equally felicitous relationship was growing, though in a different way and with a very much wider gap in age. The Prime Minister frequently exclaimed, "What have the British people done to deserve her!"

I must now describe the Maltese problems, which are amongst the most difficult to deal with in the whole world. The underlying reason which makes them so intractable is that the Maltese aspire to political independence and to financial dependence.

Life on the island on its present scale can only be sustained if financial aid is forthcoming. But whenever some control—even couched in general terms—was sought concerning the spending of this aid, whether for helping emigration, maintaining employment or promoting local industries, the Maltese Ministers fell back upon obstruction of a mediaeval complexity and drew, and possibly overdrew, on their well deserved credit as the George Cross island.

On the other hand, it is difficult for a British Government and for the House of Commons to pour out very large sums without some control, even if remote, of the ways in which these sums are to be spent.

At this time there was a considerable agitation in Malta for union with Italy. This solution would have rid us of many vexatious problems, but it would have been cynical to accept it. It would not have promoted the well-being of the islanders or for that matter of Italy herself.

The Prime Minister of Malta at this time was Dr. Borg Olivier, who only enjoyed a majority of four in the legislature. As a negotiator he, too, relied upon methods of attrition. After long protracted talks, wearisome discussions of proposals and counter-proposals, no more than a temporary *modus vivendi* could be reached.

A little time before the Coronation, Her Majesty had arranged that the High Commissioners of the self-governing dominions should each plant a tree in the Great Park at Windsor to commemorate the occasion. The Governor was to represent Malta, and when it was explained that their representative was not in the same bracket as the other High Commissioners, the Maltese at the last minute refused to take part. I had to plant the tree, as Secretary of State, and carry off the stainless steel shovel which I had used.

It is, of course, easy to laugh at the protocol, but if it is disregarded, other claims which cannot be met within the constitution and framework of the Commonwealth spring up, and what may seem a trivial concession may end in an erosion of important principles.

When the arrangements for the Coronation itself were being made, the Maltese Prime Minister insisted, though without justification by the protocol, that he must drive in the procession with the Prime Ministers of the self-governing dominions. I had at first refused this privilege, but in the middle of May had to leave for Kenya. Whilst I was away, the Prime Minister conceded it, perhaps rightly. On my return, I was glad to find that the matter had apparently been taken out of my hands, but I was immediately faced with a new crisis—the horse crisis.

Another carriage and horses had to be provided for Dr. Olivier and his wife, and the Crown Equerry in charge of these matters had no horses to spare; if any of them went lame or broke down, he only had two in reserve.

Time was short and I suggested that some other horses could surely be found, even if they had to be flown over from France. The Crown Equerry said that the risk was too great and that his horses had been trained for months to accustom them to the crowds and the cheering. Once upon a time the horses dragging the Lord Mayor's coach at the Lord Mayor's Show had broken loose into the crowd and caused some fatal casualties. At this last hour I had the delicate diplomatic task of explaining why there were no horses available in England. Though this was true it is hardly surprising that the Prime Minister, who had read of Newmarket and Epsom, regarded it as a mere pretext.

The horse crisis lasted for a day or two. The Equerry said that he could only throw in his reserve of two upon the direct order of the Queen. I said, "The horses to draw this carriage have become a matter of imperial policy. Would you ask the Queen?" Her Majesty took the very real risk, and released them. The Prime Minister drove in the procession.

IV *British Guiana*

In September 1953 grave reports were received from British
Guiana. The Ministers elected under the new constitution, framed
by the Waddington Commission of 1950/51, were trying to use the
machinery of democracy to destroy democracy and substitute rule
by one party on the Communist model.

The Ministers, while holding their portfolios, succeeded in in-
citing strikes in the sugar industry for political purposes. They
attempted to oust the trade unions, which had been established
and were still in the formative state, and to substitute unions
under their own control. The Ministers, though in office, continued to hold their official positions in these splinter trade unions.
Lastly they were neglecting their duties in a most irresponsible
manner.

At this time, the reports from our intelligence services were that
riots and bloodshed would soon break out and that there was a plot
to burn down the wooden capital—Georgetown. The sales of kero-
sene and petrol in small quantities to men and women without
cars were growing rapidly. I decided to seek the approval of my
colleagues to suspend the constitution, to divert a cruiser to
Georgetown and to land a force of about 700 men.

After studying the evidence, the Cabinet unhesitatingly supported me. The constitution was accordingly suspended by Order
in Council on October 9th, 1953. The House was not sitting at the
time, and was not due to reassemble until the last week of the
month. The Opposition, the *Daily Herald* and the *Daily Mirror* in
particular, fell upon this appetising opportunity with gusto. "Lyttelton must go" was of course the main theme; my ruthless methods and iron hands, stained with African blood, were held up to
obloquy.

The back-benchers of the Labour Party burst into violent
speeches in which their horror of the action of the Government
and their abuse of the Colonial Secretary were only equalled by
their ignorance of the events in British Guiana. They returned to
the House of Commons breathing fire and polishing their weapons, confident that an easy victory, at least of words, awaited
them.

The Commonwealth and Colonial Committees of the Labour

Party met in private in the House of Commons. The tenor of its proceedings reached my ears. When some members discovered that the Ministers in British Guiana had sought to overthrow the existing trade unions and to substitute splinter unions supported by the W.F.T.U. in Vienna, and when it was known that they had remained officials of these unions whilst being members of the Government, some Labour Members refused absolutely to support any motion of censure, at least in terms.

Somehow, the thunder of the last fortnight had to be muted. The Committees' recommendations were against condemning my actions out of hand, and some ingenious drafting had to be improvised. The Opposition amendment must needs be as mild as it could be drawn, if the differences in the party were not to be indecently exposed in public, but at the same time had to give some semblance of excuse for the strong drink with which members had been recently intoxicated. The amendment was nearly all soda water; only a drop of whisky could be risked. It ran:

[This house] whilst emphatically deploring the actions and speeches of some of the leaders of the People's Progressive Party in British Guiana, as set forth in the White Paper, Command Paper No. 8980, and condemning methods tending to the establishment of a totalitarian regime in a British Colony, nevertheless is not satisfied that the situation in British Guiana was of such a character as to justify the extreme step of suspending the constitution.[5]

It was unpromising material for Opposition speakers.

I was able to quote messages from a number of bodies representing the ordinary people of British Guiana in support of my action. Conversely, some of the statements of the Guiana Ministers struck the House as bizarre.

For example, I quoted:

He [a Minister] used these words at a public meeting:

"We do not have control of the police, which means that if we were to start a strike, the Government would call in the police and shoot us down."

I do not want to make too much of this statement, but I suggest that these words give us some insight into the twisted mentality of this Minister. In the first place, the statement says: "If we call a strike . . ." But it is a Minister speaking. For a Minister to attempt to call a strike himself is sufficiently serious, but having said that, he then deplored

[5] Hansard: House of Commons, Vol. 518, Col. 2195, October 22nd, 1953.

that the police, instead of supporting the party, might support the Government in which he himself is a Minister, and that shows that the Ministers do not regard themselves as in any way responsible for government or indeed as any part of it.[6]

The Opposition had a bad afternoon, and in particular poor Mr. Griffiths, who could make nothing of it. He had already begun to lose a great deal of support from his own benches and when he executed some figure-skating on this over-thin ice it was seen that the sobriquet given him by his own side of "the Minister of Tears" was being earned. Nor was Mr. Attlee with all his parliamentary experience able to conceal the embarrassment of his party. He could only end up in a lame and contradictory peroration.[7] What remained of the Opposition cohorts was finally torn to pieces by Mr. Macmillan, who wound up the debate. My own position in the Conservative Party was strengthened and reinforced.

Parliamentary parties are prepared to support drastic and unpopular action if they think it right but when that action gives them a happy experience they positively purr.

[6] Hansard: Vol. 518, Col. 2164.
[7] Hansard: Vol. 518, Col. 2268.

CHAPTER XXIII

FINAL CHAPTER

J UST BEFORE THE Coronation I had had a disturbing conversation with my accountants, who told me that I was rapidly exhausting my capital and savings, and that in fairness to my wife and children I should not continue in politics for much longer. I have earlier explained how disastrous office is—financially—to those who have not prepared their lives in its anticipation.

I had to meet all my commitments for life insurance, settlements on my children, and pensions for some of my dependants, out of capital. One rather ironical twist concerns life insurance. Before the war a man was allowed tax relief down to 2s. 6d. in the £ on money spent on life insurance up to a quarter of his income. I had taken full advantage of this, but when I became a Minister, instead of my premiums being a quarter they became more than a half of my income; an example of being hit twice for the same offence of becoming a Minister.

Moreover, the company of which I had been Chairman and to which I was bound by ties of loyalty, very properly sought to know my intentions. They had kept the post warm for me, but Sir George Bailey, my successor, was well advanced in years. If there was to be much further delay in my return they wished, and rightly, to appoint a permanent Chairman to take over from him.

Towards the end of the year, I wrote to the Prime Minister and explained that I must shortly leave the Government. The Prime Minister summoned a deputation of the Directors to No. 10 Downing Street, and asked them to be patient and not to press for my return until at least the end of July. They agreed.

My feelings about resignation were naturally mixed. Red boxes have little attraction for me, and seductive though it is to be listened to with respect even when talking at random, I never wholeheartedly relished the Ministerial life. At the same time I had some reason to expect other offices in the next Government which would be interesting and perhaps less controversial than the Colonial Office, such as the Ministry of Defence.

Above all, I was going to feel a terrible wrench at leaving my colleagues, although less at leaving my Chief, because I knew that he would himself shortly resign.

One of the attractions of office is the society and conversation of men of high intelligence, whether fellow Ministers, Members of Parliament or civil servants.

Dusty as are some of the paths which have to be trodden in politics—speaking in remote parts of England, never being able to order your time to your own wishes, the sudden crises, the snarling of the Opposition, particularly when you know that they do not always mean it, and the perpetual quarrelling with your fellowmen, the immense pressure of work, the complexity of the task, especially when related to policy in offices not your own—there is also much dust in commercial life.

Nowadays the social side of business has grown immeasurably and I believe unpardonably. Every association thinks it obligatory to have annual dinners and not infrequent cocktail parties. Speakers have to be found and it is a trifle humiliating to discover at over sixty that you have earned your niche in the State, which is to be the ideal guest speaker for a remote chamber of commerce or association. Often a friend implores you to come and make a speech and it is difficult to refuse invitations which are kindly meant.

The pattern of these dinners is sometimes uncivilised and places an unnecessary burden on the visiting speaker. For example, in my youth, decorations were only worn when a member of the Royal Family was present or for some other special reason. To-day white ties, tail coats and decorations are ordered with such frequency that they are reducing the value of this currency. Above all, it is the flood of speeches that is distressing.

After two or three of these dinners, I had a nightmare. I dreamt I was sitting at a table with some notes for a speech in my hand. I looked at the menu. I dreamt it was:

MENU

THICK (BROWN WINDSOR) SOUP

———

FRIED FILLETS OF HALIBUT

———

BOILED CHICKEN

(In my dream this was the colour of the hind leg of an elephant, and the athletic nature of the chicken's past life was
concealed by a thick flour-filled sauce of a sickly white
colour.)

———

PÊCHE MELBA

(In my dream a California tinned peach on which some synthetic vanilla ice cream and raspberry jam had been poised.)

Looking at the wine list, I saw that this collation was to be
washed down by some anaemic white wine claiming German origin and some burgundy which was likely to be heavily reinforced
with Algerian concentrate, topped up by a thimbleful of searing
brandy.

I then inspected the Toast List. It ran:

1. "The City of Blank"   Proposed by Alderman Harry Verdigris, JP.
                            Reply by the Lord Mayor.

(In the nightmare I guessed that this would take forty-five minutes.)

2. INTERVAL (In my dream I could hear the guests exchanging in the
   lavatory stories as scabrous as they were antique.)

I even caught the notes of

3. "Asleep in the Deep" — Baritone
   "Tosti's Farewell   — Soprano

   (I dreamt that these would be followed by a couple of encores;
   say, "Trees" and "I Seem to See Your Face" [Somerville Hasting
   Turner].)

4. "The Houses of Parliament"
                Proposed by Sir Charles Prolix Doughty Prolix, JP, LLD

5. "The Guests," etc.   Reply by the Rt. Hon. The Visitor

I had the nightmarish feeling that, by the time No. 4 on this programme was reached, not even Burke could rouse an audience or cozen them away from looking at their watches.

Then I suddenly woke up and was much relieved that none of it was true.

Of course, entertainments are not like this, but quite a number of them have one or other feature from my imaginary menu or toast list, which give a grisly verisimilitude to my dream.

In the real world, I am always grateful and honoured to have been asked, but I know that my pleasure would be much enhanced by simpler dishes and few and shorter speeches.

For example, a summer menu might be Clear Soup, Cold Ham and Summer Pudding. In the winter you might have a savoury instead of the pudding. There should be a liberal supply of a good carafe Bordeaux, and some brandy—not in an eyebath—might top it up. There should not be more than two speeches, one of which should be made by an experienced speaker who had partially lost his voice.

The attractions of business are that the problems posed even to the head of a very large company have at least the semblance of being within the compass of a single trained mind and within the compass of a seven- or eight-hour day. Finally, if your labours are successful they are expressed in a notation which allows little argument to detract from them. If you can say: Yes, the company built this plant; it employs 800 people at good wages in healthy and interesting conditions; it exports a third of the products and makes a profit of 15% on the capital, it is difficult to chip the ivory ball of achievement.

Since, as a rule, human affairs tend to deteriorate, your achievements in politics always appear transient in man's estimation. Few political decisions, and generally those that have been forgotten, are immune from the hindsight of future generations who proclaim with gusto how different would have been the state of humanity if only Mr. So-and-So had done differently.

This is another reason why Ministers who have an eye to their place in history should not fear resignation; it may even happen that someone may exclaim how different things would be if only Mr. So-and-So had been at the helm.

Many people think that it is power that attracts men to politics or urges them to strive for the summit in industry. Power is largely illusory; in politics, Ministers other than the Prime Minister have in theory wide powers but they cannot exercise them unless they are used in agreement with their colleagues or sometimes even with the party. The Prime Minister, himself, has of course great powers of patronage and is the chairman, in effect, of the Cabinet. He again must use his power with great circumspection; he sometimes has to be content with appointments which in his absolute discretion he would regard as second best. Behind him also stands the shadow of the House of Commons, and he must reef or shake out his sails with some regard to the parliamentary weather.

The myth of power finds many believers. One of the phrases sometimes put in front of a Minister, though never more than once in front of me in any office, is: "My attention has been drawn to . . ." Paraphrased, this means that this Olympian would not have known of the struggles of the groundlings unless someone had winged his way upwards with the news which has at last penetrated the lower slopes of the mountain. I saw a minute of my own the other day. A draft letter to Lord Halifax had been put in front of me concerning his work for the Commonwealth Society for the Blind. It began: "My attention has been drawn . . ." I minuted: "Never let me see this repulsive phrase again. Lord Halifax is an old friend: he has been Viceroy of India, Foreign Secretary, Ambassador to the United States and has recently been made an Earl. He may safely be treated as an equal."

In business, power is restricted by competition and by the need to conserve resources. The management of companies cannot concentrate solely on future development, however imaginative and constructive it should seem to be. The present shareholders require present dividends, and they cannot be expected to be interested only in the fortunes of their grandchildren. The chairman has to carry his board with him in the same way, though upon less significant issues, that the Prime Minister has to carry his Cabinet. On the other hand the control of promotion, which resides largely in the chairman, gives him in theory much power over his subordinates.

Nevertheless this power too is largely illusory. Unity and cohesion must be preserved; attention must be paid to the continuity of employment, and to past services. Sometimes a younger and better man has to wait his time, lest promotion should seem to be subject to wayward decisions, or even to personal favouritism.

Power thus becomes residual, and dwells in the background. It would not be far from apposite to describe it as the ability to exercise nice matters of judgement. I have heard speakers, in both walks of life, use the phrase, "I can say without fear of contradiction . . ." Anyone who says this in a modern democracy, or to the shareholders of a modern company, should see the doctor.

On my last day at the Colonial Office, I was writing a few telegrams of farewell to some of the Colonial Governors in a relaxed frame of mind, when the telephone rang and an agitated Chief Whip said, "You must come at once to the House. They are in an uproar about Cyprus. Henry has used the word 'never' about independence, but hurry."

This made me think that perhaps I should not miss politics so much. I had to face an angry House and only rode the storm by assuring them that the Minister of State had only meant "never" in the sense that we would never abandon our responsibilities until a stable life could be assured for minorities. This was precisely what Henry had meant, but some slipshod phrase or clumsy emphasis, to which all men are prone, caused the kettle to boil over.

The Opposition knew that this was the last time that they would see me and this gratifying thought no doubt calmed them down, but it was not an hour which increased any feelings of nostalgia which I might have entertained.

The last time I saw them all together I felt sad and emotional at taking leave of my colleagues. For me the atmosphere was overcharged with sentiment, and I had a lump in my throat. The Prime Minister said, "You will hand over very fully to your successor, I hope, and tell him of your thoughts and plans."

"Oh," I said, swallowing hard, "I will tell him all about the white man in the wood-pile."

The temperature fell abruptly and I escaped amidst smiles.

When I was given a peerage, my successor, Alan Lennox-Boyd, and the senior civil servants gave me a cocktail party at the Colonial Office. I made a very short and genuinely impromptu speech, in which I said how truly glad I was to see them that evening, and how truly glad I was to think that I should not be seeing them tomorrow. I could imagine what might well happen. The Permanent Secretary would come in and say, "Secretary of State, something rather awkward has occurred in Blankland. The police have disembowelled the Crown witnesses, and there is a Private Notice Question on the paper in the name of Mr. Griffiths."

Since those days, I have been offered high office by both Prime Ministers but I have refused, if only because I had contracted to give my services to my company, and was no longer a free agent. I have been happy as Chairman of A.E.I. these last seven years;

the electrical, together with the chemical, industry must remain in the forefront of industrial progress in this country. Interest in the development in these spheres is absorbing; the human relations which are involved are worthy of the greatest thought and sympathy. Of late, the going has been difficult, but I hope, when I lay down my office, to leave to my successor a streamlined company that will survive and prosper in the highly competitive world which confronts it.

I was born with outstanding health. Perhaps this is the main reason why I have always had a great zest in living. I have seldom woken up in the morning—except when about to make an important speech—without feeling how good life was, how hungry I was for breakfast and how I must do this or that before nightfall. At the end of it was there to be a game of bridge, an opera or a play in the evening, or time to read my book, or to talk to my wife, whose conversation, informed by wide reading, is illuminating and independent?

The zest still continues, and when I have to quit this life, I still feel that the moment will not be bliss, for all that the clergy say.

INDEX